MW01029906

LAWYERING PEACE

In all but the rarest circumstances, the world's deadly conflicts are ended not through outright victory, but through a series of negotiations. Not all of these negotiations, however, yield a durable peace. To successfully mitigate conflict drivers, the parties in conflict must address a number of puzzles, such as whether and how to share and/or re-establish a state's monopoly of force, reallocate the ownership and management of natural resources, modify the state structure, or provide for a path toward external self-determination. Successfully resolving these puzzles requires the parties to navigate a number of conundrums and make choices and design mechanisms that are appropriate to the particular context of the conflict, and which are most likely to lead to a durable peace. *Lawyering Peace* aims to help future negotiators build better and more durable peace agreements through a rigorous examination of how other parties have resolved these puzzles and associated conundrums.

PAUL R. WILLIAMS holds the Rebecca I. Grazier Professorship in Law and International Relations at American University where he teaches in the School of International Service and at the Washington College of Law. He is the founder of the Public International Law & Policy Group (PILPG), a pro bono law firm providing legal assistance to state and non-state parties involved in peace negotiations, post-conflict constitution drafting, and the prosecution of war criminals.

Previous Books by the Author

Treatment of Detainees: Examination of Issues Relevant to Detention by the United Nations Humans Rights Committee, Henry-Durant Institute, 1990

International Law and the Resolution of Central and East European Transboundary Environmental Disputes, Macmillan/St. Martin's Press, 2000

Indictment at the Hague: The Milosevic Regime and Crimes of the Balkan Wars, with Norman Cigar, New York University Press, 2002

Peace with Justice? War Crimes and Accountability in the Former Yugoslavia, with Michael P. Scharf, Rowman and Littlefield, 2002

Shaping Foreign Policy in Times of Crisis: The Role of International Law and the State Department Legal Adviser, with Michael P. Scharf, Cambridge University Press, 2010

The Law of International Organizations: Problems and Materials, third edition, co-authored with Michael P. Scharf, Carolina Academic Press, 2013

Research Handbook on Post-Conflict State Building, co-edited with Milena Sterio, Edward Elgar, 2020

The Syrian Conflict's Impact on International Law, with Michael P. Scharf and Milena Sterio, Cambridge University Press, 2020

Lawyering Peace

PAUL R. WILLIAMS
American University

CAMBRIDGE
UNIVERSITY PRESS

University Printing House, Cambridge CB2 8BS, United Kingdom

One Liberty Plaza, 20th Floor, New York, NY 10006, USA

477 Williamstown Road, Port Melbourne, VIC 3207, Australia

314–321, 3rd Floor, Plot 3, Splendor Forum, Jasola District Centre, New Delhi – 110025, India

103 Penang Road, #05–06/07, Visioncrest Commercial, Singapore 238467

Cambridge University Press is part of the University of Cambridge.

It furthers the University's mission by disseminating knowledge in the pursuit of education, learning, and research at the highest international levels of excellence.

www.cambridge.org
Information on this title: www.cambridge.org/9781108478236
DOI: 10.1017/9781108776264

© Paul R. Williams 2021

This publication is in copyright. Subject to statutory exception and to the provisions of relevant collective licensing agreements, no reproduction of any part may take place without the written permission of Cambridge University Press.

First published 2021

A catalogue record for this publication is available from the British Library.

Library of Congress Cataloging-in-Publication Data
NAMES: Williams, Paul R., 1965– author.
TITLE: Lawyering peace / Paul R. Williams, American University, Washington DC.
DESCRIPTION: Cambridge, United Kingdom ; New York, NY : Cambridge University Press, 2021. |
Includes bibliographical references and index.
IDENTIFIERS: LCCN 2021008424 (print) | LCCN 2021008425 (ebook) | ISBN 9781108478236 (hardback) |
ISBN 9781108745628 (paperback) | ISBN 9781108776264 (epub)
SUBJECTS: LCSH: Peace-building–Law and legislation. | International law. | Practice of law.
CLASSIFICATION: LCC KZ6787 .W55 2021 (print) | LCC KZ6787 (ebook) | DDC 341.7/3–DC23
LC record available at https://lccn.loc.gov/2021008424
LC ebook record available at https://lccn.loc.gov/2021008425

ISBN 978-1-108-47823-6 Hardback
ISBN 978-1-108-74562-8 Paperback

Cambridge University Press has no responsibility for the persistence or accuracy of URLs for external or third-party internet websites referred to in this publication and does not guarantee that any content on such websites is, or will remain, accurate or appropriate.

For Sam, Will, Jack, and Eve

Contents

About the Author

Dr. Paul R. Williams holds the Rebecca I. Grazier Professorship in Law and International Relations at American University, where he teaches in the School of International Service and at the Washington College of Law. Dr. Williams is also the founder of the Public International Law & Policy Group (PILPG), a *pro bono* law firm providing legal assistance to state and nonstate parties involved in peace negotiations, postconflict constitution drafting, and the prosecution of war criminals. As a world-renowned peace negotiation lawyer, Dr. Williams has assisted more than two dozen parties in major international peace negotiations and has advised numerous parties on the drafting and implementation of postconflict constitutions. Several of Dr. Williams' *pro bono* government clients throughout the world joined together to nominate him for the Nobel Peace Prize.

Early in his career, Dr. Williams was heavily engaged in various peace processes, including serving as a member of the Bosnian delegation at Dayton, serving on the legal team of the Kosovar delegation to the Rambouillet talks, serving on the Montenegrin delegation for the Union Treaty negotiations, advising the Albanian-Macedonian delegation to the Lake Ohrid negotiations. He then worked with the government of Armenia during the Key West negotiations on Nagorno-Karabakh, and the government of Georgia on the Abkhazia and South Ossetia negotiations. He also advised the Turkish Republic of Northern Cyprus during the Cyprus peace process.

During the Arab Spring and its aftermath, Dr. Williams advised Egypt, Libya, and Yemen during their constitution-drafting processes. He also advised the UN mediator on the Yemen peace talks, and the Syrian opposition delegation to the Geneva and Astana talks. Previously, he was in Baghdad in 2005 and 2007, advising the Iraqi Constitution Drafting Committee. In Asia, Dr. Williams provided legal assistance to parties involved in the Sri Lankan peace talks, the Nagaland negotiations, the Nepalese postconflict constitution, the Philippines–Mindanao peace process, the 2004 Afghanistan Constitution, and the Burmese ceasefire talks.

Dr. Williams provided assistance to the government of South Sudan on the implementation of the Comprehensive Peace Agreement and its secession from Sudan, and the development of an interim constitution. For over a decade he advised the Darfur delegation to the various Sudan peace negotiations, and in 2019 and 2020 he and his legal team provided support to the multiparty peace talks in Juba. He also served as co-counsel in the Abyei Arbitration before the Permanent Court of Arbitration, and provided legal assistance to the civil society delegation to the Eldoret peace talks for Somalia.

In the field of transitional justice, he has worked with a wide variety of states, including Bosnia, the Ivory Coast, Kenya, Kosovo, Libya, the Seychelles, Tanzania, and Uganda to craft mechanisms for the prosecution of war criminals and pirates.

Dr. Williams has served as a senior associate with the Carnegie Endowment for International Peace, as well as an attorney-adviser for European and Canadian affairs at the US Department of State, Office of the Legal Adviser. At the Department of State, Dr. Williams was heavily engaged in the legal dimensions of the dissolution of the Soviet Union, and with the Yugoslavian peace process. He received his JD from Stanford Law School and his PhD from the University of Cambridge. Dr. Williams is a sought-after international law and policy expert. He is frequently interviewed by major print and broadcast media and regularly contributes op-eds to major newspapers. Dr. Williams has authored eight books on various topics concerning international law and has published over four dozen scholarly articles on topics of international law and policy. He has testified before the US Congress on a number of occasions relating to specific peace processes, transitional justice, and self-determination. Dr. Williams is a member of the Council of Foreign Relations and has served as a counselor on the Executive Council of the American Society of International Law. More information about Dr. Williams can be found at www.drpaulrwilliams.com.

Acknowledgments

Years ago in Sri Lanka, Elisabeth (Beezie) Dallas planted the idea in my head that it might be valuable to put to paper the lessons we were learning on how to solve the various puzzles and associated conundrums faced by parties seeking to design durable peace agreements. Years later, in the midst of the Yemen ceasefire negotiations, and no doubt in collusion with Beezie, Yoonie Kim informed me that she had decided it was time that I find a way to crystalize and share my insights from nearly twenty-five years of lawyering peace negotiations. This prodding, coupled with the enduring partnership with Milena Sterio and Michael Scharf as my co-directors of the Public International Law & Policy Group, has made this book possible.

Over the last twenty-five years I have had the privilege of being invited by states, nonstate parties, nonstate armed actors, and mediators to lend a legal hand in their attempts to negotiate an end to conflict and draft durable peace agreements. Without exception, these individuals have genuinely and warmly welcomed me into that space behind closed doors where parties and mediators engage in fierce political bargaining processes as they try to meet the needs and interests of their constituencies while also seeking to design an agreement that will yield a resilient peace. Without their willingness to include me in these negotiations, I would never have developed an understanding of the complex and nuanced thinking and negotiating that goes into resolving armed conflicts. I hope that in some small way, future peacebuilders are able to benefit from the insights reflected in these pages.

This book would not have been possible without the tireless dedication, hard work, enthusiasm, and constant prodding by Isabela Karibjanian and Jessica Levy, two of the most brilliant young professionals I have had the opportunity and pleasure to work with. This book is indebted to their research support, thoughtful edits, inquisitive minds, and determination. I am also deeply grateful for the tireless effort, dedication, and perpetual wisdom of my research team, Sophie Pearlman, Nicole Carle, Alexandra Koch, Lisa Dicker, Carly Fabian, and Danae Paterson.

I am exceptionally grateful to the Cambridge University Press team, including the now-retired John Berger, who supported the vision for the book, and Jackie Grant for her enthusiasm and support during the drafting process. I am also grateful to Joan Dale Lace, Catherine Smith, and Divya Arjunan, for guiding me through the proofing and publication process.

Finally, I would like to thank the American University's School of International Service and Washington College of Law for institutional support, as well as the following young professionals who provided invaluable research assistance: Emma Marion, Dalya Kefi, Nicole Waterman, Jessica McKenney, Megan Masingill, Meagan DeSimone, Amanda Grau, Alexis Rossetti, Karen Kim, Ryan Westlake, Genevieve Ding Yarou, Jennifer Morris, and Gordon Ahl.

Introduction

No corner of the globe is exempt from the scourge of conflict. Every year, hundreds of thousands of civilians die as a consequence of armed conflict, and millions more are displaced. These conflicts are brutal, durable, and global. Oftentimes, they are characterized by genocide, as in Bosnia, Darfur, Iraq (ISIS), Myanmar, and Rwanda, or widespread atrocity crimes, as in the Central African Republic, the Democratic Republic of Congo, Libya, Syria, and Yemen. As is often said, it is easy to start an armed conflict, but excruciatingly difficult to end one. In any given year, there are nearly four dozen active armed conflicts around the globe. While some of these conflicts may transpire over a relatively short time (3–5 years), others remain active for a decade or more, and still others are "frozen" for decades on end, continuing to contribute to instability and insecurity.

In all but the rarest circumstances these conflicts are ended not through outright victory, but through a series of negotiations. These negotiations often relate to ceasefires, peace talks, and postconflict constitutions. Not all of these negotiations, however, yield a durable peace. Many negotiations fail to bring about an end to a conflict, and nearly half of those conflicts "resolved" through negotiations subsequently fail and slip back into armed conflict.

A number of factors contribute to the durability of a negotiated peace. One of the primary factors is the manner in which the parties to the conflict mitigate conflict drivers. In order to successfully mitigate conflict drivers, the parties must address a number of puzzles, such as whether and how to share and/or reestablish a state's monopoly of force, reallocate the ownership and management of natural resources, modify the state structure, or provide for a path toward external self-determination. Successfully resolving these puzzles requires the parties to navigate a number of conundrums and make choices and design mechanisms that are appropriate to the particular context of the conflict, and that are most likely to lead to a durable peace.

Few state and nonstate actor representatives at the negotiation table have much experience with negotiation ceasefires, peace agreements, or postconflict constitutions. This is the natural consequence of the fact that many of them are state or nonstate armed actors, and are more comfortable in the field, so to speak, than around a negotiating table. While there is frequently a great deal of intellectual capital that these actors are able to assemble on their delegations, there is seldom a depth of expertise in negotiating ceasefires, peace agreements, or constitutions for the simple reason that these types of negotiations do not occur frequently in any one state. As such, a surprising number of negotiation delegations have been led by brilliant bankers, cardiologists, commercial lawyers, dentists, historians, industrial engineers, professors of literature, and even elementary school teachers.

The purpose of this book is to help these inadvertent negotiators build better and more durable peace agreements through a rigorous examination of how other parties have resolved these puzzles and associated conundrums. The book takes a clear-eyed approach to the good, bad, and ugly of peace agreements. The book is also designed to be easily accessible to those studying conflict resolution as a path to becoming future peacebuilders, as well as those fortunate enough to be called upon to assist with mediating ceasefires and peace negotiations, or facilitating the drafting of postconflict constitutions.

The book does not propose a state-of-the-art strategy for negotiation, or posit an innovative theory for conceptualizing how to get to yes or to checkmate, nor does it recount insightful behind-the-scenes moments in key negotiations. There is a plethora of well-written and easily accessible books that already accomplish those objectives. This book is designed to help parties, practitioners, and academics work their way through the multitude of decision points they face in a negotiation, and then to draft legal text that encapsulates that agreement in a way that will promote the durability of the agreement or constitution; hence the title, "Lawyering Peace."

During the course of a peace process, the parties face a wide variety of puzzles, and any comprehensive examination of those puzzles would be a multivolume undertaking. This book seeks to add value by addressing five key puzzles relating to security, power-sharing, natural resources, self-determination, and governance. These five puzzles represent particularly fraught aspects of negotiation and reflect complex issues that are difficult to resolve in a manner that generates agreement from both parties. These puzzles often require difficult tradeoffs and, if not dealt with deftly, they stand in the way of a durable peace. Other equally perplexing puzzles meriting examination include transitional justice and accountability, refugees and internally displaced persons, human and minority rights, and transitional administrations, among others.

The five puzzles are each examined in a separate chapter. Each chapter first discusses the nature of the puzzle facing the parties. Next, the chapter provides a conceptual and legal primer for understanding the subject matter of the puzzle, in particular the relevant norms, rules, procedures, and processes the parties may rely upon to assist with resolving the puzzle. Then the chapter explores a number of instances of key state practice to analyze and highlight how parties involved in a peace process have sought to manage the conundrums they faced when seeking to solve the puzzle.

Often, a number of instances of state practice illustrate how challenging puzzles were successfully navigated. Other instances of state practice represent mixed outcomes, where certain objectives may have been achieved, but others were not. Still other instances of state practice provide illustrations of unsuccessful attempts to solve the puzzles presented. These, too, provide rich insights into potential obstacles to achieving durable peace, from which future negotiators can benefit.

Each chapter's umbrella topic encompasses a variety of related subtopics. To maximize the value of the analysis, each chapter undertakes a detailed exploration of one of those subtopics. The lessons learned from the negotiation and design of provisions formulated to facilitate a resolution of that particular puzzle are addressed such in a way as to be broadly applicable to the other related subtopics addressed during the peace process.

During the peace process, including during peace negotiations, the parties confront a variety of security-related topics, including peace enforcement; ceasefires; peacekeeping; disarmament, demobilizations, and reintegration; security sector reform; and the restoration of a state's monopoly of force. Chapter 1, "Security," explores the puzzle of whether and how to create a state-held monopoly of force in a way that ensures a durable peace. The monopoly of force relates to the state's exclusive right and ability to control and oversee the legitimate use of violence within its borders.

Chapter 1 begins with a review of the foundational principles of sovereignty, political independence, and territorial integrity and their relationship to sharing and/or reestablishing a monopoly of force. It also reviews the international frame-work for the authorization of the use of force embedded in the UN Charter. Then, the chapter reviews the peace processes related to conflicts in Angola, Bosnia, Burundi, Kosovo, Mozambique, Papua New Guinea/Bougainville, Rwanda, Sierra Leone, Sudan/South Sudan, and Sudan/Darfur in order to underscore the compli-cated tradeoffs parties face sharing and/or reestablishing the monopoly of force, including, when sharing force with the international community, questions of: the consent of the state, and often the consent of the nonstate parties; the nature and configuration of the international forces, including the command structure of the international forces; and the mandate of those forces.

The chapter also analyzes cases during which the state seeks to integrate nonstate armed actors into the national forces, when parties are faced with the questions of how best to provide for the disarmament, demobilization, and reintegration of nonstate forces, coupled with security sector reform for the national forces. It additionally examines the questions that arise when the state seeks to restore limited control over the monopoly of force by permitting nonstate actors to maintain their forces and command structure under the umbrella command of the national forces, including to what extent to promote some degree of integration among special units of the state and nonstate forces, as well as a timeline for the eventual integration of forces.

To craft a durable peace, parties to peace negotiations often also spend considerable time and effort crafting power-sharing arrangements that balance the pull of some parties for greater diffusion and devolution of political power with the pull of other parties to maintain a degree of political centralization, both for the sake of efficiency and effectiveness, and to preserve their prior political privileges. Chapter 2, "Power-Sharing," explores the puzzle of whether and how to create a vertical power-sharing arrangement that leads to a durable peace.

Chapter 2 begins with a review of the conceptual and legal primer for understanding the nature of various state structures (unified, modified unitary, federal, or confederal); the allocation of executive and legislative powers between the national government and its substate entities; and political, administrative, and fiscal decentralization. It then reviews the peace processes related to conflicts in Bosnia and Herzegovina, Colombia, Indonesia/Aceh, Iraq, Macedonia, Nepal, the Philippines/Mindanao, South Africa, Sudan, and Yemen to understand how parties have grappled with the thorny set of power-sharing conundrums, including the choice of state structure; the allocation of legislative and executive powers among the levels of government; the degree of political, administrative, and/or fiscal decision-making authority to be devolved; and the timeline for implementing any agreed plan for decentralization.

Access to natural resources and the allocation of revenue generated by resource exploitation is at the core of many conflicts and plays an important role in many others. Such natural resource conflicts are twice as likely to revert to conflict in the first five years after the signing of a peace agreement. Chapter 3, "Natural Resources," explores the puzzle of whether and how to address natural resource ownership, management, and revenue allocation in a manner that promotes durable peace. Efforts to solve the puzzle of whether and how to address natural resource ownership, management, and revenue allocation in a manner that promotes durable peace are complicated by the fact that natural resources can be both a driver of the conflict and a key factor in promoting a durable peace.

Chapter 3 begins with a review of key conceptual approaches for allocating the ownership, management, and associated revenue of natural resources, and the various legal norms, rules, processes, and procedures used to design and implement natural resource arrangements. It also reviews a number of international legal obligations relating to natural resources, including the consideration of the interests of local and indigenous populations, as well as the international Kimberley Process for the regulation of the diamond trade. The chapter then reviews the peace processes related to conflicts in Papua New Guinea and Bougainville, Indonesia and Aceh, Iraq and Kurdistan, the Philippines and Mindanao, Sierra Leone, Sudan and South Sudan, Sudan and Darfur, and Yemen to understand if and when parties broach the subject of natural resources in the peace process, and how they then decide upon matters such as ownership, management, and revenue allocation.

Self-determination and sovereignty-based conflicts are widespread throughout the globe, and are particularly durable and deadly. These conflicts may be resolved through military victory, through some form of enhanced internal self-determination, or through a path to external self-determination. Chapter 4, "Self-Determination," explores the puzzle of whether and how to provide for external self-determination as a means for ensuring a durable peace.

Chapter 4 begins with a review of the conceptual and legal framework governing self-determination, including an examination of the long-standing concepts of sovereignty, territorial integrity, and political independence, as well as the emergence and development of the now well-established principle of self-determination. It then differentiates and describes internal self-determination, a principle that guarantees a people the right to determine their own future, and external self-determination, which entails a path for a substate entity becoming independent from a parent state. Then, the chapter reviews the peace processes related to conflicts in Bosnia, Indonesia/East Timor, Israel/Palestine, Kosovo, Northern Ireland, Papua New Guinea/Bougainville, Serbia/Montenegro, Sudan/South Sudan, and Western Sahara in order to understand how the parties seek to most effectively share sovereignty in the interim; build sustainable institutions; determine final status; phase in the assumption of sovereignty; condition the assumption of this newfound sovereignty; and, if necessary, to constrain the exercise of sovereignty of the new state.

Lastly, establishing a comprehensive legal framework for postconflict governance is one of those tasks where there is seldom the time or capacity for parties to reach a full and complete agreement during a negotiation. Although decisions relating to postconflict governance are critical issues for discussion within peace negotiations, parties often are not able to determine each detail of the system for postconflict governance. Instead, parties often agree to a preliminary set of principles coupled with a general governing framework. They then set forth an agreed process for negotiating, designing, and implementing a national dialogue, the drafting or amending of a constitution, and elections. Chapter 5, "Governance," explores the puzzle of whether and how to address constitutional modification during peace negotiations in a manner that promotes a durable peace.

Chapter 5 begins with a review of the political, legal, and social nature of constitutions, and the related legal obligations to ensure that any process for modifying a constitution is inclusive and participatory. It then reviews the peace processes related to conflicts in Bosnia and Herzegovina, Colombia, East Timor, Guatemala, Iraq, Kosovo, Macedonia, Nepal, Northern Ireland, Somalia, South Africa, Syria, and Yemen to explore whether and how to address constitutional modification during the peace process; the timing of determining and executing a postconflict constitution-drafting process; whether to draft an interim constitution; whether to accomplish constitutional reform through amendments or drafting a full constitution; how to approve and finalize constitutional modifications; and whether and how to incorporate issues of human rights.

In the face of seemingly intractable conflicts, state and nonstate parties are time and again able to reach a negotiated compromise that leads to a durable peace. At other times, unfortunately, the process is rushed or misconceived and the peace is short-lived or never reached. From these successful and unsuccessful peacebuilding endeavors, the Conclusion synthesizes a number of lessons learned with regard to how to solve the various puzzles and associated conundrums faced by parties seeking to design resilient peace agreements and establish a durable peace.

The Appendix contains a brief summary of each of the key peace agreements discussed in this book. For each peace agreement, the entry sets forth the conflict drivers, including the nature of atrocity crimes, if any, the nature of the peace process, the core elements of the peace agreement, and the current status of implementation. The Appendix is designed to provide a brief snapshot of the conflicts referenced in this book in order for the reader to have the necessary context to readily move through the substance of the chapters.

1

Security

The need to restore security and rebuild the security infrastructure in a postconflict state is of paramount importance for ensuring a durable peace. Nearly all recent conflicts (thirty of thirty-three) were intrastate conflicts with nonstate armed actors eroding the monopoly of force held by the state.[1] As such, over 75 percent of the post-1989 peace agreements contain detailed provisions relating to the restoration of security, and in particular the reestablishment of a state's monopoly of force. In those agreements that did not contain security provisions, the issue of security was usually addressed in supplementary agreements.[2]

During the peace process, including during peace negotiations, a variety of security-related topics are confronted, among them: peace enforcement; ceasefires; peacekeeping; disarmament, demobilization, and reintegration (DDR); security sector reform (SSR); peacebuilding; and the restoration of a state's monopoly of force.[3]

As noted in the Introduction, each chapter undertakes a detailed exploration of one dimension of a broader set of issues needing resolution to achieve a durable peace. Under the umbrella of restoring postconflict security, this chapter focuses on the conundrums related to reestablishing a monopoly of force. The lessons learned from the negotiation and design of provisions formulated to facilitate the reestablishment of a state's monopoly of force are broadly applicable to the other security-related topics addressed during peace negotiations.

In brief, the monopoly of force relates to the state's exclusive right and ability to control and oversee the legitimate use of violence within its borders. Prior to the negotiation of a peace agreement, a state often shares its monopoly of force with international actors, such as United Nations peacekeepers, to facilitate bringing an end to the conflict. A state may then continue to share this monopoly of force with the same or different international actors during the initial stages of peace agreement implementation. This sharing of a monopoly of force by the state may be initiated by the state, or may to a degree be forced upon the state. The sharing of a monopoly of force will be addressed first in this chapter, followed by a discussion of peace agreement provisions designed to facilitate the reestablishment of a state's monopoly of force.

When properly negotiated and implemented, monopoly of force provisions can be key to ensuring a durable peace. A recent study examining peace agreements at the end of the twentieth century found that states were able to avoid a breakdown in the agreement and return to conflict in 87 percent of the cases where they had fully implemented the provisions relating to the reestablishment of a state's monopoly of force.[4]

This chapter addresses a number of challenges related to reestablishing the monopoly of force that parties face during peace negotiations and the broader peace process. First, this chapter discusses the puzzle of whether and how to create a state-held monopoly of force in a manner that ensures a durable peace. Next, it provides a conceptual and legal primer for understanding the principle of sovereignty, as well as the international framework for the authorization of the use of force centered around the United Nations Charter. Then, the chapter explores a number of instances of key state practice to analyze and highlight how parties involved in peace negotiations have sought to manage the conundrums they faced in solving the puzzle of reestablishing the monopoly of force.

THE PUZZLE: WHETHER AND HOW TO CREATE A STATE-HELD MONOPOLY OF FORCE IN A WAY THAT ENSURES A DURABLE PEACE

Prominent political theorists have espoused the idea of a monopoly of force as a key determinant of statehood. Max Weber famously defined states as "the form of human community that (successfully) lays claim to the monopoly of legitimate physical violence within a particular territory."[5] In doing so, Weber drew on a rich tradition of social contract theorists. In the *Leviathan*, Thomas Hobbes theorizes that a commonwealth must join together under the authority of a sovereign who is empowered "to do whatsoever he shall think necessary to be done, both beforehand, for the preserving of Peace and Security, by prevention of discord at home and Hostility from abroad."[6] For these political theorists, it is the common power of the sovereign that allows individuals to exist securely in a shared social condition, which in turn grants the sovereign a monopoly on the legitimate use of force.

This theoretical basis has informed much of the modern literature on the practice of peacebuilding, which generally views a monopoly of force by the state as the ideal to be pursued during peace negotiations.[7] With a monopoly of force by the central government, the state exercises control over its armed forces, police forces, and other security institutions without rival groups competing for control of such institutions. Even though a federal state may set up a system in which certain provinces maintain their own police forces or state units of a national guard, it is government entities rather than rival factions that control these forces.

Creating a monopoly of force for the state can be quite difficult, particularly in the aftermath of intrastate conflict. While the government or mediators may envision the creation or restoration of a state's monopoly of force, the nonstate armed actors are unlikely to readily or immediately agree.

For instance, in 2015, UN envoy Jamal Benomar sought a negotiated solution to the crisis in Yemen. The negotiations failed for a number of reasons, not the least of which was that none of the half a dozen heavily armed nonstate actors engaged in combat and competing for political power could conceive of granting any other party, especially not the government, a monopoly of force.[8] The UN security experts presented the UN envoy with a textbook draft security annex that set forth a traditional state-centric monopoly of force plan. Among other things, it required that the members of the Houthi militia either disarm or integrate into the national army.

Benomar responded by politely suggesting that they walk out to the front gates of the Movenpick hotel, where the envoy's team was housed, and present their plan to the Houthi militia forces, which only days before had routed the government forces, occupied the capital city, Sana'a, and were now manning security checkpoints throughout the capital, including the one in front of the Movenpick, to protect against attacks by Al Qaeda and other forces.

With the increasingly multidimensional nature of conflicts, a proliferation of nonstate armed actors is often involved in the negotiation process. Frequently, there are no clear "winners" when a conflict "ends," which makes it difficult for negotiators to identify a single party that all can agree should acquire a monopoly of force. In cases of extremely devastating civil wars, there may not even be a viable state remaining. In 2014, the Bertelsmann Transformation Index reported that only about half of countries in the midst of a postconflict transition had reestablished a full monopoly of force, with approximately 40 percent having succeeded in establishing only a partial monopoly of force, and the remaining 10 percent having no monopoly of force at all.[9]

To restore the conditions under which a state-held monopoly of force might be possible, states may decide to share force with international or regional actors. The most common source of support comes in the form of peacekeeping forces. These forces may arrive before and/or after a comprehensive peace agreement, but in each case the state will need to navigate whether and how to consent to their presence, agree a mandate for those forces, and share its claim to legitimate force until a durable peace is secured.

After sufficient conditions of peace are restored (often with international and/or regional support) and ongoing violence no longer poses an overt challenge to the state's monopoly of force, the state and nonstate actors can viably explore what form a future monopoly of force should take. Even if there is an evident choice for which group will claim the monopoly, there is frequently deep mistrust among the parties. This animosity makes "losing" parties less willing to relinquish their ability to use force. This is especially true of cases where the state's forces have committed atrocity crimes, decreasing the willingness of the nonstate armed actors to recognize the state's claim to legitimate violence. In general, since nonstate armed actors come into being specifically to challenge the state's monopoly of force, they are unlikely to readily concede a full return to a state monopoly of force.

Given the reluctance of the parties to agree to a rapid reestablishment of a state's monopoly force, parties often develop hybrid approaches that balance their interest in maintaining some interim level of armed forces with the state's interest in building integrated national-level forces for the long term. The conundrums discussed later in this chapter explore how the parties navigate these conflicting security interests revolving around the reestablishment of a state's monopoly of force.

CONCEPTUAL AND LEGAL PRIMER

The conceptual and legal primer for understanding negotiations relating to sharing and/or reestablishing a monopoly of force draws heavily from the principle of sovereignty, as well as the international framework for the authorization of the use of force centered around the UN Charter.

Sovereignty

From the perspective of a state, every peace negotiation is grounded in the precept that the state has absolute sovereign control over its territory and is entitled to operate independently of the influence of other states.[10] These foundational principles of sovereignty, political independence, and territorial integrity were recognized as early as the seventeenth century in the peace treaties of Westphalia,[11] and codified in the UN Charter.[12] These three principles are appropriately and jealously guarded by states, as is explored in greater depth in Chapter 4, on self-determination.

States consider that the principle of sovereignty grants them the exclusive right to use force within the territory of their state. As such, in all but the rarest cases a state must consent to the deployment of peacekeepers and international monitoring or assistance missions that operate on its territory. The requirement of consent permits a state to negotiate the timeline, rules of engagement, and/or standard operating procedures of a peacekeeping or observer mission. These provisions are often included within a status-of-forces agreement, or within a negotiated annex to a Security Council resolution, or a similar resolution by a regional body, authorizing the deployment of a force.[13] The host state's consent is revocable, however; thus states may, and occasionally do, terminate the sharing of their monopoly of force early.

From the perspective of a state, under the principle of sovereignty, nonstate armed actors operating in a state's territory do not have the right to maintain armed forces absent the consent of the state. During negotiations to end an intrastate conflict, states without exception refer to the principle of sovereignty to justify the restoration of a monopoly of force. In contrast, for a nonstate armed actor, the negotiation begins from the starting point that the state has abused its sovereign rights and it is now necessary to effect regime or territorial change, or to subject the state to the political supervision of an international actor prior to reestablishing any monopoly of force for the state.

United Nations Charter

The Charter of the United Nations sets forth the purposes and authorities of the organs of the United Nations.[14] The various powers and authorities of the UN and its subsidiary bodies are often invoked and relied upon to authorize the sharing of the monopoly of force with international actors during the peace process, which may occur before and/or after the negotiation of a peace agreement.

In Chapters VI, VII, and VIII, the UN Charter grants broad authority for both the peaceful and the forceful resolution conflicts that threaten international peace and security.[15] This authority includes preventing conflict recurrence, preventing cross-border spillover, post-ceasefire stabilization and monitoring, assistance with implementing peace agreements, and governance support to postconflict administrations.[16]

While United Nations missions are often referred to in a catchall way as "peace-keeping" missions, it is worth distinguishing between four different types of UN missions: peacemaking, peacekeeping, peace enforcement, and peacebuilding. The UN's 2008 Capstone Doctrine defined peacemaking as "measures to address conflicts in progress," typically involving diplomacy and negotiations to bring armed parties to the table,[17] whereas peacekeeping is "a technique designed to preserve the peace, however fragile, where fighting has been halted, and to assist in implementing agreements achieved by the peacemakers."[18]

Peacekeeping can be preceded or supplemented by peace enforcement, which features "the application, with the authorization of the Security Council, of a range of coercive measures, including the use of military force ... to restore international peace and security in situations where the Security Council has determined the existence of a threat to the peace, breach of the peace or act of aggression."[19] While peacekeeping missions can be authorized under both Chapter VI and Chapter VII, peace enforcement missions are typically authorized under the UN Security Council's Chapter VII authority. While peacekeeping missions are universally bound by host-state consent, peace enforcement operations may occasionally occur in the absence of consent.[20]

Each of these three variants of "peacekeeping" are complemented by peacebuilding, which "involves a range of measures targeted to reduce the risk of lapsing or relapsing into conflict by strengthening national capacities at all levels for conflict management, and to lay the foundation for sustainable peace and development."[21] Peacebuilding efforts underlie or are woven into almost every conundrum addressed in this book. The conundrums addressed in this chapter, however, will focus primarily on peacekeeping and peace enforcement to hone in on how states and the UN rely upon their legal authority to use force to share and/or reestablish a state's monopoly of force.

Chapter VI

Chapter VI of the UN Charter addresses the peaceful resolution of disputes and provides the legal authority for the UN to assemble, fund, and deploy military forces of its member states under the command of the United Nations.[22]

UN peacekeepers under Chapter VI mandates are not authorized to use force to resolve the dispute, but they can undertake a number of missions related to the peace process. These include: assisting with the implementation of a ceasefire in order to create the conditions necessary for the parties to negotiate a peace agreement; assisting with the implementation of a peace agreement; protecting civilians; monitoring disarmament, demobilization, and reintegration; supporting security sector reform; creating conditions for safe, free, and fair elections; and otherwise aiding with the restoration of the full monopoly of force to the state.[23]

There is some legal debate over the binding nature of Chapter VI resolutions. Article 25 within Chapter V of the UN Charter provides the Security Council the power to pass legally binding resolutions, denoting that "[t]he Members of the United Nations agree to accept and carry out the decisions of the Security Council in accordance with the present Charter."[24] Legal scholars disagree, however, as to whether or not Article 25 is sufficient to render a UN Security Council resolution, such as those implicitly taken under Chapter VI, binding without also invoking the further enforcement authority that comes in Chapter VII.[25] The predominant consensus is that Article 25 does apply to more than just Chapter VII resolutions.[26] Interestingly, when the Security Council acts under Chapter VI, it does not cite Chapter VI in the language of the resolution.[27]

Chapter VII

Chapter VII addresses the United Nation's ability to respond to threats to international peace and security.[28] In the case that peaceful measures fail to pacify the threat, Article 42 grants the Security Council the power to "take such action by air, sea, or land forces as may be necessary to maintain or restore international peace and security. Such action may include demonstrations, blockade, and other operations by air, sea, or land forces of Members of the United Nations."[29]

The UN Charter recognizes that there are limits to a state's claim to sovereignty. In Article 2, the Charter specifies: "Nothing contained in the present Charter shall authorize the United Nations to intervene in matters which are essentially within the domestic jurisdiction of any state … but this principle shall not prejudice the application of enforcement measures under Chapter VII."[30] In this way, Chapter VII provides legal authority to interfere with a state's sovereignty in order to restore peace and security.

In earlier years, the Security Council did not explicitly invoke Chapter VII in its resolutions – mirroring its omission of references to Chapter VI. The authority to intervene was taken to be understood from the context of the conflict and substance of the clauses in the resolution. As member states sought to add greater clarity and emphasis to Security Council resolutions that called upon the heightened authority present in Chapter VII, they increasingly added the phrase "acting under Chapter VII" to these resolutions – particularly those that authorized peace enforcement.[31]

In July 1950, the UN authorized the use of force by member states to repel the armed attack by North Korea against South Korea, and to "restore international peace and security in the area."[32] The UN did so in response to a request by South Korea to share its monopoly of force in order to defend itself from the attack by North Korea. In a subsequent resolution, the UN Security Council recommended that all states providing military assistance to South Korea do so under the unified command of the United States. The United States was authorized to use the UN flag at its discretion in the course of the operations.[33] Under this arrangement, the UN maintained close contact with the American command, but did not exercise any control over the action of those forces.

In 1960, the Security Council underwent a significant expansion in the authorization it granted its own peacekeepers to use force, beginning with the United Nations operation in the Congo that authorized the "use of force, if necessary, in the last resort."[34] The Security Council expanded this power further when granting missions in Cyprus and Lebanon the authority not only to use force in self-defense, but also in "defense of the mission." Eventually, the legal permission for the use of force was expansive enough that missions could use all necessary powers to defend their forces, and to implement their mandate.[35]

As illustrated in the Key State Practice and Conundrums sections, in the case of Kosovo, the Security Council invoked Chapter VII to provide the legal authority to entirely exclude a state's claim to monopolize force. UN Security Council Resolution 1244 placed Kosovo (at the time a province of Serbia) under UN interim administration and authorized North Atlantic Treaty Organization (NATO) forces to maintain the peace and security. The resolution excluded all Serbian forces from the territory of Kosovo and called for the immediate withdrawal of all forces extant in the region.[36]

Chapter VIII

Chapter VIII addresses the relationship between UN forces and those of regional bodies in peace operations. Article 52 first clarifies that action by the Security

Council does not prohibit the pacific settlement of disputes by regional entities.[37] Such action is in fact encouraged, provided that it is done in a manner that is consistent with the principles of the UN Charter.

In cases in which the Security Council is authorizing a peace operation, Article 53 also permits the Security Council to, "where appropriate, utilize such regional arrangements or agencies for enforcement action under its authority."[38] The UN may thus use Chapter VIII to call upon regional bodies to support peacekeeping or peace-enforcement measures. As we will see in the Key State Practice and Conundrums sections, the UN is increasingly authorizing peacekeeping and peace-enforcing missions by regional bodies such as NATO, Organization for Security and Co-operation in Europe (OSCE), the Economic Community of West African States, and the African Union.

KEY STATE PRACTICE

This chapter draws on the following key state practice cases for a discussion of the various conundrums the parties to a peace negotiation face when confronting the puzzle of postconflict security. The paragraphs that follow highlight the relationship between each peace process and the sharing or reestablishment of a monopoly of force. For more on these conflicts, negotiations, and agreements, consult the Appendix.

Angola achieved independence via the 1975 Alvor Agreement between Portugal and the Angolan Liberation Movements.[39] The failure of the power-sharing arrangement included in the Alvor Agreement plunged Angola into a decades-long civil war.[40] In 1991, the opposing forces signed a ceasefire agreement, the Bicesse Accord. The accord provided for the creation of a monopoly of force through the immediate integration of the state security forces and nonstate armed actors.[41] This effort failed, in part due to the compressed timeline for creating the monopoly of force through a merger of the forces.[42] In 1994, the parties signed the Lusaka Protocol, which called for a ceasefire, the sharing of the monopoly of force with a UN peacekeeping mission, and the consolidation of forces into a single national army.[43] After three iterations of a UN presence, which evolved from observing and monitoring to peacekeeping, Angola requested in January 1999 that the peacekeeping forces withdraw.[44] In 2002, the Angolan forces defeated the nonstate armed actors, and the parties signed the Luena Memorandum of Understanding, bringing an end to the armed conflict.[45]

In 1992, in the midst of the violent dissolution of the former Yugoslavia, the UN Security Council established the UN Protection Force (UNPROFOR) with the consent of the parties to the conflict. The force was initially intended for **Croatia** but soon after expanded to include **Bosnia and Herzegovina** as well as **Macedonia**.[46] The UN force's confusing and ever-changing mandate, frequently characterized as "Chapter VI and a half," repeatedly failed to adequately protect civilians. As violence peaked in 1995, the international community, acting under Chapter VII, decided to intervene and essentially assume near-total control over Bosnia's monopoly of force, with NATO authorizing airstrikes designed to bring an end to the conflict by forcing the Serbian forces into a genuine negotiation process.[47] In November 1995, the parties signed the Dayton Peace Accords.[48] The accords provided for the deployment of a NATO-led Implementation Force (IFOR), and a UN civilian police force to enforce the peace agreement. The agreement granted NATO forces near-total control over Bosnia's monopoly of force. The Dayton Accords also created a domestic military structure in which each of the entities (the Federation of Bosnia and Herzegovina, and the Republika Srpska) would in the interim maintain a separate army.[49] In 2005, a decade after the signing of the Dayton Accords, the three armies established a joint command at the national level and a national Ministry of Defense.[50]

Burundi experienced severe ethnic violence, including massacres of Hutus in 1972 and 1988, and of Tutsis following the 1993 murder of then President Ndadaye.[51] Years of negotiations eventually produced the Arusha Peace and Reconciliation Agreement in August 2000, which outlined a power-sharing agreement but did not include a ceasefire. Hutu rebel groups declined to sign the Arusha Agreement. Nevertheless, the security and defense forces integration agreements outlined in the Arusha Agreement became the basis for subsequent efforts to reestablish a monopoly of force. The transitional government of Burundi was established in November 2001, and subsequently negotiated a joint ceasefire in 2002, as well as separate ceasefires with the nonstate armed actors. Beginning in October 2003, the African Union Mission in Burundi supported the implementation of the Arusha Agreement and agreed to share Burundi's monopoly of force via monitoring of these ceasefires. In June 2004, this shared monopoly of force was transferred to a UN peacekeeping mission.[52]

Shortly after declaring independence from Portugal, **Mozambique** descended into civil war.[53] Domestic devastation plus declining international support eventually motivated the parties to sign the 1992 General Peace Agreement. The agreement established a permanent ceasefire, and provided for reestablishment of the monopoly of force through the joint creation of a new national Mozambican Defense Force, and the disarmament and demobilization of all other units.[54] The agreement also provided for a sharing of force with UN forces, which would monitor the implementation of the General Peace Agreement. Peace held for two decades, until violence erupted again in 2013 and the nonstate armed actors declared the 1992 agreement invalid.[55] New agreements between the parties in 2014 and 2019 promised a permanent ceasefire and new governance structures.[56]

From 1988 to 1998, the **Bougainville** Revolutionary Army fought an armed conflict for their right to secede, against both the **Papua New Guinea** Defense Force and Papua New Guinea's proxy force, the Bougainville Resistance Forces. In 2001, the parties signed the Bougainville Peace Agreement, which granted

Bougainville autonomous status under the newly established autonomous Bougainville government. The agreement provided for a referendum to be held on Bougainville's political status in 10–15 years. Until then, the parties agreed to cease the use of force, and restore the national government's monopoly of force. The parties also approved and annexed a weapons disposal plan.[57] In the independence referendum, held between November and December 2019, 98 percent of voters cast ballots for independence.[58]

In 1994, the **Rwandan** armed forces incited a genocide that killed an estimated 800,000 Tutsis and moderate Hutus over the course of 100 days.[59] With the Rwandan Patriotic Front's definitive defeat of the Rwandan army, and the end of the genocide, the new government under Paul Kagame secured a monopoly of force for the new government. In an effort to retain the monopoly of force and guard against a counterrevolution, the government adhered to the security provisions agreed in the earlier 1993 Arusha Peace Agreement and created an ethnically integrated national army.[60]

Between 1991 and 2002, the Revolutionary United Front (RUF), with the support of Liberian President Charles Taylor, fought a brutal civil war against **Sierra Leone**.[61] During this time Sierra Leone shared its monopoly of force with a wide range of actors, including the Kamajors militia, Executive Outcomes (a South African mercenary force), ECOMOG[62] forces from the Economic Community of West African States, the United Nations, Guinea, and the United Kingdom. The parties signed the Lomé Peace Accord in July 1999, which granted the founder of the RUF, Foday Sankoh, amnesty and the position of vice president in return for demobilizing and disarming the RUF. The accord also provided for the disarmament of the Sierra Leone army.[63] The agreement collapsed, and Sierra Leone, in concert with its international allies defeated the RUF and reestablished its monopoly of force.

The 2005 Comprehensive Peace Agreement between **Sudan** and **South Sudan**[64] sought to bring an end to the decades-long conflict by granting the south the possibility of independence after an interim period of national unity where the north and the south would seek political integration and limited democratic transformation. During the interim period, the north and south shared the monopoly of force, with the south maintaining its separate armed forces, along with the creation of a limited number of joint integrated units. There were limited provisions for DDR, and an even more limited effort to implement those provisions. The southern population voted overwhelmingly for independence, with South Sudan becoming a new state, and rather promptly descending into civil war.

In addition to the conflict with South Sudan, **Sudan** was also engaged in conflict in **Darfur** from 2003 to 2020, and with **Southern Kordofan** and **Blue Nile** from 2011 to 2020. The Abuja and Doha agreements relating to Darfur established innovative, yet ultimately unsuccessful, mechanisms for reestablishing Sudan's monopoly of force. Throughout much of the conflict, Sudan begrudgingly shared its monopoly of force with a hybrid African Union/United Nations peacekeeping force, whose mandate substantially evolved over the course of the conflict. In 2020 Sudan reached a multitrack peace agreement with the nonstate actors in Darfur, as well as some of the nonstate actors in Southern Kordofan and Blue Nile, in addition to other intra-Sudan regional parties. These agreements provided for an eclectic, and separate, array of means to share the monopoly of force in the interim, and over time to reestablish the monopoly of force for Sudan.

CONUNDRUMS

Parties to a conflict face two buckets of conundrums when they seek to resolve the question of the monopoly of force. The first relates to sharing the monopoly of force with the international community. The second relates to sharing the monopoly of force with each other.

Negotiations relating to the sharing of force with the international community are multidimensional and occur several times throughout the peace process. They often, but not always, involve all the parties to the conflict, and they often also include various representatives of the international community, including the mediators, the UN Security Council, and states providing peacekeeping or peace-enforcing forces. In some circumstances, the international community may act unilaterally to erode a state's monopoly of force.

Negotiations oftentimes initially occur when the parties are negotiating a cessation of hostilities or a ceasefire and are seeking the assistance of the international community in observing, monitoring, or enforcing the agreement. Subsequent rounds of negotiations may occur as the parties seek to evolve the depth and breadth of these initial cessation and ceasefire agreements. Negotiations also resume when the parties begin to discuss a comprehensive agreement, which nearly always includes security provisions. Frequently, one or more of the parties may require the sharing of the monopoly of force with international forces to ensure the implementation of those and other provisions of the agreement.

When negotiating the sharing of force with the international community the parties nearly always address questions of: the consent of the state, and often the consent of the nonstate actors; the nature and configuration of the international forces, including the command structure of the international forces; and the mandate of those forces.

Negotiations relating to the sharing of force between the state and nonstate actors can be grouped into three main approaches. In the first approach, the state seeks to restore full control over the monopoly of force.

In the second approach, the state restores full yet modified control over the monopoly of force via the integration of nonstate armed actors into the national forces. In these instances, the parties often develop elaborate provisions relating to the disarmament, demobilization, and reintegration of nonstate forces, coupled with security sector reform for the national forces. The parties and the international community also often establish processes for either amnesty or accountability as a condition for and as an effort to underpin the durability of the integration of the forces. The sequencing and timing of DDR, SSR, and amnesty or accountability often proves crucial to the success of efforts to integrate forces.

In the third approach, the state restores limited control over the monopoly of force by permitting nonstate actors to maintain their forces and command structure under the umbrella command of the national forces. This approach is most frequently adopted when the peace agreement envisions a future determination of final status for a party seeking external self-determination, or where one or more of the nonstate actors is not firmly convinced the agreement will be durable. This approach is often coupled with efforts to promote some degree of integration among special units of the state and nonstate forces, as well as a timeline for the eventual integration of forces.

Negotiating the Sharing of Force with the International Community

During an intrastate conflict, a state's monopoly of force is eroded by nonstate armed actors. As such, it is often impossible for a state to maintain peace and security within its borders. Notably, in many instances it is both the state and the nonstate armed actors that threaten the peace and security of the state.

In order to restore peace and security, the state, often in partnership with the nonstate armed actors, will seek the assistance of the international community, in the form of the United Nations, or a regional political or military body, such as the African Union or NATO. In some limited instances, the international community will unilaterally impose itself on a state to restore peace and security, as with the case of the humanitarian intervention by NATO in Serbia/Kosovo.

A recent scholarly survey observed that in over 60 percent of intrastate conflicts, international peacekeepers had been deployed to assist with the restoration of peace and security and the reestablishment of the state's monopoly of force.[65] The survey also noted that the engagement of the international community to restore a monopoly of force is a relatively new development, and that between the end of World War II and the end of the Cold War states only sought the assistance of international peacekeepers in less than 14 percent of the cases.[66]

When a state and nonstate actors seek to engage the international community, they do so in a variety of negotiation settings. Initially, the parties will most likely consent to and seek involvement through a negotiated ceasefire. Nearly all ceasefires contain a provision for some degree of international involvement, be it observing, monitoring, or enforcing. When seeking to commit the international community to such action, the parties invariably must include representatives of the international community. In these cases, the international community oftentimes acts as both a mediator and a party, at least with respect to the provisions relating to international engagement.

Next, the parties frequently work with the international community to craft some sort of letter or formal request for assistance. The drafting of the formal request often entails the engagement of the international community. As with the letter, the response also frequently includes the engagement of the state, and, likely to a lesser degree, the nonstate actors. The response of the United Nations nearly always takes the form of a UN Security Council Resolution, with the state having a right to participate in the debate concerning the resolution.[67] These resolutions often focus heavily on the mandate of the mission.

The intervening forces and the state then negotiate a status-of-forces agreement,[68] which sets forth the nature of the mission, the privileges and immunities of the international forces, and the rights and obligations of the state and the international forces.[69] The deploying force then drafts the Rules of Engagement for its military personnel, often with some degree of cooperation with the state.[70]

When negotiating the sharing of force with the international community, the parties nearly always address questions of: the consent of the state, and often of the nonstate actors; the nature and configuration of the international forces, including their command structure; and the mandate of those forces.

Consent of the State and Nonstate Parties

The first conundrum faced by a state in conflict is whether and how to consent to the sharing of its monopoly of force with external actors. Given that sovereignty, and the monopoly of force, are cornerstones of statehood, states are exceedingly cautious about granting consent to have international forces deploy to their territory. The decision to share this monopoly of force oftentimes occurs only after the state has fully exhausted its efforts to resolve the conflict through the use of force and/or where it is forced into ceasefire negotiations either by the success of the nonstate actors or via pressure from the international community.

The state must then contend not only with whether it shares its monopoly of force with the international community but also whether it shares its sovereign right of consent with the nonstate armed actors. Without the consent of the nonstate armed actors, the international community may be unwilling to deploy forces. Yet by granting the nonstate armed actors the right to consent, the state begins the slippery slope of diluting its sovereign authority as the price of peace.

The state must also determine if it will specify whether it is requesting Chapter VI or VII authority, though it can choose to remain silent on this question. Chapter VI is a lighter infringement on the sovereignty of a state, but may result in the state undertaking a sharing of its monopoly of force, but without sufficient authority by the international community to actually bring an end to the conflict. If the state requests Chapter VII, however, the international forces may possess all the necessary authority, and may use that authority against the state. In this case, the state has not only shared its monopoly of force, but the international forces may then use that force to further restrict the sovereign actions of the state.

The state must also consider how to share its monopoly of force in such a way that the international community does not use that initial consent to embark on an evolution of the mandate of the international forces. The state may find itself in a position where it consents to an initial deployment of lightly armed forces with a limited mandate, but the deployed forces and their political overseers interpret the mandate in expansive terms, and enhance the military capabilities of the forces. The state also runs the risk that the international community, absent the consent of the state, will formally modify the mandate and the nature of the deployed military forces.

Finally, the state must consider how it might withdraw consent for the sharing of its monopoly of force, in whole or in part. To do so could tip the state back into widespread violence, or the international community may decide that the initial consent is irrevocable and refuse to leave until the conflict is resolved, thus further eroding the state's sovereignty.

Approaches to Resolving the Consent Conundrum

In the case of Mozambique, the government initially agreed with RENAMO[71] that they would jointly express its consent to share Mozambique's monopoly of force. The government did so in a Joint Declaration in August 1992 wherein it expressed its commitment to consent to "the role of the international community, particularly the United Nations, in monitoring and guaranteeing the implementation of the General Peace Agreement, particularly the cease-fire and the electoral process."[72] Subsequently, in October 1992, the parties settled upon a general peace agreement, which provided for additional and quite extensive engagement of the United Nations, in terms of both monitoring the implementation of the agreement and carrying out specific functions in relation to the ceasefire, the elections, and humanitarian assistance. The United Nations was also charged with chairing the Supervisory and Monitoring Commission designed to oversee the implementation of the agreement.[73]

The United Nations participated in the negotiations as observers and helped to shape the specific nature of the request. To formally express consent, the president of Mozambique submitted a letter to the UN secretary-general requesting the United Nations to immediately deploy UN personnel to assist with monitoring the implementation of the agreement, and supervising the ceasefire and reintegration process. The president set an expiration time frame for the deployment as "until the holding of the General Elections," which was to take place a year later.[74] The UN secretary-general then acted upon this request and secured the authorization of the Security Council to deploy a UN mission.

Mozambique sought to navigate the conundrum of consent by involving the nonstate actor RENAMO in a general Joint Declaration, but reserved for itself the sovereign right to communicate this request to the United Nations, and to frame its consent in a presidential letter. Mozambique also set clear expectations as to the nature of the mandate, and specified a time limit for the sharing of its monopoly of force. The peace agreement also carefully framed the role of the UN in various places as observers, with a role to monitor and verify the implementation of the agreement and, when called upon, to provide material and technical assistance. In only one provision did it call upon the UN to guarantee the implementation of the agreement. To carry out its mission, the UN deployed over 6,500 military personnel, along with nearly 400 civilian staff. During the course of the mission, Mozambique and RENAMO consented to and sought an expansion of the mandate to include the oversight and reform of the police force, which resulted in the deployment of over 1,000 international police officers.[75]

Notably, Mozambique and the United Nations did not negotiate a status-of-forces agreement, which caused a number of both logistical and legal issues that delayed the full deployment of the UN forces. This lack of a status-of-forces agreement, together with other issues, ultimately set back the implementation of the DDR process and the elections by a year.[76] On the whole, Mozambique effectively managed its consent to the sharing of its monopoly of force and kept the UN largely within its original mandate, and a reasonable extension of the time frame, with monopoly of force restored at the end of the deployment.

In the case of Sudan, sharing monopoly of force with the UN and African Union in Darfur proved to be a complicated story of evolved and forced consent. As part of the Comprehensive Peace Agreement between Sudan and South Sudan, the state of Sudan consented in 2005 to the creation of a UN mission in Sudan, which resulted in the deployment of up to 10,000 UN forces in Sudan and South Sudan to help implement the peace agreement.[77] Previously, Sudan consented to the deployment of a limited number of African Union forces into Darfur with the mandate to monitor and support the humanitarian ceasefire signed in N'Djamena in April 2004.[78]

In addition to the ceasefire negotiations, the African Union also led the effort to reach a Darfur peace agreement in Abuja. In response to growing conflict in Darfur, and with the consent of Sudan, in October 2004 the African Union increased its military contingent to over 2,300 and nearly 1,000 civilian police, and then again in April 2005 to over 6,000 military personnel. The mandate was extended to include not only monitoring the ceasefire but also helping to establish a secure environment conducive to the delivery of humanitarian assistance and the return of refugees and internally displaced persons.[79]

In May 2006, Sudan and the Darfur nonstate armed actors reached agreement in Abuja on the Darfur Peace Agreement. While the agreement provided for an extensive role for the African Union forces in providing security for the civilian population, it provided for only the most minimal role for the United Nations in the areas of observing the ceasefire, providing humanitarian assistance, and aiding internally displaced persons and returning refugees.[80] Despite the lack of consent in the peace agreement for a UN military force, the UN secretary-general notified the Security Council of his recommendation that the UN deploy over 18,000 UN peacekeepers to assist with the implementation of the agreement. The secretary-general advocated for Sudan to accept such a mission on the basis that it would preserve the peace recently concluded with South Sudan.[81]

The UN Security Council acted in August 2006, and adopted Resolution 1706, which authorized, under Chapter VII, the expansion of the UN mission's mandate to include a deployment of thousands of additional forces to Darfur to aid in the protection of the civilian population. The Security Council also requested the secretary-general to work with the African Union to integrate its force into the UN force. The Security Council in its first operative paragraph of the resolution invited Sudan to consent to the deployment and this sharing of its monopoly of force.[82] Sudan did not provide the requested consent, and the UN was unable to deploy armed peacekeepers to Darfur.

In response, the UN worked to increase the troop strength of the African Union forces, and the creation of a joint African Union/United Nations peacekeeping mission. After a year of negotiations, during which time Sudan came under intense international pressure, Sudan agreed to the creation of the United Nations–African Union Hybrid Operation in Darfur, called UNAMID,[83] which consisted of over 20,000 troops.[84]

As will be discussed in the Approaches to Resolving the Nature and Configuration of Forces Conundrum section, Indonesia similarly consented to the sharing of its monopoly of force with an Australian-led Chapter VII UN force after significant political and economic pressure to do so.

Burundi, however, faced the opposite scenario. In Burundi, the state explicitly requested that the Security Council invoke a Chapter VII mandate in order to ensure a robust peacekeeping force that was to take over the peacekeeping responsibilities previously held by an African Union force (most of which was rolled into the new UN force). In a March 2004 letter from the permanent representative of Burundi to the president of the Security Council requesting a UN peacekeeping mission to support the implementation of the Arusha Accords: "In view of the work to be done, the Government of Burundi believes that such a mission should be provided with substantial means and, above all, with an adequate mandate under chapter VII of the Charter of the United Nations."[85] The letter then laid out a number of objectives for the peacekeeping mission. Many of these were granted in the Security Council's subsequent resolution, which acted under Chapter VII to deploy a United Nations operation in Burundi with the authority to "use all necessary means," including force, to carry out its mandate.[86]

In autumn 1991, Yugoslavia consented, via letter to the president of the Security Council, to the deployment of a peacekeeping mission on its territory.[87] Bosnia, which was a part of Yugoslavia at the time but was in the process, along with Croatia and Slovenia, of seeking external self-determination, also consented to the deployment of peacekeepers. The UN coupled the deployment of peacekeepers with an arms embargo on the territory of Yugoslavia.[88] Over time, as the people of Bosnia were subjected to attempted genocide,[89] Bosnia argued that the arms embargo prevented it from exercising its right of self-defense and therefore was illegal,[90] and that it no longer consented to its application or enforcement. The UN, however, refused to withdraw the embargo, and noted that it if the United States proceeded with threats to unilaterally lift the embargo then the UN forces would be withdrawn.[91]

Angola was, however, able to withdraw consent for the deployment of peacekeepers on its territory in order to regain its monopoly of force and seek to resolve the conflict through a return to violence.[92] After three iterations of a UN presence, which evolved from observing and monitoring to peacekeeping, Angola requested in January 1999 that the peacekeeping forces withdraw. In light of the unwillingness or inability of Angola and the nonstate armed actor UNITA[93] to maintain a genuine peace process, the secretary-general supported the end of the mission, and the Security Council terminated the mission in February 1999.[94] In 2002, the Angolan forces defeated UNITA, bringing an end to the armed conflict.

In some limited circumstances, the state is forced to share or surrender its monopoly of force. In August 1990, at the height of the Liberian conflict, the Economic Community of West African States authorized its ECOMOG forces to essentially fight their way into Liberia in order to force a cessation of hostilities among the parties, and to occupy Monrovia, the capital.[95] They were authorized to do so by the Economic Community of West African States and, for an initial two-year period, maintained a relatively successful ceasefire.

In the case of Kosovo, NATO forces launched an intensive seventy-eight-day air campaign against the Serbian government forces, in both Kosovo and Serbia, which were conducting a campaign of atrocity crimes against the Kosovo-Albanian population. NATO successfully defeated the Serbian forces and, through a subsequent process of negotiation and Security Council Resolution 1244, excluded Serbia's ability to exercise a monopoly of force over Kosovo territory.

In the case of Libya, the UN Security Council, under Resolution 1973, invoked the doctrine of humanitarian intervention to authorize member states to take all necessary measures, except foreign occupation, to protect civilians in Libya, including the establishment and enforcement of a no-fly zone.[96] The NATO-led intervention resulted in interim security for the population of Libya, and the subsequent overthrow and execution of Muammar Gaddafi by Libya opposition forces.

Nature and Configuration of the International Forces
When in a position where it is necessary to share the monopoly of force, states must address of the conundrum of which forces the state should share its monopoly with.

While the United Nations is the most commonly thought of, there is actually a plethora of ad hoc and standing forces with which a state can share its monopoly of force. Similarly, there are degrees of "force" that can be shared, whether it is the monitoring of the actions of the state and nonstate actors, the use of force, or the ultimate Chapter VII use of overwhelming force to initiate or secure a peace. The latter will be addressed in the next section, where mandate is discussed. Having the nature of the mandate in mind is important when deciding upon the nature of the international forces.

One question associated with this conundrum is that of "too much or too little" in terms of the ability of the force to match the challenge it is called upon to address. An unarmed, lightly resourced ad hoc monitoring mission grafted onto an existing international institution may be just the right "light" touch to share a fragment of a state's monopoly of force in an effort to appease the international community and be relieved of political and economic sanctions. Such a force is also more palatable in terms of any potential affront to sovereignty, and it may avoid the unnecessary militarization of a force mandated to simply observe or monitor.

Such an unarmed light presence could, however, be just the beginning, and could eventually lead to a heavily armed Chapter VII force. Once the door is opened to sharing the monopoly of force, the legal and political precedent is set for such a "sharing." Moreover, a light force may not possess the strength to carry out its mandate, and as time evolves the state, and/or the nonstate armed actors, may come to desire an effective monitoring force.

Another question parties face is whether the force should be from an ad hoc collection of states, or a regional force, or a truly global force – meaning the United Nations. Ad hoc collections of states, which are often neighboring states, such as the Nordic countries, are more likely to be responsive and sensitive to the sovereign interests of the state. They may also be less effective at preventing breaches by the state and nonstate armed actors. Regional bodies of which the state is a member are likely to be more responsive to prerogatives of sovereignty, and may or may not possess the necessary assertiveness and competence to accomplish the mandate, but certainly do provide the necessary political cover to ease political and economic sanctions. Recently, a handful of regional entities have sought to enhance their peace-monitoring and peacekeeping capabilities.

The state, and the nonstate armed actors, must also decide whether they seek the involvement of a purely regional political organization, a regional political organization with ability to authorize and organize an ad hoc military operation comprised of its member states, or a regional military organization like NATO. The answer again depends on the appetite of the state to share its sovereignty, and the sincerity of the parties' wish for an effective force.

Relatedly, the parties must consider who should command the force. In some instances, the organization exercises overall command consistent with its decision-making structure, while in others it may delegate the command to a member state.

When there is more than one entity engaged in the sharing of the monopoly of force, those entities may establish a dual-key approach to authorizing activities such as the use of force. Streamlined command structures tend to be more effective, but are more of a threat to the forces of the state and nonstate armed actors when it comes to decisions to use force.

Finally, parties must determine whether to seek the overlay of a UN Security Council resolution when they decide to engage a non-UN force. In the event the Security Council adopts a resolution under Chapter VIII, that resolution can modify through expansion or limitation the mandate of the force. If it chooses to declare that it is taking this action under Chapter VII, it may provide definitive authority to use military force. Having a Security Council overlay has the benefit of providing the nonstate armed actors additional assurance that the ad hoc collection of states, or a regional force, will be subject to some degree of oversight by the UN to offset any tilt toward the sovereign interests of the state. The engagement of the Security Council, though, will remove control over the mandate and actions of the force even further from the state and nonstate actors.

Approaches to Resolving the Nature and Configuration Conundrum

In some instances, the state and the nonstate actors have a shared interest in creating an ad hoc monitoring mission with which to share a sliver of the state's monopoly of force in order to secure the implementation of a ceasefire. In the case of Sri Lanka, the state had a previous negative experience with the Indian peacekeeping force that operated on Sri Lankan territory from 1987 to 1990 with the mission to guarantee the implementation of the Indo-Sri Lanka Accord. Sri Lanka was also generally sensitive to infringements on its sovereignty. The Tamil Tigers, on the other hand, objected to the involvement of any state that listed the militant group as a terrorist organization, which included a vast number of states in the international community. Thus, when Sri Lanka and the Tamil Tigers reached a ceasefire in 2002, they invited Norway, Sweden, Finland, Denmark, and Iceland to form an unarmed, sixty-person Sri Lanka mission to monitor its implementation. Remarkably, the agreement provided that the head of the mission would possess final authority regarding interpretation of the agreement.[97]

The mission failed for a number of reasons. First and foremost, both Sri Lanka and the Tamil Tigers ultimately determined it was in their interests to seek a final resolution of the conflict through the use of force. Notable pressures on the monitoring mission included the demand by the Tamil Tigers in June 2006 to exclude Swedish, Finnish, and Danish monitors on the basis that their countries had imposed antiterrorism sanctions on the militant group,[98] leaving just twenty monitors from Norway and Iceland. Sri Lanka also grew increasingly anxious about the monitoring mission as it deemed the mission to be infringing on its sovereignty outside the scope of "monitoring." For instance, in 2003 the Sri Lankan navy notified the monitoring mission that, under the ceasefire agreement, it was intending to interdict a Tamil Tigers arms supply naval vessel. The monitors notified the militant group, which then diverted the ship and avoided capture.[99] Sri Lanka also took sovereign offense when the monitors facilitated a "diplomatic" visit from an Icelandic Foreign Ministry official with the head of the militant group.[100]

In January 2008, Sri Lanka formally withdrew from the ceasefire and terminated the monitoring mission.[101] In May 2009, Sri Lanka defeated the Tamil Tigers, amid credible allegations of atrocity crimes committed by Sri Lankan forces.[102]

In El Salvador, on the other hand, the state and the Farabundo Martí National Liberation Front agreed to a UN observer mission during the initial stages of their peace process to monitor the protection of human rights and investigate any violations. The parties signed a human rights accord in July 1990,[103] and requested the UN to prepare to deploy a light mission to observe the forthcoming ceasefire. The parties then requested that the UN preemptively deploy a peacekeeping force to monitor the implementation of the human rights accord, which it did in 1991.[104]

The parties then agreed twice more to expand the mission, first to support the Chapultepec Peace Agreement signed in Mexico City to monitor the ceasefire, and second to monitor and assist with the transformation of the national police force.[105] The UN, acting under Chapter VI,[106] deployed approximately 350 military observers and 315 civilian police to accomplish this task. As the peace process moved forward with implementation, the UN correspondingly drew down its forces. Second, in response to a request by El Salvador to the UN secretary-general to monitor elections,[107] the UN then deployed about 900 electoral observers.[108]

In April 1995, the UN mission ended with the withdrawal of the remaining monitors. Both the UN mission and the peace agreement were generally considered to be successful;[109] nearly all the provisions were deemed fully implemented, with an overall implementation score of 95.83 out of 100 by the University of Notre Dame's Kroc Institute for International Peace Studies.[110]

In the case of the dissolution of the former Yugoslavia, the parties consented, via the Brioni Declaration in July 1991,[111] to the creation of an ad hoc European Community monitoring mission. The declaration was followed a few days later with a memorandum of understanding, which was essentially a status-of-forces agreement, signed in Belgrade.[112] The Brioni Declaration launched what was to become a long and tortuous series of negotiations to first forestall and then to end the war in Yugoslavia, culminating in the Dayton Accords.

The monitoring mission agreed to by Yugoslavia, and authorized by the declaration, was initially intended to monitor the ceasefire agreement and the withdrawal of Yugoslav national army forces from Slovenia. The mission was comprised of a small number of military and civilian personnel from the European Community and the Conference on Security and Cooperation in Europe. Each observer team was to be escorted at all times by a liaison officer of each of the opposing parties.

Interestingly, the first monitors deployed were from the Dutch navy and were dressed completely in white. White became the color of the mission, and all subsequent monitors were dressed in white and drove unmarked white vehicles, earning them the Yugoslav nickname of "ice cream men."

Over the course of its operation from July 1991 to December 2007, the scope of the mission expanded to include Bosnia, Croatia, Macedonia, Montenegro, and Serbia, with the mandate to collect and report to the EU on the military situation, engage in negotiations to resolve local conflicts, assist humanitarian organizations, monitor the human rights situation, and eventually report on violations of the Bosnian no-fly zone.[113] Building from the establishment of this extremely light monitoring mission, the nature and configuration of the international community's sharing of the monopoly of force, first with Yugoslavia, and then with its successor states, haltingly evolved to become increasingly militarized.

During this time, the international community moved from a deployment of 50 military liaison officers, to the deployment of 39,000 peacekeepers as part of UN Protection Force I (UNPROFOR), to an additional deployment of peacekeepers and an expanded mandate of UN Protection Force II. The international community then augmented the peacekeepers with an ad hoc, heavily armed Rapid Reaction Force with troops from France, the United Kingdom, and the Netherlands. And then further augmented the force to include the use of NATO air power: first to enforce a no-fly zone and then to provide air support for UN peacekeepers. Finally, as authorized by the Dayton peace negotiations, NATO deployed 50,000 troops, anchored by America's First Armored Division, to secure the implementation of the agreement.

The mandate correspondingly evolved from Chapter VI to so-called "Chapter VI and a half," to Chapter VII. Significantly, in August 1992, the Security Council passed Resolution 770, which, acting under Chapter VII, called on "states to take nationally or through regional agencies all measures necessary to facilitate in coordination with the United Nations" the delivery of humanitarian assistance in Bosnia.[114] Yet in September 1992 the Security Council authorized UNPROFOR to carry out this task with the assistance of member states, downgrading the resolution to a Chapter VI.[115]

The situation in Kosovo saw a similar dramatic evolution of the nature and configuration of international forces sharing the monopoly of force with Serbia. The basis for the initial sharing of the monopoly of force is somewhat murky. With the increasing violence in Kosovo in the summer of 1998, and with the memory of the wars in Croatia and Bosnia as a backdrop, the international community feared another Balkan war with the accompanying humanitarian crisis and atrocity crimes.

In June 1998, five member states of the international community created the ad hoc mission known as the Kosovo Diplomatic Observer Mission to monitor levels of violence in Kosovo. The mission was created by the European Union and five other states (with Canada, the United States, Russia, France, and the United Kingdom operating as their own missions) increasing their military and civilian presence in their embassies in Belgrade, Serbia, and sending out staff to travel throughout Kosovo, and in some cases stationing staff there permanently. The five missions did not have an overall coordinating structure, but did share information widely among interested states. Rather than seeking the consent of Serbia, the missions used their diplomatic status as the legal authority for the missions.

In September 1998, the United States negotiated a ceasefire agreement with Serbia. The agreement provided that Serbia would permit the creation of the unarmed Kosovo Verification Mission.[116] The agreement also provided for the creation of operation Eagle Eye, which would permit NATO to fly oversight missions throughout the territory of Kosovo. The Security Council, acting under Chapter VII, endorsed both of these missions and mandated the Commission on Security and Cooperation in Europe to staff the Kosovo Verification Mission, and NATO to conduct the overflight operation.[117] The Kosovo Verification Mission selected orange as the color for its vehicles to distinguish it from previous monitoring and peacekeeping missions.[118]

To support the exchange of information between the Kosovo Verification Mission and operation Eagle Eye, NATO established the Kosovo Verification Coordination Centre in Macedonia. The center was essential for collecting data that would be used for future political and military planning. NATO, learning the lessons of the sometimes-hapless UNPROFOR efforts, where peacekeepers were routinely taken hostage, also created a 1,500 strong extraction force to rescue any monitors under threat.[119]

The Kosovo Verification Mission was led by retired US ambassador William Walker, creating an opportunity for a turning point for NATO engagement in Kosovo in terms of piercing Serbia's monopoly of force. In January 1999, Serbian forces killed forty-five Albanian Kosovar men and boys aged between fourteen and ninety-nine in the town of Racak.[120] Ambassador Walker led a team of monitors to the site, accompanied by journalists. After examining the site, he announced that it was clearly a crime against humanity, and that it was committed by Serbian forces. During the course of the Croatian and Bosnia wars, the UN peacekeeping force had contorted itself in any way possible to avoid tagging something an atrocity crime, or to assign responsibility to Serb forces.

Ambassador Walker's unequivocal identification of the crime and the forces responsible, and the failure of Serbia to participate in good faith in the Rambouillet peace talks, galvanized NATO support for a humanitarian intervention to end the conflict. The massacre also formed part of the basis for the subsequent indictment of President Slobodan Milošević by the International Criminal Tribunal for the Former Yugoslavia for crimes against humanity in Kosovo.[121] Eventually the Security Council adopted Resolution 1244, which effectively replaced Serbian sovereignty over Kosovo with that of the UN mission, and fully replaced Serbia's monopoly of force with a monopoly held by NATO peacekeeping forces. The resolution was based upon, and contained annexed to it, a statement of principles proposed by the former president of Finland Martti Ahtisaari and former prime minister of Russia Viktor Chernomyrdin and was accepted by Slobodan Milošević.[122]

The conflict in Sierra Leone illustrates the sharing of a monopoly of force with international forces to aid in the neutralization or defeat of the nonstate armed actors. In Sierra Leone, state shared its monopoly of force with a plethora of actors for this purpose. This case also illustrates that sometimes the "state" is a less stable entity than is often hoped and it may itself change sides in a conflict.

The war in Sierra Leone began in March 1991 when the Revolutionary United Front, with the support of Liberian revolutionary forces under the command of Charles Taylor, sought to take control of Sierra Leone. In light of the successes of the RUF, the Sierra Leone army staged a coup in April 1992, and undertook a relatively effective campaign against the RUF. During this time, Sierra Leone also shared its monopoly of force with the Kamajors militia, which sought to defend villages against both RUF and Sierra Leone army attacks and looting.

The RUF, however, regrouped and reoccupied much of Sierra Leone. In March 1995, the president of Sierra Leone hired the South African Executive Outcomes mercenary force to share in the exercise of its monopoly of force to repel the RUF. Executive Outcomes was highly successful in pushing back the territorial gains of the RUF and forcing them into peace negotiations in Abidjan. During this time, Sierra Leone also returned to democratic governance with the holding of parliamentary and presidential elections in the spring of 1996.

In November 1996, Sierra Leone and the RUF signed the Abidjan Peace Accord. The accord provided for the creation of a neutral monitoring group,[123] but its composition could never be fully agreed upon and it did not come into existence.[124] The accord also provided that the forces of Executive Outcomes would be withdrawn five weeks after the deployment of the neutral monitoring group.[125] Despite the fact that the monitoring group never deployed, the UN and the IMF pressured Sierra Leone to terminate its relationship with Executive Outcomes. The IMF went as far as to withdraw funds from Sierra Leone due to the presence of Executive Outcomes forces, which some say contributed to the later destabilization of the state.[126]

In May 1997, with the failure to implement the peace agreement and the resurgence of the RUF, the Sierra Leone army again staged a coup, but this time joined forces with the RUF to occupy nearly all the territory of Sierra Leone, including the capital of Freetown. The army and the RUF then launched a wave of atrocity crimes against the people of Sierra Leone.

In response, the government in exile, claiming to continue to hold the right to a monopoly of force, asked the Economic Community of West African States to send in its military force, the Economic Community Ceasefire Monitoring Group, to retake the capital. ECOMOG had previously intervened in a similar situation in

Liberia.[127] The ECOMOG force successfully secured Freetown, enabling the government to return. The force was, however, unable to extend its reach much beyond the capital. The returned government of Sierra Leone and the RUF entered into negotiations leading to the Lomé Peace Accord in March 1999.[128] The accord created a power-sharing arrangement granting the leader of the RUF, Foday Sankoh, the vice presidency and the chairmanship of the wealth-sharing committee, with control over the revenue generated by the mining industry. He was also granted amnesty for atrocity crimes.[129] The Lomé Accords also provided for the disarmament of both the RUF and the Sierra Leone army.[130]

The accords further provided for the deployment of a joint ECOMOG–UN peacekeeping force to monitor the implementation of the agreement, and to oversee the disarmament process.[131] The Security Council, acting under Chapter VII, created the UN Mission in Sierra Leone.[132] The peacekeeping force was initially authorized at 6,000. The force was heavily militarized, yet subject to intra-command power struggles and was largely ineffective in its early deployment. At one point, over 500 peacekeepers were taken hostage by the RUF.

The RUF largely ignored the Lomé Agreement and launched an offensive to retake Freetown in May 2000. In August 2000, the Security Council adopted Resolution 1313, which shifted the mandate of the UN forces from one of neutrality to one of supporting the government forces in their fight against the RUF, specifically authorizing the force to "deter and, where necessary, decisively counter the threat of RUF attack by responding robustly to any hostile actions or threat of imminent and direct use of force."[133] The Security Council also imposed an embargo on Liberian and Sierra Leonean diamonds, which served as the primary source of funding for the RUF.[134] Shortly thereafter, the Security Council authorized an increase in the force size to 17,500.[135]

In May 2000, the United Kingdom, with the consent of Sierra Leone, deployed a military force initially to assist with the evacuation of civilians, but which subsequently shifted its mandate to assist the UN force, and to train and re-equip the Sierra Leone army. The British forces aggressively engaged the RUF, with the assistance of air strikes from the neighboring state of Guinea against RUF strongholds. While the UN sought to have the British forces integrated into its command, the United Kingdom refused and insisted on operating under its own command.

The combined action of forces from Sierra Leone, ECOMOG, the UN, Guinea, and the United Kingdom pushed the RUF to surrender via a ceasefire agreement providing for their complete disarmament and demobilization, with the conflict coming to an end in January 2002.

The Special Court for Sierra Leone, a hybrid tribunal, subsequently indicted both Foday Sankoh and Charles Taylor for atrocity crimes in Sierra Leone. The tribunal ruled the Lomé amnesty inapplicable to international laws prohibiting atrocity crimes. Foday Sankoh died while awaiting trial, and Charles Taylor was convicted and sentenced to fifty years' imprisonment.

In some instances, the UN will configure the command structure to provide a single member state with unified command. In the case of East Timor, with the consent of Indonesia, the UN Security Council authorized Australia in September 1999 to undertake a Chapter VII mission leading a multinational force to restore peace and security. The force was to be subsequently replaced by a more traditional UN peacekeeping mission.[136] The Australian command led a combined force of nearly 12,000 troops from twenty-two nations and rapidly deployed throughout East Timor to secure the territory. During the mission, the forces engaged in combat operations with pro-Indonesian paramilitary forces and occasionally with Indonesian police forces, and suspected Indonesian military forces. Six months after their deployment, the multinational force handed over control to a UN peacekeeping force. Notably, in 2006, heavily armed Australian forces returned to the island at the request of East Timor to restore order following a coup attempt.

A much less successful dual-key approach to the authorization of military force was utilized in Bosnia. The system created in Bosnia required the authorization of the UN secretary-general's envoy to Yugoslavia for any NATO enforcement action. This system substantially constrained the ability of NATO to effectively use force as a deterrent to the atrocity crimes being committed in Bosnia, and is widely credited with playing an essential role in the massacres associated with the Serbian government forces' annihilation of the UN safe areas in Gorazde, Srebrenica, and Zepa.[137] During the Dayton peace negotiations NATO insisted on, and was granted, exclusive authority to determine when and how to use force to secure the implementation of the agreement.

The Mandate of the International Forces

When sharing a monopoly of force with an international force, it is necessary for parties to precisely determine the mandate of that force. The parties and the international organization usually define the mandate at the same time they establish consent and determine the nature and configuration of the force. In nearly all instances, the parties consent to the initial scope of the mandate, and the nature and configuration of the force is tailored to that initial mandate.

The mandate is comprised both of a set of goals that the international force is expected to achieve and a set of tools which that force is authorized to employ in order to facilitate the achievement of those goals.[138] The goals may include facilitating the negotiation process, protecting civilians, reducing or pausing the use of force by the parties, and promoting the durability of a peace agreement.

The tools to accomplish this include deploying peacekeepers or police officers to observe, monitor, and/or report on compliance with ceasefires and peace agreements, providing humanitarian assistance, protecting safe areas, enforcing weapons exclusion zones, enforcing no-fly zones, arresting individuals indicted for war crimes, assisting with DDR, assisting with elections, and establishing the rule of law.[139] When setting the mandate, as noted above, it is necessary to match the nature and configuration of the international force to the mandate.

There are two distinct phases of any mandate. The first relates to the pre-negotiation phase where the state shares its monopoly of force in order to facilitate either getting to yes or getting to checkmate with the nonstate actors. The second relates to sharing the monopoly of force in order to secure the implementation of a peace agreement, or to secure stability after the defeat of the nonstate armed actors.

The primary conundrum is to determine how much of a sharing of the monopoly of force is absolutely necessary to facilitate the desired outcome. If insufficient force is shared, the conflict continues on, accomplishing only the introduction of yet another dimension into the conflict. If too much of the monopoly of force is shared, then the state, or the nonstate actors, may lose control over their destiny and ability to shape the outcome in a way they desire. The international force also has an interest in ensuring that its mandate is sufficiently tailored so that it is able to accomplish the goals of its mission with the most efficient and effective use of specified tools. No international force wants to preside over a failed mandate, or inadvertently be pulled into an expanded mandate for which it may not have a properly configured force.

During this first phase, the goals will likely evolve, and the parties, including the international force, are continuously challenged to match the tools and the force configuration with the evolving mandate, and to assess whether they in fact consent to this evolution.

In the second phase, the parties again face the conundrum of determining how much of the monopoly of force is absolutely necessary to share in order to ensure the durability of a peace agreement. States are frequently in a hurry to reestablish their monopoly of force, but nonstate armed actors are often deeply reluctant to permit that reestablishment unless their security is fully ensured for a period of time within which they can establish a trusting relationship with the state. From the perspective of the nonstate actors, that period of time can be quite lengthy.

International forces are similarly quite interested in ensuring that they are not called upon to undertake undefined, unnecessarily dangerous, or expensive tasks that are more appropriately situated with the parties, or for which their force is not suitably configured. The state, on the other hand, would often like to move various tasks to the international force so as to shift the burden, responsibility, and public accountability for implementation to it and the funding sources that generally accompany such a force.

For both phases, the parties must determine whether the mandate should be authorized under Chapter VI or VII. The conundrum here becomes how best to match the goals of the mandate with the authorized level of force. Essentially, what degree of force must the UN authorize its peacekeepers or regional forces to use in order to successfully carry out their mandate? Given the variation in the mission's legal authority to use force, the failure to clarify the legal parameters of the peacekeepers' mandate can have significant consequences.

A related conundrum parties face is how to ensure that the international force will actually exercise the level of force authorized to accomplish the mandate, and correspondingly to ensure that the international force does not exceed the use of force mandated.

Approaches to Resolving the Mandate Conundrum

Given the over three dozen UN Security Council resolutions that addressed the ever-evolving mandate of the UN and other forces operating in the territory of the former Yugoslavia, this section will address the approaches to resolving the mandate-based conundrums with an exclusive focus on the former Yugoslavia.[140]

In the early stages of the conflict, the UN sought to accomplish the goal of supporting the resolution of the conflict through peace negotiations by authorizing the deployment of a peacekeeping force to Croatia to monitor a ceasefire and a preliminary political agreement designed to reintegrate back under Croatian state control those territories occupied by Serbian paramilitaries.[141] The mandate subsequently was expanded to charge the UN forces with "creating the conditions necessary" for successful peace negotiations with specific authority to monitor the unblocking of the Yugoslav People's Army forces and their return to barracks, and to assist with providing humanitarian aid.[142]

With the failure of the ceasefire and the collapse of the preliminary agreement, the UN then evolved the mandate to include the demilitarization of four "UN Protected Areas," which were Serbian-populated enclaves within Croatia that remained occupied by the Yugoslav army, and from which non-Serbian civilians had been ethnically cleansed. In response to changed facts on the ground brought about by various military acts, the UN further expanded the territorial mandate of the UN forces to so-called pink zones adjacent to the UN Protected Areas.[143] Facing resistance from Serb paramilitary forces to demilitarize, the UN then extended the mandate to include controlling the international border between these protected areas and Serbia and Bosnia, taking on immigration and customs functions.[144]

In light of the limited success of these efforts, Croatia requested that the UN peacekeepers be authorized to use force. The UN secretary-general objected to the evolution of the mandate on the grounds it would push the peacekeepers into direct military conflict with the Serb paramilitary forces, and that the troops were not configured for such a confrontation. The Security Council struck a compromise, and upgraded the status of the force from Chapter VI to Chapter VII, and authorized the peacekeepers to use force to defend themselves.[145] This resolution put the UN force on the erratic path to the eventual use of air strikes to bring Serbia to the Dayton peace negotiations. The second step along this path was to authorize close air support by NATO member states to defend the UN peacekeepers,[146] followed by authorizing the use of all necessary measures, including air support, to protect UN humanitarian aid convoys.[147]

In light of the failure of the UN peacekeeping force to successfully reintegrate the UN-protected areas back into Croatian state control, Croatia withdrew its consent for nearly all of the mandated authorities of the peacekeeping force. Once it reclaimed its near monopoly of force, Croatia undertook a successful military campaign to reintegrate these territories.

In Bosnia, the mandate evolved similarly, and so did the nature and configuration of the international force, as discussed earlier.[148] As noted by one commentator, through dozens of resolutions, the Security Council "entrusted UNPROFOR with increasingly complex and dangerous tasks that suggested a mix of traditional peace-keeping, 'wider peacekeeping' and peace enforcement."[149]

As a first step in the evolution of the mandate, the Security Council modified and expanded the mandate,[150] acting under Chapter VII to call upon states to take measures nationally or through regional arrangements to facilitate the successful delivery of humanitarian aid in Bosnia.[151] This modification of the mandate was designed to allow the peacekeepers to call on NATO to provide air support to protect UN personnel, UN aid convoys, and civilian populations.[152] The Security Council then expanded the mandate to create a no-fly zone for military aircraft over Bosnia and authorized the peacekeepers to monitor compliance. After 465 violations, the Security Council again evolved the mandate to permit member states and/or regional organizations to coordinate "all necessary measures" to ensure compliance with the no-fly zone.[153] NATO began immediate enforcement operations, eventually shooting down a number of Serbian fighter planes.

The UN also authorized the creation, and subsequent protection of, "safe areas" in and around six besieged cities.[154] As noted above, France, the United Kingdom, and the Netherlands created an ad hoc heavily armed Rapid Reaction Force to supplement the capabilities of the UN peacekeepers. After the safe areas of Zepa and Srebrenica were overrun, and after the Serbian forces took a number of UN peacekeepers hostage, NATO undertook an extensive air campaign, coupled with counter-battery artillery from the Rapid Reaction Force.

Throughout the evolution of the mandate, NATO force commanders, member states of the Security Council, the UN secretary-general and the UN envoy constantly debated and negotiated. While some members of the Security Council and the NATO force commanders emphasized the Chapter VII nature of the mandate, and the authority to use force to protect civilians, the secretary-general and his special representative characterized the mandate as "VI and a half," and sought to limit the use of force to protecting UN forces and personnel. As such, the consequences of the timid and tardy approach of the UN Security Council were amplified by the narrow, and inaccurate, interpretation of the mandate by the secretary-general and his special representative. As noted earlier, the establishment of the dual-key approach for the use of force further undermined the effectiveness of the mandate, and led to the ultimate failure of UN forces to protect civilians from massacres, including the one at Srebrenica.[155]

In Macedonia, the UN forces took on the role of a preventative deployment – essentially a trip wire. At the request of the president of Macedonia, in November 1992 the UN agreed to share Macedonia's monopoly of force, and deploy peace-keepers for the purpose of monitoring threats to Macedonia's territorial integrity. This was the first time such a mandate was authorized for UN peacekeeping troops, and in fact a similar request from Bosnia in January 1992 had been denied.[156] To augment the "trip-wire" nature of the force, in March 1995 the UN expanded the configuration of the UN force to include American soldiers.[157]

During the Dayton negotiations, NATO sought to avoid the consequences of UN engagement in interpreting the mandate, and insisted that any sharing of the monopoly of force for the purposes of territorial integrity and security be with an ad hoc implementation force comprised almost exclusively of NATO forces, and under the command of the North Atlantic Council (the civilian command structure for NATO). The first annex of the agreement was the IFOR annex, which provided that the UN would transfer its sharing of Bosnia's monopoly of force to IFOR. The annex also laid out explicit authority for IFOR to use force to accomplish the objective set forth in the annex, and to protect its own forces.[158]

The Bosnian delegation sought to include explicit authority to provide security for elections and to arrest indicated war criminals in the mandate. General Wesley Clark, who was negotiating on behalf of NATO, refused these requests, arguing that the broad mandate provided sufficient authority to take on these tasks should NATO wish to do so. During the initial years of IFOR's deployment the NATO refused to arrest war criminals. Only after intense pressure from human rights organizations and a number of rather humiliating encounters with indicted war criminals[159] did NATO exercise its authority to arrest war criminals.[160]

Negotiations Relating to the Sharing of Force between the State and Nonstate Actors

Negotiations relating to the sharing of force between the state and nonstate actors can be grouped into three main approaches. In some instances, the state restores full control over the monopoly of force. In others, the state restores full yet modified control over the monopoly of force via the integration of nonstate actor forces into the national forces. In still others, the state restores limited control over the monop-oly of force by permitting nonstate actors to maintain their forces and command structure under the umbrella command of the national forces.

Once a temporary peace has been secured – or, in some cases, concurrently with peacekeeping efforts to restore the conditions under which a monopoly of force could be possible – the parties must decide whether they will establish a state-held monopoly of force. Most often, this means negotiating whether they will aim to create a single, unified national army, police, and security infrastructure.

The nature of the conflict at the time of the negotiations influences the willingness of the parties to agree to, or refuse, a state monopoly of force. If the nonstate actors were defeated, or if they were victorious and are now poised to become the state actors, they are likely to be more willing to embrace a state monopoly of force.

When peace negotiations occur in the midst of intrastate conflict, or mere days or weeks after a preliminary ceasefire, the nonstate actors can be deeply reluctant to agree upon or even envision a state-centric monopoly of force arrangement. In cases where the conflict ends in a stalemate, is characterized by a high level of atrocity crimes, or is part of a wider series of recurring conflicts between the parties, the nonstate actors are much less likely to embrace the state monopoly of force. In the event that the parties do not agree on the state-held monopoly of force as a long-term goal, they will then need to create a structure that allows for two or more armed forces to operate on the territory of the state.

The Restoration of Full Control over the Monopoly of Force
In some cases, the state restores full control over the monopoly of force through the defeat of the nonstate armed actors, while in others the nonstate armed actors are victorious. In still others, neither side is militarily successful, but the parties accomplish their objectives through the peace negotiations, and agree that the state should regain its full control over the monopoly of force.[161]

In any of these cases, the parties face a number of conundrums. First, they face the conundrum of how to create security arrangements that account for any state or nonstate armed forces that are not going to be a part of the armed forces. These former combatants often have difficulty envisioning a return to civilian life and relinquishing their arms.

Parties typically decide to facilitate this transition by undergoing a process of disarmament, demobilization, and reintegration (DDR) into society. DDR is designed to move armed parties toward a state monopoly of force, primarily by removing weapons from combatants, removing combatants from alternate military structures, and reintegrating combatants into civilian and economic life. DDR provides a "face-saving process for rebel groups to lay down their arms without being seen as losers" and establishing a "safety net" for former combatants as they work to transition into a civilian lifestyle.[162]

When approaching DDR, the parties often disagree on how to time the stages of disarmament, demobilization, and reintegration. While the national government is usually keen to have the nonstate actors disarm immediately, such actors often seek assurances that certain conditions or benchmarks in other areas of the peace agreement will be met before they begin or progress along the path of disarming. The reality is that often parties enter into a peace agreement because a balance of power among forces has occurred on the battlefield. Once the nonstate actors begin to disarm, that balance of power shifts in favor of the national forces and this may induce the national forces to return to the use of force in order to press this advantage.

When undertaking the disarmament of former combatants, the parties must agree on which weapons to surrender. While medium and heavy weapons are almost always relinquished, parties often engage in substantial debate as to whether small arms and light weapons such as AK-47s must be surrendered. Such weapons are often used for personal protection in unstable postconflict environments, but are highly destabilizing as their retention can enable a paramilitary group to remobilize quickly. Small arms and light weapons are oftentimes sufficient to enable a group of former combatants to turn to organized crime such as narcotics trafficking. Further complicating this conundrum, in some instances the possession of light weapons is integral to tribal and cultural structures.[163]

The forces called to disarm may also include government-sponsored paramilitaries and irregular forces that share a common interest with the government, but are not directly supported or controlled by the government. The government is often reluctant to acknowledge that it sponsors paramilitary forces, and may in fact have little control over these irregular forces. Similarly, the government, or the nonstate armed actors, may be supported in-country by foreign forces, either from a foreign state or by individuals from abroad. These forces may or may not be responsive to the requests of the parties to leave the state.

A second set of conundrums relates to the question of how and when to demobilize the combatants, be they excess state forces or the forces of the nonstate armed actors. Armed actors are usually initially gathered into cantonment sites, sometimes with and sometimes without their weapons.[164] Members of national armed forces are returned to their barracks.[165] Ideally, these zones are away from major civilian areas.[166] As with disarmament, mutually distrusting parties often call upon international observers to monitor these cantonment areas.[167]

Demobilized combatants have an array of possible paths to pursue. They may return to their civilian communities; but they may join other militias not part of the peace agreement, turn to organized crime, be hired out as mercenaries, or engage in narcotics or human trafficking. The key to avoiding the latter destabilizing activities is to ensure that former combatants are integrated into civilian life and that they are able to secure stable, income-generating employment.[168] The conundrum is that illicit activity is often more instantaneously profitable for former combatants, and may be more in tune with their warrior ethos. Heightened economic incentives for former combatants are often resisted by civilians who suffered during the war, frequently at the hands of these very same former combatants.

Approaches to Resolving the Reestablishment of Full Monopoly of Force Conundrum

In the case of Papua New Guinea and Bougainville, the Bougainville Revolutionary Army agreed, in August 2001, to the state of monopoly of force by Papua New Guinea in the Rotokas Record agreement,[169] and the subsequent Bougainville

Peace Agreement.[170] Specifically, the Revolutionary Army agreed to a weapons disposal plan,[171] and subsequently to the disbanding of its armed groups.[172] The Rotokas Record also required the state-aligned paramilitary Bougainville Resistance Force to disarm and demobilize.[173]

The armed groups and the political leaders of the Bougainville resistance forces agreed to reestablish the state monopoly of force in exchange for a commitment by Papua New Guinea to set Bougainville on a path to external self-determination through increased autonomy and eventually a referendum on the region's independence.[174] In the end, not all the forces disbanded, and a small group followed the former leader of the Revolutionary Army into the jungle where an official no-go zone was established. The group remained isolated and eventually dissolved when the breakaway leader died of malaria.[175]

In the case of Colombia, under the November 2016 Final Agreement to End the Armed Conflict and Build a Stable and Lasting Peace, the state regained the monopoly of force. The agreement did not provide for the integration of the Revolutionary Armed Forces of Colombia (Fuerzas Armadas Revolucionarias de Colombia, FARC) members, but rather for the disarmament and demobilization of the militia members and their integration into society. The agreement also provided for the transformation of the FARC into a political party and set aside seats in the national parliament for the new party.[176]

In a prior related effort in 1990 to disarm and demobilize paramilitary forces associated with the government, nearly a fifth of the members of the paramilitary group that disarmed were later assassinated by other armed groups or by members of the national army.[177] As a consequence, the agreement contained elaborate provisions for the security of the FARC forces being disarmed and demobilized.

The members of the FARC agreed to turn over their weapons to the United Nations within six months of the signature of the agreement. The weapons were to be transformed by the UN into three historical monuments. The demobilized members, along with their families, assembled in a number of newly formed villages throughout Colombia. Each of these villages was deemed a special economic zone, and the former combatants were allocated a monthly stipend of 90 percent of the minimum wage and given access to various social programs, training, and educational opportunities. Security for the villages was provided by the national army. In addition, a special security force was created to protect members of the newly formed FARC political party, and it was deemed permissible for former members of the FARC to serve in this security force.[178]

Soon after the beginning of the implementation of the agreement, approximately 1,200 so-called FARC dissidents returned to armed conflict, and narcotics trafficking. The dissidents were led by a number of former mid-level commanders, and operated mostly in remote areas where they are engaged in active conflict with the national army.[179]

Rwanda faced a more decisive transition to a state-held monopoly of force than occurs in most postconflict contexts. In 1994, the armed wing of the nonstate Rwandan Patriotic Front overwhelmingly defeated the Rwandan army. These non-state armed actors then became the state and replaced the former army as the holder of Rwanda's monopoly of force. Although the new government integrated the new national army, with two-thirds Hutu and one-third Tutsi (honoring the commitment that had been previously agreed in the 1993 Arusha Accords), they appointed former members of the Rwandan Patriotic Army to nearly all the senior positions.[180]

In Yemen, the state failed to establish a full monopoly of force despite the aspirations and outcomes of the National Dialogue. Yemen's 2014 National Dialogue Outcomes explicitly declared: "The constitution shall provide that the State has monopoly on the use of power and force in accordance with the powers vested on them by law and in pursuant to the constitution."[181] That clear articulation was further supplemented a few pages later, when the document stipulated: "The armed forces belong to the people; its mission is to protect the country, maintain security, unity and territorial integrity, sovereignty and the Republican System. The State has the exclusive right to establish such forces. An individual, body, party, agency, group, organization or a tribe are prohibited from establishing such forma-tions, bands, military or Para-military organizations under any name."[182]

Despite the conclusions of the National Dialogue, Yemen's nonstate armed actors had no interest in relinquishing their arms and disbanding their forces.[183] In particular, the Houthi forces rejected the attempts to codify the National Dialogue Outcomes in new governance structures and continued armed conflict, tipping Yemen into a devastating civil war. The push for a state-held monopoly of force, among other issues, contributed to the decision of the Houthis to pursue change on the battlefield rather than through the political process.

A key element of restoring a state's monopoly of force is ensuring the removal of foreign forces, including those supporting the state as well as those supporting the nonstate armed actors. In the case of Angola, the first in the series of agreements bringing an end to the conflict was dedicated to the phased redeployment, followed by the withdrawal, of Cuban forces from Angolan territory. The agreement also applied to South African forces, which had previously withdrawn.[184] The withdrawal of forces was monitored and verified by a United Nations force.[185] Similarly, the Lomé Peace Agreement for Sierra Leone required the withdrawal of all "mercenar-ies,"[186] and the Framework for a Comprehensive Political Settlement of the Cambodia Conflict detailed plans for the removal and verification of "any foreign forces, advisers, and military personnel remaining in Cambodia, together with their weapons, ammunition, and equipment."[187]

When restoring the monopoly of force, the parties often must create a program for disarming the nonstate combatants, and reintegrating them into civilian society. In the case of Mozambique, for instance, the agreement provided that the armed actors would "revert for all purposes to the status of civilians," in increments of 20 percent of the force per thirty days.[188] This was accompanied by a detailed program for disarmament. The parties to the Burundi agreement structured the demobilization such that those deemed to be suitable for civilian reintegration disarmed, while those deemed suitable for integration into the new armed forces were allowed to keep their weapons and bring them with them into the new security forces.[189]

As noted earlier, the parties often seek the assistance of the international community when dealing with the restoration of the monopoly of force. The disarmament process is no different. Oftentimes, the nonstate armed actors seek assistance and monitoring of their disarmament by UN peacekeepers or other neutral third parties in order to guard against retaliation by the government. This neutral engagement is designed to increase their trust in the weapons collection process. In the case of Angola's Bicesse Accords, nonstate forces surrendered their weapons to a joint monitoring entity, rather than transferring their arms to the government forces.[190] In El Salvador, the armed actors surrendered their weapons under the watch of the UN Observer Mission in El Salvador.[191] In the case of Liberia, the weapons were surrendered to the Economic Community of West African States Monitoring Group in Liberia.[192]

The handover of weapons can involve quite a quixotic process. Frequently the state will lead with a request for the disarmament of the nonstate armed actors in the first phase of the negotiations. Such a demand by Sudan during the Doha negotiations in 2011 substantially delayed the talks and undermined the trust of the Justice and Equality Movement armed actors to such an extent that they left the talks.

In the case of Aceh, Indonesia asserted during the initial phases of the talks that the Free Aceh Movement must disarm. The Free Aceh Movement refused to hand over its weapons on the basis that there was no means to secure the safety of its forces unless the government also redeployed its forces. The government was unwilling to undertake such a redeployment while the Free Aceh Movement retained its weapons and remained an effective fighting force.[193] Ultimately, the 2004 tsunami, and the willingness of Indonesia to grant substantial asymmetrical autonomy to Aceh prompted the Free Aceh Movement to agree to demobilize.[194] But even then, the rebel leaders of the Free Aceh Movement substantially delayed complying with the requirement in the agreement to provide a list of their members that had demobilized. Moreover, they refused to join the Indonesian armed forces, an option provided in the agreement, preferring to return to civilian life.[195]

In the case of Northern Ireland, the disarmament of the Irish Republican Army was one of the most contentious issues in the peace process, with the parties reaching a number of understandings on political issues before reaching agreement on disarmament. Even then, it was not until eight years after the signing of the agreement that the Irish Republican Army formally decommissioned its weapons.[196] In South Africa's peace process, the African National Congress disarmed and demobilized four years after signing the National Peace Accord, by which time the ANC had won the elections and become the governing party.[197] In El Salvador, even with the participation of the UN observer mission, the Farabundo Martí National Liberation Front stashed a sizable number of weapons in caches, just in case the peace process was not successful.[198]

In some cases, such as the early ceasefires of the Doha peace negotiations on Sudan, the parties opt for simple disbandment, without detailed provisions relating to the disarmament of those forces. The initial agreements at Doha also provided for a lengthy period of time for their integration, thus permitting the rebel forces to retain combat-ready units in the event the government failed to fulfill its obligations. This ultimately turned out to be the case, with the parties returning to conflict rather quickly.[199]

Even when not formally mandated by a peace agreement, the possibility of continuing to operate in the security sector may be an appealing path for many combatants who worry about their economic prospects in civilian life. Many demobilized members of the Kosovo Liberation Army took new positions in the reformed Kosovo Police Service.[200] The UN Mission in Kosovo also created a new institution, the Kosovo Protection Corps, to accommodate former combatants looking for new jobs. It was a civilian emergency service agency that employed many former members of the Kosovo Liberation Army and provided humanitarian aid, disaster response, and postconflict reconstruction.[201] It provided a "stop-gap" solution for demobilized combatants, a formalized entity in which former combatants could stably operate.[202]

The Reestablishment of Full, yet Modified, Control over the Monopoly of Force via the Integration of Nonstate Forces into the National Forces

In conflicts that do not have clear victors, but in which the parties do seek a state-held monopoly of force, the parties are likely to move toward integrating their forces into unified security apparatuses. To accomplish this objective, the parties create a plan that addresses the timing and sequencing of integration, and often couple this plan with security sector reform.

One of the first conundrums the parties face is determining when to begin integrating armed forces and how long the process of integration should last. States seeking to reclaim their monopoly of force are often inclined to move quickly toward the creation of a unified armed force, whereas the nonstate armed actors that have been challenging the state in conflict are unlikely to possess high levels of trust and may want to proceed more gradually. Nonstate actors may also refuse to immediately break apart their command structures, worrying that they may need to return to armed conflict if the state fails to uphold its other commitments in the peace agreement, such as power-sharing, wealth-sharing, and protecting human rights. At the same time, the state may be reluctant to move forward with those commitments before the nonstate forces have begun integrating.

While an integration process works to transition the nonstate forces back to arrangements that do not challenge the state-held monopoly on force, the nonstate actors (and often mediators or the international community) will typically demand that the state also undergo a broad reform process to remedy the initial drivers of conflict that prompted the militarization of opposition groups.[203] Many of these are reforms related to governance, natural resources, and sovereignty arrangements that are discussed in depth in the other chapters of this book. The reform of the security sector is no exception.

The reform of the security sector, at any time, can be a complicated and fragile process. Reforming the security sector, while integrating former nonstate armed actors, and providing security for the implementation of a peace agreement, can be particularly challenging.[204] Such reform is necessary, however, to enable the previously warring parties to confer political legitimacy upon the new armed forces and security apparatuses, as well as the institutions that support those entities. Importantly, security sector reform (SSR) can also address impunity for violations and abuses of human rights in postconflict contexts, contributing to the rule of law.[205]

While SSR clearly includes the reform of armed security forces, it may also include the reform of a range of related state institutions.[206] Some commentators have gone so far as to argue that SSR should be an expansive undertaking that aims to "create a secure environment that facilitates development, poverty reduction, good governance and the consolidation of democracy based on the rule of law."[207]

During the course of a peace negotiation, it can be difficult for parties to determine where to draw the line with reforms. While it is often crucial to reform the army, the police, and the intelligence services, it is tempting to take the opportunity of a negotiation to propose agreement on the comprehensive restructuring of all things related to security in order to promote a peaceful, democratic, and rule of law-based society. Yet doing so diverts attention and resources from the reform of the core security services, and it may have the unintended and counterproductive effect of framing the provisions as aspirational rather than obligatory.

Notably, strong support for security sector reform is not always present in peace negotiations. The state may be somewhat reluctant to engage in intensive or wideranging reforms, viewing significant changes, particularly when done at the behest of international or mediator pressure, as an infringement on its sovereignty. At the same time, the state may recognize change is necessary to resolve the armed challenge to that very sovereignty, which may be relaunched by the armed groups with which the state is negotiating the peace agreement. Even when the parties both agree that incorporating certain aspects of SSR within a peace process is necessary, they may face difficulties determining the scope of the reforms.[208]

Approaches to Resolving the Integration of Nonstate Forces
into the National Forces Conundrum

For parties reestablishing the state's monopoly of force by pursuing the integration of nonstate armed actors into the national security forces, there are a number of approaches that they can pursue.

The first option is for the nonstate armed actors to integrate into the national security structure. As noted above, the Doha agreement between the Liberation and Justice Movement and Sudan provided for such an integration over a rather lengthy period of time.[209]

In the case of Angola's Bicesse Accords of 1991, the parties sought to integrate the UNITA nonstate armed actors into the national army and state police forces immediately following the start of the ceasefire and prior to holding elections, so that those elections could have a better chance of being free and fair.[210] This rushed timeline proved problematic. The accords provided an unrealistic timeline of only sixty days for the cantonment of hundreds of thousands of combatants and simultaneous creation of a new army of 50,000. Instead of complying, the rebel UNITA forces used the period to regroup and prepare to resume fighting should the election result not be in its favor. By the day of the 1992 election, only 8,800 of the anticipated 40,000 combatants that were meant to integrate into the Angolan Armed Forces had reported for duty.[211] When UNITA lost the election, they disavowed the accords and the civil war resumed.

In the case of the Philippines, the Moro National Liberation Front used the integration program as a way of retiring older or injured members into the armed forces, where they received a regular pay check and retirement benefits. The Moro National Liberation Front retained much of its force structure outside of the integrated army to operate as an informal guarantor of the peace agreement. Interestingly, unlike the case of Burundi, those integrating into the armed forces needed to turn over their weapons. Since cultural norms essentially required males to be armed, those integrating would take loans against their future military pay to purchase old or dysfunctional weapons to turn in.[212] Notably, the agreement did permit the Moro National Liberation Front to retain its status as a "revolutionary organization" and thus to keep its heavy weapons. The only fighters who were actually "disarmed" during this process were those that integrated into the Philippines' national security forces.

The second option for integration is to create a new national security force composed of members of the former state army and the former nonstate armed groups. For instance, in August 2000, multiple parties fighting in Burundi's civil war signed the Arusha Peace and Reconciliation Agreement, which provided for the creation of national defense and national police forces.[213] The new national security forces were to "include members of the Burundian armed forces and combatants of the political parties and movements in existence at the time of restructuring of the army, as well as other citizens who wish to enlist."[214] The provisions also expressly stipulated that no ethnic group would compose more than 50 percent of either the national defense force or national police force.[215]

The Arusha negotiations occurred before a definite end to the conflict in Burundi, and it would be years before key ceasefires were signed. Codifying a firm agreement on integrated monopoly of force arrangements, however, helped guide the subsequent security negotiations during the end of conflict and postconflict periods. Even for the parties that did not sign the Arusha Agreement, the provisions provided a crucial framework against which those groups eventually negotiated and signed agreements in the years that followed.[216] The parties signing the Arusha Agreement were aware that its integration protocols would not be immediately implemented, but their codification within the agreement paved the way for eventual military integration.

Integrating the officer corps can be more complicated given the qualifications required of senior commanders. Nonetheless, parties often allocate substantial space for commanders from the nonstate actors for the purpose of ensuring a durable peace, rather than have disaffected senior leadership outside the national forces and potentially posing a threat of renewed conflict. For instance, the Pretoria Protocol on Political, Defence, and Security Power Sharing in Burundi provided that the National Defence Force would be composed of 60 percent officers from the governmental army and 40 percent from the nonstate armed actors.[217] The Pretoria Protocol also transformed the former armed party into a political party, thus creating space for leadership to move off the battlefield into the political arena.[218] The Colombian peace process similarly permitted the transformation of the FARC into a political party, and set aside an initial percentage of parliamentary seats for the new party.[219]

When integrating forces into an existing or new security force structure, the parties must address whether to integrate individuals or units. Individuals often feel less secure, but are also less likely to break away from an integrated security force and return to violence. Mozambique addressed this quandary by creating a new national army, and initially integrating whole units from the existing forces of each party until the army was at full strength. At that point, the previous units would be dissolved and reformed into new units.[220] Any forces controlled by the parties not intended to be integrated into the new army would be demobilized under a comprehensive DDR program.[221] In the case of Nepal, the Maoist forces sought to have almost their entire military structure absorbed into the state army. The army insisted on only integrating individuals, and argued against integrating any officers.[222]

A third option is for a nonstate armed force to transition into a fully functional force within the state's security structure. In Sudan, the pro-government militia known as the Janjaweed, which was responsible for much of the genocide in Darfur, transformed in 2019 into the Rapid Support Forces administered by Sudan's National Intelligence and Security Service. This transformation occurred despite an explicit government commitment to disarm those forces.[223] The Rapid Support Forces were relocated from Darfur to Khartoum to bolster the government of Omar al-Bashir. Those forces were widely accused of being responsible for the Khartoum massacre of unarmed protestors on June 3, 2019, which then led to the toppling of the Bashir regime.[224]

In the case of the August 2020 Juba Agreement between Sudan and the Sudan People's Liberation Movement–North/Sudan Revolutionary Front (SPLM-N/SRF), the parties coupled a ceasefire with an integration plan that included substantial SSR. The implementation of the agreement would be carried out and supervised by a series of joint committees composed of members of the two parties and neutral third parties. These committees would exercise command and control over the forces undergoing integration.[225]

The plan for integration into a single national professional army consisted of three year-long phases wherein the SPLM-N/SRF forces would be integrated first at the battalion level, then the company level, and then finally at the individual level at the conclusion of a roughly three-year period. The agreement provided for an elaborate process of demobilizing the elderly, young, and disabled, coupled with the registration and assessment of those interested in serving in the security forces of Sudan. Through the joint mechanisms, the parties would agree on the optimal number of individuals to serve in the security forces. The security forces included in this agreement consisted not only of the army and the police, but also the intelligence services.[226]

The program of SSR was designed to dramatically reshape the Sudanese army, which was for decades used as a tool for President al-Bashir to maintain his hold on power, and was implicated in genocide in Darfur and numerous other atrocity crimes throughout Sudan. Under the agreement, the parties agreed to transform the army and other security institutions to reflect the diversity and aspirations of the democratic revolution in Sudan; free these institutions from any ideological, political, regional, or tribal affiliation; and adopt best practices of modern democratically controlled armed forces. The state of Sudan would exercise the sole monopoly of force. The agreement does, however, seem to indicate that this restructuring of the security forces would occur after the three-year period of integration.[227]

In a parallel agreement between Sudan and the Darfur nonstate actors, the parties agreed to the rapid integration of the Darfuri rebel forces beginning with the assembly and vetting of forces within ninety days of the signing of the peace agreement. The integration process was to start immediately upon the agreement of requirements and qualifications for integration, and be completed within fifteen months of signing the peace agreement. The parties negotiated an additional requirement that forces, which were to be integrated at the unit level, would remain deployed in Darfur for forty months, after which time they could be deployed to other parts of Sudan. No integrated soldier could be terminated before six years of service, except with good cause.[228]

The agreement further provided that Sudan would pay to the Darfuri nonstate armed actors the value of the weapons surrendered. The value would be determined by a joint specialized technical committee.[229] And, as with the SPLM-N/SRF agreement, this agreement provided for a fairly radical overhaul of Sudan's security services.

The Reestablishment of Limited Control over the Monopoly of Force by Permitting Nonstate Actors to Maintain Their Forces and Command Structure under the Umbrella Command of the National Forces

In some rare instances, the state restores limited control over the monopoly of force by permitting nonstate actors to maintain their forces and command structure under the umbrella command of the national forces.

This approach is most frequently adopted when the peace agreement envisions a future determination of final status for a party seeking external self-determination. If a state is contemplating, or if the peace agreement specifically provided for the exercise of the right of external self-determination, the party is likely to wish to maintain effective security forces so as to be able to protect any newly acquired territorial integrity and sovereignty. The conundrum parties face when considering this context is how to maintain security throughout the territory of the state when there are two or more functional armies.

The parties to a peace negotiation often attempt to secure a durable peace by creating some degree of joint command at the highest level and/or by creating joint integrated units at the operational level. The joint integrated units could either become models for future integration of the multiple armies, or they may become flashpoints leading to renewed hostilities.

Approaches to Resolving the Limited Control over Monopoly of Force Conundrum

The Comprehensive Peace Agreement, which brought an end to the Sudanese civil war in 2005, provided that South Sudan would be entitled to hold a referendum within six years to decide whether it wished to remain a part of Sudan or to become an independent state.[230] Over the course of the conflict, South Sudan had developed a substantial armed force, and it wished to maintain this force in the event there was a return to conflict before the referendum, or in the event it attained statehood after the six-year period.

The Comprehensive Peace Agreement therefore provided that both the army of Sudan (Sudanese Armed Forces) and the army of South Sudan (the Sudan People's Liberation Army) would continue to exist. The president of Sudan would be the commander in chief of the Sudanese Armed Forces, and the first vice president, who would represent South Sudan, would be the commander in chief of the Sudan People's Liberation Army.[231] Both armies were to be considered and treated equally as Sudan's National Armed Forces during the interim period prior to the referendum.[232] In the event South Sudan opted to remain a part of Sudan, the two armies would be merged into a single national army.

The agreement also provided that each army would redeploy to its respective territory within two and a half years.[233] This redeployment proved difficult to implement. Several thousand troops that fought for the Sudan People's Liberation Army, yet were originally from northern regions, ended up remaining in those northern regions. After the south's resounding vote for secession in the 2011 referendum, many of these troops reformed as the Sudan People's Liberation Army-North, which would continue the fight against the northern government of Sudan.[234]

To prepare the groundwork for a future integrated army in the event the south voted to remain in Sudan, and also to provide security for hot spots during the interim period, the parties agreed to create joint integrated units (JIU). These units would each contain an equal number of soldiers from the north and the south. If the outcome of the 2011 referendum was Sudanese and South Sudanese unity, then these units would be greatly expanded to create a future Sudan national army. Conversely, if the outcome of the vote was independence, then the forces would be dissolved and would return to their respective armies. Nearly 40,000 troops were to participate in these joint integrated units.[235]

To command this "third force," the parties agreed to establish a Joint Defense Board that would be comprised of the chiefs of staff of the two forces, their deputies, and an agreed number of senior officers. The board was to take its decisions by consensus and be chaired on a rotating basis by the respective chiefs of staff.[236] This approach of rotating command was applied all the way through the chain of command down to the unit level.[237]

The rotating nature of the command, the unwillingness of many troops to serve in joint units, and the fact that the units were destined to return to their respective armies in the event of independence substantially undermined the ability of the units to operate in an efficient and effective manner. In fact, "the three most serious breaches of the CPA's permanent ceasefire resulted directly from the actions of JIU battalions and brigades."[238] The north also developed a habit of incorporating state-aligned paramilitary forces into the joint integrated units in place of its regular armed forces. This substantially undermined the trust relationship with the southern forces.[239]

In the case of Bosnia, at the time of the signing of the Dayton Accords in December 1995, the parties were set on maintaining separate armies. At the time of the peace talks in Dayton, none of the parties envisioned a full monopoly of force as the long-term goal, so the agreement designated one army for the Republika Srpska, and two within the Federation – one Croatian and one Bosnian.[240] The Dayton Accords established that the Federation and the Republika Srpska would retain entity-level armies as well as their own Ministries of Defense, with some limited coordination at the national level.[241]

During the early days of the implementation of the Dayton Accords, the United States undertook a train-and-equip program for the Bosnian army, but only for the army of the Federation. Notably, throughout this time, security in Bosnia was provided via 50,000 NATO troops, and thus it did not suffer from the sporadic post-agreement violence that tended to plague Sudan decades later.

In 2005, a decade after the signing of the Dayton Accords, the three armies established a joint command at the national level and a national Ministry of Defense.[242] The army maintains both multinational and single ethnic battalions, but all brigades are multinational. The integration was driven in large part by an interest in joining NATO's partnership for peace.[243] Eventually, the Bosnian forces themselves shared the monopoly of force with other states as they participated in peace support operations in Mali, Afghanistan, Congo, and Iraq.[244]

During the Juba negotiations, Sudan accepted in a pre-agreement statement of principles titled a "Joint Agreement" that the Sudan People's Liberation Army-North/Al-Hilu could retain its own security forces until final security arrangements were agreed, and until the "separation between religion and state is actualized."[245] The nonstate actors thereby tied the retention of their armed forces to the implementation of one of their top political objectives.

In a variant of the limited control over the monopoly of force, Sudan and the Darfur parties to the Juba negotiations agreed to create a unique "security keeping force" to provide civilian protection in Darfur. The force was to be comprised of 6,000 members from the Darfuri nonstate armed actors, and 6,000 from a mix of Sudanese Armed Forces, Janjaweed/RSF forces, and state police and state intelligence forces. While this force would operate in an integrated manner within the framework of the Sudanese army, the 6,000 Darfuri members would not necessarily be considered part of the Sudanese armed forces. The force would operate for a renewable period of two years. It was designed to essentially replace the functions of the UNAMID peacekeeping force. Sudan thus sought to create a separate internal peacekeeping force charged with more or less the same mandate as the joint UN and African Union peacekeeping force.[246]

CONCLUSION

Negotiating and agreeing upon the reestablishment of a monopoly of force, and broader security arrangements, is a fundamental component of achieving a durable peace. Without creating the conditions for an end to armed conflict, de-escalating violence, and reestablishing a monopoly of force, resolving the other puzzles discussed in this book would be impossible. The monopoly of force provides the basis for state legitimacy, a key component of establishing power-sharing arrangements, creating resource-sharing structures, enabling postconflict governance, and if necessary, allowing a smooth path to external self-determination.

As discussed in this chapter, to achieve a monopoly of force and promote postconflict security, the parties must navigate the need for international forces to assist with establishing the conditions for peace, overcoming mistrust between formerly warring parties, and developing a common understanding on the future of security and the nature of the forces necessary to provide that security. This chapter examined the opportunity presented to parties in postconflict peace negotiations to design innovative frameworks for reestablishing the monopoly of force in such a way as to mitigate conflict drivers.

This chapter has also discussed the consequences of rushing the process of determining security arrangements or with the oversharing or imprecise sharing of a state's monopoly of force with international actors. The rushed armed forces unification timeline in Angola and the unclear mandate for peacekeeping forces in Bosnia both contributed to a resurgence of violence and further set back those peace processes. If each conundrum related to the creation of a secure postconflict state is not carefully considered, the missteps committed can derail any hope for a durable peace.

The case studies highlighted in this chapter – Angola, Bosnia, Burundi, Kosovo, Mozambique, Papua New Guinea/Bougainville, Rwanda, Sierra Leone, Sudan/South Sudan, and Sudan/Darfur – underscore the complicated tradeoffs parties face when confronting conflicting visions for a future state, including the composition of its armed forces, the scope of activities for international forces keeping the peace, and the role of former combatants in society. Each approach parties take when resolving numerous security-related conundrums poses a potential for lasting peace as well as a danger for provoking future conflict.

The next chapter will explore a subject that often goes hand in hand with the reestablishment of a monopoly of force and a sense of genuine security throughout the state: power-sharing.

2

Power-Sharing

Nearly all contemporary conflicts are driven in part by political marginalization. This political marginalization amplifies the consequences of economic and cultural marginalization. To craft a durable peace, the parties to peace negotiations often spend considerable time and effort crafting power-sharing arrangements that balance the pull of some parties for greater diffusion and devolution of political power, with the pull of other parties to maintain a degree of political centralization, for the sake of efficiency and effectiveness, and to preserve their prior political privileges.

A recent study indicates that over 80 percent of modern intrastate peace agreements include arrangements to share power among various political constituencies.[1] These arrangements include both horizontal power-sharing and vertical power-sharing. In some instances, the parties negotiated a balanced and rational set of arrangements for power-sharing that led to a durable peace. In other instances, the parties negotiated an array of disconnected or inconsistent arrangements that led to political dysfunction and gridlock, or a return to conflict.

Horizontal power-sharing is intended to facilitate the participation of several political constituencies in the decision-making process at the national, and sometimes regional, level. Diverse political participation in a postconflict state is expected both to constrain the ability of any one political constituency to monopolize state power and to allow previously marginalized constituencies to attain and sustain greater access to political power, and accompanying access to economic resources.

Horizontal power-sharing arrangements at the national and regional level nearly always address power-sharing in the executive, legislative, and judicial branches of government. These arrangements may include co-presidents or co-prime ministers; allocation of the position of "first" vice president to a specific constituency; a rotating presidency; the creation of a bicameral legislature with membership in the second chamber based on membership in a designated political constituency; specific set-asides for guaranteed legislative representation; special executive or legislative veto privileges for a minority constituency; and quotas for membership on the constitutional court.[2]

Vertical power-sharing is intended to complement horizontal power-sharing by empowering previously marginalized political constituencies at the local level. The devolution of political power to the local level is expected to build the foundation for a durable peace by shielding local constituencies from the abuse of political power by political constituencies entrenched at the national level. Vertical power-sharing is also intended to allow previously marginalized constituencies to attain internal self-determination and control their political future on matters of direct local importance, such as use of their traditional language, cultural preservation, education, and the exploitation and management of natural resources. Effective vertical power-sharing may quell calls for external self-determination and secession.

Vertical power-sharing arrangements seek to accomplish these objectives by devolving various powers from the national government to substate levels of government, such as the regional, provincial, or municipal levels.[3] These powers often encompass political, administrative, and/or fiscal powers and may be devolved in a symmetrical or asymmetrical fashion. In order to create a system for vertical power-sharing, it is often necessary to redesign some elements of a state's structure, which may even include the complete transformation from a unitary to a federal state.

In keeping with the overall approach of the book, this chapter undertakes a detailed exploration of one dimension of power-sharing – in this case, vertical power-sharing. This chapter notes where applicable how the parties to a peace negotiation coordinated their design of vertical power-sharing arrangements with those of horizontal power-sharing.[4] The lessons learned from the negotiation and design of vertical power-sharing arrangements are also broadly applicable to horizontal power-sharing arrangements addressed during peace negotiations.[5]

This chapter addresses a number of conundrums related to vertical power-sharing that the parties face during peace negotiations and peace processes. First, the chapter discusses the puzzle of whether and how to create a vertical power-sharing arrangement that leads to a durable peace. Next, the chapter provides a conceptual and legal primer for understanding the basic elements of vertical power-sharing mechanisms. Then, the chapter explores a number of instances of key state practice to analyze and highlight how the parties involved in peace negotiations have sought to manage the conundrums they faced when seeking to solve the puzzle of vertical power-sharing.

THE PUZZLE: WHETHER AND HOW TO CREATE A VERTICAL POWER-SHARING ARRANGEMENT THAT LEADS TO A DURABLE PEACE

As noted in the Introduction to this book, during peace negotiations the parties are first and foremost seeking to protect their interests, either through the devolution or through the centralization of political power, depending on whether they are a marginalized constituency or an entrenched political elite. Secondarily, the parties may be seeking to establish the foundation for a durable peace. The mediator, in some circumstances, may play an instrumental role in harmonizing these interests.

If these interests are not effectively harmonized, and the agreement not carefully crafted, the hoped-for benefits of a vertical power-sharing arrangement may in fact increase the likelihood of a return to armed conflict. Vertical power-sharing is often a tempting panacea to some of the most prominent underlying causes of conflict, including unequal access to resources, inadequate political representation, and social marginalization. Yet a poorly conceived vertical power-sharing arrangement may paralyze the national government, fail to meet the reasonable expectations of the constituents of substate entities, or even embolden substate entities to seek external self-determination.

Opportunity to Support Durable Peace

A well-crafted vertical power-sharing arrangement can significantly contribute to a durable peace. The devolution of power increases the likelihood that the primary parties to the conflict are absorbed into the postconflict governance structure and thereby generate an interest in the success of those governance structures.[6]

Vertical power-sharing enhances the durability of a peace agreement in three primary ways. First, vertical power-sharing increases "opportunities for citizen participation and ownership" of political processes, which is particularly important in postconflict states.[7] The potential for greater input into government decision-making processes at the local or national level can bring groups previously disengaged from the political process into the fold of formal governing structures. Scholars of power-sharing and democratic governance have found that increased participation by citizens can positively shape the government itself, leading to greater stability.[8]

Second, vertical power-sharing minimizes the risks of tension and conflict between groups in ethnically or religiously heterogeneous societies. Vertical power-sharing provides opportunities for identity-based groups to practice local governance and "exercise local customs and religious beliefs without fear of persecution."[9] Scholars generally agree that postconflict states that have devolved substantial political power generally experience less organized minority violence, less religious militancy,[10] fewer secessionist movements,[11] and less ethnic tension.[12]

Third, vertical power-sharing can also address certain root causes of conflict, such as tensions relating to control over revenue flow or the historic exclusion of certain groups from decision-making positions. Indeed, in certain contexts, vertical power-sharing may be the only feasible alternative to the immediate secession of a substate entity.[13] In cases where the conflict is driven at least in part by a party seeking self-determination, vertical power-sharing is a tempting option for the parties to agree upon in order to avoid the potentially more destabilizing option of external self-determination. If the state categorically opposes external self-determination, a peace process is unlikely to produce an agreement absent some measure of autonomy or enhanced power for the substate entity eyeing independence.

Threat to Durable Peace

Vertical power-sharing can raise a multitude of challenges to the durability of a peace agreement and, in some instances, risk a return to conflict. First, vertical power-sharing may be used by some parties to a negotiation as a disingenuous means to retain their disproportionate access to political power and economic resources. The entrenched political elite controlling the government, for instance, may offer substantial devolution of power as a method for facilitating an opposition group's signature to a peace agreement, with the intent of then stalling, obfuscating, and otherwise blocking implementation to ensure that its level of authority is not meaningfully diluted. Opposition parties, on the other hand, may agree to various vertical power-sharing arrangements while in fact intending for the agreement, and the associated devolution of power, to serve as a step towards external self-determination. When only one, or potentially neither, party has the genuine intent to implement vertical power-sharing arrangements, the arrangements are likely to be hastily or incompletely developed, risking their ability to contribute to durable peace.

Second, postconflict decentralization often takes a problematic form: an inversion of the process by which many "model" decentralized states were developed. Many of these "model" states did not devolve power from a highly centralized state down to substate entities, such as provinces or regions, but, rather, coalesced preexisting entities into a federal state. In contrast, postconflict states that were previously heavily centralized seek to devolve political power down to substate entities, the boundaries for which may not have formally existed prior to the conflict. In this way, modeling decentralization of a postconflict state after Germany, for instance, may not adequately or appropriately address the unique circumstances of that postconflict state. Overreliance on these "model" case studies can even risk misleading states into believing that federalism is an instant remedy for corruption, a lack of democratic norms, inequitable resource allocation, and the abuse of power by entrenched elites.

Third, once the parties achieve agreement on vertical power-sharing arrangements, they may agree to a process or timeline that the state and/or the parties do not have the capacity to implement. If authorities at the local level do not have the requisite fiscal and administrative power and resources to execute their duties, decentralization is likely to fail or encounter significant difficulties.[14] Similarly, if decentralization is conducted in a piecemeal fashion, by devolving political authorities without devolving at least a minimum threshold of administrative and fiscal authorities, local governments may be unable to effectively exercise the political powers devolved to them. In effect, this can lead to disenfranchisement. This aspect of the puzzle is further intensified by the fact that marginalized parties often seek a maximalist devolution of power given their historical relationship with the national government. They may find that they are effective at negotiating a substantial redistribution of power, but are unable effectively to implement those powers.

Fourth, vertical power-sharing can be used as a simple bargaining chip to entice the parties to agree to end the violence, which differs from an intentionally sequenced and detailed process. When addressed as part of a peace process, the parties may be forced to negotiate complex vertical power-sharing details in a chaotic, politically charged, and unplanned process in an effort to appease certain actors or interests. When implemented in a rushed or unsystematic fashion, vertical power-sharing can generate new problems within the very governing structure it was attempting to reform, or even collapse it entirely.[15]

CONCEPTUAL AND LEGAL PRIMER

There are over two dozen federal states around the globe, dozens more decentralized unitary states, and even a handful of confederations. These states provide a rich body of comparative state practice from which to identify the key conceptual approaches to vertical power-sharing, and the various legal norms, rules, processes, and procedures used to design and implement vertical power-sharing arrangements.

The conceptual and legal primer for understanding vertical power-sharing involves the nature of the state structure (modified unitary, federal, or confederal); the allocation of executive and legislative powers between the national government and its substate entities; and political, administrative, and fiscal decentralization.

State Structure: Unitary, Devolved Unitary, Federal, or Confederal?

State structures generally fall into the four broad categories of unitary, devolved unitary, federal, and confederal. The latter three may be asymmetric.

Where states fall on this spectrum of decentralization dictates the degree to which power is devolved, as well as the exact nature of the vertical power-sharing arrangement between the national government and the substate entity. A greater devolution of power to lower levels of government results in increased sharing of governing authority between the state and substate entities, and thus a more decentralized system of government.[16]

Unitary

A unitary state is not a form of decentralized state structure, but in weighing the options in a postconflict context, it often remains an attractive option for certain parties to a peace negotiation. Nonstate parties seldom seek to maintain a unitary state structure; however, the preconflict ruling party or government often initially proposes the maintenance of a unitary structure to centralize power or to maintain a hold on resources. A brief review of the unitary state structure is useful as it forms the foundation for the creation of a devolved unitary state structure, which will be discussed immediately below.

Unitary states are organized around a single central source of authority.[17] Administrative units exercise their rights primarily through the common organs of the national government rather than through parallel government structures. While regional political mechanisms may be established, they are constitutionally subordinate to and receive all their political authority from the national government. These mechanisms do not independently represent citizens or undertake independent legislative or executive decisions. The national government has a monopoly over the constitutional sovereignty of the state and significant powers are generally not devolved to lower-level entities.[18] Instances of unitary states include: Albania, Angola, Armenia, Bulgaria, Cuba, Honduras, Hungary, Iran, Ireland, Norway, Romania, Singapore, Sri Lanka, and Uganda.

In cases where the parties have agreed to continue a unitary state structure in the aftermath of a conflict, they are likely to have agreed only by securing other mechanisms to address drivers of conflict, such as by incorporating provisions related to monopoly of force, human rights, or accountability for atrocity crimes in the agreement. As a unitary state structure does not involve vertical power-sharing, it will not be further discussed in this chapter.

Devolved Unitary

In postconflict contexts, the parties often seek to modify a unitary state structure. One such way is by creating a devolved unitary state structure. Devolved unitary systems are, in essence, unitary states that incorporate some aspects of federalism. A unitary state may decide, via statute or constitutional modification, to devolve certain powers from the national government to the local governments of substate entities. The national government may also authorize the creation of representative bodies, such as parliaments, at the substate entity level.

Some states, such as France, have taken a light approach to devolution, with elected local assemblies exercising devolved powers in areas such as the maintenance of local infrastructure, including schools, and the provision of certain social services.

Other states, such as Spain and Italy, have taken a more intense approach to devolution and are often mistakenly considered federal states. In Spain, for instance, the national government has devolved substantial powers to elected governments of its seventeen autonomous communities and two autonomous cities.[19] These powers are asymmetric, generally cover the management of local finances, education, health, and social services, and may include the operation of a local police force and the use of a local official language.

In the case of Italy, the state is unitary, but with the substate entities organized into regions, provinces, and municipalities, with each level possessing substantial powers devolved from the national government, including all powers not specifically reserved by the national government.[20] Each of Italy's twenty regions has an elected parliament and an executive branch headed by a governor.[21] In all but two regions, the governor is directly elected. Notably, five of the regions possess an asymmetric devolution of additional authority, designed primarily to prevent their secession from Italy. In addition, similar to federal state structures, Italy has a bicameral parliament, with the second house, the Senate, elected on a regional basis.[22]

Other devolved unitary states include Azerbaijan, Bolivia, Chile, the Czech Republic, Georgia, Japan, the Netherlands, New Zealand, Peru, South Korea, Ukraine, the United Kingdom, and Uzbekistan.

Devolved unitary states are distinct from those with federal structures, as the powers devolved to substate entities like regions or provinces are less protected than in a federal system. In devolved unitary states, the national government often retains the ability to dissolve or override the decisions made by local governments. In a unitary state, the national government may also retract a measure of the power that was devolved to the local level, whereas a federal system typically protects against this retraction of devolved power.

Federal

In societies where ethnic, cultural, or linguistic heterogeneity exists, federalism has emerged as an often attractive alternative to a unitary or devolved unitary state structure, as it recognizes both regional or cultural differences and common national interests and identity.[23] States thus frequently rely upon a federal state structure to protect minority rights, culture, and language. This is usually done in a strategic manner, to minimize the risk of conflict between groups or to satiate secessionist movements.

A federal state structure is characterized by a division of power between the state and substate entities, such as regions or provinces.[24] Though there are common characteristics for federal systems, there is no "pure model" for federalism.[25] Federal states generally have a minimum of two levels of government organized into self-governing federal units that are united through the national government.[26] In federal systems, the local governments of substate entities possess a degree of autonomy, while sharing certain responsibilities with the national government.

Substate entities in federal structures nearly always have constitutions, popularly elected legislative and executive bodies, and judicial systems to decide on matters under the jurisdiction of the substate entity. Substate entities are also usually represented in some form in the national legislature,[27] which is often bicameral.

In Canada, for instance, each of its ten provincial governments has powers derived from the Constitution Act of 1867, which divided legislative powers between the national parliament and the provincial legislatures for them to exercise exclusively.[28] Canada also includes three territorial governments,[29] whose powers are delegated to them by the national parliament, as well as municipal governments, whose powers are delegated to them by the province or territory.[30] Elected members to the House of Commons and Senate represent each province and territory at the national level.

Malaysia, like Canada, is a federal state. Malaysia is composed of thirteen states, each with an assembly and a state-level government headed by a chief minister, and three federal territories with special status. The federal territories are delegated less authority than the states and lack their own legislative assemblies and heads of state. In the territories, executive powers are held by mayors that are appointed by the monarch on the advice of the prime minister, with the federal legislature adopting legislation concerning the territories.[31]

The United Arab Emirates represents one of the most extreme forms of a federal state structure, and is often considered a de facto confederal state. Each of the state's seven emirates has its own head of state. Each of these emirates existed as an independent emirate prior to coalescing to form the United Arab Emirates. The emirates retain significant individual authority, including revenue and natural resources-related powers. The nucleus of the national government is composed of the top officials from each emirate, who amongst them elect the president and vice president of the state.[32]

There are currently more than two dozen federal states, including Argentina, Australia, Austria, Brazil, Ethiopia, Germany, India, Mexico, Nigeria, Pakistan, Russia, and the United States. Roughly, an eighth of the states in the world are federal, and seven of the largest states are governed by federal structures.

Confederal

The most extreme form of a devolved state structure is confederal. A confederation is a collection of two or more sovereign substate entities that are linked together for the purpose of engaging in certain forms of common activity, such as foreign relations.

In a confederation, a national government is granted few powers and is typically weaker than the national government in a federal state. Often, substate entities in a confederation retain a de facto right to secession. A number of current federal states were initially confederations, such as the United States of America under its initial Articles of Confederation.

Switzerland, one of the few contemporary confederations, is comprised of a federal government, 26 cantons, and around 2,250 communes. The national government, known as the "Confederation," includes a directly elected parliament and a federal council elected by parliament.[33] The national government possess powers relating to international relations, defense, the national road network, nuclear energy, and a few other areas that require national-level agencies that cannot be maintained by cantons alone or that require uniform regulation. The cantons each have their own constitutions, parliaments, courts, and government, taking on the vast majority of authorities within the Swiss structure of governance. Each canton determines the division of responsibilities between itself and its communes, which typically maintain schools, energy, roads, planning, and taxation at the local level.[34] Some communes have their own parliaments.[35]

Asymmetric

In both a devolved unitary and federal state structure, there may be an asymmetrical devolution of powers to one or more substate entities. States oftentimes design an asymmetrical structure to account for historical differences, to meet the interest of a localized minority, or to forestall secessionist tendencies.

The asymmetric nature of the relationship may include varying degrees of the devolution of political power, the establishment of substate legislative and executive bodies, the application of a distinct form of local law (e.g., civil law vs. common law), the maintenance of an additional official language, rights to natural resources, separate police and security forces, and in some cases the right to external self-determination.

The unitary state of Denmark, for instance, maintains an asymmetrical relationship with Greenland, created under the 1978 Greenland Home Rule Act. Under this system, Greenland operates as an autonomous region within Denmark, maintaining control over issues including taxes, religious affairs, education, and health services.[36] In the unitary state of the United Kingdom, while England is subject to direct rule by the British Parliament, Scotland[37] and Wales[38] have their own parliaments and, along with Northern Ireland,[39] each possesses a set of unique devolved powers.

In Canada, the province of Québec maintains asymmetrically devolved powers in order to protect and develop its distinct culture.[40] Canada's government has broad powers at the central level, including those related to public debt, the census, currency, prisons, and immigration.[41] The Constitutional Act establishes a federal structure, provides for devolution of power to provinces, and enumerates the specific provincial government powers.[42] There are particular asymmetric powers given to the province of Québec, including power over official language and the operation of a French civil law system.[43]

In India, a number of its twenty-eight states and eight union territories possess widely varying asymmetric rights and privileges.[44] Notably, the national government has extensive power to modify not only the rights and privileges of the substate entities, but also to create, disband or merge states, as well as to change their borders or downgrade their status to that of a union territory.[45] The varying degrees of the rights and privileges are so extensive that India's 200-plus-page constitution is the longest in the world.

Allocating Legislative and Executive Powers

To ensure the effective functioning of government, decentralized states must specify which legislative and executive powers are exercised by the national government and which are exercised by the local governments of the substate entities. They must also specify which, if any, powers are exercised concurrently, and whether powers not specifically assigned are "reserved" for either the national or substate level. Importantly, some states devolve power to only one lower level of government, whereas others devolve to two or more levels.

A clear division of powers between the national and local government entities can strengthen state stability, prevent disputes over authority, encourage cooperation, and signify both local character and national identity. Explicitly delineating the authorities pertaining to each level of government through a legal mechanism such as a constitution or basic law can avoid confusion and disputes between different levels of government.

National governments generally, at a minimum, retain power over foreign affairs, the central bank, currency, fiscal policy, national elections, citizenship, immigration, trade policy, defense, air transport, postal and telecommunications services, maritime fisheries, social policy, environmental regulation, and national standards and statistics. For instance, the Netherlands is a decentralized unitary state, with extensive powers devolved to provinces and municipalities. The national government is vested with authority over national infrastructure such as roads and railways, public health, education, agriculture, price and incomes policy, defense, and international policymaking.[46]

Substate entities at the provincial level may possess a widely varying degree of legislative and executive power, which may relate to education, health, local environmental regulation, local policing, natural resource management, tourism, recreation, culture, language, water management, inland fisheries, agriculture and forestry, economic development, sports, and youth. For instance, France's regions are responsible for regional transport, civil airports, departmental transport (along with the departmental governing authorities), education, vocational training, cultural heritage, regional planning, economic development, environmental concerns, and scientific development. Its departments, another intermediary level of substate entity between the national and local level, similarly have authority over a wide range of fields, including departmental transport, education, social aid, public health, complementary economic planning along with regions, environmental concerns, tourism, agricultural aid, and business development.[47]

Powers held by local or municipal levels of government frequently include public lighting, waste collection, local public road maintenance, traffic management, drinking water supply systems, public parks, libraries, fire-fighting services, urban planning, and some social services.

Powers concurrently held by the national government and the substate entity often include fiscal powers such as collecting taxes, industrial and agricultural regulation, environmental policy, natural resources, infrastructure projects, criminal, civil and, administrative justice, economic regulation, transportation, and protecting public health. Traditional national government powers are seldom, if

ever, held concurrently, but those traditionally held by the substate entity are often
alternatively classified as concurrent powers. Oftentimes, the constitution will provide that the national government adopts framework legislation, and then the local
governments adopt more specific legislation within that framework in a way that
meets the unique or particular needs of the substate entity.

In Germany, a number of powers are concurrently shared between the national
government and provincial (*Länder*) governments, including those related to criminal and civil law; the administration of courts and notaries; economic matters; labor
law; land laws; disease control; and federation-wide transportation and shipping.[48]

Implementing concurrent authorities can lead to substantial discord between the
levels of government. As a result, states generally establish mechanisms for dispute
resolution and cooperation between levels of government in the exercise of concurrent authorities, such as a review process by a constitutional court. Further, executing concurrent authorities can prove to be complicated if deliberate guidance is not
included in an agreement or constitution.

States may also establish "residual clauses" by which any authorities that are not
explicitly designated are retained by either the national or local governments. For
instance, the German Constitution reserved authority over areas that are the pre-
rogative of a sovereign state, such as foreign affairs and defense, national citizenship,
customs and trading, and currency for the national government.[49] All authorities not
vested in the national government through the constitution are granted to
Germany's provinces.[50] Conversely, in Canada, residual powers are reserved for
the national government.[51] This can in many instances be one of the most important
clauses when addressing the allocation of legislative and executive powers.

Political, Administrative, and Fiscal Decentralization

In the context of devolution, there are generally three categories of devolved powers:
political, administrative, and fiscal.

Political Decentralization

Political decentralization involves the devolution of governing responsibilities and
decision-making authority to substate entities. These powers are devolved to local
executive and parliamentary bodies, which may be elected by the population of the
substate entity. These local bodies are then empowered to decide on policies, rules,
and regulations regarding the issues that have been assigned to the substate entity in
the peace agreement and/or constitution.

The purpose of political decentralization is to bring decision-making closer to the
people affected by those decisions. The central tenet of this approach is the belief
that the people affected by political decisions are the most well-informed about their
consequences, and that decision-makers themselves will be better informed if they
are accountable to the local populations. It is also understood that local

decision-making better reflects the interests of diverse populations, which are often the minority at the national level, but may be the majority at the local level.[52]

Take the case of Switzerland, a state that, as noted, is highly decentralized due to its history, heterogeneity, and pluralism.[53] Switzerland has nearly two dozen cantons, each of which has its own government, constitution, legislature, and courts.[54] Cantons then frequently devolve power to more localized governments, known as communes. In Switzerland's system, the cantons are the dominant political actors and decision-makers and hold the most political power.

In some instances, the national government devolves power to the provincial governments, which may then decide whether to devolve power to local/municipal governments. In other instances, the national government devolves power directly both to provincial governments and directly to local municipal governments.[55]

In devolving political power, states frequently create mechanisms to facilitate citizen participation in governance. Most states that engage in political decentralization allow for direct local elections, contrasting with centralized political systems where local officials are often appointed by the national government.

Administrative Decentralization

Administrative decentralization involves the transfer of the authority and responsibility to provide public services to the local governments of substate entities.[56] Administrative decentralization also involves the authority to implement the policies, rules, and regulations adopted by the local legislative bodies.

Functions over which substate entities often assume administrative responsibility include health services, sanitation, land use and natural resources protection, education, local infrastructure maintenance, and the operation of public utilities. For instance, Ethiopia devolved power to the lowest level of government to maintain local policing units, provide utilities and water, ensure sanitation services, and implement health and education services.[57]

As with political decentralization, states may set forth the agreed framework for administrative decentralization in their constitution, or they may set out a few constitutional principles and leave the details to subsequent legislation – usually in the form of a Local Government Act. In some instances, the legislation sets out national guidelines within which a substate entity must act, as in the case of Ghana, while in others it permits the substate entities to exercise any powers necessary to implement their administrative functions.[58]

Notably, political devolution does not require administrative devolution. A devolved unitary state may devolve some political decision-making to substate entities but retain the power to implement those decisions through existing state administrative bodies. Similarly, a province may delegate political decision-making to a municipality but implement those local decisions through provincial administrative bodies.

Administrative decentralization often entails the redistribution of civil service personnel or funding for such personnel.[59] This can include reallocating jobs from the national government to substate entities, creating a new workforce at the substate level to carry out administrative functions, and designing local capacity-building or training projects.

Fiscal Decentralization

Fiscal decentralization involves the devolution of fiscal authority with respect to allocating expenditure authority and revenue authority between the national government and substate entities; creating mechanisms to prevent and mitigate vertical imbalances; and establishing forums to debate and adjust fiscal policy and any conditions placed on the distribution of revenue.[60]

With respect to expenditure authority, the national government generally assumes expenditure authority for certain national-level public services such as the postal service, national security and defense, immigration, regulation of trade and commerce, foreign affairs, and some state-wide social programs.[61] Local governments typically take on expenditure authority in areas such as education, local law enforcement, transportation, communication, housing, healthcare services, and other population-specific areas.[62]

The allocation of revenue collection authority between levels of government determines the ability of a particular level of government to generate funds from citizens, businesses, and activities performed within its jurisdiction. Aspects of revenue collection authority include the ability to determine tax bases and rates, collect tax revenue, and set and collect fees for services provided by the government.

Some states have centrally concentrated revenue collection systems, allowing lower levels of government limited avenues for revenue generation. For instance, in Mexico the national government retains the vast majority of revenue collection authority. Local governments are authorized to collect property taxes, automobile taxes, and limited fees or user charges; the national government retains all other revenue collection powers. As a result, local governments in Mexico rely on the national government to transfer revenue to fulfill 80–90 percent of the local government's budget.[63] While this can help strengthen bonds between levels of government, it can also weaken local accountability and ownership over fiscal policy.

Other states grant wide authority to the various levels of government to generate revenue. In Switzerland, all three levels of government – federal, cantonal, and municipal – collect their own taxes.[64] At the federal level, taxes are directly collected on personal income and corporate profit, and indirectly on a number of other items. Each canton has fiscal autonomy,[65] and as a result the taxation rates and tax legislation of each canton vary significantly.[66] Cantons can levy taxes on personal income, personal property, corporate profit, and corporate capital, for instance.

Local governments in Switzerland can then levy taxes assigned to them by cantons.[67]

Nearly all states that devolve fiscal authority also create mechanisms to prevent and mitigate vertical imbalances through fiscal equalization. Some states opt to establish intergovernmental transfers, grants made between levels of government to ensure sufficient resources, decrease service delivery inequality, and/or offset economic inefficiencies between and among local governments. States often establish policy adjustment mechanisms to discuss and adjust fiscal policy and any conditions placed on the distribution of revenue.[68]

Spain's regional governments and autonomous communities, for instance, receive financial support from the national government. Regional governments receive an equalization transfer from the national government. The regions themselves also finance some equalization grants to autonomous communities with lower fiscal capacity. The autonomous communities have a much greater level of fiscal autonomy than the regions, and the current asymmetrical system creates an imbalance in revenue distribution, as well as asymmetric tax competition. Imbalances remain a contentious issue, as some regional governments claim not to receive sufficient funding from the national government.[69]

KEY STATE PRACTICE

This chapter draws on the following key state practice for a discussion of the various conundrums that the parties to a peace negotiation face when confronting the puzzle of negotiating vertical power-sharing. The paragraphs that follow highlight the relationship between each peace process and vertical power-sharing arrangements. For more on these conflicts, negotiations, and agreements, consult the Appendix.

The Dayton Accords for **Bosnia and Herzegovina** created a constitution for Bosnia and Herzegovina and a system of extensive vertical power-sharing. Bosnia's structure is characterized by limited central power, substantially devolved authorities, and a highly complex system of political devolution. Bosnia's two substate entities, which generally align with ethnicity, form a confederal state.[70] Under the framework established by the Dayton Accords, the Republic of Bosnia and Herzegovina is comprised of the Federation of Bosnia and Herzegovina and the Republika Srpska.[71] These two entities have their own constitutions and, while there are some authorities afforded only to the national government, powers are largely devolved to each of the substate entities. This is complemented by a system of extensive horizontal power-sharing, including a rotating presidency, a vital interest veto, a House of Peoples, and regional quotas in the national government.[72]

In 1991, **Colombia** drafted a new constitution that intended to decentralize power as part of the peace process, creating a devolved unitary state structure. This constitution included a number of provisions related to decentralization, including direct elections for mayors, governors, and legislative bodies, as well as significant fiscal and administrative decentralization. Despite these efforts at devolution, the conflict continued, with the insurgent groups infiltrating and manipulating the new vertical power-sharing structures.[73] In 2016, the parties' final peace agreement reaffirmed the devolution established in the 1991 constitution.[74]

The 2005 **Indonesia/Aceh** Memorandum of Understanding provided for asymmetrical devolution of all powers related to "public affairs" to the region of Aceh, as well as a number of other power-sharing arrangements. The central Indonesian government retained specific authority over foreign affairs, external defense, national security, fiscal matters, and freedom of religion.[75] After the signing of the agreement, Indonesia remained a unitary state, but with asymmetrically devolved power to the region of Aceh. No horizontal power-sharing arrangements were established by the agreement.

The 2005 **Iraq** Constitution and its predecessor, the Transitional Administrative Law, created a federal state with substantial vertical power-sharing.[76] The Iraqi constitution provided for a state with "a decentralized capital, regions and governorates, and local administrations" that each have particular powers – in other words, an asymmetric federal structure.[77] The constitution specified a number of exclusive and shared powers for regions and the national government, such as the right of regions to exercise executive, legislative, and judicial authority in accordance with regional constitutions.[78] These arrangements complemented a system of both formal and informal horizontal power-sharing arrangements.

The 2001 Ohrid Framework Agreement for **Macedonia** established a devolved unitary system of vertical power-sharing in Macedonia, aiming to establish equality for ethnic Albanians while preserving the territorial integrity of Macedonia. Section 3 of the agreement set forth the process for vertical power-sharing, devolving powers to local officials in areas including public services, urban planning, education, finance, and healthcare,[79] while retaining a unitary system of government. The Ohrid Agreement also included select horizontal power-sharing mechanisms, such as a requirement for a double majority on particular issues of importance to ethnic minorities, as well as enhanced status for Albanian as an official language of Macedonia.

The 2006 Comprehensive Peace Agreement for **Nepal** provided for the "progressive restructuring of the state by ending the current centralized and unitary form of the state." This was interpreted to mean Nepal would shift to a federal form of government with substantial devolution of political, economic, and social decision-making to the republic level. The powers defined during this peace process were often vague, with unclear demarcation of jurisdiction between levels of government and uncertain territorial demarcation of substate entities. In 2015, Nepal adopted a new constitution that devolved power to eight provinces.[80]

The 1987 Constitution of the **Philippines** provided for the creation of the Autonomous Region in Muslim **Mindanao**, subsequently implemented through domestic legislation. The constitution devolved a number of administrative powers to the autonomous region.[81] Nonetheless, a degree of violence continued between the Philippines government and the Moro Islamic Liberation Front. In 2012, the government signed the Framework Agreement on the Bangsamoro and in 2014 the government and the Moro Islamic Liberation Front signed the Comprehensive Agreement on the Bangsamoro, which provided for an enhanced asymmetric unitary structure for the region. These agreements, and the subsequent Bangsamoro Organic Law, which formalized the creation of the autonomous region, devolved enhanced fiscal and administrative powers.[82] The asymmetric powers devolved to Mindanao (now Bangsamoro) reflected a desire for greater autonomy and culturally influenced governing practices among the predominately Muslim population of the region, such as Sharia courts. No horizontal power-sharing arrangements were established by the agreement.

The 1996 Constitution of **South Africa** provided for provincial-level governance, and mandated the formation of local governments.[83] South Africa's devolved unitary system (which is often mischaracterized as a federal system) involves distinctively "cooperative" mechanisms to allow for three interdependent areas of government: national, provincial, and municipal. The constitution also lists powers that the lower governments hold both exclusively and concurrently with the state government. In practice, South Africa has faced challenges with the devolution of power at the provincial level due to political obstacles and resource disparities.[84]

In 2020, **Sudan** concluded the multitrack Juba Peace Agreement with nonstate parties representing **Darfur**, some of the nonstate parties in **Southern Kordofan** and **Blue Nile**, in addition to other intra-Sudan regional parties. These agreements required Sudan to reestablish a federal state and to provide for substantial vertical power-sharing in the form of devolved powers, residual powers, and the ability to create asymmetric relationships with the national government. The agreement also provided some innovative criteria for dispute resolution relating to the vertical power-sharing. With respect to horizontal power-sharing, the agreement provided for precise regional set-asides for seats in the executive, legislative, and judicial bodies.

In **Yemen**, the Gulf Cooperation Council Agreement of 2011, the Outcomes of the National Dialogue, and the 2014 draft constitution moved Yemen from a unitary to a federal state. The outcomes recommended, and the draft constitution provided for, the substantial sharing of political, administrative, and fiscal decision-making among four levels of government. Notably, federal decision-making was limited mostly to establishing policy, and all powers not specified in the constitution reverted to the regions. The draft constitution also restructured the administrative boundaries by creating six new regions – four in the north and two in the south – as well as granting the cities of Aden and Sana'a the same powers and responsibilities as the regions and lower levels of government. This vertical devolution was coupled with horizontal power-sharing such as a vital interest veto for the representatives of the south on specified legislative actions, an initial 40 percent representation in the House of Representatives, and a Federal Council designed to represent the interests of the regions.

Although overwhelmingly popular in peace processes, power-sharing introduces a host of potential challenges. The parties to the conflict regularly grapple with a thorny set of key conundrums, including the choice of state structure; the allocation of legislative and executive powers among the levels of government; the degree of political, administrative, and/or fiscal decision-making authority to be devolved; and the timeline for implementing decentralization.

Choosing a State Structure

In the context of determining a postconflict vertical power-sharing arrangement, the parties are first confronted with the conundrum of selecting an appropriate state structure for decentralization while balancing the distinct interests of the national government and local parties.

There are many approaches from which the parties may choose, each of which reflects a somewhat different set of interests and desired outcomes. Opposing parties may favor different or even conflicting approaches depending on their current access to power and the quality of that power, creating complications and imperfect compromises. For instance, the party representing the national government may favor a unitary state with a degree of devolution, as this allows the incumbent government to retain a significant level of authority. A substate entity, meanwhile, may prefer a more aggressive form of decentralization, such as federalism.

National governments are more often willing to share power at the national level, proposing horizontal power-sharing in a unitary structure without fundamentally redesigning the structure of their state. This would allow the national government to retain greater powers within a familiar structure, while potentially expanding the legislative body or setting aside some cabinet positions for the former combatants or their representatives.

Negotiating parties often reach a compromise by agreeing to a devolved unitary structure. A devolved unitary state structure is frequently an easier transition to implement for states in a postconflict context, as the state largely remains central-ized; but, as a result, it is often easier to reverse and easier for states to slip back into conflict.

The parties in postconflict contexts may also face pressure to agree to a system of federalism to satiate demands for autonomy and minority representation. Certain parties choose to pursue federalism because it can present an opportunity for unity while still ensuring respect of and protections for important differences among the population. In this way, federalism may also appear to be an attractive option in cases where minorities, especially those attached to a specific geographic territory, have suffered from underrepresentation, insufficient protections at the national government level, or systemic human rights abuses.[85]

If the parties choose to implement federalism as a method of vertical power-sharing, doing so comes with several risks. For instance, transitioning to federalism can raise serious potential for gridlock and governing inefficiency, slowing essential governance processes and potentially delaying other key reforms.[86] Additionally, federalism may not succeed in neutralizing corruption; the devolution of governing power does not guarantee that corruption simply will not devolve to the local level.

The parties must also grapple with how to pivot to a federalist structure without immediately unraveling an already-fragile state that may not have sufficient resources or governing capacity to implement a significant transformation. Because of the complexity and heightened political and cultural sensitivities involved in a postconflict transition from a unitary to a federal system of government, states may be unable complete this transition in a gradual or deliberate way. Federalism may be more durable in the long term, but it is difficult for the parties to agree to such sweeping decentralization, and it is exceedingly complex to implement.

In states with strong secessionist impulses, federalism can be a tempting option for mollifying secessionists with enhanced autonomy. Enhancing the strength of local authorities, however, can inflame secessionist movements elsewhere and generate unintended conflict. Additionally, attempting to institute an approach of this nature can deepen divisions in a state, as it often incentivizes local governments to break with the priorities of the national government when they feel that this is in the best interests of their local constituents.[87] Conversely, national governments may struggle to fully relinquish to local governments those powers and prerogatives previously held at the national level. This may also deepen divisions or otherwise impede implementation.

In instances where one substate entity is especially focused on decentralization and the remainder of the state's regions are in favor of a unitary system, the parties can opt for an asymmetric state structure. The parties must be careful not to undermine the interests of those substate entities not assuming decentralized powers, however, while maintaining the ability of the state to govern effectively.

States may find asymmetric structures to be particularly beneficial in facilitating decentralization in a manner that is responsive to the differing capacities of substate entities. An asymmetric devolved unitary or federal structure can enable efficiency by ensuring that weaker substate entities have sufficient support from the national government, while allowing regions with higher capacities to take on greater authority.[88] This can ensure that citizens receive sufficient levels of service delivery while still allowing for at least a measure of decentralization.

The parties are likely to seek to ensure that devolving power asymmetrically to one substate entity does not entice previously uninterested substate entities into pushing for their own devolved powers. An asymmetric structure can also breed resentment between substate entities if some entities perceive that others are receiving rights and benefits that they are not afforded. This can lead to animosity toward both the negotiating parties agreeing to an asymmetric structure, as well as toward minority groups given authority through the asymmetric structure.[89]

Although exceptionally rare today, some parties may determine that a confederal structure would best suit the needs of their particular postconflict context. A formal, or de facto, confederal state structure may deftly balance the needs of conflicting groups, but there are serious risks that it will create overlapping spheres of jurisdiction and contribute to and perpetuate dysfunctional governance.

Approaches to Resolving the State Structure Conundrum

This section discusses four primary approaches to resolving the state structure conundrum: designing a devolved unitary, federal, or confederal state, or designing an asymmetric version of one of these structures to provide for specific regional or sectarian needs.

Devolved Unitary

Macedonia's 2001 Lake Ohrid Agreement created a devolved unitary structure following the conflict between ethnic Albanians, who fought for greater rights and representation, and Slavic Macedonians.

Macedonia's ethnic Albanian population is located primarily in the north and west of Macedonia close to the Albanian border, and concentrated in the areas surrounding the capital of Skopje and in the city of Tetovo.[90] Given the geographic concentration of the population, an Albanian territory within Macedonia would have been a prime candidate for external self-determination. In resolving the conflict, the parties decided that rather than set a path of secession for the Macedonian Albanians, they would instead agree upon substantial devolution of legislative and executive power, and expanding local political, administrative, and fiscal decision-making.[91]

The parties to the Ohrid negotiations adopted a three-pronged approach to modifying the state structure for Macedonia. First, they explicitly reaffirmed the unitary character of the Macedonian state. They then committed to preserving the multiethnic character of Macedonia and further committed to taking steps to better reflect that character in the public life of Macedonia. Finally, they agreed to undertake the enhanced "development of local self-government in order to encourage the participation of citizens in democratic life, and promote the respect for the identity of communities."[92]

The parties coupled this approach with an explicit affirmation of the principle of subsidiary as applied in the European Union, which essentially provides that decision-making shall occur at the most effective level of government, with a preference for the local level. The parties also agreed to modify municipal boundaries to ensure the fair and equitable political organization and representation of the minority Albanian community, as well as other minority communities.

Notably, the parties devolved executive and legislative power, and decision-making authority, directly from the national government to municipal governments. The parties did not create new regions or districts.

The parties then coupled the modification of the state structure to a devolved unitary state with the adoption of select horizontal power-sharing mechanisms, designed to further integrate ethnic minorities into the political process. For instance, the agreement stipulated that a double majority is required for votes on certain issue areas, such as education, which gave minority groups the power to block legislation when they would otherwise be outvoted in a simple majoritarian system.[93] The Ohrid Agreement also increased the use of Albanian as an official language within government institutions and called for the expansion of multiethnic media.[94] The agreement also provided that one-third of the judges on the constitutional court would be selected by the representatives of those not in the majority, meaning those representing the ethnic Albanian population.

The agreement itself reflected this moderate approach to redesigning the state structure. It consisted of a few pages of principles followed by precisely drafted constitutional amendments. The agreement also provided for the future adoption of specific laws to accomplish the agreed principles. These laws were to be adopted using "majority of the minority" voting procedures as an additional form of power-sharing.[95]

Federal

As a reaction to the highly corrupt and highly centralized state structure of Yemen, the parties engaged in the peace process sought to transform Yemen into a federal state. While the draft constitution was never fully adopted, as the secretary of the constitution-drafting committee was kidnapped by Houthi forces while in transit to deliver the draft to the interim parliament for a vote, the Yemen case study is important for two reasons. First, the draft constitution resulting from the negotiation represents a highly detailed blueprint for the transition from a unitary to federal state, and for the operation of the newly created postconflict federal state. Second, Yemen starkly illustrates the risks negotiating parties undertake when they pursue dramatic and rapid changes in state structure.

Following a popular uprising and civil war in Yemen, the Gulf Cooperation Council, comprised of Bahrain, Kuwait, Oman, Qatar, Saudi Arabia, and the United Arab Emirates, outlined a process for a transitional government and a new constitution for Yemen. This process included several months for a national dialogue conference, followed by a constitution-drafting process, a constitutional referendum, and elections.[96] The process was designed to balance competing desires from southern secessionists, northern rebels, and a national government wishing to retain a unified state.

Two months after the end of the National Dialogue, President Hadi, the interim president, appointed a seventeen-member Constitution Drafting Committee to draft the new constitution based on the outcomes of the National Dialogue. During the first series of meetings, the drafting committee identified over 1,200 recommendations made by the National Dialogue that were deemed constitutional in nature.

There were six key dimensions of the Yemeni plan for a new federal state. First, the parties agreed on the need to create a new level of political entity, the regions, to which most of the legislative and executive power would be devolved. The regions would be comprised of existing *wilayas*, which themselves would be comprised of existing districts. The territorial delineation of the regions was hotly contested by the members of the National Dialogue and they were unable to agree upon either the number of regions, or their territorial scope. The tension was primarily, though not exclusively, driven by the desire of the south to regain much of the political power it had lost when the independent state of South Yemen[97] merged with North Yemen to create the current Republic of Yemen in 1990.

Given the inability of the parties to reach agreement during the National Dialogue, they agreed that the president of Yemen, who was also the president of the National Dialogue, would create and chair a committee to make a binding determination as to the number and territorial scope of the regions. The committee was charged with considering the option of "six (6) regions (four (4) in the North and two (2) in the South), the option of two (2) regions, and any option between these two options that can achieve consensus."[98]

Second, and as discussed in the Resolving the Political/Administrative/Fiscal Decentralization Conundrum section, substantial legislative and executive power would be devolved to the regions and *wilayas*, with the federal powers being limited in a significant way to establishing nationwide policies and standards. The regions were also entitled to adopt their own constitutions.

Third, the parties agreed to the creation of a hybrid federal judiciary with a path of district level courts, *wilaya* appellate courts, and newly created regional supreme courts, coupled with a federal supreme court and a national constitutional court. The regional courts' decisions were to be final, unless the matter was specifically within the competence of the Federal Supreme Court. There appeared to be no provision for lower federal courts.

Fourth, in order to create parity between the north and the south, and to appease the interests of the established political and economic elite, the constitution granted the cities of Sana'a and Aden status comparable to the regions. Sana'a would serve as a federal city not subject to any regional authorities. The city of Aden would operate autonomous legislative and executive authorities within, but not subject to the jurisdiction of, the region of Aden.[99]

Fifth, on the level of horizontal power-sharing, the constitution created a bicameral legislative body with a House of Representatives elected on a nationwide basis, and a Federal Council with members elected from within the regions and the cities of Sana'a and Aden. All legislation would require an affirmative vote in both bodies. The parties designed the Federal Council to play a prominent role in ensuring adequate representation of the interests of the regions in federal bodies, as well as independent institutions and specialized courts; the confirmation of cabinet appointments and senior civil and military positions; and serving as the forum for the southern provinces to exercise their vital interest veto.

Sixth, the federal structure provided for substantial asymmetrical rights for the southern provinces. Specifically, they were entitled to an initial 40 percent representation in the House of Representatives. They were also entitled to exercise a vital interest veto in the Federal Council (through the opposition of two-thirds of the representatives of the southern regions). The vital interest veto was applicable to matters such as modification of electoral constituencies, the division of revenue from natural resources, the shape of the federal state, the delineation of boundary regions, and the special status of Aden, and any constitutional amendments that might impact the representation of the south.

As the drafting committee continued to work on the constitution, Yemen's economy, as well as its security situation, rapidly deteriorated.[100] Negotiations reached a tipping point when the special committee created by the president to determine the boundaries of the regions released its conclusions. The committee created two regions in the south, which reduced the potential for future secession. The committee also created a region, associated primarily with Houthi territory, that had limited access to important economic assets in the form of oil and coastal resources.[101] The party of former president Saleh also rejected the six-region solution, arguing instead for the creation of more numerous and smaller governorates, which would be less likely to seek self-determination.

Two days after the details of the constitution were leaked, the Houthis rejected the proposed federalist structure,[102] and abducted the secretary of the Constitution Drafting Committee, who was on his way to deliver the draft for approval to the interim parliament.[103] Yemen then slipped into a multidimensional armed conflict characterized by deep political dysfunction and humanitarian catastrophe.[104]

In the case of Sudan and the Juba Agreement, the parties agreed to reestablish the federal state. The parties were so intent on securing federalism that the essential character of the state is described in paragraph one of the agreement as "a federal, independent and sovereign state in which sovereignty is vested in the people."[105] The agreement subsequently elaborated that the parties have agreed to "restore the regional-federal system of governance."[106] The transitional government of Sudan was given a short deadline of sixty days from the signing of the peace agreement to adopt legislation to restore the previous system of region-based federalism. The state then has six months from the date of the agreement to hold a constitutional conference to review the "administrative division of the various regions and levels of governance as well as the structures, powers and jurisdictions thereof."[107] Importantly, the parties to the peace agreement were empowered to agree on the participants in the constitutional conference. As a failsafe against delay, the agreement provided that in the event the conference is not held within six months, "the government of Darfur Region shall be activated in all its authorities and powers."[108] Presumably, the activation would default to the authorities and powers provided in the earlier Doha Peace Agreement.

Confederal

In the case of Bosnia and Herzegovina, the parties created an essentially de facto confederal state consisting of the two ethnoterritorial entities, the Republika Srpska and the Federation of Bosnia and Herzegovina, which itself consisted of ten autonomous cantons.[109]

Prior to the Yugoslav conflict, Bosnia and Herzegovina was a multiethnic republic within Yugoslavia. During the course of the conflict, Bosnia became essentially divided into two territories. One of these territories was the Republika Srpska, which, through a campaign of genocide and crimes against humanity, ethnically cleansed Bosniaks and Croats from that territory.[110] The second territory was the Federation of Bosnia and Herzegovina, which consisted primarily, but not exclusively, of Bosniaks and Croatians.

During the Dayton peace negotiations, the parties agreed to this bi-entity arrangement under immense pressure. The borders of the two entities essentially reflected the battle lines at the time of the negotiations, and as such ratified the results of ethnic cleansing. As will be discussed in the Allocating Legislative and Executive Powers Conundrum section, the peace agreement delegated substantial powers to the two entities, with very limited powers remaining with the central state.

At Dayton, the Republika Srpska, represented primarily by Slobodan Milošević, the president of neighboring Serbia, argued for this two-entity solution to ensure the ethnic Serbian population would have nearly exclusive political and economic control over what happened within its territory, and that it would preserve the option for that entity to someday separate from Bosnia and join Serbia.[111] In fact, the Dayton Accords specifically provided for the two entities to maintain "parallel special relationships" with Bosnia's neighboring states.

The Croatian population of Bosnia, represented in part by Franjo Tudjman, the president of neighboring Croatia, argued for the two-entity approach to protect the political gains of the substantially smaller Croatian population arising from the earlier creation of the Federation of Bosnia and Herzegovina.

The Bosniaks, the majority population in Bosnia, represented by President Alija Izetbegović, were constrained by the need to maintain the Federation in order to preserve their alliance with Croatia, and the leverage this position provided the Republika Srpska to argue for parity. President Izetbegović therefore sought to limit the devolution of authority to the two entities and maintain a functional national government, with rather limited success.

During the early stages of the war, the Srpska entity established a government structure with a president, prime minister, unicameral national assembly, and judiciary. The Federation was created in the midst of the Bosnian war by the multi-part Washington Agreement in an effort to maintain the fragile and intermittent alliance between the Bosnian and Croatian forces.[112]

The first part of the agreement, the Framework Agreement for the Federation, provided for a government structure of a bicameral parliament with a house of representatives (lower house) and a house of peoples (upper house). The framework also provided for a president and vice president, who alternate positions every year during a four-year term, a prime minister and deputy prime minister each from a different constituent people, and a judiciary. It further provided for the creation of ten cantons, whose boundaries were largely determined along postwar ethnic lines. Each canton was apportioned a president, cantonal legislature, and judiciary. The cantons were also entitled to establish cantonal councils among cantons that shared the same Bosniak-majority or Croat-majority.

Notably, the cantons were designed around the precepts of the earlier Vance–Owen Plan agreement relating to Bosnia and Herzegovina, which proposed maximum devolution of power to what were to be newly created "provinces" of Bosnia.[113] The Vance–Owen Plan is credited with inflaming the conflict and associated ethnic cleansing as it signaled the willingness of the international community to rebuild a Bosnian state based on ethnoterritorial entities.

The second part of the Washington Agreement, an outline of a preliminary agreement for a confederation between the Republic of Croatia and the Federation, captured the agreement of the parties to create a confederation between the state of Croatia and the Federation, which at the time did not possess statehood.[114] The outline essentially envisioned the eventual partition of Bosnia into the Federation, which would then join a confederation with Croatia, and the Republika Srpska, which would presumably then be incorporated into Serbia. By limiting the agreement to an outline of a preliminary agreement, the Bosnian government, as well as the United States, hoped to keep open the option of a unified Bosnian state.

The drafters of the Dayton Accords paired this confederal framework with a complex system of horizontal power-sharing. This system divides power between entities and according to ethnicity through ethnic quotas within the House of Peoples, House of Representatives, and within the state ministries.[115] A primary component of this horizontal power-sharing system is Bosnia's rotating presidency, an arrangement by which a Bosniak and a Croat are elected from the Federation and a Serb from the Republika Srpska. Whichever president receives a plurality of the vote becomes the chair. The position then rotates every six months. Additionally, the Dayton Accords provided for a vital interest veto. If a majority of the members of an ethnic group declares a decision "destructive of a vital interest," the chair of the

House of Peoples must create a joint commission, with one delegate from each of the three ethnic groups to rule on the matter. A similar veto exists for presidency decisions.[116] This system not only excludes members of the smaller minority groups from holding public office, but also entrenches ethnic-based political decision-making.[117]

As a consequence of the horizontal and vertical power-sharing systems, Bosnia's national government is often deadlocked since each of its entities, which have significant political authority, champions competing priorities based on ethnic policies.[118] Further, as political authority is greatly devolved, there is often confusion over which entities are empowered to make which decisions, compounded by a lack of coordination between a multitude of governing entities exercising devolved powers. This contributed to corruption, dysfunction, and the high cost of government.

Though the Dayton Accords put an end to a devastating conflict by creating ethnoterritorial entities and ensuring representation and political power for the three main ethnic groups, when power-sharing is implemented in a rushed manner, it can create new problems within the very governing structures it sought to reform. In the context of postconflict peace processes, completely reforming a state may seem appealing, but, as Bosnia demonstrates, the realities of the postconflict context and the capacities of existing institutions can lead to debilitating dysfunction.

Asymmetric

When designing a devolved unitary, federal, or confederal state structure, the parties to the negotiation may additionally decide that the structure should be asymmetrical.

In the case of the negotiations between Indonesia and Aceh, the unitary state of Indonesia was highly reluctant to create any nationwide adjustments to the state structure, as it did not want to encourage or advance self-determination movements in other regions, such as West Papua. The parties thus agreed that the arrangements set forth in the peace agreement would only be applicable to Aceh, and that there would be no horizontal power-sharing with Aceh at the national level. As will be discussed in Chapter 3: Natural Resources, Aceh accepted this limited degree of horizontal power-sharing in exchange for near-total control over the oil and other resources on its territory, and the right to implement Sharia law. Aceh was also induced to accept asymmetrical unitary devolution rather than independence as a consequence of the devastating humanitarian and economic effects of the 2004 tsunami.[119]

Under the 2005 agreement, Aceh would "exercise authority within all sectors of public affairs," while Indonesia retained responsibility for "foreign affairs, external defense, national security, monetary and fiscal matters, justice and freedom of religion."[120] The phrase "public affairs" was later interpreted to refer to local jurisdiction over most civil, judicial, and religious matters, as well as the administration of local police, but there have been substantial disagreements in the course of the implementation of this concept.[121] A provincial government runs Aceh, with the governor serving as the chief executive and a local parliament serving as the legislative body.

In the case of the 2005 constitutional negotiations in Iraq, the parties agreed to transform Iraq from a unitary state to a federal state, and to permit the exercise of certain asymmetrical rights and powers.[122] The Kurdish representatives led the drive for an asymmetrical federation to the negotiations primarily as an added layer of protection against a repeat of political and economic abuse suffered at the hands of Baghdad.[123] The Kurdish representatives also saw this asymmetrical federation as a way to formalize expanded autonomy gained in the mid-1990s as a result of the Gulf War, and as a tradeoff for setting aside Kurdish demands for independence.[124]

Other parties, skeptical of whether the democratic transformation would take hold, also supported the Kurds in their push for asymmetrical federalism. In particular, the Shia, who had been politically disenfranchised under Saddam Hussein, were keen that they have the opportunity to form regions among the governorates they controlled, and for those regions to possess the same rights and privileges as the Kurdish Regional Government (KRG). On the other hand, the Sunni, who had exercised substantial political power under Saddam Hussein, were unenthusiastic about the creation of regions as they worried about Kurdish secession, the devolution of power to political entities incapable of effectively exercising that power, and to some degree hoped for a return to power in the future.[125]

Ahead of the finalized 2005 Constitution, the Kurds proposed a constitution that would provide greater powers to Iraq's regions and governorates.[126] The Kurds aimed to create a "voluntary federation," with each governorate possessing the power to protect borders with other states using "self-defense forces," and the right to have a democratic constitution.[127] This Kurdish draft also included the possibility of secession through a referendum after eight years under the federal constitution, if Iraq altered its federal system, or if the region of Kurdistan was subject to "aggression or oppression, or the seizure of any of its lands."

The negotiation position of the Kurds was enhanced by the fact that the Transitional Administrative Law (TAL), adopted as an interim constitution in 2004 by the Iraqi Governing Council, provided that the three provinces that were under the protection of the UK, French, and US no-fly zone from 1992 onward had formed a de facto Kurdish regional government.[128] This region would continue and maintain special rights and privileges under the TAL's newly created federal structure.[129] The subsequent constitution also continued these special rights and privileges, and further provided that any laws, decrees, or contracts (presumably including oil contracts) adopted since 1992 would continue in force.[130]

In ultimately authorizing the Kurdish region, the TAL, and subsequently the constitution drafting committee, was cautious to limit the ability of other governorates to create regions. The TAL limited to three the number of governorates that could join to form a region.[131] This was designed to prevent the nine southern Shia governorates from joining in a mega-region, which would control the vast majority of Iraq's oil resources, and which might be subject to substantial Iranian political influence.[132]

While the constitution grandfathered in the KRG as a region, it essentially sidestepped the establishment of a process for creating additional regions, rather noting that a subsequent law would address the issue within the first six months of the National Assembly's term.[133] The constitution did, however, provide for the procedure of initiating the process for creating a region: either a request by one-third of the council members of each governorate intending to form a region, or a request by one-tenth of the voters in each of the governorates intending to form a region.[134] Since 2008, the oil-producing governorate of Basra has made halting attempts to initiate the process for becoming a region in order to grain greater control over oil revenue.[135]

The constitution authorized regions to maintain executive, legislative, and judicial bodies. As such, the KRG maintained its internal governing structure of a president, prime minister, legislative assembly, and independent judiciary. The KRG, as a region, possesses a number of special powers, including those related to regional budget allocation, policing and security, education and health policies, natural resources management, and infrastructure development.[136] The KRG also possesses the power to invalidate federal legislation that addresses any power not expressly designated as a federal power.[137]

The TAL prohibited Baghdad and Kirkuk from joining regions.[138] Kirkuk was a formerly Kurdish and Turkmen city that had been Arabized through forced population transfers under Saddam Hussein. The constitution, at the insistence of the Kurds, provided there would be a referendum in Kirkuk approximately two years after its adoption.[139] The referendum was to determine whether the citizens of Kirkuk wished to join the city with the KRG.[140] It was never held, and in part this contributed to the Kurdish referendum on independence in 2017.[141] The government of Iraq responded by militarily occupying Kirkuk to prevent its annexation to the KRG, and by imposing a temporary travel and economic blockade on the KRG.[142] The Supreme Court ruled the referendum illegal under the Iraqi Constitution.[143]

After the adoption of the 2005 Constitution, a system of horizontal power-sharing emerged to facilitate a functional system of governance among the Kurd, Shia, and Sunni groups. Though not stipulated in the constitution, by convention Iraq's prime minister is Shia, its president is Kurdish, and its parliamentary speaker is Sunni.[144] In practice, parliamentary coalitions of these three sectarian groups collectively agree to the selection of these three positions.[145]

Determining the basic structure of a system for power-sharing triggers a vast number of other complex challenges, raising further conundrums for the parties, including the allocation of legislative and executive powers.

Allocating Legislative and Executive Powers

Once the parties have determined the state structure, the next compelling question is the allocation of legislative and executive powers among the various levels of government.

The negotiation over the allocation of authorities among levels of government in a postconflict context reflects the macro-power struggle between the national government, which wishes to retain its grip on power, and nonstate actors, which agitate for greater autonomy and power. The conundrum negotiating parties face is how to reconcile the differing demands of the national government and nonstate actors, while constructing a functional system for vertical power-sharing.

Often, nonstate actors point to drivers of conflict such as marginalization, lack of autonomy, and underrepresentation in government to support their claims for greater devolution of powers to the substate level in a postconflict system of vertical power-sharing. Meanwhile, the national government often asserts that newly established substate entities lack the capacity to execute the powers devolved to them, supporting its desire to retain power at the national level and transfer powers down to the local governments of substate entities at a later time.

In many instances, the parties may seek a compromise through an extended list of powers concurrently held by national and local governments. Concurrent powers may be especially useful in contexts where substate entities are new or have limited governing ability, as is often the case in postconflict states. Concurrent powers may also be needed to handle governance issues in which both the state and substate entities have a significant interest.

Yet concurrent powers can lead to significant gridlock and destabilization within the state if not effectively managed. As states transition to a decentralized framework, a lack of clarity in defining the authorities allocated to each level of government creates confusion, dysfunction, and a general lack of coordination between jurisdictions.

One approach to coordination is to facilitate formal representation between levels of government. For instance, entities within the national government can be tasked with implementing certain policies at the local level. This approach is especially common in states that devolve administrative authorities and have central departments that are designated to help local governments manage issues such as healthcare, sanitation, and/or economic development.[146] Alternatively, the parties can create a mechanism by which representatives from various levels of government liaise or even formally sit with representative entities at other levels. Under this framework, local governments may embed representatives at the national government level, and vice versa.

Consultations between levels of government often help supplement these representative "exchanges." The parties can establish a general framework to ensure consistency across local policies that may impact the state at large. Some states also create dispute resolution mechanisms or joint councils to manage any conflict or facilitate consultation between levels of government. These councils include representatives from all levels of government, in the form of independent commissions or other intergovernmental fora.

Approaches to Resolving the Allocation Conundrum

In the case of Bosnia, the parties pursued a path of maximum devolution. A variety of factors contributed to this decision, but it was mostly driven by the preexisting federation between the Bosnian and Croatian parties. This federation blocked the ability of the Bosnian delegation at Dayton to argue for robust powers at the national level, as it would be perceived as surrendering these powers up to the national level. The Serbian delegation saw the structures created by the Dayton Accords as a way station to the eventual independence of the Republika Srpska, and thus had little interest in surrendering substantial powers to the national level.

Given these circumstances, the national government was assigned limited competencies over only ten matters, which included foreign policy, national defense, intelligence and security, foreign trade and customs policy, immigration, and air traffic control.[147] The agreement delegated all other powers to the Republika Srpska and the Federation of Bosnia and Herzegovina.

Fearing that they had created a hollow state, the mediators, under pressure from the Bosnian delegation, added a separate section to the constitution titled "Additional Responsibilities," which contained three provisions that could serve as backdoor ways of assigning powers to the national level.[148]

The first of these three provisions was that Bosnia shall "assume responsibility for such other matters as are" necessary to "preserve the sovereignty, territorial integrity, political independence, and international personality of Bosnia and Herzegovina."[149] The constitution provided that additional national institutions could be created to carry out these responsibilities.[150]

Second, Articles 5–8 of the General Framework Agreement stipulated that the national institutions were also to assume responsibility for matters related to the arbitration of disputes between the entities, the protection of human rights, the promotion of the return of refugees and displaced persons, and efforts to preserve national monuments.[151]

Third, the parties agreed that the national level of government could assume responsibility for additional matters as are agreed by the entities, and that within six months of the entry into force of the constitution the entities were to begin negotiations on including such matters, specifically those relating to the utilization of energy resources and cooperative economic projects.[152]

Notably, the horizontal power-sharing mechanisms that were adopted in Dayton allowed the representatives of the Republika Srpska to veto any efforts to use these "Additional Responsibilities" to shift more powers to the national level. Other provisions of the Dayton Accords further diluted the limited powers assigned to the national level. For instance, the Dayton Accords allocated the authority to the

Federation and Republika Srpska to establish special parallel relationships with neighboring states, maintain law enforcement agencies, and enter into certain agreements with states and international organizations.[153]

The Dayton Accords provided for further devolution within the two entities. The Federation was given exclusive authority over areas including economic policy, financial institutions, and energy policy. Along with its cantons, the Federation was allocated concurrent authority over such areas as enforcing human rights, health, environmental policy, communications and transport infrastructure, social welfare policy, tourism, and use of natural resources. The Federation's cantons were given the ability to delegate authority in the fields of education, culture, tourism, local business, and radio and television to municipalities. Its local self-governing units were given such authorities as local budgeting, spatial planning, local natural resource management, local infrastructure management, sanitation, and community self-government.[154]

Meanwhile, the Dayton Accords gave the Republika Srpska authority over security, protection of human rights, property obligations, banking, taxation, public services, environmental protections, worker safety and social care, police, and local media. With its municipalities, the Republika Srpska was allocated concurrent authorities including education, public administration, culture, and tourism. Its authorities also included regulatory competencies such as natural resource management, use of public goods, health care, public health, organization of local police, and adoption of local budgets and spatial plans.[155]

By nearly all accounts, the maximum devolution approach substantially stunted Bosnia's political development. As succinctly put by a 2019 Congressional Research Service study, the constitution created by the Dayton Accords, including its ethnic power-sharing arrangements and veto powers, fosters sustained gridlock within Bosnia's political system.[156] Along with this gridlock, the scale of Bosnia's decentralization prevents the successful implementation of reforms needed for Bosnia to join the EU and NATO, as well as the implementation of international and domestic court rulings against provisions in the constitution itself.[157]

In the case of Nepal, the parties sought to solve this conundrum by developing a fairly elaborate and specific allocation of powers among the three levels of government. At the federal level, the state possesses the standard powers relating to foreign affairs, defense, intelligence and economic regulation, international trade and environmental regulation. In addition to the thirty-five specified powers, the federal level retains authority over all powers not specifically assigned to the provinces and local authorities, or designated as concurrent powers.[158]

The constitution specified a similarly expansive and detailed list of powers held by the provincial governments relating to provincial-level institutions, economic matters, and natural resources. This is followed by a similarly detailed list of concurrent powers between the federal and provincial levels. Notably, the constitution then set out detailed powers for the local level, and a list of concurrent powers between the provincial and local levels.[159]

Some observers have criticized these lists of powers as being overlapping and vague.[160] Given the high level of distrust among the parties and the geographic regions they represented, however, it was necessary both to precisely specify the allocation of powers and to provide that many of these powers would be concurrently held. This way, no one level of government could impose its will on the other levels and thereby undermine the goals of the new federal state structure.

South Africa took a two-phase approach to resolving this conundrum, and eventually settled on a rather unique devolved unitary system. The postapartheid constitution aimed to reflect a cooperative, concurrent approach to power-sharing desired by the parties at the negotiating table, which would serve as a break from the years of deep division in South Africa.[161]

Rather than initially setting out a specific list of powers, South Africa's 1993 interim constitution, which essentially served as a peace agreement, instead set out criteria for determining which powers would be federal and which provincial in the final constitution. Interestingly, at the last minute the parties added an extensive list of provincial powers to the interim constitution.[162]

The criteria for determining which powers were to be federal included the efficacy of decision-making related to the quality and rendering of service; the need to maintain or establish uniform essential national standards and unity; and the need to create nationwide policies and enable interprovincial relationships. In the event of disputes related to concurrent legislative powers that could be resolved by courts, precedence would be given to the national government.[163]

South Africa's permanent constitution of 1996 did not list a specific set of national powers, but rather provided a detailed list of concurrent powers, and then established the relationship between the federal government and the provincial governments with respect to those powers. The constitution also provided a detailed list of relatively minor, exclusive powers for the provinces. It stipulated that the federal powers could supersede concurrent powers or powers of the provinces to maintain national security, economic unity, national standards, or to prevent "unreasonable action taken by a province" that directly conflicts with the interests of another province or of South Africa as a whole.[164] The constitution intended for the federal government to adopt legislation that would create standards and set national policy with the aim of harmonizing the laws, rules, and actions of the provinces.

The parties drafting the South Africa Constitution coupled this unique system of vertical power-sharing with a bicameral legislature, with the second chamber being the Council of Provinces comprised of ten representatives elected by province-level governments. Additionally, the constitution established a Local Government Association to formally represent local governments in the upper chamber of parliament, with an allocation ten non-voting seats.[165] The Local Government Association also established offices in each province with the aim of acting as the voice of local governments in the upper chamber of parliament.

Recent scholarly analysis indicates that due to the power disparity between the federal government and the provinces in South Africa, the federal government has used this concurrency structure essentially to centralize power away from the provinces. Notably this analysis also finds that the municipalities too have been able to pull power from the provinces, resulting in the federal government and the municipalities (in specifically defined areas) exercising most of the executive and legislative power in South Africa.[166]

In the case of Sudan, the parties to the 2020 Juba Peace Agreement agreed upon a highly asymmetric federal state. The parties representing the north and the east, as well as the central regions of Sudan had little interest in the devolution of political power, as they did not possess the institutions to absorb that power. Their concerns related more to economic marginalization, which they sought to address through aggressive wealth-sharing provisions in the peace agreement.

The multiple parties representing the Darfur region, which had been subjected to genocide under the Bashir regime, sought a highly devolved system of power-sharing coupled with the right for the three provinces of Darfur to form a single region (much like the Kurds in Iraq). This position represented, to a degree, the continuation of the achievements in the 2011 Doha peace accords, which provided for a referendum to decide whether Darfur should become a single region.[167] The referendum on Darfur's status was delayed until April 2016, five years after the signing of the Doha Document for Peace in Darfur, and ten years after the signing of the Abuja Agreement.[168] Of votes cast, 97.72 percent favored maintaining Darfur as individual states rather than forming one region.[169]

In the Juba Peace Agreement, the parties decided to create an arrangement whereby within the region of Darfur the nonstate parties representing Darfur in the peace negotiations would hold "40% of the power in Darfur," and the components of Sudan's transitional government, which included a mix of national level constituents would hold 30 percent.[170] Ten percent of the power would be allocated to Darfur nonstate actors who subsequently joined the Juba Agreement, and the remaining 20 percent would go to other Darfuri "stakeholders," as agreed by the parties.[171] The representatives selected were to "reflect the geographic, social and civil diversity in Darfur to ensure social coexistence and durability of peace."[172] It is not entirely clear from the agreement whether this allocation of representation was temporary, or permanent. Significantly, it was agreed that the leadership of the government would be selected by the nonstate parties representing Darfur in the peace negotiations.[173]

With respect to the allocation of specific executive and legislative powers, the agreement for the Darfur track did not spell out any powers for the national government, but rather listed, in great detail, over two dozen clauses setting out the powers of the region, and nearly three dozen clauses setting out concurrent powers. The agreement then provided, in the form of a residual powers clause, that "should any residual powers or competencies arise," the federal government would exercise those powers "of a federal nature," and the regional government would exercise those powers "of a regional nature," and that powers of a concurrent nature would be exercised concurrently.[174] The agreement did not specify criteria for determining the nature of specific powers. It did, however, provide criteria for the resolution of disputes relating to the conflicting laws. In this event, the law that most effectively deals with the subject matter would prevail, while taking into consideration the balance between the sovereignty of Sudan and the autonomy of Darfur; the need for national standards and norms; the principle of subsidiary; and the need to promote the welfare of the people and protect human rights and fundamental freedoms.[175] While quite innovative, it remains to be seen whether this set of criteria facilitates the resolution of disputes or leads to endless judicial review.

With respect to horizontal power-sharing, the parties agreed that the regions of Sudan would be represented at the national-level institutions in proportion to their population size, and that this representation could be augmented to account for "the principle of positive discrimination for the most underdeveloped and war-affected regions."[176] The Darfuri parties also sought substantial horizontal power-sharing in the form of representational set-asides in the interim Sovereign Council, as well as the executive and the legislative bodies. The parties agreed that the signatories to the agreement would hold three of the eleven seats on the Sovereign Council, and 25 percent of the seats on the Council of Ministers and in the Transitional Legislative Council.[177] The parties also agreed that within six months of the signing of the agreement, Darfuri men and women would make up 20 percent of the national judiciary.[178]

To ensure what was achieved in the Juba Peace Agreement was not undone or diluted in subsequent constitutional negotiations, the Darfuri parties also insisted that whatever was agreed in the peace negotiations would be binding in subsequent constitutional negotiations, and that the agreement itself would be included in the Constitutional Decree. In the event there was a conflict between the constitution and the agreement, the Constitutional Decree would be amended.[179] Thus, a subset of the body politic would be designing the new federal structure for Sudan, which was deemed necessary to reach a final and durable peace.

With respect to the so-called Two Areas of Southern Kordofan and the Blue Nile, two different delegations represented the interests of the people in those areas. One, which participated in the main negotiations, sought maximum devolution of power to the two areas, with little interest in horizontal power-sharing. This delegation sought full and exclusive jurisdiction over the social, political, and economic life, governed by its own constitution, and executive, judicial, and legislative structures, within its territorial boundaries under a special status arrangement. The delegation proposed a small list of concurrent powers with the government of Sudan, such as for taxation and electoral regulation purposes, but proposed much longer lists of powers to be held by the regions alone, including delivery of social services, economic regulation, law enforcement, and urban development. Nearly all these objectives were achieved in the final agreement.[180]

The second delegation reflected much the same opinion, but also sought a clear right to self-determination for the two areas, the declaration of Sudan as a secular state, and the right to maintain an independent army. The drive for self-determination arose largely from the belief that the two areas were promised a form of self-determination in the Comprehensive Peace Agreement, via a popular consultation, that would have enabled them to join South Sudan when it separated from Sudan, and that this was denied them by the Bashir regime. To make the point clearly that the two areas would be essentially self-governing under a federal Sudan, they proposed the term "autonomous federalism" to describe the arrangement. In September 2020 a joint agreement provided that Sudan would become a democratic state with a constitution "based on the principle of separation of religion and state, and in the absence of which the right to self-determination must be respected."[181]

Political, Administrative, and Fiscal Decentralization

Once the parties to a peace negotiation decide which levels of government will possess decision-making authority over which powers, they must decide whether that authority includes political, administrative, and fiscal decision-making, or a subset of these three. The debate among the parties often revolves around effectiveness versus effective change. Determining which of these three categories of authorities will be devolved and how they will or will not relate to one another impacts the likelihood of a durable peace.

Initially, the parties representing the substate entities often focus almost exclusively on political decentralization, as they want to reverse political marginalization and exclusion by possessing the power to make decisions on matters of central importance to their region. While there may be horizontal power-sharing mechanisms on the negotiating table, the parties are often most comfortable with simply arguing that important powers should be devolved to the substate entity, and that they would then ensure their rights and privileges are effectively implemented and protected. National government officials are often reluctant to devolve too much political decision-making to the substate entities, as this creates an inconsistent patchwork of laws, rules, and regulations across the state, and increases the financial burden on the state to maintain the various parliamentary and executive bodies necessary to carry out this local decision-making.

At some point in the negotiation, the parties will begin to discuss who will be responsible for implementing or administering the decisions made by the substate entities. Here again, the parties representing the substate entities will seek to obtain as much control as possible over the implementation of the devolved powers. Often, though, substate entities have a serious lack of capacity to operationalize the powers devolved to them by the national government, creating new governance challenges and gridlock in the provision of basic services. This is a bit of a catch-22. Local governments often lack capacity due to long-term marginalization, and to allocate decision-making authority, but deny the authority to implement those decisions due to a lack of technical capacity, will only serve to perpetuate that lack of technical capacity. Further, doing so will provide the national government with the perceived ability to undermine the political decisions through lax or divergent implementation. Negotiating parties can overcome this by designing a gradual transfer of administrative authority or transfer of national-level personnel coupled with the training of local-level personnel.

Negotiating parties soon realize that the thorniest issue is not the devolution of political or administrative authority, but rather how this devolution of power will be funded. At times, this negotiation merges into a parallel negotiation on wealth-sharing.

Successful fiscal decentralization relies on a baseline level of trust between local governments and the national government, something that is often lacking in postconflict states, especially where a substate entity maintains a long-term interest in external self-determination. Without this trust, national control over revenue authority limits the autonomy of substate entities to drive their own policy and may negatively impact their ability to execute political and administrative authorities.

Likewise, in the view of the national government, substate entities must prove to be capable and accountable partners;[182] otherwise, corruption or misuse of funds may be a risk.[183] In contexts where the capacity of local governments to implement fiscal responsibilities is in question, services may be disrupted and local officials may struggle to implement their policies. Additionally, local capacities to collect revenue may differ, leading to unintentional fiscal inequalities between regions.

A major challenge facing the parties is to devolve commensurate levels of financial authority with the devolved political and administrative authorities. An unbalanced devolution can undermine the durability of an agreement by granting a substate entity political and administrative authority that it is simply unable to implement. Too much fiscal devolution can bankrupt a state and inhibit the ability of the national government to undertake the multitude of reforms often necessary to ensure more inclusive governance and security sector reform. To ameliorate these tensions, states often create joint commissions, formal mechanisms for local integration in national institutions, budgeting committees, or other mechanisms for vertical integration of local representatives at the national level of government.

Approaches to Resolving the Political/Administrative/Fiscal Decentralization Conundrum

The parties to peace negotiations have tried a number of approaches to balancing their competing interests related to the devolution of political, administrative, and fiscal authority. They have also sought to resolve the vexing question of balancing the varying levels of authority for each of the three areas to promote and not undermine a durable peace.

As discussed earlier, prior to the implementation of the decentralization framework set out in the Ohrid Agreement, the concentration of powers in Macedonia's national government limited the ability of local authorities to provide efficient services to local communities. This undermined their ability to be responsive to ethnic grievances within their communities as well as to address basic development issues.[184]

The Ohrid Agreement provided for a law on local self-government that would "[reinforce] the powers of elected local officials and [enlarge] substantially their competencies in conformity with the Constitution."[185] Specifically, the agreement mandated that the law would include authorities for municipalities to administer public services, urban and rural planning, environmental protection, culture, social welfare, and healthcare.[186] It also stipulated the devolution of authority to local governments related to administering local policing and developing local public safety policy.[187]

The Ohrid Agreement also sought to develop innovative ways to share political and administrative authority on sensitive security issues, such as control of the local police forces. For instance, it specified a constitutional amendment empowering municipal councils to select local heads of police, drawn from lists of candidates proposed by the Ministry of Interior.[188] Though the national government would propose the lists, it would ultimately be the municipal-level government that selected its own local police chief. This enabled Macedonia to maintain its unitary state structure, but to provide the municipalities with a level of confidence in the operation of the police.

The drafters of the Ohrid Agreement matched the devolution of political and administrative authorities with a devolution of fiscal authority deemed "essential for ... promoting the respect for the identity of communities."[189] The Ohrid Agreement prescribed that local governments should be responsible for raising a "substantial" amount of tax revenue and that they should be autonomous and responsible for budgeting within their particular areas of competence, as defined by devolved political and administrative authorities.[190]

Macedonia experienced a number of unforeseen complications with its approach to fiscal devolution. Since the implementation of the Ohrid Agreement, rural municipalities have struggled to generate enough funding to meet the needs of their citizens, likely due to smaller populations and a broader distribution of financial resources. For instance, in 2012 rural municipalities in Macedonia generated only 13.1 percent of local revenues while urban areas generated the remaining 86.9 percent.[191] As a result of differences in the quantity of revenue collected following decentralization, rural local governments were able to deliver fewer public services to their constituents than urban local governments.[192]

Similarly, although capital grants were allocated to Macedonia's municipalities to supplement their revenue, the municipalities needed to apply for these resources, and some municipalities, particularly those that are rural, had lesser capacities to develop successful applications.[193] Combined with the limited tax revenue base, this puts the rural units of municipal governance at a disadvantage as it provides them with fewer resources to successfully govern.

As noted, to accomplish the aim of mitigating violent ethnic tensions and competing ethnic groups' demands for Bosnia's partition,[194] the Dayton Peace Accords set forth a system of maximum political decentralization in Bosnia. To accomplish this, the Federation and the Republika Srpska have directly elected legislative bodies and executives (a prime minister for the Federation and a president for the Republika Srpska). Each canton in the Federation has its own governing structures as well.[195]

The devolution of political authority to so many substate entities in Bosnia created gridlock, confusion, and dysfunction.[196] Though Bosnia has a population of under 4 million, it has 5 presidents, 4 vice presidents, 13 prime ministers, 14 parliaments, 147 ministers, and 700 members of parliament.[197] In the early years of implementation, Bosnia spent nearly 40 percent of its annual GDP to support these structures. Although the state has not suffered a return to conflict under this arrangement, many analysts emphasize that this decentralization framework is unsustainable.[198]

Bosnia also suffers from a substantial issue of inequality in revenue collected between substate entities. After the Dayton Accords were signed to end the conflict in Bosnia and the state was transformed into a de facto confederal structure, the national government no longer had the formal authority to tax, only to collect revenue from limited sources such as passport fees. This framework contributed to tax competition between the substate entities created by the accords, leading to a lack of coordination between them that ultimately facilitated tax evasion and fueled corruption.[199]

The absence of coordinated rules between the Bosnian entities created avenues for exploitation by which companies could avoid paying taxes. This system also led to inequality between governing entities and municipalities.[200] The lack of coordination has contributed to the underfunding of services and undeveloped accountability measures, leading to underperforming basic service provision.[201]

Furthermore, because the national Bosnian government sets tax policy but is not responsible for implementing that policy, it has been able to escape the consequences of its tax decisions.[202] This has contributed to poor central tax policymaking that has often left local governing structures without enough revenue to meet their expenditures.

The case of the Philippines and Mindanao illustrates a lengthy process of trial and error to achieve the right balance of political, administrative, and fiscal decentralization. Throughout the fifty years of conflict between the Philippines, the Moro National Liberation Front, and the Moro Islamic Liberation Front, the Philippines took several steps to devolve greater authorities to the region in an effort to quell tensions.

In 1977, the Philippines enacted narrowly tailored devolution through Presidential Decree No. 1083, which established Sharia courts for the predominately Muslim provinces of Mindanao. The jurisdiction of these courts was limited to the administration of marriage, divorce, child custody, wills, trusts, estates, and contracts between Muslims.[203] The Moro National Liberation Front embraced the agreement, but a portion of the leadership split and created the Moro Islamic Liberation Front.

In 1987, the Philippines sought to quell the conflict through enhanced devolution by providing for the creation of an autonomous region in Muslim Mindanao. The amended constitution, followed by legislation in 1989, devolved a number of political powers to the newly established autonomous Mindanao, such as authority over administrative organization; regional urban and rural planning development; ancestral domain and natural resources; economic, social, and tourism development; educational policies; and preservation and development of cultural heritage.[204]

The constitution, and the act that followed, also devolved all powers, functions, and responsibilities that the national government formerly possessed to Mindanao, excluding those specifically enumerated. Those powers stipulated in the constitution and the act included foreign affairs, national defense and security, coinage, fiscal and monetary policies, the administration of justice, elections, and citizenship.[205]

Notably, the Philippines did not devolve fiscal authorities to Mindanao at this time, thus depriving the newly created autonomous region of the ability to effectively actualize its autonomy and the provision of public services. Though the Moro National Liberation Front accepted the agreement, it was rejected by the Moro Islamic Liberation Front. The conflict continued and the desire for genuine autonomy continued unabated.

In 1996, the parties again attempted to cement a durable peace through the Mindanao Final Agreement. The agreement provided for the devolution of even more political authority, coupled this time with fiscal authority. The Mindanao Final Agreement allowed the provincial government to enact a local tax code, and to "[budget] its own revenue resources and block subsidies granted to it by the National Government and foreign donors."[206] The agreement, however, did retain for the national government the power over fiscal and monetary policies.[207] This enhanced decentralization framework, which paired fiscal powers with the previously devolved political powers, set the region on a path for a more successful transition.

After several years of negotiations with the Philippines government, the Moro Islamic Liberation Front abandoned its claim for external self-determination, and the parties reached a comprehensive agreement in 2014,[208] and later an Organic Law.[209] The new autonomous entity was formally established formally in 2019 following a plebiscite.[210] The entity, called the Bangsamoro Autonomous Region, has its own parliament, fiscal autonomy, and over fifty enumerated exclusive powers, marking a significant expansion from the previous Organic Act.[211] Most notably, the Bangsamoro Autonomous Region planned to have a justice system based on Islamic law extending beyond the jurisdiction of the Sharia courts previously established in the region.[212] Since this increased devolution of administrative authorities, the insurgency, which had started in 1969, has substantially subsided.

In the case of Yemen, the proposed constitution, which was intended to transform Yemen from a unitary to a federal state, provided for the devolution of substantial political and fiscal authority. In particular, the draft constitution provided that each of the regions, *wilaya*, and districts would enjoy financial independence, as well as the ability to levy fees, fines, and service charges, including particular taxes. The draft constitution also provided for the creation of a National Revenue Fund, to be managed by a board that included representatives from each level of government.[213]

The constitution also provided, however, that revenues generated from natural resources and national revenues would be shared by all three levels of government in a "fair and equitable manner."[214] To this end, all national revenues were to be deposited with the National Revenue Fund, including taxes and natural resource revenues.[215] Under the proposed Revenue Division Act, these national revenues would be divided by paying attention to the "national interest," the "responsibilities and needs" of local governments determined by "objective criteria," the financial capacity of the local governments, and the responsibilities of the local governments that produce or exploit resources.[216]

The southern regions, which were the two highest oil-producing regions, saw the National Revenue Fund as an effort to redistribute revenue from the south to the north, and thus deprive them of what they considered fair and adequate fiscal devolution. This dissention was one of the many factors contributing to the failure of the constitutional process and the return to conflict.

Colombia's 1991 Constitution, prompted by a reform movement amidst ongoing guerilla violence, devolved political, administrative, and fiscal authority.[217] The process, coupled with other efforts to end the ongoing conflict, sought to increase opportunities for underrepresented groups to participate in politics and to counter guerilla narratives related to political participation. The absence of formal state power in many rural areas had created a power vacuum, filled by insurgent groups. By devolving powers and expanding access to government services, the Colombian government attempted to create buy-in for the official political process rather than the parallel structures run by insurgents.[218]

Politically, Colombia's constitution called for direct elections for mayors, governors, and legislative bodies.[219] Administratively, Colombia's constitution granted authorities to local governments, including those related to education, health, irrigation, and budget preparation and execution. Fiscally, Colombia's constitution stipulated that "50 percent of all revenues collected at the national level were to be transferred to municipalities and the bulk of this spent on health and education," as well as equitable natural resource revenue distribution.[220]

Colombia's substate entities assumed greater administrative authorities, but the national government maintained its authority over sectoral spending decisions. Though Colombia was able to successfully devolve most of these authorities, this program of decentralization, and the expansion of service provision meant to contribute to pacification, created an environment conducive to armed clientelism by insurgent groups. Ultimately, "the national government lacked the presence and capacity to prevent irregular groups from taking over and controlling many departments and municipalities," and as a result the conflict and related violence continued.[221] Without a strong monopoly of force, the national government's effort at devolution created conditions for the deepening of a parallel state operated by armed groups.

To confront the conundrum of coordination between levels of government, South Africa created formal institutions to promote collaboration between its provincial, local, and national governments, such as its Budget Council and Budget Forum.[222] The South African Constitution ensured representation for provincial and local governments in the Budget Council, a forum in which the minister of finance discusses the proposed budget.[223] This forum for consultations on the budget between local, provincial, and federal levels of government contributed to the larger goal of the postconflict 1996 Constitution of "ensuring the provision of services to communities in a sustainable manner" and rebuilding local communities to create a new democratic, deracialized system of governance following apartheid.[224]

Once the parties have sorted through these thorny conundrums associated with designing a state structure, devolving decision-making authority, balancing the devolution of political, administrative, and fiscal authority, they must determine a timeline for implementation.

Timeline for Decentralization

The timeline for decentralization poses a challenging conundrum for the parties to a peace process: what timeline will be sufficient to allow the parties to effectively implement their chosen approach to decentralization without delaying implementation so long that one or more of the parties loses confidence in the process and returns to conflict?

The parties typically need to decide whether the peace agreement will define a specific timeline. If they decide to determine a timeline, the parties are then confronted with choosing whether this timeline will include a series of benchmark deadlines by which certain tasks must be completed.

A consistent undercurrent surrounding each of these decisions is the larger issue of whether decentralization will be immediately implemented, or if the state will slowly introduce components of decentralization over time. This challenge raises a tense tradeoff: the state may not have the capacity or the infrastructure successfully

90   *Power-Sharing*

to devolve powers immediately, increasing the likelihood that decentralization destabilizes or overwhelms the state.

A sequenced timeline can allow for the effective implementation of a transition in stages, with each stage containing steps necessary to lay the foundation for the next stage of the transition.

Longer timelines for decentralization can allow incumbents, including the state's political elite, to retain power for a substantial period of time. In instances where the current governing powers or frameworks were significant causes of the conflict, a longer timeline and delayed reform may cause resentment, allow the incumbent political elite to further delay, divert, or obstruct reforms, or otherwise damage the implementation of the peace agreement. This can lead to diminishing confidence and may erode the likelihood of achieving durable peace.

Similarly, a more drawn-out timeline often damages the credibility of the peace agreement and can lead to its rejection, or otherwise undermine the credibility of the decentralization process and the effectiveness of the postconflict government. This is especially true in contexts where states have deep ethnic and political tensions that prevent consensus.

Approaches to Resolving the Timeline for Decentralization Conundrum

In South Africa, the postapartheid multiparty negotiations finalized a formal guide to a transition to a devolved unitary state structure, including a timeline to govern aspects of the interim period.[225] South Africa's 1993 interim constitution included a two-year period of transition to the permanent constitution, which would commence upon the election of the Constitutional Assembly. The interim constitution also recognized that decentralization would occur at different speeds in different regions, accounting for the specific contexts of particular regions.[226]

During this period, South Africa maintained national and regional ombudsman offices to serve as a government accountability mechanism and ensure continuity across all government sectors during the transition.[227] South Africa also established legal mechanisms to coordinate the new devolved unitary system across the state, including mechanisms to facilitate intergovernmental relations, implementation of federal statutes in provincial and local governments, fiscal coordination, and intergovernmental dispute resolution.[228]

This longer timeline for decentralization allowed for a more formalized, structured transition. Since all negotiating parties were invested in forging a new South African state following a violent and divisive past, the longer timeline did not prove to be a liability in the decentralization process.

Longer timelines are not, however, a guarantee of successful decentralization. The Philippines attempted to mollify Moro National Liberation Front insurgents' desire for autonomy by establishing Mindanao as an autonomous region through a 1989 Organic Act, but the violence continued as the armed insurgents agitated for more autonomy. In 1996, the parties came to a final agreement, which created a longer timeline and aimed for the successful devolution of powers to Mindanao and an end to the decades-long conflict.

Phase I ("The Transitional Period") was due to last three years and focused on investments in "intensive peace and development efforts" in conflict-affected provinces.[229] During Phase I, a joint monitoring committee was established between the government of the Philippines and the Moro National Liberation Front to monitor the implementation of the agreement. Following this, Phase II, as specified in the final agreement, would create the structures for autonomous governance and entail a plebiscite vote for other areas' incorporation into the autonomous region.[230] Despite implementing a best practice of a deliberately staggered timeline for greater decentralization spanning from 1996 to 2001,[231] violence reignited due to a lack of representation in the region's governance structures for the Moro Islamic Liberation Front, another militant organization seeking autonomy for Mindanao.[232]

Shorter timeframes can also lead to implementation challenges. As emphasized throughout this chapter, Yemen illustrates the very real dangers of rushing a decentralization process in an attempt to prevent an impending conflict. Furthermore, the attempt to implement an unrealistically short timeline can lead to inevitable delays as the parties attempt to engage in a multilayered decentralization process, potentially while also implementing a number of other postconflict mechanisms provided for in the peace agreement in relation to other key issue areas.

One delay can impose a potential domino effect in a timeline for decentralization, even if the parties initially agree to a short and urgent timeframe. A memorandum of understanding signed between the Free Aceh Movement and Indonesia in 2005 provided that the formation of Aceh's local government and political parties would be formed within 12–18 months. The memorandum also specified when local elections were to take place.[233] Despite this detailed timeline, Aceh's local elections were pushed back eight months as a result of a delay in passing the Law on the Governing of Aceh, which was tasked with outlining the details of devolution and thus was necessary in order for the elections to occur.[234] While this delay did not undermine the implementation process, it did inject a degree of uncertainty and distrust at a crucial point in the implementation process.

Delays can also contribute to destabilization in fragile postconflict contexts. In the case of Macedonia, though the parties agreed to a short timeline for devolving powers to local entities, the process of decentralization had not even begun years after the signing of the agreement.[235] This was in part due to the longstanding ethnic tensions between Slavic Macedonians and ethnic Albanians, but also in part due to intraparty competition within the Slavic Macedonian and ethnic Albanian constituencies, which complicated the timeline as the multiethnic coalition government struggled to reach agreement on a number of issues.

Implementing legislation was not adopted until 2004, more than three years after the signing of the agreement. Although Macedonia managed to stabilize despite the delays in establishing a devolved unitary structure, in general delays of this nature can erode the public's confidence in the state's ability (or willingness) to implement key reforms promised via the peace process.

Just as challenging, however, are instances in which the timeline was neither too short nor too long, but rather remained unspecified. Nepal's 2006 Comprehensive Peace Agreement, which ended an insurgency against the monarchy, provided that the parties would pursue a political system that deconstructs the unitary state of the past and creates a new structure in an "inclusive, democratic and forward looking manner."[236] The agreement did not specify a timeline for accomplishing this decentralization.

Nepal's 2007 interim constitution provided more details about the nature of decentralization that should take place and stipulated that a high-level commission should be created to recommend a structure for decentralization, again without a timeline for implementation.[237] Divisions over the degree of autonomy certain provinces would possess, as well as the number of provinces that would be created, coupled with political and ethnic infighting, prevented state restructuring from occurring following the adoption of the interim constitution.[238]

These divisions persisted for several years, exacerbated by delays in producing a new constitution for Nepal. Ultimately, following the severe April 2015 earthquake, four of Nepal's major political parties reached an agreement to create eight provinces, and enshrined those provinces in the new constitution.[239] This protracted process suggests that the lack of specificity in the timeline may have contributed to the early failure to decentralize.

Each decision that negotiating parties make in relation to power-sharing has a significant impact on the prospect for durable peace and successful postconflict governance. Though certain choices may move the negotiations along at a faster rate, they may come back to severely affect the implementation of a power-sharing arrangement.

CONCLUSION

Vertical power-sharing can provide a useful mechanism for forging compromise between the parties engaged in peace negotiations, addressing certain root causes of conflict, providing an alternative to external self-determination, and protecting the interests of vulnerable groups in a postconflict setting. Crafting a vertical power-sharing arrangement that successfully accomplishes those goals, while ensuring a functional government and guarding against the relapse of conflict is a highly complex task and involves deliberate decisions on a number of technical details. Despite the risks, the vast majority of peace agreements signed since 1989 have included language related to power-sharing,[240] illustrating how many parties believe that constructing power-sharing arrangements is necessary for ensuring durable peace.

This chapter has discussed how the parties in postconflict peace negotiations have taken the unique opportunity to innovate within frameworks of power-sharing, both horizontal and vertical. The parties in Macedonia and Indonesia recognized the potential for moving away from the enticing one-size-fits-all model of federalism often promoted by external international actors, and the successes and sticking points of devolved unitary and asymmetric unitary structures, respectively. The thoughtful, deliberate choices made to tailor decentralization to the specific contexts of the conflict drivers in Macedonia and Indonesia set these two cases apart from those states that attempted to reach too far with sweeping programs of decentralization.

This chapter has also illuminated the very real potential for negotiations relating to power-sharing to tip states back into conflict. For instance, despite an inclusive peace process and extensive constitution creating a new, federal Yemen, the state tipped from the brink of peace back into war because of disagreements about how the federal structure should be implemented. The plan for power-sharing in Yemen was too wide-ranging, while at the same time it was rejected because of dispute over fundamental details. Similarly, the Philippines spent nearly thirty years negotiating with separatists in Mindanao, proposing various power-sharing arrangements and descending back into violent insurgency, until the parties accepted an agreement providing greater autonomy for the region.

The case studies highlighted in this chapter – Bosnia, Colombia, Indonesia/Aceh, Iraq, Macedonia, Nepal, the Philippines/Mindanao, South Africa, Sudan/Darfur, and Yemen – underscore the need to carefully consider each component of the decentralization process and its relationship to the unique challenges of a particular postconflict setting. If chosen appropriately, the method of decentralization, the authorities devolved, the selection of concurrent powers, and the timeline for the decentralization process can augment the chances for a lasting peace.

The next chapter will explore a subject that often intertwines with the vertical power-sharing conundrums examined in this chapter: natural resources.

3

Natural Resources

Access to natural resources and the allocation of revenue generated by resource exploitation is at the core of many conflicts and plays an important role in many others. Since 1990, there have been nearly twenty conflicts related to the exploitation of natural resources, and in the last sixty years, over 40 percent of intrastate conflicts have been related to the exploitation of natural resources.[1]

As a result, between 1989 and 2004 nearly half of all peace agreements included detailed provisions addressing natural resources.[2] From 2005 to 2014, all major peace agreements included provisions relating to the ownership or management of natural resources and/or the allocation of revenue derived from those resources.[3] This was likely the case given that in many fragile states the exploitation of oil, gas, minerals, and timber provide a fairly significant percentage of national revenue.[4]

Notably, conflicts related to natural resources are twice as likely to revert to conflict in the first five years after the signing of a peace agreement.[5] When a fragile state possesses an abundance of natural resources (oil and gas particularly), there is a substantially increased likelihood of intrastate armed conflict, and an increased likelihood that the substate entity involved in the conflict will seek external self-determination as a means to resolve the conflict.[6] Political elites frequently capture resources, which leads to unaccountable governance structures, which then in turn act as a conflict driver.[7] Moreover, when a state depends on natural resources for a significant share of its GDP, this will frequently "increase the likelihood of underdevelopment, fragility and conflict."[8]

There are three main types of natural resource-based conflicts: those that relate to extractive resources such as oil, gas, minerals, diamonds and timber; those that relate to land; and those that relate to water.[9]

Resource-based conflicts can relate to either the high-value abundance or the scarcity of a particular resource. Extractive natural resource conflicts tend to relate to abundance. For instance, the conflicts in Liberia, Angola, and the Democratic Republic of Congo were heavily based around on "high-value" extractive resources, such as diamonds, gold, minerals, and oil that were rich and abundant in the regions. Land- and water-based conflicts, on the other hand, tend to relate to scarcity. This was the case in Darfur and has been the case for a number of conflicts in the Middle East.[10] Additionally, conflicts will often relate to more than one category of natural resources.

Sometimes the conflict directly relates to the question of who owns or controls a natural resource. In other situations, the conflict may be only tangentially related to the ownership and control of the resources, but the availability of revenue from natural resources acts as a driver of the conflict by fueling access to weapons and influence.

The tension relating to the ownership or control of the natural resource often mirrors and is interwoven with other conflict drivers, such as political and economic disenfranchisement. If a general governance issue exists, then there will certainly be a governance issue relating to the ownership and management of natural resources. As such, over time, what starts as a conflict over political rights may evolve into a conflict over the ownership of natural resources.[11]

In keeping with the overall approach of the book, this chapter undertakes a detailed exploration of one dimension of natural resources – in this case, the development of peace agreement provisions relating to extractive natural resources. The lessons learned from the negotiation and design of extractive resource provisions are broadly applicable to disputes relating to land and to water.

This chapter addresses a number of conundrums related to the ownership, management, and associated revenue of extractive natural resources that the parties face during peace negotiations and peace processes. First, this chapter discusses the puzzle of whether and how to address extractive resource ownership, management, and revenue allocation in a manner that promotes durable peace. Next, it provides a conceptual and legal primer for understanding the frameworks states have used to govern the ownership, management, and associated revenue of extractive resources. Then it explores a number of instances of key state practice to analyze and highlight how the parties involved in peace negotiations have sought to manage the conundrums they faced when seeking to solve the puzzle of extractive resources.

THE PUZZLE: WHETHER AND HOW TO ADDRESS EXTRACTIVE NATURAL RESOURCE OWNERSHIP, MANAGEMENT, AND REVENUE ALLOCATION IN A MANNER THAT PROMOTES DURABLE PEACE

Efforts to solve the puzzle of whether and how to address extractive natural resource ownership, management, and revenue allocation in a manner that promotes durable peace are complicated by the fact that natural resources can be both a driver of the conflict and a key factor in promoting a durable peace. A number of factors make the negotiated resolution of extractive natural resource-based conflicts a highly complex endeavor.

Conflict Drivers

Natural resources drive conflict in a number of ways. Natural resources can fuel unfair distribution of wealth resulting from extraction and demand of scarce resources that exceeds supply, both of which can drive conflict.[12] Oftentimes the ownership of natural resources and the associated revenues are captured by the by national government or the dominant political actor and associated political elites. This leads to substantial real or perceived economic disenfranchisement of large sectors of the population, and in particular regional authorities and actors. Those disenfranchised populations then often take up arms in an effort to wrest control of those resources away from the national government, as was the case of Aceh in Indonesia, where the national government appropriated nearly all of the revenue from the Acehnese oil fields.

Frequently, the national government will engage in an unequal distribution of the revenue associated with natural resources, benefiting one regional, religious, or ethnic group over the rest of the population, as was the case with Iraq and the favored treatment of the Sunni.

The controlling authority also may choose to undertake very little, if any, distribution of the revenue among stakeholders. In these instances, those in power use funds garnered from natural resources not for the benefit of the state, but for the personal enrichment of the political elite, as was the case with Sierra Leone[13] and Angola.[14] Many parties have a "strategic interest in maintaining instability in order to profit from illegal exploitation and trade of natural resources."[15]

Relatedly, states may access the resources to fund the conflict, as with the government of Sudan relying heavily on oil revenue to fund the conflict with South Sudan and Darfur. In some cases, nonstate armed actors access resources to sustain the armed conflict. In Sierra Leone, the Revolutionary United Front (RUF) used the sale of blood diamonds to fund its revolutionary movement. During the confusion and disarray of a conflict, resources are also extracted and sold by illicit actors for personal gain. These illicit actors then become stakeholders in the conflict, and seek to resist or undermine the efforts of the parties to negotiate a peace. This was the case in Sierra Leone, where many illicit diamond miners and smugglers became additional parties to the conflict.[16]

The conflict may transform from a political conflict to one associated primarily with economic gain, as was the case with timber extraction by the Khmer Rouge on the border between Thailand and Cambodia after their expulsion from Cambodia.[17] Because of the geographic nature of the distribution of extractive natural resources, in cases where these unequal distributions correspond to ethic, religious, or other divides, they may substantially augment the difficulty of resolving the conflict.[18]

Moreover, if there tends to be a high concentration of resources in the territory of a substate entity with a marginalized population, this may fuel the drive for external self-determination, as was the case in South Sudan.[19]

This can also be seen in the case of Ethiopia, where all land and natural resources belong to the state, rather than to the regional units or individuals.[20] The resource-rich Gambella region is home to the Anuak people,[21] who perceive government and private industry extraction of resources[22] as a threat to their political power and culture.[23] The seizure of land has led to reports of violence between the local citizens and federal government agents.[24] In response to the perceived threat, militant groups such as the Anuak-led Gambella Peoples' Liberation Front have conducted raids on state infrastructure.[25]

In many cases, the centralized control of the resources is coupled with a localization of the negative environmental and social impacts associated with the extraction of the resources, as was the case with Bougainville and Papua New Guinea. The copper mine in Bougainville generated minimal economic benefit for the people of Bougainville, but they were wholly and exclusively subjected to the quite substantial negative environmental and social impacts. Moreover, in some conflicts, natural resources are governed by customary institutions rather than legal structures, making resources a conflict driver related to the historical and customary extraction practices.[26]

Opportunity to Support Durable Peace

The effective management of natural resources as a result of a peace agreement can substantially promote the durability of that agreement in a number of ways. The revenue generated from the extraction of those resources serves as a near-immediate and highly visible peace dividend that demonstrates the real and practical value of peace.[27] The revenue generated from the extraction of the natural resources also provides a fund to pay for reconstruction and the implementation of various aspects of the peace agreement.[28] While the international community invariably provides resources for peace process implementation, the marshaling of these resources can often be slow, conditional, and driven by the specific interest of each donor. Ready access to revenue generated by a state's own resources provides the state with the ability to respond quickly and to prioritize projects that it deems are necessary to secure the peace. In the case of a party exercising an agreed path to external self-determination, such as South Sudan, natural resources in theory can provide a source of income to help stabilize the economy of the new state.

A properly designed peace agreement can create a system for more professional and efficient management of the resources and expand their value. Increasing the value of the resource, assuming it is equitably shared, creates a greater opportunity cost of a return to conflict.[29]

Undertaking equitable access to the benefits of the resource is a concrete and tangible means of removing a driver of conflict, and demonstrating the willingness and ability to undertake equitable arrangements in the political, security, and other sectors of governance covered by the peace agreement. State control of resources, particularly under an effective power-sharing arrangement, can exclude illicit actors or spoilers from accessing the resources to fund any efforts to undermine the implementation of the peace agreement.[30]

While extractive industries present an opportunity to fund peace in the short term, without the existence of strong safeguards and the institutions necessary to support them, they also present significant risks to the development of a durable peace. Optimism about the potential of extractive resources to fund redevelopment often outpaces the development of regulations and safeguards against corruption, abuse of local communities, and environmental pollution.[31] Consequently, corrupt and poorly regulated extractive industries can continue to provide funding to existing or new nonstate armed actors, as was the case with the Khmer Rouge's illicit timber trade.[32] The rapid postconflict development of large-scale mines, and the attendant community displacement, pollution, and private security forces, can also lead to immediate local grievances and reduce opportunities to develop sustainable livelihoods.[33]

Without trusted mechanisms in place to resolve grievances, local communities may turn again to insurgent groups and violence. This was the case in Afghanistan, where local grievances surrounding the rapid development of multinational mines pushed communities closer to insurgent groups and reignited violence in previously peaceful areas.[34]

Heightened Complexity of a Negotiated Resolution

There are a number of factors that complicate the natural resource puzzle when it comes to determining whether and how to allocate the ownership, management, and associated revenues of extractive natural resources in a manner that promotes durable peace.

This puzzle is particularly difficult for mediators and nonstate parties given the complex technical nature of regimes for the management of questions relating to natural resources. Mediators are often skilled at political negotiations and frequently have experience with governance and security in a prior professional capacity. International mediators, however, seldom have an expertise in natural resource management.

Nonstate actors and, in some instances, state actors, often do not possess the background knowledge to fully understand the implications of decisions related to natural resources made during the peace negotiations.[35] As will be discussed, the decisions relating to natural resources can translate into the allocation of billions of dollars in revenue. While it is possible for the mediator to bring technical experts onboard to the peace negotiations, it is much more difficult for the nonstate parties to do so.

This puzzle is further complicated by the plethora of relevant actors and stake-holders party to any given natural resource conflict. Negotiators must consider actors who may not be at the table but will ultimately shape the long-term impact of the agreement.[36] The interests of local and indigenous communities, in particular, may differ from the interests of actors represented at the table.[37] While the parties at the negotiating table are frequently focused on the potential benefits to be gained from extractive resources, local and indigenous communities may be equally or even more concerned about the significant potential socio-environmental costs, as they will frequently endure the highest costs.[38] If the peace agreement fails to anticipate these concerns and address the responsibility to mitigate associated risks, future local grievances over socio-environmental damage may reignite the conflict.[39]

Negotiations over globally traded oil and other fungible resources do not take place in a vacuum, but rather in a broader political economy in which neighboring states, multinational companies, and international regulatory bodies each play a key role.[40] Without sufficient global support for market regulation at both the regional and international level, domestic peace agreements may be insufficient to meaning-ful alter the role of extractive resources in conflict, as was the case with Sierra Leone's domestically focused Lomé Agreement.[41]

External actors not officially present at the table may also play an active role in shaping the process. While likely not formally part of a negotiation process, the national oil company, international oil companies, and those involved in the illegal extraction and sale of resources will no doubt exert influence on the peace process. In the case of Yemen, the French oil company TOTAL played an outsized role in the National Dialogue and constitutional process. Despite the fact that the state parties had agreed on a federal state structure, TOTAL, working with the French government, continued to press for a unitary state, even to the extent of seconding a French expert to advise the National Dialogue on the constitutional aspects of a unitary state. For TOTAL, it was more economically efficient to negotiate and contract with a single government than to have to negotiate with provincial governments.

The peace process as it relates to natural resources is also complicated by the near-myopic focus on the question of ownership, with substantially less attention paid to the details of management and revenue distribution. Mediators are complicit in this omission, as they tend to favor moving the "technical issues" into a post-peace agreement process.[42] This is understandable given the many competing priorities during the brief window of a peace negotiation, such as the need to establish a monopoly of force, plan for internal or external self-determination, create conditions for the return of refugees, design power-sharing arrangements, and create govern-ance structures, among other challenges.

Because conflict is often primarily related to securing or continuing access to financial resources for a dominant political group, reallocation of natural resources is significantly more difficult to negotiate than topics in the political and security arenas. It is also exceptionally difficult to engage with and negotiate a change in behavior for the illicit operators and the spoilers who are destined to lose out with the establishment of a functional and professional process for managing natural resources.[43]

A negotiated outcome to a conflict based around extractive natural resources entails not only an arrangement between the substate entities and the state, but also between substate entities, as natural resource wealth is frequently redistributed to some degree among the substate entities.[44] This gives substate entities without actual geographic possession of the natural resources a stake in negotiating ownership, management, and allocation of revenue. This was the case in Yemen, where the six-region structure for the state proposed in the draft constitution prevented the Houthis from accessing the land that held rich oil and coastal resources.[45] The topic, much like power-sharing, becomes more multidimensional than other topics on the agenda during the peace negotiations, and can create an outsized role for certain, non-resource-rich substate entities beyond what one might have originally anticipated.

CONCEPTUAL AND LEGAL PRIMER

There are a substantial number of both resource-rich and resource-scarce states around the globe. These states provide a rich body of comparative state practice from which to identify the key conceptual approaches for allocating the ownership, management, and associated revenue of extractive natural resources, and the various legal norms, rules, processes, and procedures used to design and implement natural resource arrangements. A number of international legal obligations relate to natural resources, including the consideration of the interests of local and indigenous populations, as well as the international Kimberly Process for the regulation of the diamond trade.

Ownership, Management, Revenue Allocation

This section will explore comparative state practice relating to natural resource ownership, management, and revenue allocation.

Ownership
Generally, states utilize three methods to allocate ownership of extractive natural resources: national ownership, local ownership, and shared ownership.

NATIONAL OWNERSHIP Prior to the nineteenth century, natural resources largely existed in the legal domain of private landowners or substate entities. During this time, nation-states were created out of substates opting to join in political union. Hence, as will be discussed, Canada, the United Arab Emirates, and the United

States have a higher degree of local ownership of natural resources. Many other states, however, came into being as unitary states or were initially unitary and then undertook a degree of devolution of power. These states, which are by far the majority, exercise national ownership of natural resources, and claim to utilize those resources for the benefit of the entire nation.[46]

Many states maintain national ownership of their extractive natural resources, and in a large number of these states this system is constitutionally protected, including in Kazakhstan,[47] Russia, Norway, Indonesia, Venezuela,[48] and many of the Middle Eastern and African oil-producing states, such as Kuwait,[49] Nigeria,[50] Qatar,[51] and Syria.[52] In fact, of the fourteen Middle Eastern and African oil-producing states,[53] thirteen exert complete national ownership. States that maintain national ownership over extractive natural resources commonly have highly centralized governments. Most of the Gulf States are monarchies while the other Middle Eastern oil-producing states are highly centralized (e.g., Egypt and Iran). A significant number of the non-Gulf States are represented by a republican form of government, yet often these governments are weak democracies (e.g., Indonesia, Russia, and Venezuela), nondemocratic (e.g., Chad), or former de facto military dictatorships (e.g., Libya and Angola).

LOCAL OWNERSHIP Very few states vest ownership of natural resources with substate entities. Such ownership generally exists in federal states, mirroring the general framework of decentralized government. Notably, local ownership is often accompanied by other means of indirect national government involvement in tax structures or regulations related to foreign direct investment.

By way of example, the United Arab Emirates is a federation of seven emirates, with political power concentrated in Abu Dhabi, which controls the vast majority of the state's economic and resource wealth.[54] Under the constitution, each emirate owns its own oil resources and controls oil production and development within its respective territory, although the constitution does vest the emirates with the responsibility of utilizing these oil resources "for the benefit of the national economy."[55] Argentina also vests ownership of natural resources with the province in which those resources are located.[56] Notably, these provinces possess the right to enter into related international agreements "with the knowledge of Congress," so long as they do not infringe on the powers of the national government and are consistent with the country's foreign policy.[57]

SHARED OWNERSHIP Some states have a system of shared state and local ownership of natural resources. The shared ownership approach often comes about as a compromise between substate entities that would prefer to have ownership rights, and a national government unwilling to relinquish potentially wide-reaching control over valuable and strategically important resources. In a shared ownership system, laws, regulations, and other agreements between the national and local governments typically provide different levels of government with varying levels of authority over the use and management of the resources or different avenues for providing direct streams of revenue to the national government.

Canada is often cited as an example of complex, asymmetrically shared control over natural resources. In Canada, each province owns and administers the extractive natural resources within its borders.[58] The provinces levy taxes and collect royalties from the resources extracted from within the territory of the province. The federal government retains control over interprovincial and international aspects of the trade in natural resources.[59] The federal government also owns and administers natural resources on Canada's frontier lands and offshore resources, though this is subject to occasional disputes by some provinces.

While the revenue from natural resources belongs to the province within which it lies, the Canadian government undertakes equalization payments to provinces to ensure that each province maintains the capacity to provide comparable levels of public services at comparable levels of taxation.[60] When determining the amount of equalization payments that a province should receive, the government considers a province's need based on its revenue from many different sectors, including natural resources.[61]

Management

While ownership and management issues are closely linked, ownership is not in fact synonymous with management authority, and many agreements address these two issues separately. The entity that owns the resource may, but does not always, have the authority to manage the extraction and sale of those resources.

The management of natural resources entails determining which resources may be exploited and when, issuing exploration permits, issuing licenses for the extraction of resources, negotiating revenue contracts, revoking licenses and terminating contracts, creating macrodevelopment plans for the resources, ensuring the health and safety of workers, and environmental protection.[62]

Notably, the question of the management of natural resources is as important as, if not more important than, the question of ownership. While the parties are certain to focus on the question of ownership during peace negotiations, they seldom address the question of management. In fact, "fewer than a quarter of peace negotiations aiming to resolve conflicts linked to natural resources have addressed resource management mechanisms."[63]

National ownership generally results in a management scheme designed at the state (rather than local) level, and where it exists, local ownership is often curtailed in some manner by national government management through regulations, taxation, or other revenue-sharing requirements.

Although the party that owns the resource may also manage it, many states also design an entity in which representatives from both the national and local governments possess joint authority to manage natural resources. One such entity is a joint natural resource authority, which is generally an independent institution acting without exclusive national or local oversight, but is rather composed of representatives of different levels of government. Joint authorities are most commonly found in federal states that have significant power-sharing between the national government and substate entities.

Composition of a joint authority may vary depending on the particular circumstances of the state and the interests represented. Some states have one single joint management authority that represents national government and all the substate entities, while other states have multiple authorities, and each authority manages the relationship between a particular substate entity and the region and the national government.

States may allocate varying levels of authority to joint natural resource authorities. In some states, the authority has near-complete control over maintenance, regulation, and licensing of natural resources, while other states create a more limited role for the authority. States often take into account the particular governmental structure of the state, the location of resources, and the capabilities of the parties involved when allocating power to the joint authority.

In Australia, the joint authority is essentially a bilateral committee with one representative of the Australian government's minister for resources and one counterpart from the provincial ministry.[64] The Australian joint authority has fairly wide-ranging powers and may issue grants, revoke licenses, and regulate existing license agreements to explore, drill, and extract oil.[65]

In 1990, Canada created the Canada–Nova Scotia Offshore Petroleum Board as a joint authority to manage Nova Scotia's offshore petroleum resources. The board, which was established through an accord between the federal government and the Nova Scotia provincial government, and which is comprised of representatives of both governments, has the authority to manage nearly all aspects of the exploitation of petroleum resources.[66] This authority is subject to a limited right of veto held by both the federal government and the Nova Scotia government.[67]

Prior to 2009, Greenland and Denmark operated a Joint Committee on Mineral Resources in Greenland, which served to facilitate discussion between and provide advice to the governments of Denmark and Greenland on the exploitation of natural resources. Although not responsible for licensing and contracting, the joint committee was encouraged to comment on the granting of prospecting, exploration, or production licenses.[68]

Revenue Allocation

Oil-producing states have implemented numerous formulas for revenue allocation revenue. Some states apply the same formula to share oil revenue as used for other budgetary distributions, while others favor the derivation principle, whereby each substate entity's share relates to the oil revenue originating in its territory. Still others follow different criteria such as population, social needs, or tax capacity.[69]

A state's approach to revenue allocation is generally informed by the ownership and management structure, as well as the unique characteristics of the state. As such, the approaches states have employed to allocate oil revenue do not readily fall into discrete categories; nor is there a systematic method of addressing the issue of revenue allocation.

In the United Arab Emirates, for instance, each emirate collects the revenue from oil produced in the emirate, but a certain percentage must be shared with the national government.[70] In Canada, each province owns and controls natural resources in its territory and allocates revenue as it chooses[71] but, as noted earlier, the federal government provides equalization grants to the non-resource-rich provinces through other sources of federal revenue.[72]

In Indonesia, since 2001, the national government has received 85 percent of revenue from oil production, while the producing province receives 15 percent.[73] The 15 percent allocation of resources to the producing provinces corresponded to an increased devolution of political authority and obligations relating to health, education, and public works.[74] In Saudi Arabia, as well as the other oil-producing Gulf monarchies, the ruling family directly controls the allocation of oil revenue, and no clear set formula for allocation of oil revenue can be discerned.

Notably, when in 1998 the World Bank agreed to fund the Petroleum Development and Pipeline Project to develop and export Chad's oil resources, the World Bank required Chad to adopt a Petroleum Revenues Management Law. Under the law, the government was obligated to utilize 80 percent of the oil revenues on its "priority sectors" (education, health, social services, environment, and infrastructure development). The remaining 20 percent was apportioned as 5 percent for the oil-producing region of Doba, 10 percent for an escrow account for future generations, and 5 percent left to the government's discretion.[75] The government of Chad, however, did not ultimately apportion oil revenues as per the law. In 2008, the government of Chad paid off its outstanding World Bank loans and extracted itself from the obligation to allocate the revenue according to the law.

Many oil-producing states also implement stabilization and/or intergenerational funds as a way to address possible fluctuations in production levels and related revenue, and to ensure that wealth from the resource is reserved for future generations.

A stabilization fund aims to minimize the effects of fluctuations in oil prices or production levels. Such fluctuations can create large differences from one year to another in the revenue of oil-producing states. With a stabilization fund, the state directs all or a portion of yearly oil revenue into the fund, and the government then accesses the fund for state expenditures. This ensures that the governmental budget does not fluctuate significantly from year to year, especially in countries where budgets are highly dependent on oil revenues. Access to the fund may also be permitted in the case of a national economic crisis or in order to develop non-oil industries.

In contrast to a stabilization fund, the purpose of an intergenerational fund is to conserve a portion of resource wealth specifically for future generations. Such funds can ensure that the state's citizens continue to benefit from the non-renewable oil resource. While some oil-producing states maintain separate stabilization and intergenerational funds, other states implement intrastate oil funds that fulfill both objectives.

For instance, in 1990, the Norwegian government established the Government Petroleum Fund of Norway to minimize the impacts of short-term variations in oil revenues.[76] The fund also acts as a mechanism to address the long-term challenge of continuing government expenditure after oil resources are exhausted. Specifically, the Norwegian government seeks to secure funding for future government pension payments.[77] The government of Kazakhstan created a similar National Fund of Kazakhstan to reduce economic volatility from fluctuating oil prices, and to serve as a savings fund for future generations.[78]

The state of Alaska in the United States maintains a specialized oil fund that operates as a stabilization fund and a type of modified intergenerational fund. Revenue from the Alaska Permanent Fund is only distributed for two purposes: an annual dividend payment made directly to qualifying residents of Alaska[79] and protection against inflation.[80]

The Rights of Local Populations

UN General Assembly Resolution 1803 (XVII) provided that peoples have a right to "permanent sovereignty over their natural wealth and resources" and that "the exploration, development and disposition of such resources ... should be in conformity with the rules and conditions which the peoples and nations freely consider to be necessary or desirable."[81] This Resolution was initially applied to interstate conflicts in the context of decolonization, but is increasingly applied to intrastate conflicts as well.[82]

While international law relating to natural resources has historically applied to interstate conflicts, there is increasing attention paid to the impact of international law on natural resource allocation in intrastate conflicts, particularly as it relates to a people's "collective cultural attachment" to land and resources.[83]

Free, prior, and informed consent is the right of indigenous peoples to "give or withhold consent to a project that may affect them or their territories."[84] The right to free, prior, and informed consent is set forth in a variety of international instruments, including the United Nations Declaration on the Rights of Indigenous Peoples, the International Labor Organization Convention No. 169, and the Convention on Biological Diversity.[85] Free, prior, and informed consent involves an ongoing process with indigenous peoples in the consultation and implementation of procedures that will directly affect them. This can include practices such as participatory mapping and data collection.[86] This framework, which helps to ensure that the territories and resources of indigenous peoples are not exploited, is often relevant in peace processes for conflicts relating to resources.

Kimberley Process

Conflict diamonds, often referred to as blood diamonds, are rough diamonds traded by state and nonstate armed actors to finance armed conflict.[87] Blood diamonds financed and exacerbated a number of post-Cold War conflicts, including in Sierra Leone, in which somewhere between US$300 million and US$450 million worth of diamonds were sold by various factions to fuel the conflict.[88]

To address this growing scourge, in the late 1990s, the United Nations and a number of nongovernmental organizations met for a series of negotiations called the Kimberley Process. The negotiations produced the Kimberley Process Certification Scheme, "a voluntary international agreement regulating the diamond trade through certification of legitimate diamonds."[89] The Kimberley Process requires that its members certify shipments of diamonds as conflict-free, pass national legislation related to conflict-free diamonds, and commit to being transparent about their diamond-related data. To date, the Kimberley Process, established in 2003, has been joined by eighty-one states, which represent 99.8 percent of the global production of rough diamonds.[90] The initial negotiations and meetings of the Kimberley Process were supplemented by the adoption of UN General Assembly Resolution 55/56 in 2000, which "mandated an expanded Kimberley Process, giving the forum the task of drawing up detailed proposals for an international certification scheme for rough diamonds."[91]

KEY STATE PRACTICE

This chapter draws on the following instances of key state practice for a discussion of the various conundrums the parties to a peace negotiation face when confronting the puzzle of negotiating extractive natural resource ownership, management, and revenue allocation. The paragraphs that follow highlight the relationship between each peace process and natural resource arrangements. For more on these conflicts, negotiations, and agreements, consult the Appendix.

The conflict between **Aceh** and **Indonesia** was rooted in claims that the Acehnese community was not reaping the benefits of the exploitation of the region's widespread oil and gas resources.[92] The 2005 Memorandum of Understanding (MOU) that ended the conflict provided for special autonomy for Aceh, including Aceh's exercise of authority over its public affairs. The agreement aimed to provide Aceh with a more direct benefit from the exploitation of its resources, such as by stipulating that "Aceh would have control of over 70 percent of revenues from the province's oil and gas production."[93] The Indonesian parliament subsequently enacted legislation implementing the principles of self-government set forth by the MOU in 2005.

In **Iraq**, 95 percent of government revenues are generated by oil. Iraq's oil resources are not evenly distributed throughout the state, but rather are concentrated in the Kurdish north and Shia Arab south. During the constitution-drafting process in 2005, federalism and wealth-sharing related to oil were at the forefront of the conversation. Ultimately, the new Iraqi constitution provided the autonomous Kurdistan region, as well as potential future regions, greater control over their own oil management and revenues.[94] At the same time, the constitution vested ownership of oil in "all the people of Iraq in all regions and governorates."[95]

While the 2001 peace agreement between **Papua New Guinea** and **Bougainville** granted autonomy to the region of Bougainville, it left the question of extractive resources to be addressed in the subsequent constitution-drafting process. In 2004, the Bougainville Constitution granted customary rights over all natural resources to the "People of Bougainville."[96] The Bougainville Constitution also explicitly addressed the legacy of environmental damage and instructed the autonomous Bougainville government to "take all possible measures to prevent or minimize damage and destruction" and to manage the resources to meet the "development and environmental needs of present and future generations."[97]

The Comprehensive Agreement on the Bangsamoro, signed in 2014 by the government of the **Philippines** and the **Mindanao**-based Moro Islamic Liberation Front, detailed a process for establishing an autonomous Bangsamoro region in exchange for disarmament that built upon a number of other agreements and negotiations between the parties. The 2001 Tripoli Agreement contained a number of provisions relating to the shared control and management of the region's oil resources.

Between 1991 and 1999, **Sierra Leone's** supply of "blood diamonds" incentivized and prolonged a devastating conflict over their extraction that claimed the lives of over 75,000 people and displaced half of the country's population.[98] In 1999, the Lomé Peace Agreement gave the Sierra Leone government control over diamonds and designated the profits from those resources as public money to be spent on development and postwar rehabilitation and reconstruction. To oversee this arrangement, the agreement created a "Commission for the Management of Strategic Resources, National Reconstruction and Development," an autonomous body in charge of monitoring compliance with the agreement's provisions.[99] Notably, the agreement also appointed as chairman of the commission the leader of the Revolutionary United Front (RUF), Foday Sankoh, who ultimately ignored this responsibility and continued to fund the RUF through the illicit trade of diamonds.[100]

The adoption of the 2005 Comprehensive Peace Agreement between **Sudan** and **South Sudan** ended the long war, which was substantially, but not exclusively, driven by competition over oil resources. Oil was used "as a rallying cry by the South, which charged the Sudanese government with exploiting the resource without providing tangible benefits to local populations."[101] The vast majority of Sudan's oil originates from the state's central and southern regions. After extraction, Sudanese oil travels north, via pipelines, to Sudan's oil refineries and export terminals. The Agreement on Wealth Sharing, one of the six protocols of the agreement, set out detailed provisions for natural resource management and revenue allocation.[102] Notably, the agreement did not address the question of ownership.

In 2020, **Sudan** concluded a multitrack Juba peace agreement with nonstate parties representing **Darfur** and some of the nonstate parties in **Southern Kordofan** and **Blue Nile**, in addition to other intra-Sudan regional parties. These agreements provided for the ownership of natural resources, in particular oil and gold, by the people of Sudan, but with special dispensation of revenue for previously marginalized areas. The agreements also set forth detailed arrangements for the cooperative management of resources, the review of existing contracts, and the allocation of revenue.

Prior to the outbreak of a civil war in 2015, the government of **Yemen** relied heavily on dwindling oil resources to provide the majority of government revenue.[103] Chronic corruption and mismanagement in this sector helped fuel the outbreak of fighting in 2014, and the instability and resulting depletion of revenue has presented an obstacle to resolving the conflict.[104] The draft constitution of 2015 attempted to ward off a civil war by creating a federal system where power would be shared among the federal government, regional governments, and local *wilayas*. The constitution outlined general principles for a formula for the allocation of future revenue, and to manage resources; it called for future federal legislation to create an "independent national council made up of representatives of the federal government, regions and wilayas."[105] It also ambiguously provided that both the *wilayas* and this independent national body (on which *wilayas* would be represented) would be responsible for managing natural resources and awarding contracts.[106] Partly due to ambiguities such as this one over power-sharing, the draft constitution was never adopted, and Yemen tipped into a wide-ranging civil war.[107]

CONUNDRUMS

When the parties seek to negotiate a durable peace in a conflict that entails extractive natural resources, they must first determine if and when to broach the subject in the peace process. Once the parties determine the timing of discussing natural resources in the broader context of negotiations, they oftentimes address the technical matters of ownership, management, and revenue allocation.[108] Each of these four issues presents a number of conundrums.

Timing

Before entering the more technical aspects of a natural resource-based negotiation, the parties must decide at what point in the peace process to incorporate discussion

of natural resources. Negotiating the ownership, management, and revenue allocation of natural resources during a peace process can help the parties to achieve a
durable agreement, especially if tensions over resources drove conflict. Alternatively,
including discussions relating to natural resources can derail the peace process if it is
too contentious of an issue among the parties.

A main conundrum the parties face is where to place this discussion of natural
resources on the timeline of the negotiation process. Laying the foundation for the
negotiation of natural resources by determining precisely when the topic is introduced
into the larger peace process has tangible consequences for the outcome of negotiations and the prospects for durable peace. Determining the order of agenda items in
a negotiation, if done thoughtfully, can create momentum to achieve durable agreements on topics including natural resources. Alternatively, including natural resource
negotiations too early in the process can forestall debate over other important issue
areas or derail any momentum that has been created by previous discussions.

Approaches to Resolving the Timing Conundrum

In Aceh, the conflict itself was rooted in the unequal distribution of resource-related
wealth, which, in effect, marginalized the Acehnese community.[109] Natural
resources were at the heart of the conflict that claimed tens of thousands of lives
and were prioritized before the parties resolved issues of demobilization, disarmament, and reintegration) or external self-determination.

Questions of demobilization, disarmament, and reintegration and self-
determination were predicated on the issue of resource distribution. Acehnese
nonstate armed actors would not consider incorporating a program of demobilization, disarmament, and reintegration into the agreement until the main cause for
which they fought had been secured. Similarly, one of the goals of external self-
determination is economic independence and the ownership of the resources
within the confines of a state's territory. From the perspective of the Indonesian
government, by resolving the question of resources first, the Acehnese desire for self-
determination would be reduced. In this way, it proved to be mutually advantageous
to begin the peace negotiations with the subject of natural resources.

The destruction caused by the 2004 Indian Ocean tsunami further induced both
parties to achieve an agreement despite the contentiousness of the conflict. Located
ninety miles from the epicenter of the earthquake which triggered the tsunami,
Aceh suffered tens of thousands of casualties and widespread destruction. The
nonstate armed actors agreed to a ceasefire four days after the tsunami, and shortly
thereafter entered into peace talks with Indonesia. Because reconstruction was a
paramount and pressing concern, external self-determination became less of a
priority than the revenue stream to be derived from natural resources.[110]

In contrast to Aceh and Indonesia, wealth-sharing of natural resource revenue was
discussed at the very end of the peace process between Sudan and South Sudan.[111]

Unlike the largely single-issue conflict in Aceh, the South Sudanese conflict was driven by a number of factors, including the misallocation of oil resources, racism, tribal conflict, and political disenfranchisement. To start peace negotiations with the emotionally charged, highly technical issue of natural resource distribution would have absorbed all of the energy in the talks, likely becoming an immediate barrier to agreement on other issue areas.

Devising a mutually agreed formula for resource-sharing would prove to be complicated and fraught with risk. In the context of the conflict, oil ownership was an existential question for both Sudan and South Sudan, and, given the perceived inequitable existing arrangement between Sudan and South Sudan, it was an issue area fraught with mistrust on both sides. Information asymmetry regarding the contracts between Sudan and foreign investors such as China and Malaysia created an unequal bargaining position for South Sudan and further complicated the situation.

To build momentum in the peace process, Sudan and South Sudan negotiated issues of self-determination and religion prior to broaching the topic of natural resources. The Machakos Protocol, agreed in 2002, set forth principles of a phased process of self-determination for South Sudan, mechanisms for power-sharing, a ceasefire, and an agreement on the role of religion, among other topics.[112] Discussion of oil is noticeably absent from this agreement. By agreeing to a substantive protocol on a number of other contentious issues, the parties built mechanisms for information-sharing and trust with each other, as well as with mediators, such as Norway, that had preexisting expertise in natural resource management. This strategy proved successful, as ultimately the parties reached a detailed set of agreements on certain aspects of natural resource management, which were set forth in the sixteen-page 2004 Agreement of Wealth Sharing, that was incorporated into the 2005 Comprehensive Peace Agreement.[113]

The Bougainville Peace Agreement also left the question of extractive resources to be addressed later. The agreement did not include mention of natural resources, focusing instead on the conflict driver of autonomy and laying out a process for a future independence referendum and weapons disposal.[114] Because natural resource extraction was a central driver of the conflict and could serve as a spoiler of a peace agreement, the parties decided to delay negotiating this question until after the agreement was signed.[115]

The parties to the conflict in Bougainville postponed addressing the question of resources until three years later. In 2004, the Bougainville Constitution partially resolved the conflict over natural resources by granting customary rights to the "People of Bougainville in relation to the land and the sea and natural, mineral and oil resource."[116] After the majority stakeholder of the mine transferred its holdings to both Papua New Guinea and the government of Bougainville, each was given an equal 36.4 percent ownership interest in the mine.[117]

In 2019, to prepare for a vote likely to be in favor of independence, Papua New Guinea pressured the Bougainville government to achieve fiscal self-reliance and reopen the mine, which would have the potential to also reopen the wounds of the conflict. Strong public resistance in Bougainville kept attempts to reopen the mine at bay.[118] With the arrival of the referendum date, however, the forces coalescing around the reopening of the mine redoubled their efforts to overcome this public resistance. Amid this pressure, rather than resolving the conflict, the referendum's narrow focus on political independence may instead reignite it.

At no point in this slow and elongated peace negotiation process did natural resources, the core driver of the conflict, receive direct attention. As Bougainville illustrates, leaving decisions related to natural resources to be decided later in the peace process does not always ensure that the issue will be resolved.

At whatever point a party decides to negotiate natural resources in a peace process, at the beginning or the end, or even in a parallel process or in a subsequent constitutional law, they will likely turn first to the instinctual question of ownership. As will be discussed in the next section, just as timing proved to be a deceptively complicated question, ownership, too, can be an equally surprising and perplexing issue.

Ownership

The conundrum of determining natural resource ownership is the highest profile and most emotional that the parties to a peace negotiation can face, yet it is often the least important question they address, making it immensely difficult to negotiate.

Ownership is the preeminent question that the parties seek to address when resolving a conflict featuring disagreement over natural resources, and it often sets the framework for how natural resources are addressed throughout the peace agreement. Often, each party to a conflict desires to have complete ownership of the contested natural resource. No party to the conflict wants to concede ownership of a resource that could prove to be immensely valuable in the future.

While the parties may know, or have an idea of, the extent of the existing resource reserves, by their nature it is not possible to have full knowledge of future reserves. Reserves could be minimal, substantial, or in an unclear location. This can create complications if a substate entity agrees to share ownership with the national government, only to discover years later that greater oil reserves exist elsewhere, suddenly shifting the incentive to share ownership with the state.

The parties to a conflict have generally pursued four main approaches to addressing the ownership conundrum: ownership by the people; the state; a substate entity; or shared ownership between the state and one or more substate entities. States may opt for a fifth approach, which involves agreeing not to decide the question of ownership during the process of conflict resolution and peace negotiations, instead shifting the conversation to topics of management and revenue allocation.

Opaque language about ownership "by the people" often helps achieve an agreement and serves a symbolic function in unifying disparate parties around a set of principles. Nonetheless, it is exceedingly difficult to implement natural resource ownership by "the people" in a postconflict context.

In opting for national ownership of a resource in a postconflict context, the parties face this issue of underdeveloped government institutions and likely issues of corruption. In a conflict-ridden state without strong institutions, exclusive ownership of the natural resource by the state creates friction among national and local governments over revenue, geographic boundaries, and/or regional wealth disparities. In recent postconflict contexts, the parties to peace negotiations rarely agree to exclusive ownership of a resource by the state itself, unless the state defeats a party and forces them to the negotiation table. For the same reasons, the parties also seldom agree to exclusive ownership by the substate entity.

An alternative to national or local ownership is shared national–local ownership. In a functional federal state, shared ownership can be effective because it enables regional entities to maintain a high level of autonomy from the national government. Shared ownership may also enable a higher degree of community and local involvement in exploitation policies and greater control of revenues to spurn local development. Though shared ownership, particularly if associated with local management, requires the local government to have sufficient capacity to carry out its responsibilities effectively, oftentimes this capacity either does not exist or has been destroyed over the course of conflict.

In certain contexts, the parties agree to asymmetrical ownership, which is a form of shared ownership in which one substate entity owns significantly more of a resource than other substate entities, and may have a greater share than the state. Asymmetrical shared ownership and management, which often translates into increased revenue for the producing substate entities, may become a driver of conflict if there are not adequate mechanisms to equalize development between oil-rich and non-oil-producing substate entities.

With shared ownership, substate entities maintain control over substantial portions of their oil resources, while also allowing the national government to regulate the transportation of oil interregionally and internationally. Another disadvantage to shared ownership, however, is the difficulty in deciding how to implement joint ownership of oil resources between the national government and substate entities to the satisfaction of all parties involved.

In other cases, the parties leave ownership undetermined in peace agreements despite, and perhaps because of, their position at the heart of the conflict at hand.

Approaches to Resolving the Ownership Conundrum

In some cases, the parties agree to a form of opaquely described national ownership that is noted in a constitution or peace agreement as vesting ownership in "the people." For instance, the Iraqi Constitution of 2005 vested the ownership of oil resources in "all the people of Iraq in all regions and governorates."[119]

As the 2005 Iraqi constitutional negotiations ended, oil and gas became the linchpin issue, stalling negotiation of all other unresolved subjects until an agreement was reached on these resources.[120] Iraq's seventy-one-member constitutional committee, faced with approaching deadlines and under pressure from international actors,[121] sought to move forward with a final agreement, and consequently opted for vague language on ownership by "all the people" that would allow discussion on other matters to continue. Rather than elaborating on what this ownership by "all the people" entails, the constitution provided more specific language on the management of natural resources and associated revenue allocation.[122]

This vague language may have helped to move the constitution-drafting processes forward, but uncertainty over oil ownership continued to bedevil Iraqi efforts to manage its natural resources. A series of oil management laws stalled in parliament in 2007 due to disagreement between Kurdistan and the national Iraqi government over ownership of those resources. In 2018, a new Iraqi oil law was passed, but it again focused on resource management, not ownership.[123]

Yemen's 2014 National Dialogue Conference Outcomes Document, which outlined the results of a transitional dialogue process, similarly declared that "natural resources are the property of the people of Yemen," before shifting to a more detailed conversation about the management and development of natural resources.[124]

By framing this in terms of "the people" of Yemen rather than the state or substate entities, the rhetoric surrounding resource ownership sought to posit it as a unifying factor for the Yemeni people. Because the outcomes document did not refer to discrete political or ethnic groups when discussing oil ownership, and rather mentioned ownership by a singular and unified Yemeni people, the document did not validate claims of particular groups' legitimacy and claims to territory where those resources may be based. This notably reflects the fractious political context in which the document was negotiated. The 2015 draft constitution, which aimed to prevent a civil war, followed suit and described water as "owned by the people of Yemen," before it discussed the specifics of water management and preservation.[125]

The Philippines opted for asymmetrical regional ownership of natural resources in face of self-determination movements and conflicts. For decades, the Moro people agitated for self-determination in the region of Mindanao, calling for the creation of separate Muslim political structures to reflect their distinct cultural characteristics.[126]

In addressing this decades-long insurgency, the Philippines Constitution of 1987 provided that all natural resources are the property of the federal state and are nontransferable, with the "exploration, development, and utilization of natural resources ... under the full control and supervision of the State," excluding agricultural lands, with an explicit exception for the Autonomous Region of Muslim Mindanao.[127] In particular, the constitution granted the autonomous region legislative authority over all "ancestral domain and natural resources" within its respective territory.[128]

In addition to regional legislative authority, the Moro National Liberation Front, and later the Moro Islamic Liberation Front, pushed strongly for the region to achieve fiscal autonomy, which it perceived to be central to autonomous governance. During the protracted peace process between Mindanao and the Philippines, the Moro Islamic Liberation Front negotiated with the goal of steadily increasing the amount of natural resource revenue it was able to generate on its own over the course of several years.[129] Ultimately, the 2017 Bangsamoro Organic Law, which established the Bangsamoro Autonomous Region, replacing the Autonomous Region of Muslim Mindanao, codified regional ownership and authority over natural resources.[130]

The question of natural resources was particularly acute during the conflict in Aceh between the Free Aceh Movement and Indonesia, and was resolved through asymmetrical ownership.[131] Aceh is rich in natural resources, and provides 15–20 percent of Indonesia's oil and gas output, along with other resources such as timber and minerals.[132] The contrast between Aceh's economic potential and its pervasive and persistent poverty embodied for the people of Aceh the extent of the Indonesian government's neglect and indifference,[133] and inspired the drive for external self-determination.[134]

The 2005 Memorandum of Understanding ending the conflict outlined asymmetrical ownership of natural resources. The MOU granted Aceh "sole jurisdiction," which may mean ownership, over natural resources in the territorial sea surrounding Acehnese territory.[135] The context of the devastating tsunami in the months prior, mentioned previously, contributed to both parties' willingness to accept this arrangement.

In the Sudan/South Sudan conflict, ownership of oil resources was among "the most contentious issues, going right to the heart of the dispute over the government's sovereignty and self-determination of the South, was the ownership of land and natural resources."[136] The parties left this topic for the end of the negotiation process for this very reason. South Sudan claimed that the community living on a particular plot of land owned the resources of that land. Sudan alternatively "argued that the state ownership of surface and subsurface land was the prerequisite for an equitable and legitimate redistribution of natural resources."[137]

Because oil ownership could derail the possibility for peace in Sudan, the wealth-sharing protocol of the Comprehensive Peace Agreement explicitly provided that it was "not intended to address the ownership," affirming the establishment of a future process to resolve ownership disputes.[138] The parties recognized that an impasse on oil ownership would prevent agreements on other issues such as revenue-sharing.[139] The issue of ownership between the two groups was so complicated that it was only hardened after the secession of South Sudan in 2011. In the Comprehensive Peace Agreement, the parties instead focused on oil management and revenue allocation.

In the case of the 2020 Juba Agreement between Sudan and a number in intrastate parties, the parties broadly agreed that the land and natural resources in Sudan shall be utilized for the benefit of all the people of Sudan.[140] More specifically, the agreement provided that the "[t]he Sudanese people shall own the natural resources found on its soil and underground," but that the people of the regions where such resources are located shall have "special rights that must be met according to specific agreements and percentages."[141] Throughout the agreement, the parties sought to provide ownership to the people, but with special dispensation for the previously marginalized populations. As discussed below, the parties also sought to tap the natural resource wealth of Sudan to pay for the implementation of the agreement and to save for future generations.

As these instances of state practice illustrate, though natural resource ownership is often perceived to be the crux of conflict between the parties and a straightforward transactional negotiation, in practice the parties rarely negotiate it in a detailed fashion. Instead, the parties turn to the complicated and technical questions of resource management and revenue allocation.

Management

The conundrum the parties face when incorporating provisions related to natural resource management into peace agreements center around how to provide for efficient management when there is an eclectic array of interested parties each seeking to have a role in management processes. Delegating the power of management to a single party may be more efficient, but it is not inclusive of all the interests at play in a peace process.

While the precise framework for managing natural resources may not be the first question negotiating parties seek to answer during peace talks, management can be a key both to neutralizing the drivers of conflict and to establishing durable peace. Though, as stated previously, because of the detailed and technical nature of management discussion, they are often pushed to post-peace agreement processes.[142] Indeed, only a quarter of negotiations linked to natural resources address specific resource management mechanisms.[143]

If the parties decide to negotiate natural resource management in the context of conflict resolution, there are several component parts that are often included in the negotiations, each of which can be negotiated separately and requires a degree of background technical knowledge, including extraction management; existing and future contracts; the authority to contract; and the creation of joint mechanisms. Each component of natural resource management can fall under the purview of national, regional, or local governments, or a combination.

Approaches to Resolving the Management Conundrum

One method of resolving the management conundrum is to bring the responsibility of management under the control of the national government. Following a devastating conflict incited and exacerbated by the extraction of diamonds, Sierra Leone and the Revolutionary United Front agreed that the national government "shall exercise full control over the exploitation of gold, diamonds and other resources, for the benefit of the people of Sierra Leone."[144]

The Lomé Agreement also stipulated the creation of a Commission for the Management of Strategic Resources, National Reconstruction and Development by the national government, which would monitor the legitimate exploitation and export of extractive resources such as gold and diamonds. Through this commission, "all exports of Sierra Leonean gold and diamonds shall be transacted by the Government."[145]

This centralized control over resource management formally shifted control of these natural resources away from nonstate armed actors. To achieve an agreement, the parties appointed as chairman of the commission the RUF leader Foday Sankoh, who ultimately ignored the responsibilities of this role and the requirements of the agreement, and continued to fund the RUF through the illicit resources trade. This tradeoff may have been necessary given the stalemate nature of the war, the failures of previous attempts at peace agreements, and calls for increased power-sharing on behalf of the RUF, but it enabled a continuation of past resource management tactics that sustained the conflict.[146]

Instead of vesting control over resource management in one national body, the parties to a peace negotiation can choose to share management authority among federal and regional groups, through management councils or commissions. Iraq's 2005 constitution established a combined approach for resource extraction management, providing that "the federal government, with the producing governorates and regional governments, shall undertake the management of oil and gas extracted from present fields."[147] The constitution also applied this national–regional management technique to the creation of a draft joint management council, the Federal Oil and Gas Council, which was given the power to determine and administer Iraq's oil and gas policies and plans.[148] The constitution stipulated membership of both national and regional government authorities on the council,[149] which could coordinate federal and regional laws within the framework of the federal legislative framework.[150] This shared management tactic reflects Iraq's ownership "by all people" principle, discussed earlier.

By creating a joint management system, Iraq's draft legislation addressed several issues closely related to federalism disputes, such as whether regional governments can sign oil development contracts without direct interference from Iraq's national government.[151] Though the draft framework legislation did not become official, Iraq's Kurdistan regional government adopted legislation within the draft framework that tracked its regional oil and gas provisions, and created a model contract for oil production agreements with outside investors.[152]

Uncertainties over whether Iraq's national or regional governments would maintain natural resource contracting authorities under the federal system led to lengthy disputes between Iraq's national government and the regional Kurdistan government. Foreign oil companies were attracted to the "superior" contract terms offered by the autonomous Kurdistan government, but Iraq's national government refused to recognize or enforce natural resource contracts between foreign companies and the Kurdistan government.[153] Iraq's national government even declared many contracts between private oil companies and the regional Kurdistan government to be illegal.[154]

Yemen, too, sought joint management of its natural resources, including water and oil.[155] The National Dialogue Conference outcomes document provided that the natural resources owned by "all the people" would be managed and developed by producing *wilayas* along with regional and national authorities.[156] This was enshrined in the 2015 draft constitution. The 2015 draft constitution also provided for a natural resources management council, "composed of representatives of the federal government, regions and wilayas," which would create relevant policy, conduct evaluations, and liaise with *wilayas* and regions on the topic of natural resource management.[157]

The Yemen draft constitution further provided that *wilayas* would be responsible for local oil and gas service contracts,[158] building off the National Dialogue Conference outcomes document, which called for the "cancelation of all monopoly contracts in oil exploitation and related services including the transport of oil derivatives in a manner that achieves public interest."[159] Ultimately, the constitution's provisions never came to fruition, due to disagreements over the federal structure.

Sudan's Comprehensive Peace Agreement, which avoided any discussion of ownership, established the National Petroleum Commission. The commission was created to be a joint management body for oil management, specifically for contract management.[160] The commission consisted of the president of the Republic, the president of the government of Southern Sudan, a group of eight permanent members, and a group of nonpermanent regional representatives.[161] Four of the permanent members were to be representatives of the national government and four of South Sudan, with up to three to come from the producing regions in which the development is being considered.[162] The commission was designed to balance the interests of three distinct groups, the national government, the secessionist-minded South Sudan, and the oil-producing regions.

In the Juba Agreement, the parties sought to by and large mimic the mechanisms set forth in the Comprehensive Peace Agreement, but to improve upon its failings. The agreement provided that the regions would be a "genuine partner" with the national government with respect to managing natural resources extracted from the territory of the regions. The Darfuri parties were precise in ensuring the region of Darfur would be engaged "throughout all the phases of allotment, awarding, contracting, production and marketing."[163] The agreement also prioritized environmental protection, providing the regions with the primary responsibility for environmental regulation in order to ensure public health.[164]

Given the history of corruption associated with prior natural resource contracts, the parties agreed that the regions would be entitled to review all of the existing natural resource exploitation contracts relating to their territory. Pending the review, they would be "entitled to make adjustments to these contracts to ensure the fair and equitable allocation of revenue, as well as sufficient environmental protections."[165] The regions were also entitled to participate in the negotiation of any new contracts, and those contracts would be governed both by regional law and national law.[166]

Aceh also approached natural resource management from a shared national–regional perspective, but did not initially include specific provisions for a joint management commission like Yemen or Sudan. The Law on the Governing of Aceh, which came after the signing of the peace agreement, provided that future contracts "may be executed provided that the entire content of such cooperation contract agreements has been jointly agreed by the Government and Aceh Government."[167] This law indicated that all future oil and gas projects would be jointly managed between the government of Indonesia and the Aceh government, and included the potential future creation of a joint implementing agency.[168] The law respected existing contracts, allowing them to stay in effect until the natural termination date for the contract.[169]

The opportunity to design a functional approach to managing the development of natural resources may also serve as an opportunity to build support for other dimensions of the negotiations, such as those relating to state structure, power-sharing, and mitigating the consequences of prior marginalization. Similarly, the question of how to collect and allocate revenue can be addressed in ways that support or frustrate agreement on these other dimensions

Revenue Allocation

When considering the allocation of revenue derived from extractive natural resources in a peace negotiation, the primary conundrum the parties face is how to allocate revenue in a way that is fair and equitable for each of the parties that believe they have an entitlement to a share of those resources.

The parties must also identify and assess what constitutes a "valid" claim of entitlement to natural resource revenue while deciding how to prioritize these claims during negotiations. Complicating these primary revenue allocation questions even further is the common misperception that there are more resources or revenue to be had than may actually exist. Relatedly, the parties must consider how to find a balance between fair and equitable allocation of finite revenue with the need to fund the effective operation of the national government.

Though it is beyond the scope of this chapter, the parties must also determine how to match the allocation of resource revenue with the state's governance structure. Whether a state is unitary or federal can alter revenue allocation mechanisms and the considerations of those involved in the peace negotiations.

There are three core approaches to collecting and distributing oil revenue: direct collection and retention by national or local governments; collection into a single account and then subsequent sharing based on an agreed formula; or a hybrid approach.[170]

Direct collection and retention often is established through a provision in a peace agreement or constitution that establishes the authority of a national or local government to collect and retain revenue.[171] Single point collection involves the collection of all revenue from oil extraction into a single account. That revenue is then divided and redistributed between the national and local governments based on a formula typically agreed on through a peace agreement, constitution, or subsequent legislation.[172] The parties are often highly concerned with revenue collection and allocation because the collecting or allocating authority has the potential to retain an unfair share of the revenue, or in other cases, guard against graft and corruption.

Approaches to Resolving the Revenue Allocation Conundrum

Sierra Leone adopted a direct collection and retention approach. The Lomé Peace Agreement designated revenue garnered from the sale of gold and diamonds as public funds, to be put in an account used for public works, education, and health projects in primarily rural areas. The agreement also provided that funds from resource revenue should be appropriated to incapacitated victims of war and other postwar reconstruction efforts.[173] As previously mentioned, RUF leader Foday Sankoh was appointed chairman of the Commission for the Management of Strategic Resources and continued to fund the RUF through the trade of illegal diamonds.[174] After his arrest for atrocity crimes, the commission was disbanded.[175]

In 2009, ten years after the Lomé Peace Agreement, Sierra Leone implemented a Mining Act. This act included extensive provisions for community development, such as revenue-sharing and communal governance.[176] Implementation lagged, however, and the act has had a minimal impact on the allocation of natural resource wealth to the local communities.[177]

Other states approach revenue-sharing from a formula-based perspective. The peace agreement between Sudan and the Sudanese People's Liberation Movement/ Army allocated revenue to three separate entities. The agreement provided that oil revenue would be channeled from exports above an annually established benchmark price into a national Oil Stabilization Account. The agreement provided that after this payment is made, revenue would be allocated to the oil-producing region based on the proportion of oil it contributed, with each region receiving a minimum of 2 percent of the revenue. Then, the remaining oil revenue would be divided equally between the government of southern Sudan and the national government in northern Sudan.[178]

Soon after the signing of the agreement, the application of this article became a source of conflict between Sudan and South Sudan. In 2006, for example, Sudan claimed that the oil production rate was 330,000 barrels per day while the south claimed that production was as much as 450,000 barrels per day.[179] The south subsequently viewed the payment it received, which was based on Sudan's oil production rate, as woefully inadequate.[180]

After South Sudan gained independence from Sudan under the terms of the Comprehensive Peace Agreement, it assumed control of over 75 percent of Sudan's oil production.[181] Despite South Sudan's independence and the fact that it had two-thirds of the former unified state's oil fields, export facilities remain in the north.[182] In late 2011, South Sudan accused the Sudanese government of stealing oil from South Sudan as it was being transported through the north and being held in export terminals there.[183] South Sudan's lead negotiator accused Sudan of stealing over $600 million of oil.[184] In early 2012, Sudan claimed responsibility for confiscating oil, but argued that it did so because South Sudan was not paying its appropriate transit fees.[185] South Sudan then shut down virtually all of its oil production because of this dispute with Sudan over transit fees, a topic that was not discussed in depth in the original agreement.

On September 27, 2012, the presidents of Sudan and South Sudan signed the Cooperation Agreement, beginning a lengthy process for the resolution of this dispute.[186] This agreement included language describing eight future agreements to be implemented, including an "Agreement concerning Oil and related Economic Matters."[187] This agreement determined the specific payments from South Sudan to Sudan for processing and transporting oil, as well as a payment the government of South Sudan must pay to Sudan for lost revenue due to its secession. The agreement also established "mutual forgiveness" of past oil-related claims and joint evaluation of facilities.[188]

As with the management of resources, the parties to the Juba Agreement track relating to Darfur sought to learn the lessons from and improve upon the arrangements from the Comprehensive Peace Agreement. The parties thus set forth a very precise formula that 40 percent of the revenue from the mineral and petroleum resources in Darfur would belong to the region for an initial ten-year period. Local populations would be entitled to 3 percent of that revenue. The parties also agreed that the national government and the local governments would consider the needs of future generations and invest a specified percentage of revenue for the benefit of future generations.[189]

Some parties have addressed revenue-sharing in peace negotiations through a combination of formula-based revenue-sharing and direct ownership. In Aceh, the 2005 Memorandum of Understanding granted Aceh the right to retain 70 percent of its revenues from current and future oil and gas extraction, attempting to address a key conflict driver. The MOU also includes an ambiguous provision stipulating that the Indonesian and Acehnese governments will manage the resources jointly.[190]

At the time, Acehnese civil society objected to this combined revenue-sharing approach. The method by which revenue was first collected by the Indonesian national government and then distributed to the local government fomented suspicion of revenue as a tool of political influence, rather than of regional reconstruction and development.[191] A further complicating factor was that the extraction of oil and gas in Aceh was on the decline from 2001,[192] with one of the largest gas fields ceasing production in 2014.[193] The rather dramatic resource and revenue depletion was not foreseen or adequately taken into consideration in the text of the peace agreement or subsequent law on the governing of Aceh.[194]

Yemen's 2015 Constitution also provided for a program of revenue-sharing among the various levels of local government after an initial collection by the federal government. The constitution provided that a federal law shall ensure that "annual national revenues shall be divided amongst the federal and regional governments, wilayas, districts and the cities of Sana'a and Aden,"[195] taking into consideration "transparency and equitable distribution," the needs of producing regions, and allocation of a share of revenues to the federal government.[196]

This law was never drafted, as the 2015 Constitution was rejected quickly and "categorically" by Yemen's Houthi opposition movement.[197] The process to approve the constitution was notably fraught with sectarian tensions. For instance, the Yemeni president's chief of staff was kidnapped by armed members of the Houthi movement while on his way to present the draft constitution to parliament.[198] The Houthis strongly opposed the constitution and the revenue-sharing approach as their three delineated provinces would not have access to the coast or to oil resources. These tensions contributed to civil war, the very outcome the constitution sought to avert.

The Iraqi Constitution defined a program of sharing oil revenues through a hybrid approach as well. Article 112 of the Iraq Constitution set forth two conditions on the distribution of oil revenue. First, revenue from "present" fields must be distributed in a fair manner to all parts of the country, based on population, and in a manner that would ensure balanced development throughout Iraq.[199] Second, an allotment must be made for regions that were "unjustly deprived" under the former regime and for regions damaged afterwards.[200] The constitution mandated that an equitable share of the national revenues be allocated to the regions and governorates sufficient to discharge their responsibilities and duties.[201]

Since the implementation of the Iraqi constitution, controversy over the implementation of joint ownership and related revenue-sharing has continued, especially with regard to the authority of the Kurdish regional government to independently sign contracts and manage the oil reserves in the region. These disputes caused Iraq's national government to limit its revenue payments to the Kurdistan region, revenue that was necessary to pay private oil companies operating in the region. The national government maintained it was the only authority entitled to export oil from Iraq. After nearly six months of dispute, the national government agreed to pay $560 million to Kurdish oil producers so that exports could continue.[202] The dispute over these payments contributed in part to the Kurdish referendum on independence, and its destabilizing consequences.

CONCLUSION

At once both emotionally laden and inaccessibly technical in nature, negotiated approaches to natural resource ownership, management, and revenue allocation can serve to mitigate the drivers of conflict and achieve durable peace, or they may have the opposite effect. The proper management of valuable extractive resources such as oil and diamonds can create opportunities for reconciliation, trust-building, and empowerment. Revenue-sharing systems can provide much-needed resources to conflict-stricken regions, investment in public services, and a highly public peace dividend. Agreements on natural resource ownership, management, and revenue allocation can just as easily catalyze the return of conflict, as each decision the parties face in negotiating these subjects can set the stage for mounting tensions.

This chapter has sought to illustrate that parties in peace negotiations are provided with a unique moment to draft language that can reshape a state's economy, relationship to resources, budget priorities, and relations between segments of its population. Assigning ownership by a region over the natural resources that exist within its territorial bounds, as in the case of Philippines and Mindanao, can accelerate the end of an entrenched, decades-long insurgency. Describing oil ownership as "by the people" of a state, as in Iraq, can smooth over lingering tensions between groups demanding ownership of natural resources, while paving the way for more technical discussions related to management and revenue-sharing.

This chapter has also illustrated how decisions hastily made in good faith during peace negotiations on the topic of natural resources can tip states back into conflict and erode hopes for a durable peace. The case of Sierra Leone illustrated how formally shifting the control of natural resources away from nonstate armed actors who had used them to fund insurgencies, and towards a centralized commission, did not prevent the armed actors from accessing diamonds. Though the decision to appoint RUF leader Foday Sankoh as head of the commission was an essential compromise to achieve an agreement, it set the stage for a return to the very practices that fueled the conflict. In Sudan, the imprecision in the agreement contributed to continued tensions between Sudan and southern Sudan, tensions that were only resolved years after South Sudan's secession in 2011, and a destabilizing oil shut-in.

The instances of key state practice highlighted in this chapter – Papua New Guinea/Bougainville, Indonesia/Aceh, Iraq/Kurdistan, the Philippines/Mindanao, Sierra Leone, Sudan/South Sudan, Sudan/Darfur, and Yemen – illustrate the impact of each component of natural resource ownership, management, and revenue allocation on the prospects for a durable peace. Each technical detail must be acknowledged by the parties to a peace negotiation, with each conundrum deliberately confronted according to the specific context of the conflict. Decisions to address and negotiate or to avoid the subject of natural resources must be undertaken with careful consideration and an understanding of how particular choices fit into the larger landscape of the conflict.

The next chapter will explore a closely related topic: self-determination.

4

Self-Determination

Self-determination and sovereignty-based conflicts are widespread throughout the globe. Since 1950, over seventy ethnic groups on five continents have engaged in armed conflict for autonomy or independence (excluding sovereignty-based conflicts for peoples under colonial rule).[1] Self-determination conflicts tend to be durable and deadly. A recent study indicated that of the eighty-two self-determination conflicts studied since 1956 only twenty-eight were settled, while another twenty-nine were merely contained, usually through the deployment of international peacekeepers, and twenty-five remained ongoing. With respect to the twenty-five ongoing conflicts, their average duration was twenty-seven years.[2]

Sovereignty-based conflicts can be resolved in any number of ways. In some instances, the parent state defeats the military forces of the substate entity and quashes the substate entity's movement for self-determination. This was the case in Sri Lanka, where the government forces defeated the Tamil Tigers and essentially ended, for the time being, the aspirations of the Tamil people for a devolution of power to the northern and eastern provinces, or a possible independent state of Tamil Eelam.

In other instances, the substate entity is able to defeat the forces of the parent state, often with the support of a sponsoring state. After defeating their parent states, many states attain recognition by the international community, as was the case with Slovenia and Croatia's separation from the former Yugoslavia. Other states, however, have defeated their parent state's forces but remained unrecognized by the international community, as is the case with Nagorno-Karabakh and Azerbaijan, or were absorbed into the sponsoring state, such as Russia's illegal annexation of Crimea from Ukraine.

If there is no military solution to the conflict, then the parties will attempt to negotiate a resolution. In a limited number of cases, the parties negotiate the continuation of a unitary state, with some degree of power-sharing among the various constituent units of the state.

In other cases, the state and substate entity agree on the substantial asymmetrical devolution of power to the substate entity. This occurred when Indonesia and Aceh agreed to resolve their decades-long conflict by devolving a moderate degree of political power to Aceh, coupled with the right of Aceh to retain 70 percent of the revenue from oil resources on its territory.[3] In other cases, such as Yemen, the state may agree to transform from a unitary to a federal state.[4]

In the remainder of cases of sovereignty-based conflicts, the parties reach an agreement on external self-determination as a means of resolving the conflict. In these cases, the substate entity becomes, through a peace agreement, entitled to decide whether it will remain a part of the parent state or will become independent.

Some instances involving an agreement on the option of external self-determination as a means to resolve an armed conflict include Sudan/South Sudan, Indonesia/East Timor, Papua New Guinea/Bougainville, United Kingdom/Northern Ireland, and Serbia/Montenegro. In the case of Kosovo, the path to external self-determination came about through a UN Security Council resolution. A managed process for external self-determination was also proposed for Morocco/Western Sahara and Israel/Palestine.

A number of recent instances of non-armed conflict resolved sovereignty-based claims by the substate entity when the parties peacefully agreed to consider external self-determination. These include Canada/Québec; United Kingdom/Scotland; the dissolution of Czechoslovakia; the dissolution of Soviet Union; Ethiopia/Eritrea; France/New Caledonia; New Zealand/Tokelau; Nevis/St. Kitts and Nevis; and the dissolution of the Dutch Antilles. While not central to the discussion in this chapter, these cases provide useful precedent for sorting out some of the practical issues that arise when a state and substate entity seek to structure an agreement on external self-determination.[5]

This chapter addresses a number of conundrums related to external self-determination that parties face during peace negotiations and peace processes. First, this chapter discusses the puzzle of whether and how to provide for external self-determination as a means for ensuring a durable peace. Next, it provides a conceptual and legal primer for understanding the right to external self-determination as well as its conflict with the principles of sovereignty and territorial integrity under international law. Then, the chapter explores a number of instances of key state practice to analyze and highlight how parties involved in peace negotiations have sought to manage the conundrums they faced when seeking to solve the puzzle of external self-determination.

THE PUZZLE: WHETHER AND HOW TO PROVIDE FOR EXTERNAL SELF-DETERMINATION AS A MEANS FOR ENSURING A DURABLE PEACE

Given that competing claims over sovereignty are often at the root of violent conflict, peace negotiations frequently address the question of whether providing for a right to and a process for external self-determination is essential to create a durable peace. In the event it is deemed necessary to provide for the possibility of self-determination, the question becomes how to do it in such a way as to promote a durable peace and not contribute to greater instability in the parent state or substate entity, or in the neighboring region.

In many, though not necessarily all, peace negotiations, the substate entity will seek to establish protections for internal self-determination as well as provide for the possibility of some form of external self-determination. The state is often willing to consider varying degrees of internal self-determination, but is often highly reluctant to envision an agreement where the substate entity can pursue external self-determination, allowing the substate entity to break away and become independent.

Mediators and third-party states are also often extremely reluctant to consider or participate in efforts that create a process for possible external self-determination unless they perceive it as absolutely necessary in order to end the conflict. Even then, mediators and third-party states seek to have the process highly managed and regulated. Mediating states and third-party states are reluctant to consider a path for external self-determination as they fear that allowing too many instances of self-determination would facilitate secessionist movements in their own states, or undermine the Westphalian international order. Unfortunately, mediators who adopt this approach often find themselves in a position of accommodating, and sometimes even appeasing, aggressor regimes.[6]

CONCEPTUAL AND LEGAL PRIMER

This section will examine the conceptual and legal framework that governs self-determination. First, it will provide an overview of the longstanding concepts of sovereignty, territorial integrity, and political independence. Next, it will describe the emergence and development of the now well-established principle of self-determination. Then it will then differentiate and describe internal self-determination, a principle that guarantees a people the right to determine their own future, and external self-determination, which entails a substate entity becoming independent from a parent state.

Sovereignty, Territorial Integrity, and Political Independence

Since the conclusion of the Treaty of Westphalia in 1648, the principles of territorial integrity and political independence have formed the core of the international structure relating to sovereignty.[7]

A central attribute of sovereignty under international law is the exclusive jurisdiction of a state to exercise authority within its own borders to preserve its territorial integrity from external and internal threats.[8] Territorial integrity is a fundamental principle of international law that protects the indivisibility of a state. This principle is established and codified through the UN Charter Chapter I Article 2(4), which provided that "All Members shall refrain in their international relations from the threat of use of force against the territorial integrity or political independence of any state."[9]

At its core, the principle of territorial integrity holds that a state is entitled to maintain the whole of its territory and that this territory cannot be diminished. Other states cannot seek forcibly to acquire parts of one state's territory, nor may other states promote the separation of a substate entity (either to become independent or to join with another state).[10] Doing so is viewed as an act of aggression under international law.

Similarly, it is generally held that, absent a few exceptions, a substate entity may not simply detach its territory from that of the parent state and become an independent state itself. The consent of the parent state is required before other states may recognize the new state as distinct from the territory of the parent state. This is, in part, due to the international community's anxieties that allowing for the universal exercise of self-determination would destabilize the international order.[11]

Notably, the International Court of Justice in its Advisory Opinion about the accordance with international law of the unilateral declaration of independence in respect of Kosovo held that it was not a violation of Serbia's territorial integrity for Kosovo to declare independence, as "general international law contains no applicable prohibition of declarations of independence." The court reasoned so on the basis that the right to territorial integrity exists between states, and as Kosovo was not a state, it could not be deemed to be infringing on Serbia's right. Given the nature of the question posed by the General Assembly, the court did not address the issue of whether other states' recognition of Kosovo's independence absent Serbia's consent violated Serbia's territorial integrity.

The Law of Self-Determination

The principle of self-determination has joined the principles of sovereignty, territorial integrity, and political independence as one of the foundational principles that govern state behavior.

The principle of self-determination can be broadly defined as a people's right to determine their own political destiny.[12] The principle of self-determination is tridimensional, with two dimensions being settled law and the third remaining unsettled. It is settled that former colonies are entitled to independence, that distinct peoples have a right to internal self-government (internal self-determination), and it remains unsettled as to whether noncolonial distinct peoples are entitled to independence.

Decolonization
The principle of self-determination provides that colonies are entitled to become independent states. During the twentieth century's wave of decolonization, nearly 100 former colonies became independent states.

The basic legal structure for the independence of colonies is set forth in the UN Declaration on the Granting of Independence to Colonial Countries and Peoples, which provided that "All peoples have the right to self-determination; by virtue of that right they freely determine their political status and freely pursue their economic, social and cultural development."[13] The declaration also called for the immediate "transfer [of] all powers to the peoples of those territories."[14] The Annex to the Declaration on the Granting of Independence to Colonial Countries and Peoples, outlined in UN General Assembly Resolution 1541, as a follow-up to the declaration, established principles to guide members in the determination of whether a territory is non-self-governing and thus can achieve sovereignty and determine its own governance.[15] Essentially, the UN mandated the colonial states to share governing responsibilities with their colonies in such a way that would build their colonies' capacity for self-government and prepare for their eventual independence, if that were to be the will of the people of the colony.[16]

The International Court of Justice reaffirmed the principle of self-determination a number of times during the process of decolonization. Specifically, in the Advisory Opinion on Western Sahara, the court, having established the existence of a distinct Sahrawi people in Western Sahara prior to colonization, decided that Western Sahara was "entitled to exercise the right of self-determination."[17]

During the course of decolonization, a number of important principles or practices developed that are relevant to efforts by the parties to negotiate external self-determination. These include assessing the will of the people; *uti possidetis*; the phased transfer of governing authority; associated state status; and trusteeship.

Assessment of the will of the people: In a number of instances, referenda asked the people of various colonies whether they desired to become an independent state or whether they wished to retain some association with the colonial state. While assessing the will of the people through a referendum was not a required or consistent practice, the French used it in 1958 in a referendum taken across many of its colonies concerning a new French constitution, designed primarily to reaffirm a commitment to remain a French colony. The French held subsequent referenda in Algeria, Djibouti, Comoros, and New Caledonia, among other French colonies. The British also relied upon referenda in Malta, Bahrain, and Bermuda to assess the will of the people for independence or association.

Uti possidetis: During the course of decolonization, the principle of *uti possidetis* was established, which provided that a colony would assume its colonial border as its international borders upon independence. In only the rarest circumstances could these borders be adjusted. As noted by the International Court of Justice in *Burkina-Faso v. Mali*, the rationale for the principle is simple and clear:

[*Uti possidetis*] is a general principle, which is logically connected with the phenomenon of obtaining independence, wherever it occurs. Its obvious purpose is to prevent the independence and stability of new states being endangered by fratricidal struggles provoked by the changing of frontiers following the withdrawal of the administering power.[18]

Phased transfer of governing authority: During the process of decolonization and in the lead-up to independence, the colonial powers frequently devolved governing authority over a period of time. This process allowed for the gradual development of self-governing institutions and responsible governments before extending sovereignty rights.[19] Colonies were often given internal autonomy with representative governments and sovereignty in internal affairs, while authority over defense and foreign affairs remained in the hands of the colonial administration. In Singapore, for example, the British colonial administration created the Rendel Commission to serve as an interim body for Singapore's eventual independence. The Rendel Commission paved the way for internal self-government while allowing the British to retain interim control over security and foreign affairs.[20]

Associated states: A number of colonies or former trusteeships, often called microstates, opted for free association with their former colonial states. Colonies and former trusteeships in this relationship are called associated states, and the conditions of the association differ depending on the parent state with which it is affiliated. Under an association, the former colony becomes an independent state, but the parent state maintains responsibility for specified areas of competence such as defense and foreign affairs. The United States refers to these relationships as compacts of free association.[21] The United States has such a relationship with the Federated States of Micronesia, the Republic of the Marshall Islands, and Palau.[22]

Trusteeships: The United Nations also employed trusteeship as a means for transitioning territories or colonies formerly occupied by the Axis powers in World War II to independence. Trusteeship territories, primarily in the Pacific, were placed under the authority of states designated as administering authorities. These authorities were responsible for promoting the "political, economic, social and educational advancement" of trustee territories so that they may achieve full self-governance or independence, depending on the wishes of the people concerned.[23] These administering authorities were then subject to the oversight of the UN Trusteeship Council. As of May 1994, all trustee territories had achieved self-governance (through association) or independence.[24]

Algeria bridge case study: The case of Algerian independence from France provides insight into how a number of provisions in contemporary peace agreements addressing external self-determination were key to resolving questions arising in the decolonization context. The case of Algeria is particularly insightful because from the perspective of the Algerians, it was a case of decolonization, whereas from the perspective of the French, it was a case of external self-determination, with a "department" of France, Algeria, seceding from France.[25]

To establish the authority to launch negotiations on self-determination, the French government held a referendum in January 1961 in the territories of both France and Algeria. The referendum passed by over 75 percent in France and over 69 percent in Algeria.[26] Shortly thereafter, negotiations were held in Évian, France. They were successfully concluded in March 1962, and came to be known as the Évian Accords. The accords settled a number of key issues related to the self-determination of Algeria, and set the parameters for Algerian independence.[27]

The primary foci of the Évian Accords included providing for a referendum on the question of self-determination; the creation of an interim government; settling the borders of Algeria, coupled with an agreement on preferential terms for French access to Algeria's oil resources; guarantees for the "European" population living in Algeria; the status of French military bases postindependence; and a framework for French–Algerian economic and political cooperation.[28]

As provided for in the accords, a referendum by the people of Algeria would determine the question of whether the country would become independent or remain a part of France. The yes/no question was framed as whether or not the people of Algeria wished for Algeria to become an "independent state, co-operating with France under the conditions defined in the declarations of 19 March 1962."[29] The referendum was required to be held no sooner than three months and no later than six months after the adoption of the accords.[30]

The accords created an interim government with executive powers that had the authority to manage the referendum. France was to be represented by a high commissioner during this interim period. The high commissioner was the "custodian" of matters of defense and security and "the maintenance of law and order in the last resort."[31] Notably, the court of public law was to consist of an equal number of European and Muslim judges.[32]

With the discovery of oil in the Algerian desert in 1956, French President Charles De Gaulle proposed that the littoral territory, where most of the population lived, become the territory of an independent Algeria, and that the Algerian desert remain part of France. This was rejected as a violation of *uti possidetis*, and an unfair limitation on Algeria's prospects for economic viability. France did, however, negotiate substantial concessions relating to the extraction and sale of oil that were highly beneficial to French oil companies.[33] After independence, Algeria would rapidly become one of the ten largest oil-producing states in the world.[34]

The Évian Accords also provided for a three-year transition period in which the "European" population living in Algeria would be entitled to continue to possess, without discrimination, all the rights and privileges they possessed before independence. By the time of the expiration of the interim period, those individuals would need to acquire Algerian citizenship, or be considered resident aliens.

Finally, the accords provided that France would be entitled to maintain certain military bases deemed necessary by France, and in particular to maintain for a period of fifteen years its naval facilities at Mers-el-Kébir, which played a role in

France's nuclear testing. The accords also provided extensive measures for French–Algerian economic and political cooperation postindependence in an effort to maintain the deep integration of the two economies.

The question of independence, in line with the parameters set forth in the accords, was put to the people of Algeria on July 1, 1962, and was approved by an affirmative vote of over 99 percent. France recognized Algeria as independent on July 3, 1962, and this was immediately followed by recognition from the member states of the international community. Algeria became a member of the United Nations on October 8, 1962.

Internal Self-Determination

Internal self-determination is a principle of international law that guarantees a people the right to determine their own future. Specifically, internal self-determination "allows a people broader control over their political, economic, social and cultural development, while stopping short of secession."[35]

The principle of internal self-determination is codified in both the International Covenant on Civil and Political Rights,[36] and the International Covenant on Economic, Social and Cultural Rights.[37] Article I of both covenants provides that "All peoples have the right of self-determination. By virtue of that right they freely determine their political status and freely pursue their economic, social and cultural development."[38]

In order to qualify for internal self-determination, and as will be explained with external self-determination, a group must possess a united identity that is sufficient for it to attain distinctiveness as a people. The factors for determining this include (1) the extent to which members of the group share a common racial background, ethnicity, language, religion, history, and cultural heritage; and (2) the territorial integrity of the region the group is claiming.[39] It is also important for the group to demonstrate to a significant extent a self-perception of the group as distinct, possessing a shared sense of values, and the potential to form a viable political entity.[40]

In granting rights of internal self-determination, states are often explicit that this right does not equate with a right to declare independence. The Spanish constitution, for instance, reaffirms "the indissoluble unity of the Spanish nation, the common and indivisible homeland of all Spaniards, and recognizes and guarantees the right to autonomy of the nationalities and regions which make it up and the solidarity among all of them."[41] Finland, which provides substantial internal self-determination to the Åland Islands, and is often seen as a model for dealing with modern self-determination conflicts, provides in its constitution that "the territory of Finland shall be indivisible," and that "its boundaries may not be altered except by Parliamentary consent."[42] Similarly, while Greenland has substantial autonomy under the Danish Home Rule Act, it may exercise this power only "within the framework of the unity of the Realm."[43]

When faced with a claim for external self-determination, a state with the goal of protecting its territorial integrity will almost invariably propose enhanced internal self-determination as an alternative coupled with a denial of the "right" of the substate entity to claim external self-determination.

External Self-Determination

External self-determination entails a substate entity becoming independent from the parent state in much the same way that a colony would become independent from the colonial state. Since 1991, twenty-seven new states have been created, either from the dissolution of states or state secession.[44]

External self-determination exists at the point of conflict between the right of self-determination and the right of territorial integrity. While international law is clear that peoples have a right of self-determination and that states have a right of territorial integrity, it is an unsettled question of law as to whether people on the territory of a substate entity may exercise their right of self-determination to the point of securing independence from the parent state, without the consent of the parent state.

In 1975, the United States and the Soviet Union, along with their European allies, attempted to bridge the gap between territorial integrity and self-determination. In the Helsinki Final Act, they provided that "[t]he participating States will respect the equal rights of peoples and their right to self-determination, acting at all times in conformity with the purposes and principles of the Charter of the United Nations and with the relevant norms of international law, including those relating to territorial integrity of States."[45]

The Canadian Constitutional Court, in addressing the question of the right of Québec to hold a referendum and to secede from Canada, succinctly answered the question of whether a substate entity possesses the right to external self-determination. According to the court,

> a right to secession only arises under the principle of self-determination of peoples at international law where "a people" is governed as part of a colonial empire; where "a people" is subject to alien subjugation, domination, or exploitation; and possibly where "a people" is denied any meaningful exercise of its right to self-determination within the state of which it forms a part.

The court then further explained: "[a] state whose government represents the whole of the people or peoples resident within its territory, on a basis of equality and without discrimination, and respects the principles of self-determination in its internal arrangements, is entitled to maintain its territorial integrity under international law and to have the territorial integrity recognized by other states."[46]

Despite the Helsinki Final Act, or maybe because of it, and the efforts of the Canadian Constitutional Court precisely to articulate the parameters of the right of external self-determination, state actors and legal scholars continue to debate whether the principle of self-determination constitutes a legal "right" for a substate entity to attain independence. The precise nature of such a right remains an open question, and is beyond the scope of this chapter.

In the course of a peace negotiation, the parties may agree upon a path for external self-determination. In this case, the requirement of consent is met and the secession is deemed legal. In some cases, as in the former Yugoslavia, the parent state will be deemed to have dissolved and therefore be incapable of providing consent, and thus that requirement is waived. While in others, the international community may deem the parent state to have lost the capacity to provide meaningful consent, as in situations where the institutions of that state are committing atrocity crimes against the people of the substate entity. This latter category is called remedial secession and is less settled in international law.

Importantly, the focus of this chapter is not on the legal status of external self-determination, but rather on the question of how the parties will structure the process that will lead to an option for external self-determination in such a way as to minimize the drivers of conflict and instability, and set the foundation for a durable peace.

KEY STATE PRACTICE

This chapter draws on the following instances of key state practice for a discussion of the various conundrums the parties to a peace negotiation face when confronting the puzzle of self-determination. The paragraphs that follow highlight the relationship between each peace process and the agreed arrangements relating to external self-determination. For more on these conflicts, negotiations, and agreements, consult the Appendix.

The 1995 Dayton Accords, which brought an end to conflict in **Bosnia and Herzegovina**, mandated an internationally appointed high representative to oversee the civilian implementation of the agreement and made provisions for the deployment of a security presence by a NATO implementation force. By the provisions of the accords, the high representative had authority to manage many of the sovereign authorities and functions of the independent state of Bosnia for an indeterminate period.[47] To avoid delayed or obstructed implementation of the Dayton Accords by local nationalist politicians, the Peace Implementation Council granted further substantial powers to the Office of the High Representative over Bosnian institutions.[48] While conditional sovereignty is not explicit, the pattern of practice in Bosnia indicates that the international civilian authority will be discontinued only upon a showing that Bosnia can adequately function as an ethnically integrated state. As of 2020 the high representative continued to operate in Bosnia.

The Comprehensive Agreement for **Bougainville**, signed in August 2001, established an autonomous interim arrangement for the region of Bougainville within **Papua New Guinea**. Bougainville shared authority and certain functions with

Papua New Guinea during this interim period. The agreement provided that Bougainville would gradually gain authority over a wide range of powers and functions under the newly established autonomous Bougainville government. This sovereign authority, however, was conditioned on the implementation of a weapons disposal plan and on the achievement of good governance standards. The Comprehensive Agreement for Bougainville provided that within a period of 10–15 years, and after meeting the aforementioned conditions, Bougainville could hold a referendum on secession from Papua New Guinea.[49] In a referendum held between late November and early December 2019, 98 percent of voters opted for independence from Papua New Guinea.[50]

In 1999, **East Timor** rejected, by referendum, Indonesia's proposal for East Timorese autonomy within Indonesia in favor of independence.[51] Following this vote, pro-integration East Timorese militia, supported by elements of the Indonesia military, propelled East Timor into conflict.[52] In response to this violence, the UN Security Council passed Resolution 1272, which provided for the creation of the UN administration of East Timor.[53] The resolution provided authority for a two-and-a-half-year period of shared sovereignty between the United Nations and East Timor through the establishment of the interim United Nations transitional administration of East Timor, during which time East Timor was able to build and strengthen the institutions necessary for independent self-governance.[54] After successfully meeting a number of benchmarks, East Timor was recognized as an independent country by the international community in May 2020.

The United States, the European Union, the United Nations, and Russia ("the Quartet") developed the "Roadmap" for Middle East peace in 2003. The roadmap aimed to resolve the conflict in the Middle East through a three-phase plan that sought to ensure the security of **Israel** and simultaneously created a process for the establishment of an independent **Palestine**.[55] The roadmap proposed a two-state solution to the Israeli–Palestinian conflict through Israel's withdrawal from Palestinian areas occupied since September 2000, the creation of Palestinian institutions of self-government, followed by the international recognition of an independent Palestine with provisional borders.[56] This proposed phased sovereignty was contingent on the Palestinian authorities meeting a number of conditions relating to democratization and an end to violence.[57] In addition, the roadmap called for a subsequent agreement that would detail the final borders of Israel and Palestine, as well as address other controversial issues at the heart of the conflict.

UN Security Council Resolution 1244, with reference to the terms of the Rambouillet Agreement, provided for the administration of **Kosovo** under the provisional authority of the United Nations Interim Administration Mission in Kosovo (UNMIK) and the deployment of a NATO-led force to oversee the withdrawal of Serbian military forces from Kosovo.[58] Resolution 1244 vested UNMIK with near-absolute authority over the territory and people of Kosovo, including all legislative and executive powers and administration of the judiciary, in order to build democratic institutions that would allow for autonomous governance for Kosovo.[59] The United Nations-led interim administration was established with the goal of transferring certain sovereign authorities and functions to the Kosovar government pending a political settlement and the capacity of established institutions to exercise their own authority.[60] The full devolution of authority and the determination of final status depended on Kosovo's compliance with standards of democracy and good governance. In February 2008, Kosovo declared independence. Over 115 states recognize Kosovo as an independent state. To date, Serbia has not recognized the independence of Kosovo.

The 1998 Good Friday Agreement provided for the creation of institutions for **Northern Ireland** and the interim conditional devolution of substantial power to those institutions. The agreement contained provisions for the status and system of government of Northern Ireland within the United Kingdom, the institutional and constitutional arrangements between Northern Ireland and the Republic of Ireland, and the relationship between the Republic of Ireland and the United Kingdom.[61] The Good Friday Agreement also provided the people of Northern Ireland with the right to decide the issue of unification with the Irish Republic via a referendum at a point later than seven years from the signing of the agreement.[62]

The Constitutional Charter of the State Union between **Serbia** and **Montenegro** brokered by the European Union in February of 2003, created a confederacy between the two states that provided for the sharing and devolution of sovereign authority under a joint government. The constitutional charter provided that after three years of shared sovereignty between Serbia and Montenegro, during which the states were to strengthen their economic and governance systems, the final status of the state union would be determined through a referendum.[63] The referendum was held in 2006 with 55.5 percent of the vote in favor of Montenegrin independence from the Union.[64]

The 2005 Comprehensive Peace Agreement provided for the cessation of hostilities between the forces of northern **Sudan** and forces of southern Sudan and established a transitional governing framework for a unified Sudan. The agreement provided for **South Sudan** to determine its political status at the end of the six-year interim period through an internationally monitored referendum, jointly organized by the governments of Sudan and South Sudan. Via the referendum, the people of South Sudan could vote for secession or adopt the system of government established under the agreement.[65]

The Baker peace plans of 2000 and 2003 for the resolution of the **Western Sahara** were initiatives to provide for the creation of self-governing institutions in the Western Sahara under the auspices, and with the assistance, of the United Nations.[66] The plans called for a period of autonomy for the Western Sahara, including the devolution of numerous sovereign powers and functions to the Western Sahara Authority. Specifically, the plans offered exclusive competence over local government administration to the population of Western Sahara, and foreign relations, national security, and external defense to the government of Morocco.[67]

The plans did not detail options for the final status of Western Sahara, but instead called for a referendum to be held within five years to determine the status of the territory if the final plan was adopted. The Baker Plan, which was perceived to be in favor of Western Saharan self-determination, was endorsed unanimously in the United Nations Security Council Resolution 1495, and adopted in July 2003. In response, Morocco presented a counterproposal to the Baker Plan, known as the Draft Autonomy Status, which diluted key elements of the Baker Plan. Specifically, the Moroccan proposal excluded independence as an option for the status of Western Sahara. The Baker Plan was not implemented due to a lack of mutually acceptable political solution from all parties involved.[68]

CONUNDRUMS

When seeking to negotiate a path towards external self-determination, the parties and mediators are often guided by four pressing goals. First, the state usually seeks to design a path that will ultimately preserve the option of retaining the unity of the state. Second, the substate entity seeks to design a path that will preserve the option for independence, while also ensuring that if the final status is unity, there is extensive internal self-determination for the people of that substate entity. Third, the mediator and the substate entity, and to a degree the national government, are also guided by the desire to ensure that in the event the substate entity achieves independence, the newly formed state is functional. Fourth, both parties and the mediator seek to design the path for external self-determination in such a way that it does not destabilize neighboring states or lead to further conflict between or within the state and substate entity.[69]

To accomplish these four goals, the parties often address up to six conundrums, including how best to share sovereignty, build institutions, determine final status, phase in the assumption of sovereignty, condition the assumption of sovereignty, and constrain the exercise of sovereignty.

Sharing Sovereignty

To create the possibility of a durable peace, the parties to an agreement may seek to provide for a period of shared sovereignty in the time between the conclusion of a peace agreement and the point at which the substate entity decides whether to exercise the option to become independent.

When a state and substate entity share sovereignty, the state devolves to the substate entity specified political, administrative and financial authority and functions. These may include domestic authority and functions, such as taxation, policing and internal security, economic development, commercial regulation, resource development, environmental protection, agricultural policy, education, health, infrastructure, and social welfare.[70] In some cases, the powers devolved are ones typically associated with a highly autonomous province. In others, such as East Timor and Kosovo, nearly all the powers of the state were allocated to the substate entity in partnership with the international community.

With each peace negotiation, the relevant provisions for shared sovereignty may vary according to the duration of the window of shared sovereignty; the substantive nature of the powers shared; whether the powers are also shared with an international entity; and the purpose of sharing those powers, be it to create an opportunity for capacity-building and institution-building and/or to induce the substate entity to remain a part of the parent state. It is often the task of the parties and the mediator to balance these variables to create a package that provides enough shared sovereignty to placate the substate entity, but not so much or so little that the substate entity is prompted to return to a call for immediate independence.

The state may also devolve authority and functions relating to the international prerogatives of the state, such as entering into treaties, establishing relationships with other states, or joining international organizations. This was the case with Montenegro and Serbia under the Constitutional Charter of the State Union of Serbia and Montenegro, which united the two states. The powers of the union were restricted to such matters as immigration, selection of the flag and anthem, and working with the European Union on economic harmonization.[71] Notably, under the Constitutional Charter, the appointment of all diplomatic representatives required the consent of both Serbia and Montenegro.[72] The state may also equally share sovereign powers, such as the right to maintain an army, as was the case with Sudan and South Sudan under the Comprehensive Peace Agreement, where both the state and the substate entity maintained their separate armies during the interim period.

The sharing of sovereignty can occur between the state and the substate entity or between the substate entity and one or more international entities or organizations, or among all three. In the case of East Timor, sovereignty was shared symbolically with Indonesia, but functionally with the United Nations. In the case of Kosovo, sovereignty was shared with the United Nations, NATO, Organization for Security and Co-operation in Europe, and the European Union. International organizations exercise this shared sovereignty when the parent state has been precluded from exercising those functions on the territory of the substate entity, often because of its commission of atrocity crimes, and the substate entity is not yet capable of exercising those functions on its own.

In instances such as East Timor and Kosovo, shared sovereignty was used to assist the substate entity in establishing the necessary institutions for self-government. As discussed in the Determining Final Status section of this chapter, sometimes the state and substate entity fail to utilize the period of shared sovereignty to build effective institutions, but rather run down the clock to the referendum.

The state may be motivated to share sovereignty as a means for lessening the substate entity's interest in seeking independence or as a means to eliminate the causes of conflict by creating some form of perpetual autonomy. This possibility seemed to be the assumption of Papua New Guinea and of international mediators, as reflected in the Bougainville Agreement, which provided for a separate Bougainville constitution governing the authority of Bougainville to generate its own revenue and establish separate Bougainville courts, public service institutions, and police force. The delegation of these powers is embedded in the constitution of Papua New Guinea and can only be amended with the consent of Bougainville. The parties then agreed on a 10–15-year period before a referendum on independence,[73] the assumption being that within this window of time, the people of Bougainville would grow accustomed to this degree of internal self-determination and vote against independence, or choose not to hold the referendum. There was a similar, albeit unrealistic, assumption that underpinned the Comprehensive Peace Agreement for Sudan and South Sudan. In both cases, voters chose independence in their referendums.

In cases where it is likely the state and substate entity will remain together, or where they envision a close political and economic relationship following substate entity independence, the sharing of sovereign functions may assist with building confidence and promoting institutional reconciliation between the parties. For instance, in Northern Ireland, shared sovereignty has been considered necessary for the state and substate entity to establish a viable relationship that will survive the independence of Northern Ireland, or that will dampen the drivers of conflict should it continue to remain a part of the United Kingdom.[74]

Finally, the parties may also intend to undertake a period of shared sovereignty as an interim step to independence, with the substate entity exercising nearly all the power and authority of an independent state and sharing equally any remaining authority. The Constitutional Charter of the State Union of Serbia and Montenegro provided that the union exercised almost no original authority and merely served as a conduit between the member states and the international community, in particular the European Union and the international financial institutions.[75] In the case of East Timor, the international community intended to share sovereignty with local institutions only so long as necessary to ensure that those institutions could support a stable independent East Timor.

Building Institutions

In order to carry out shared functions and authorities, it is necessary for the substate entity to establish effective institutions of governance. It is doubly important for the substate entity to create those institutions in the event it opts for independence after the period of shared sovereignty. Effective institutions of democratic governance are also necessary to prevent a return to conflict or to prevent the emergence of a new conflict within a newly independent state. Given the importance of institution-building, peace agreements often seek to provide for the creation of effective institutions from the initial stages of any interim period, and often involve the support or engagement of the international community.

The institutions created are often those needed for shared powers. Montenegro, for instance, created a parallel Ministry of Foreign Affairs, Ministry of Finance, and a central bank in order effectively to implement its shared powers. Sometimes, it is less necessary to create administrative institutions and more necessary to create political institutions to provide effective representation at the sub-state level. For example, in the case of Northern Ireland, there was no need to provide for the creation of new administrative institutions, but there was a need to create political institutions and to reform many of the key existing administrative institutions to increase stability. The Good Friday Agreement addressed this need by creating the Northern Ireland Assembly, which would be able to absorb the sovereign functions and authority to be devolved from the United Kingdom.[76]

Notably, the Good Friday Agreement for Northern Ireland also provided for the creation of new institutions that would function on state-to-state and substate-to-foreign-state levels. Specifically, the agreement also provided for the creation of two consultative mechanisms, a North/South Ministerial Council and a British–Irish Council intended to facilitate political stability during the period of shared sovereignty and the transfer of sovereign functions and authority to Northern Ireland.[77]

Often, the international community is called upon to provide assistance as the substate entity mistrusts the motives of the parent state, and it is often the failure of the parent state to create its own effective institutions of democratic government that served as an initial conflict driver. The ability of the international community to assist with institution-building is often quite limited, and is hampered by high turnover in personnel, its own limited institutional capacity, and a lack of local knowledge or context. The authority by which the international community participates in institution-building is often found in the peace agreement itself, or in more limited cases, in a UN Security Council resolution.

In some cases, the international community engages quite extensively. In East Timor and Kosovo, the international community was called upon to create the foundation for nearly all political and security institutions to allow East Timor and Kosovo to effectively operate as independent states.[78] The Baker peace plan for the Western Sahara called upon the United Nations to assist with the creation of a Western Sahara government that included a chief executive, a legislative assembly, and a supreme court.[79]

In other cases, such as the Israeli–Palestinian Roadmap, specific members of the international community were to be called upon in a more limited capacity to create and monitor key institutions necessary for democratic development.[80] In particular, the roadmap provided for the restructuring of security services, the establishment of an Interior Ministry, the appointment of an interim prime minister or cabinet with executive decision-making capacity, the adoption of a Palestinian constitution, and the creation of an electoral commission.[81]

In some cases, however, the international community has sought to distance itself from institution-building for fear that it would be seen as seeking to prejudice the outcome of any decision on whether or not the substate entity would pursue independence. For instance in the case of South Sudan, the international community adopted a policy of attempting to "make unity attractive" as a means for enticing the south to stay unified with Sudan.[82] Unfortunately, the international community feared that if it invested heavily in the institutions that would be needed by South Sudan to operate effectively as an independent state, this would be perceived as an effort to make separation more attractive than unity. There was also the concern that if these institutions were created, they would in fact not only appear to, but would actually make separation more attractive as the people of South Sudan would have a greater degree of confidence in the ability of South Sudan to survive and prosper as an independent state.

The concerns of the international community were misguided, as it was clear to nearly all close observers that after twenty years of conflict the people of South Sudan would most definitely vote for independence. In fact, over 99 percent of the population voted in favor of independence when the referendum was conducted. Within two years, South Sudan entered its own brutal civil war, attributed largely to the failure of any functional democratic institutions.

Phasing Sovereignty

Depending upon the nature and characteristics of the conflict, it may not always be possible to achieve even preliminary power-sharing arrangements. Thus, to enhance the relationship between shared sovereignty and institution-building, some peace agreements have incorporated the element of phased sovereignty. Phased sovereignty involves the measured devolution of sovereign functions and authority from the parent state or international community to the substate entity during the period of shared sovereignty. Phased sovereignty can be useful to promote a smooth transition in those contexts where the adversarial claims of the parties do not allow for immediate devolution of powers. The timing and extent of the devolution of authority and functions may be correlated with the development of institutional capacity and/or conditioned on the fulfillment of certain benchmarks, such as democratic reform and the protection of human rights.

Kosovo presents the most comprehensive example of the use of phased sovereignty to manage the devolution of sovereign authority and functions. Subsequent to Resolution 1244, the United Nations endorsed a provisional constitutional framework for Kosovo. This provided that both the UN Mission in Kosovo and Kosovar entities would share most of the functions typically associated with an independent state, including foreign relations.[83] UNMIK then began a slow but steady process of transferring power to Kosovo's national government institutions. The degree of transfer was determined by an informal mix of institutional capacity on the part of Kosovo, and the coordination of the timing of devolution with progress being made towards resolving the final status of Kosovo.

Other agreements that included an element of phased sovereignty are the Good Friday Agreement, the Israeli–Palestinian Roadmap, and the Bougainville Agreement. In the Good Friday Agreement, the United Kingdom was entitled to manage the rate of devolution, and even reverse the devolution by suspending parliament, if the Irish Republican Army failed to comply with its obligations to demobilize and decommission its weapons.[84] The Israeli–Palestinian Roadmap provided for the phased accumulation of sovereign attributes, beginning with the adoption of a new constitution and elections for a prime minister and cabinet, and ending with the possible creation of an independent Palestinian state.[85] The Bougainville Agreement also provided that the Bougainville government would assume increased control over a wide range of powers, functions, personnel, and resources during the interim period prior to the determination of final status.[86]

It is worth noting that not all instances of external self-determination include the element of phased sovereignty. For example, upon ratification of the agreement for the creation of the Union of Serbia and Montenegro, both member states immediately assumed the sovereign authority and functions allocated to them under the agreement.[87] In fact, Montenegro had exercised many of those functions prior to the adoption of the agreement.

Conditioning Sovereignty

To promote effective implementation of power-sharing through functioning democratic institutions, the transfer of sovereign authority to the substate entity, or the determination of final status, may be conditioned upon the fulfillment of certain benchmarks. Some peace agreements condition the phasing of sovereignty on the achievement of a satisfactory level of good governance and legal guarantees. This includes protection of human and minority rights, disarmament and demobilization, development of democratic institutions, establishment of the rule of law, and promotion of regional stability.

The notion of conditional sovereignty originated in the European approach of earned recognition of the successor states of the former Soviet Union and the former Yugoslavia. In response to calls for international recognition by the republics of the Soviet Union and Yugoslavia, on December 16, 1991, the European Community Council of Foreign Ministers developed a policy of earned recognition. Under this approach, states seeking recognition by the European Community were required to meet a set of detailed criteria. The European Community then adopted additional criteria to be applied specifically to the republics of Yugoslavia, and required that the republics seeking recognition submit an application to the Yugoslav Peace Conference being conducted by the United Nations and European Union at that time. The co-chairs of the Peace Conference would then seek a determination from the Arbitration Commission as to whether the applicant states fulfilled the criteria for recognition.[88]

The conditions will necessarily vary depending on the context of the conflict, and will particularly aim to eradicate what is identified as the major obstacle to peace. For example, the Roadmap for Peace in the Middle East is conditioned on the cessation of terrorism.[89] In the case of Northern Ireland, the continued devolution of authority was conditioned on the decommissioning of paramilitary forces and the surrender of weapons.[90] In Kosovo, the United Nations adopted an approach of "standards before status," which provided that before Kosovo could undertake final-status negotiations to secure independence, it must meet a number of standards or benchmarks,[91] with an emphasis on the protection of human rights and the return of refugees. The Bougainville Peace Agreement provided that the referendum on final status would only be held if the Bougainville government ensured the decommissioning and disposal of weapons and undertook good governance, including the development of democracy, transparency, and accountability, as well as respect for human rights and the rule of law.[92] Not all phased agreements contain the element of conditional sovereignty, however. For instance, the Baker Peace Plan for Western Sahara and the Machakos Protocol in the Sudan set specific dates for the devolution of sovereign authority and functions, as well as the determination of final status without conditions.[93]

Determining Final Status

The most hotly contested conundrum is how to assess the "will of the people" to determine whether a substate entity should remain an autonomous part of the parent state or become an independent state. The answer in its simplest form is that there should be a referendum; from there, it becomes complicated. When should the referendum be held? Who is eligible to vote in the referendum? What is the precise question to be put to the people? What percentage of the people must vote in favor of the question, and is there a minimum voter turnout required? Is the outcome of the referendum binding on the parent state? Is it binding on the international community? Can the referendum be repeated at a later time? If a new state is established through the referendum, what are the boundaries of the new state?

When Should the Referendum Be Held?

Sometimes, as in the cases of East Timor and Bosnia, it is the referendum that launches the process of external self-determination followed then by some form of shared sovereignty or phased independence. In most cases, however, the parties agree upon a period of time designed to balance the need for the dissipation of conflict drivers and institution-building with the desire to resolve the question of continued association or independence in a timely way so as not to prompt disenchantment and a return to violence.

Each case balances a unique set of factors, and there is no apparent best practice in terms of timing. Serbia and Montenegro adopted a relatively brief period of three years,[94] as did the Rambouillet Accords, whereas Papua New Guinea and Bougainville adopted a window of 10–15 years.[95] Other agreements or proposed agreements provided for timelines within those two limits. The Baker Peace Plan provided that the final status of Western Sahara shall be determined by referendum no earlier than four and no later than five years after the adoption of the peace plan[96] and the Machakos Protocol for South Sudan provided for a referendum after six years.[97]

In Northern Ireland, the Good Friday Agreement took a rather innovative approach. It provided that the British secretary of state would call for a referendum on independence in seven-year intervals if it was "likely" that the majority of those voting would express a wish that Northern Ireland should cease to be part of the United Kingdom and form part of a united Ireland.[98] The agreement provided as its rationale that the "the present wish of a majority of the people of Northern Ireland . . . is to maintain the Union" with the United Kingdom, and that the status of Northern Ireland would not be modified without the consent of the people.[99]

Who Is Eligible to Vote in the Referendum?

There are two core questions relating to voting on the question of external self-determination. The first is whether the parent state is entitled to conduct a referendum of its citizens on the question of whether the substate entity should be permitted to secede. The second relates to who in the substate entity should be able to participate in the referendum.

On the first question, the parties frequently raise in negotiations that the citizens of the parent state should have a voice in whether the substate entity should secede. The parties deploy arguments of sovereignty and territorial integrity to support this demand. The Rambouillet Accords, for instance, provided that there would be an assessment of the "will of the people," presumably via a referendum, but did not define who would constitute "the people," leaving open the possibility that the people of Serbia as well as those of Kosovo would have a say in the referendum. The mediators rejected a request by the Kosovo delegation that the provision specifically note that there would be an assessment of the "will of the people of Kosovo."[100]

The standard compromise is that the citizens of the parent state may be involved in a referendum to approve the peace agreement itself, and thus "consent" to the eventual referendum to be held on the territory of the substate entity. This harkens back to the Algeria case, where French voters approved the Évian Accords, which contained the provision for an Algerian referendum, and then only residents of Algeria participated in the referendum on self-determination. In the case of the Good Friday Agreement, the people of Ireland participated in a referendum on the accords, as well as the citizens of Northern Ireland, but it was not put to a referendum in Great Britain.

On the second question – who in the substate entity should be able to participate in the referendum – the substate entity is often anxious that if put to a referendum where a large number of residents hail from other parts of the parent state, the population may vote to remain a part of the parent state. In the case of Montenegro, for instance, nearly 30 percent of the population self-identified as Serbian, and there were many Serbian nationals with second residences in Montenegro.

This is where the legal principle that self-determination as a right possessed by a "people" becomes relevant. Substate entities are able to use the principle to seek to ensure that only those people that share common characteristics and are attached to the particular territory of the substate entity participate in the referendum. This then also raises the question of whether members of the group living outside the substate entity but within the parent state are entitled to participate in the referendum.

The eligibility requirements negotiated in peace agreements span a wide spectrum. In Montenegro, those who were registered to vote in Montenegro, which required having resided in the country for at least two years, were entitled to participate in the referendum, regardless of whether they identified themselves as Montenegrin or Serbian. Despite the fact that a number of political parties strongly advocated for the right of Montenegrin-born citizens living in Serbia to participate in the referendum, this option was not included in the Montenegrin referendum law. This was in part due to the opposition of such a provision by the Organization for Security and Co-operation in Europe because it would entitle these individuals to double-vote, though there was in fact no referendum on the territory of Serbia.[101]

Other peace agreements have similarly provided that the voter eligibility will mirror the voter eligibility requirements of national elections. For instance, the referendum outlined in the Bougainville Peace Agreement provided that the "eligibility to vote in the referendum will be the same as for national elections in Bougainville."[102] Alternatively, the parties may seek to provide for eligibility requirements to vote that are specific to the referendum, as was the case in East Timor's referendum. In that case, the agreement specified that anyone over the age of seventeen was eligible to vote if they were born in East Timor, had at least one parent born in East Timor, or were married to someone who fell into one of the previous two categories.[103]

In some cases, the historical connection to the territory is even more precisely constrained. In South Sudan, the referendum law, following the parameters of the Comprehensive Peace Agreement, provided that eligible voters were those who were at least eighteen years old, "of sound mind," and registered in the Referendum Register. Additionally, eligible voters needed to meet one of the following two categories: (1) "born to parents both or one of them belonging to one of the indigenous communities that settled in South Sudan on or before the 1st of January 1956" or (2) a permanent resident or someone whose "parents or grandparents are residing permanently . . . in South Sudan since the 1st of January 1956."[104]

What Is the Precise Question to Be Put to the People?

The wording of the referendum is also often hotly contested. In some instances, a confusing question can bias a referendum one way or another, or a multipart question can lead to imprecise results. Public referenda frequently rely on legal terminology that is difficult for the average voter to understand. When voters do not fully understand the question, they are more likely to be influenced by the structure of the question rather than just the content. For example, the order of a two-option question can prejudice which answer the voters select; less-informed voters often go for the first option.[105] A simple yes/no question is preferred from a technical view due to the ease of the phrasing, but the parties often contest whether the question is "Do you prefer independence?" or "Do you prefer unity?"

Sometimes the questions are set forth in the peace agreement, whereas in other instances, the substate entity adopts a referendum law that sets out the question, and in still others, there is a subsequent mini-negotiation over the phrasing of the question.

The question put to the people of Montenegro was straightforward: "Do you want the Republic of Montenegro to be an independent state with full international and legal personality?"[106] Indonesia and East Timor opted for an either/or question of "Do you accept the proposed special autonomy for East Timor within the Unitary State of the Republic of Indonesia?" or "Do you reject the proposed special autonomy for East Timor leading to East Timor's separation from Indonesia?"[107] Papua New Guinea and Bougainville reached an agreement in 2018 for the referendum in 2019 to be held on the question of "Do you agree for Bougainville to have: (1) Greater Autonomy (2) Independence?"[108] South Sudan had a simple two-word referendum, with a box next to the word "unity" and a box next to the word "separation" and the voter put a thumb print in the relevant box.[109] South Sudan also had a visual option, with the voter able to make a thumb print on a pictogram of two hands clasped together or to make a thumb print on a single palm-facing hand.

What Percentage of the People Must Vote in Favor of the Question, and Is a Minimum Voter Turnout Required?

Another hotly contested question is what percentage of the voters must vote in favor of independence. In some cases, it is a simple majority, while in others it is a higher threshold or supermajority, such as two-thirds. The parties must also consider whether or not there will be a minimum voter turnout requirement. There is no established consensus on either of the two questions. Frequently, the turnout rate for self-determination referenda is high. Of the thirty-seven secession referendums from

1991 to 2011, thirty-one had voter turnout rates of more than 70 percent, far higher than in general elections.[110]

Substate entities have wide discretion on referenda issues. Notably, neither the European Convention for the Protection of Human Rights and Fundamental Freedoms[111] nor the International Covenant on Civil and Political Rights,[112] or any other international convention or treaty, establishes binding standards relating specifically to voter threshold or quorum requirements in referendum laws.[113]

As such, peace agreements themselves frequently do not specify voter threshold or quorum requirements. These are more often provided for in subsequent referendum laws. For instance, the agreements concerning East Timor,[114] Sudan,[115] and Bougainville[116] do not contain any provisions requiring a specific threshold or quorum.

Despite the fact that a referendum on independence sets in motion a significant, potentially irreversible, decision, a surprising number of substate entities provide for a simple majority. The Baker Plan for the Western Sahara, for instance, envisaged a referendum on self-determination to be decided by a simple majority of votes cast.[117] There are ad hoc determinations, such as Montenegro's 55 percent requirement, which seemed fairly random, and was essentially imposed as a condition by the European Union. Additionally, there are then cases such as Bougainville, for which the referendum law requires a two-thirds vote in favor of independence.

A minimum voter turnout can empower the party opposed to independence. Specifically, if they choose to boycott rather than vote no, it combines their opposition votes with the non-votes of those who simply choose not to participate. Most agreements therefore do not require a quorum – the minimum number – of registered voters. Montenegro, however, required that "the decision in a referendum is taken by the majority vote of the citizens who have voted, provided that the majority of citizens with voting rights has voted."[118]

In some cases, a state party will try to argue for an even higher threshold for the percentage of the registered voters needed to vote in favor of external self-determination. Overly stringent quorum requirements can harm, rather than enhance, the legitimacy of independence referenda. In April 1990, for example, the Soviet Union's legislative body, the Supreme Soviet, enacted a law "Concerning the Procedure of Secession of a Soviet Republic from the Union of Soviet Socialist Republics."[119] Among other conditions, this law required that before a republic could leave the Soviet Union, the republic needed to hold a referendum in which 66 percent of eligible voters cast their ballots in favor of independence.[120] This elevated quorum requirement was in line with other restrictive provisions of the law, which one contemporary commentator described as "establishing a myriad of pre-conditions to secession and vesting Moscow, rather than the republics, with the authority to decide whether secession can take place."[121] Despite this law, Ukraine held a referendum on independence in 1991 and required a simple majority plus a quorum requirement of 50 percent.[122]

Is the Outcome of the Referendum Binding on the Substate Entity and the Parent State?

Peace is more durable when peace agreements clearly specify whether the outcome of the referendum is binding on the substate entity and on the parent state. Lack of clarity could destabilize the peace implementation process at the very moment it enters its final phase.

In the case of South Sudan, it was clear the referendum outcome would be binding, while in Bougainville, independence could only occur after a referendum supporting independence, and with the consent of the government of Papua New Guinea. In the case of Kosovo, the Rambouillet Accords provided that the final status of Kosovo be determined by an international conference, which would consider the will of the people for independence.[123] This language seemed to imply that the referendum would merely inform the decision of the international conference, and not bind it to a particular outcome.

In some cases, the parent state commits to the binding nature of a referendum and then changes its mind. For instance, the government of Indonesia indicated that, if the special autonomy proposal were rejected, it would grant East Timor independence.[124] After the people of East Timor voted to reject the Indonesian proposal, rather than accepting these results, the government of Indonesia supported loyalist militias in East Timor in an attempt to destabilize the substate entity and forestall its commitment to grant independence.[125]

Nearly all constitutions require a constitutional amendment to occur via a vote of the parliament for a referendum to be binding. Some states and international organizations have used these domestic law provisions to assert that given that external self-determination of a substate entity would constitute a change in the constitutional structure of a state; this must be approved by the parent state's parliament via a constitutional amendment or, alternatively, by the parliament of the substate entity. In the case of Montenegro, for instance, the Organization for Security and Co-operation in Europe recommended that after the referendum, the parliament of Montenegro should formally amend its constitution prior to declaring independence. Under the existing constitution, it would have been necessary to hold the referendum, followed by a parliamentary approval of the result by a two-thirds majority, then the dissolution of the parliament, then elections, and then a new parliament charged with approving the result with a two-thirds majority within ninety days.[126] Such cumbersome procedures could in fact destabilize a peace process by delaying the implementation of the will of the people, and by moving the threshold from a simple majority of voters to a higher parliamentary majority.

Can the Referendum Be Repeated at a Later Time?

In some instances, the parties provide that the referendum may be repeated at a future point in time. In Montenegro, for example, a second referendum could be held no sooner than three years after the first referendum. In the case of Northern Ireland, the referendum could be held every seven years. The possibility of a repeat referendum is designed to alleviate any pressure for a return to conflict. The obvious downside is that it keeps in limbo the question of the eventual final status of a substate entity and makes it difficult effectively to implement internal self-determination.

What Are the Boundaries of the New State?

If a new state is established through a referendum, the boundaries of the new state must be decided. The principle of *uti possidetis* was adopted to answer this question by requiring newly independent countries to inherit the borders of their predecessor.[127] This principle was first applied in the late nineteenth century to newly independent countries in Latin America, and then adopted during decolonization in Africa, where new countries inherited their former colonial administrative borders as they gained independence. In some cases, such as in Somalia and Morocco, new states resisted adopting the old borders and attempted to carve out borders that included all the members of their ethnic group.[128] The international community, however, universally insisted on compliance with the principle of *uti possidetis*.[129]

In the case of the dissolution of Yugoslavia, Serbia sought a change in the borders of both Croatia and Bosnia. The Badinter Arbitration Committee rejected this approach, and in Opinion No. 2 reaffirmed the principle of *uti possidetis* and its applicability to the states emerging from the former Yugoslavia. Each of the twenty-seven new states since 1991 have been recognized within their preexisting provincial borders.

Constraining Sovereignty

In order for a substate entity to become a state, it is necessary that it be recognized by other member states of the international community. The debate over constitutive or declaratory recognition is beyond the scope of this chapter, as is the question of how many states must recognize a substate entity in order for it to be considered a state.[130] However, given that states that are not parties to the peace agreement play a role via recognition in the transformation of a substate entity to a state, and because the emergence of new states may be destabilizing to the immediate region, the sovereignty of the new state may sometimes be constrained by the international community. The potential for destabilization arises from the fact that the state, even after a lengthy period of institution-building, remains incapable of exercising effective authority, or from the new state's existence in and of itself, which can create a destabilizing political dynamic.

Constrained sovereignty involves the imposition of continued limitations on the sovereign authority and functions of the new state. Such constraints include prolonged international administrative and/or military presence and limits on the right of the state to merge with another state.

In some cases, such as Bosnia, an independent state may be forced to share sovereign authority and functions with an international organization. The 1995 Dayton Peace Accords, which ended the Bosnian conflict with Serbia, in effect established a regime whereby the independent state of Bosnia was put in a de facto trustee relationship with the international community through the creation of the Office of the High Representative. The Bosnian government shared functions with an international high representative from a Western European country and with a NATO-led force to ensure security.[131] In this case, the international community determined that constrained sovereignty was necessary to ensure the territorial integrity of Bosnia, as it was believed that without an international presence the Republika Srpska would have sought to secede.

East Timor also remained under a soft form of constrained sovereignty for a period of time, as the international community – in the form of the United Nations Mission of Support for East Timor, a UN follow-up mission – provided continued assistance in the areas of civilian administration, law and order (police and development of a law enforcement agency), and military security (maintaining internal and external security).[132]

CONCLUSION

Drafting provisions related to the transfer of sovereignty and authority to substate entities is often an essential step for the parties to take during a peace negotiation. When power-sharing mechanisms do not quell demands for increased autonomy, or are impossible to embed in the peace agreement, providing for external self-determination, shared sovereignty, phased sovereignty, conditional sovereignty, and/or a future independence referendum can create the conditions needed to ensure a durable peace. As with all of the conflict drivers examined in this book, there is no one-size-fits-all model for resolving the thorny issue of sovereignty and demands for self-determination. Nevertheless, in the more than half a century since the start of the massive wave of decolonization, the sovereignty and autonomy of substate entities remains at the forefront of many armed conflicts.

This chapter has discussed how the parties to postconflict peace negotiations have developed new approaches to the concept of sovereignty by innovating timelines for earned sovereignty or implementing international administrative governing bodies, as in the case of Kosovo. In the case of Papua New Guinea and Bougainville, following the protracted conflict for Bougainvillean autonomy, the state and substate entity agreed to establish a system of good governance benchmarks including weapons disposal that would allow for increased autonomy for the substate entity. As previously mentioned, this successful process in Bougainville culminated in an independence referendum in 2019, which passed with over 98 percent of voters choosing independence from Papua New Guinea. The thoughtful choices made to tailor processes for increased self-determination for substate entities included throughout this chapter illustrate how a well-drafted agreement can resolve seemingly intractable sovereignty-based conflict and lead to a durable peace.

This chapter has also sought to illustrate that even when the negotiating parties forge detailed agreements or plans for self-determination or earned sovereignty, issues of self-determination can continue to divide the parties and prevent a durable resolution of conflict. For instance, even if a peace plan, such as the Baker Plan for Western Sahara or the Roadmap for Israel and Palestine, provides for self-determination and phased sovereignty and has the support of the international community, if it lacks political will in the region in question, it can lead to a continuation of conflict and unresolved tensions. Similarly, though UNMIK has transferred authorities to the government of Kosovo, and the state of Kosovo declared independence in 2008, certain functions of the Kosovar state remain under international jurisdiction and just over half of UN member states recognize its independence.

The case studies highlighted in this chapter: Bosnia, Indonesia/East Timor, Israel/Palestine, Kosovo, Northern Ireland, Papua New Guinea/Bougainville, Serbia/Montenegro, Sudan/South Sudan, and Morocco/Western Sahara each illuminate the complexity of crafting a durable agreement to resolve a sovereignty-based conflict. If drafted in a suitably nuanced fashion, provisions for increased self-determination, autonomy, phased sovereignty, and independence referendums can serve as a check against further conflict.

The next chapter will consider questions of postconflict governance, a topic which relies upon the key concepts of sovereignty, legitimacy, and self-determination discussed in this chapter.

5

Governance

INTRODUCTION

During a peace negotiation, the negotiating parties must reach agreement on a multitude of issues. As explored in previous chapters, the parties need to establish security arrangements and a monopoly of force, create power-sharing arrangements, determine natural resource ownership and management, and sort out questions of external self-determination. In addition to addressing these core issues, many other issues arise throughout the process of negotiating peace that parties may not have the time or capacity to fully resolve during the formal negotiations.

Establishing a comprehensive legal framework for postconflict governance is one of those tasks where there is seldom the time or capacity for the parties to reach a full and complete agreement during a negotiation.

Though decisions relating to postconflict governance are critical issues for discussion within peace negotiations, the parties often are not able to determine each detail of the system for postconflict governance. Instead, the parties often agree to a preliminary set of principles coupled with a general governing framework. They then set forth an agreed process for negotiating, designing, and implementing a national dialogue, the drafting or amending of a constitution, and elections.

The parties to peace negotiations are increasingly agreeing to hold national dialogues as a prelude to the preparation of a new or amended constitution. The national dialogue is intended to assess the will of the people as it relates to the structure and substance of the constitution. A national dialogue, also known as a popular consultation or national conference, is a process in which representatives from multiple parties discuss the issues and challenges related to a political transition.[1] A post-peace-agreement national dialogue can provide the negotiating parties with the time and opportunity to build confidence and increase participation, as well as a platform to develop the political, economic, and social principles that will guide a state's transition.[2]

The parties to a peace negotiation generally also either directly address constitutional modification during the negotiations, via an articulation of principles,
agreed amendments, or, in rare cases, a new constitution embedded in the agreement. The parties may also create a process for the post-agreement development of a
new or amended constitution. Since 1991, provisions for a constitution-drafting
process or components of a new constitution have been included in over thirty
peace agreements.

Negotiating a constitution-drafting process during the peace process allows the
parties to lock in the objective, timeframe, scope, and structure of the process. As a
state's constitution is its founding legal document and is often the supreme law of
the land,[3] developing a postconflict constitution-drafting process is one of the most
important steps in the formation of a new or reformed structure for governance.[4]
Notably, a recent study indicates that when parties draft a postconflict constitution,
which occurs in about a quarter of conflicts, the peace is more durable.[5]

In many instances, the parties will also decide during the negotiations to set
parameters around how the system of postconflict governance will operate, such as
by affirming specific human rights protections. In some postconflict contexts, there
are principles that are so important to the resolution of the conflict that the parties
articulate them specifically in the peace agreement. The parties may also create
supremacy clauses in the peace agreement that provide priority legal status in
relation to the new or amended constitution.

Generally, once a constitution is agreed, but occasionally prior to a new or
amended constitution, there will be elections. During the peace negotiations, the
parties usually decide on the process for holding these elections. The parties also
generally cover such issues as the selection and mandate of an election commission,
the type of electoral system to be implemented, the nature of voting rights for
domestic and displaced citizens, timetables for the administration of the electoral
process, dispute resolution mechanisms to resolve potential electoral disagreements,
and regulations for political financing.

In keeping with the overall approach of the book, this chapter undertakes a
detailed exploration of one dimension of the process for creating and implementing
a system for postconflict governance.[6] In this case, the chapter will address how the
parties approach achieving changes to the constitutional structure of a state during
the negotiations. As in the previous chapters, this chapter notes along the way how
the parties to the peace negotiation harmonized their approach to constitutional
modification with other components of postconflict governance. The chapter
undertakes an analysis of approaches to constitutional modification from an array
of peace negotiations, providing useful insights into the broader topic of establishing
a comprehensive legal framework for postconflict governance.

This chapter addresses a number of conundrums related to constitutional modification that parties face during peace negotiations and the broader peace process.
First, the chapter discusses the puzzle of whether and how to address constitutional

modification during peace negotiations in a manner that promotes a durable peace. Next, the chapter provides a conceptual and legal primer for understanding how the negotiating parties design postconflict constitution-drafting processes. Then the chapter explores a number of instances of key state practice to analyze and highlight how the parties involved in peace negotiations have sought to manage the conundrums they faced when seeking to solve the puzzle of constitutional modification.

THE PUZZLE: WHETHER AND HOW TO ADDRESS CONSTITUTIONAL MODIFICATION DURING PEACE NEGOTIATIONS IN A MANNER THAT PROMOTES A DURABLE PEACE

Parties to peace negotiations naturally primarily act out of their own self-interest, including when determining a process for creating and implementing a system for postconflict governance. When negotiating a modification of the constitution, or a process for post-agreement modification of the constitution, it can be exceedingly difficult for the negotiating parties to foresee which options will best suit their self-interest or the interests of their constituency. With other topics in a peace negotiation, such as external self-determination or a monopoly of force, the consequences of particular choices are more apparent to most of the parties to the negotiation.

Unlike other cornerstone issues for durable peace discussed elsewhere in this book, the decisions parties to a peace negotiation make regarding postconflict governance and constitutional modification are less clearly detrimental or beneficial both to their own interests and to the prospects for a durable peace. The parties oftentimes find it exceptionally difficult to address constitutional modification and agree to the ultimate substance of a postconflict constitution without fully knowing whether these decisions suit their interests or ameliorate the drivers of conflict. The long-term consequences of constitutional modification and the process by which it is brought about may be unclear to the parties even as they are negotiating these issues at the rapid speed often required by a peace process, contributing to a potentially flawed arrangement that the state may then be forced to contend with for years to come.

Despite the risks of not knowing the long-term consequences of constitutional modification, and the process by which it is brought about, addressing governance-related conflict drivers remains essential for the successful implementation of any peace agreement.

The parties to a peace negotiation face the challenge of determining how much substance related to postconflict governance will be determined by the peace agreement and how much will be left for a later point in time. Issues related to governance, deep structural flaws within a state's nature such as disenfranchisement or the failure to protect certain groups or classes of individuals, are often conflict drivers and therefore priorities to resolve during negotiations.[7] Peace negotiations themselves, though, are inherently time-limited and may not include all possible governance experts at the table to support the parties in attendance. Despite these limitations, the parties face immense pressure in peace negotiations to include specific principles for postconflict governance, such as the text of a constitution, in their agreement. If the parties decide to draft a constitution during the peace negotiation, they will likely face an overwhelming number of challenging decisions, including vertical power-sharing, horizontal power-sharing, oversight mechanisms, human rights protections, fundamental freedoms, military structures, and electoral reform.

Precisely because of the constraints inherent to peace negotiations, the parties may instead opt to design a postconflict constitution-drafting process. This process can serve as the conduit for key structural reforms that may have been impossible to resolve within the confines of a peace negotiation. The parties to a peace negotiation must also determine the relationship between the peace agreement and any future constitution: whether the text of what is agreed to in the peace agreement will be binding on the constitution-drafting process. Though deciding on a later constitution-drafting process may permit the parties to sign an agreement, designing the constitution-drafting process itself requires expertise and deft negotiation.

This overarching decision, choosing whether to draft or amend a constitution during the peace negotiations, or agree on fundamental principles and a select number of key mechanisms related to governance, and/or agree a process for subsequent constitution-drafting, can either lead to a durable peace or contribute to a relapse into conflict, depending on the circumstances.

Additionally, peace processes do not always include all of the primary decision-makers or influencers in a particular state whose buy-in is needed to ensure that any constitution ultimately produced is in fact implemented. Peace processes tend to include certain powerful stakeholders but not others, excluding key groups from the table. If the constitution-drafting process is relegated to a later forum, the same parties engaged in the peace process may or may not have a seat at that table, or they may find themselves sharing it with a much wider group of stakeholders. This may dilute their influence over the outcomes of any such process and either promote or threaten a durable peace.

Often the parties to a peace negotiation are not entirely inclusive or representative of the wide range of constituent interests in a state, and disproportionately represent security actors. Whenever constitutional issues arise, these security actors will have an outsized influence on the constitution that is drafted or the process by which it is drafted. As such, these stakeholders may seek to cement authoritarian power, establish a primary role for the military in postconflict governance, or forge institutions and structures that perpetuate the marginalization of less powerful stakeholders. On the other hand, it is not necessarily a given that the security environment will allow for widespread public engagement and deliberative negotiation in constitution-drafting and approval processes immediately after the signing of a peace agreement.[8] A substantial delay to wait for the security environment to improve may undermine what limited stability is created by the agreement.

The intensity of negotiation over constitutional principles and the cooptation of ongoing constitution-drafting processes by belligerents to achieve political objectives under the threat of force has led some authors to refer to such negotiations as "conflict constitution-making."[9] A conflict constitution-making process transforms constitution-drafting into a so-called battlefield, deepening divisions among drafters, preventing consensus, and leading to boycotts or rejections by stakeholders.[10] Though the parties to a peace negotiation may outwardly strive for a participatory constitution-drafting process, if the conditions within the state remain highly contentious, constitution-drafting embeds the conflict in the new legal framework of a state, rather than alleviating the conflict drivers.[11]

CONCEPTUAL AND LEGAL PRIMER

With respect to the issue of constitutional modification, there are a variety of legal norms that are relevant and important. Constitutions are a foundation for the domestic rule of law within a state, specifying "the rules by which law is made, interpreted, applied, enforced, and changed."[12] Creating these legal structures is at the core of a state's legitimacy, asserting a commitment to rule of law and a larger legal framework of norms, principles, and customary practice.[13]

An essential element of this legal framework of norms, principles, and customary practice is the notion of "participatory" constitution-drafting. The International Covenant on Civil and Political Rights, Article 25(a) codified this norm of participation.[14] The covenant provided that every citizen shall have the right and opportunity "to take part in the conduct of public affairs, directly or through freely chosen representatives."[15] A formal interpretation of this article, from the UN Office of the High Commissioner for Human Rights, more concretely ties its contents to constitution-drafting. The high commissioner formally noted that "citizens also participate directly in the conduct of public affairs when they choose or change their constitution or decide public issues through a referendum."[16]

Moreover, the UN Human Rights Committee has concluded that constitutional conferences and participatory constitutional reform processes align with Article 25(a) of the covenant.[17] In *Marshall v. Canada*, a case brought before the UN Human Rights Committee, representatives from the Mikmaq tribal society argued that their exclusion from the Canadian constitutional conferences was in violation of the International Covenant on Civil and Political Rights' Article 25(a).[18] These particular constitutional conferences had the objective of identifying and clarifying the rights of indigenous peoples in Canada.[19] The committee found that the constitutional conferences constituted the conduct of public affairs and required the representation of those interests, albeit approving indirect representation through elected representatives, and denying an absolute right to direct representation.[20]

The Human Rights Committee's 2006 state report on Bosnia similarly reinforced Article 25(a). The report indicated concern that the Bosnian constitution, and its election law, excludes "Others," persons who do not belong to the Bosniak, Croat, or Serb "constituent peoples" groups, from being elected to the House of Peoples and to the presidency.[21] The Human Rights Committee formally recommended that Bosnia "reopen talks on constitutional reform in a transparent process and on a wide participatory basis, including all stakeholders" under Article 25 of the International Covenant on Civil and Political Rights.[22]

In postconflict contexts since the late twentieth century, participatory constitution-making has increased.[23] This method rooted in international human rights norms can forge societal acceptance of a postconflict regime or constitutional order, allowing for more successful transitions out of civil conflict. Broad participation within decision-making processes, as endorsed by the covenant and the high commissioner, may assist with forging consensus and create a broadly accepted postconflict legal order following violent conflict.[24]

A number of parties have sought to act consistently with the International Covenant on Civil and Political Rights, and with Article 25(a)'s interpretation by the high commissioner in more recent constitution-drafting processes,[25] as in Kenya, the stalled Syrian Constitution Drafting Committee process, and in the case of South Africa. A number of global agreements[26] and every regional human rights charter also include language pertaining to the right to participation in state decision-making.[27]

Because of the nature of the puzzle and the focus specifically on constitutional modification, this chapter will not be engaging in a review of comparative state practice drawing from more established states that have created legal processes and procedures for constitutional modification.

This state practice, from which this book has drawn in previous chapters' sections on conceptual and legal primers, did not address processes for creating and implementing a system for postconflict governance in the same way, as we will see in our key state practice and conundrums sections below. Any type of historical analysis assuming what processes states such as Canada, Germany, Switzerland, or the United States devised to craft their constitutions will make sweeping assumptions about what those processes entailed and project lessons learned that are unlikely to apply to the key state practice we will examine in this chapter. Oftentimes, lawyers will project too great an importance onto historical case studies while neglecting to acknowledge the important differences between historical cases and contemporary realities, as well as the lack of definite information available about those historical processes.

As will be apparent with the following instances of key state practice and the conundrums, postconflict states are actively creating legal processes and procedures that govern how postconflict governance reforms are created and implemented. For practitioners and scholars, it is this comparative analysis that will prove most useful.

KEY STATE PRACTICE

This chapter draws on the following key state practice cases for a discussion of the various conundrums that the parties to a peace negotiation face when confronting the puzzle of whether and how to undertake constitutional modification in a way that contributes to a durable peace. The paragraphs that follow highlight the relationship between each peace process and constitutional modification. For more on these conflicts, negotiations, and agreements, consult the Appendix.

The mediators of the **Bosnian** Dayton Accords, a negotiation made possible by NATO airstrikes, a military stalemate, and successful shuttle negotiation, designed a dramatic, all-or-nothing negotiation strategy to put an end to the violent dissolution of the former Yugoslavia.[28] After being forced into isolation in Dayton, Ohio for three weeks in November 1995, the parties agreed to a sweeping set of accords. These accords included a complete constitution in Annex 4, containing twelve multipart articles and two sub-annexes.[29] The constitution negotiated at Dayton provided for new power-sharing arrangements, decentralization, citizenship rules, the rights of refugees, and human rights protections. The constitution and the peace agreement were accomplished through the drafting of one comprehensive set of accords, capitalizing off the momentum established by isolating the parties from the ongoing conflict.

In 1991, **Colombia** sought to end the conflict with the Revolutionary Armed Forces of Colombia (FARC) and other nonstate armed actors by modifying its constitution to provide for extensive devolution of power to the local level. These efforts failed, and the conflict continued until 2016 when the parties reached an agreement on a wide package of constitutional modifications. The agreement stipulated constitutional and legal reforms to ensure the political representation of the new political movement or party constituted by former FARC members.[30] Notably, the agreement mandated that the provisions within it that created the Special Jurisdiction for Peace, the cornerstone of the peace and reconciliation process, be incorporated into the Colombian constitution as a "transitional article."[31] The agreement was put to a referendum and was rejected by the Colombian people. The Colombian parliament then amended the agreement, which was approved by the Colombian Constitutional Court, and then implemented it without putting the agreement to a second referendum.

Following a civil war and a public referendum on the question of self-determination in **East Timor**, the United Nations Security Council established the United Nations Transitional Administration in East Timor to oversee East Timor's transition to independence in 1999. The transitional administration was granted a significant number of administrative authorities, including judicial, legislative, and executive powers.[32] In exercising these authorities, the transitional administration created a rapid, six-month-long constitution-drafting process, which included elections in 2001. While the process produced a constitution that entered into force a year later in 2002, a number of commentators noted that since the process moved so quickly the outcome suffered from a lack of full public participation.[33]

In December 1996, the parties to the conflict in **Guatemala** signed a comprehensive peace agreement that provided for the implementation of ten accords previously signed during the peace process from 1994 to 1996.[34] The agreement included a series of constitutional amendments, which intended to give marginalized and indigenous communities greater rights, representation, and recognition, as well as accomplish key democratic reforms.[35] After the peace agreement was signed, voters participated in a subsequent constitutional amendment referendum process. Voters faced an overwhelming number of amendments, misrepresentation, and oversimplification of particular amendments in the campaigning process, and the referendum failed.[36]

The Transitional Administrative Law for **Iraq**, decreed in 2004 by the Coalition Provisional Authority, served as an interim constitution for Iraq. This interim constitution set the process for creating a permanent constitution. The law set a period of six and a half months, with the possibility of an extension. A constitutional assembly was formed, made up of 55 members drawn from the 275 members of the Transitional National Assembly.[37] After the constitution was drafted, it was presented to the National Assembly and submitted to a public referendum. In October 2005, the constitution was approved by a majority vote. To ensure participation in the referendum by the Sunnis, who had threatened a boycott, the constitution-drafting committee agreed to add an amendment that created a constitutional review body after the referendum process had finished.[38] In 2007, the constitutional review body made further amendments to the constitution. The referendum process was designed to ensure a minimum level of support among the three main constituent populations of Iraq.

In an effort to end the conflict between the ethnic Albanians of **Kosovo** and Serbian forces in the territory of Kosovo, the international community convened mediation efforts in 1999. The mediators proposed a peace agreement, the Rambouillet Agreement, which contained a detailed interim constitution for Kosovo that established new democratic institutions to be overseen by an international administration. The Rambouillet process failed, and the war was only ended after a NATO humanitarian intervention. The United Nations Security Council adopted a resolution later that year that placed Kosovo under the administration of the United Nations Interim Mission in Kosovo. The UN gradually transferred its administrative responsibilities to interim authorities and, later, a permanent Kosovo government. In 2001, the United Nations created a Constitutional Framework for Provisional Self-Government in Kosovo to facilitate this transition. After violent demonstrations in 2004, and UN-mediated negotiations between Kosovar and Serbian officials, Kosovo's authorities declared independence in 2008.[39] A constitution was formally adopted later that year, after a drafting process one year prior.[40]

Following ethnic conflict between Slavic Macedonians and ethnic Albanians a decade after **Macedonia** achieved its independence from Yugoslavia, representatives from four Macedonian political parties negotiated the Ohrid Framework Agreement in 2001. The Ohrid Agreement ended the conflict and set forth specific modifications to Macedonia's constitution to address the root drivers of the conflict between the Slavic and ethnic Albanian Macedonian populations. The amendments focused on recognizing languages spoken by at least 20 percent of the population as additional state languages, mandating minority representation in government, goals for decentralizing the national government, and enhancing local governing bodies.[41]

In 2006, **Nepal's** Comprehensive Peace Agreement ended a twenty-year-long armed conflict between the Nepalese government and the Communist Party of Nepal.[42] The agreement provided the parties would draft an interim constitution based on an earlier twelve-point understanding.[43] In 2007, the reinstated parliament created the interim constitution. The interim constitution outlined the procedure for the negotiation and adoption of the future constitution.[44] After several failed attempts to establish the Constituent Assembly designated by the interim constitution to draft the permanent constitution, a permanent constitution was eventually completed in June 2015.[45] The constitution was approved by two-thirds of the second Constitutional Assembly, absent the Madhesh party representing much of southern Nepal.[46]

For three decades, **Northern Ireland** faced ethnonationalist conflict between Catholic Republicans and Protestant Unionists. After a series of deliberate steps to allow for an environment conducive to a successful peace agreement, the parties to the decades-long conflict engaged in multiyear talks to establish a political agreement tied to constitutional reform. The parties decided that the agreement, dubbed the 1998 Good Friday Agreement, would be put to a referendum in both Northern Ireland and Ireland. After a one-month campaign period, this agreement was approved in successful referendums in both Northern Ireland and Ireland.[47] The agreement created new power-sharing mechanisms and political reforms for the governance of Northern Ireland, which ended the seemingly intractable conflict.

Marking the end of the era of apartheid in **South Africa**, the parties to the peace process signed the 1993 interim constitution, which guided South Africa's transition to an inclusive, democratic state. As part of the peace negotiations, the parties agreed upon an interim constitution, which served as the peace agreement, and set forth a process for negotiating a permanent constitution. Elected Constitutional Assembly members and the Constitutional Court held hearings and consulted civil society and political representatives to gather input on the draft constitution.[48] After extensive public submissions from and consultation with individuals and public bodies, the Constitutional Court ratified the draft in 1996.[49] The constitution-drafting process was highly inclusive and deliberately planned. It resulted in a constitution that provided for significant human rights protections and a quasi-federal system of decentralization.

The 2005 Comprehensive Peace Agreement between **Sudan** and **South Sudan** set forth an interim constitution for Sudan, which provided for rather elaborate modifications to the governing structure of Sudan to allow for substantial power-sharing. The agreement also established separate institutions and governing arrangements for South Sudan.[50] The interim constitution served as the governing framework for South Sudan until it formalized its independence in 2011 through a referendum, a process also stipulated in the agreement.[51] At that point, South Sudan negotiated yet another interim constitution, which was perpetually extended through 2020.

Yemen's most recent constitution-drafting process began with the transition brokered by the Gulf Cooperation Council in 2011, aimed at resolving the Arab Spring-related uprising. The agreement called for a National Dialogue Conference to discuss key issues related to constitutional modification. The National Dialogue Conference then authorized the creation of a thirty-member Constitution Drafting Committee to draft the constitution according to the outcomes produced by the conference. The drafting committee was tasked with completing the constitution in six months. Amidst a Houthi insurgency, President Hadi announced the formation of the Constitution Drafting Committee. The committee was comprised of seventeen members who would deliberate over the course of a year,[52] a decision that was criticized for both expanding the timeframe and reducing the number of representatives from the National Dialogue's plan. Though the committee completed a draft constitution in 2015, due to the persistent lack of consensus, the constitution was never signed by all the parties and Yemen tipped back into a multiparty civil war.

CONUNDRUMS

When attempting to address the question of constitutional modification during the peace negotiations, the parties to the conflict regularly grapple with a thorny set of key conundrums, including: whether and how to address constitutional modification during the peace process; the timing of determining and executing a postconflict constitution-drafting process; whether to draft an interim constitution; whether to accomplish constitutional reform through amendments or drafting a full constitution; how to approve and finalize constitutional modifications; and whether and how to incorporate issues of human rights.

Addressing Constitutional Modification during the Peace Process

The first conundrum the parties face is whether and how to address constitutional modification during the peace process. Constitutional modifications that are focused on resolving the immediate conflict may cripple the long-term legitimacy and efficacy of the constitution. A peace process that spends too much time on difficult and contentious constitutional issues may also prolong the conflict or lead an otherwise stable peace process to relapse into conflict.

The contradictory needs of these two approaches require the parties to strike a difficult balance. The parties to peace negotiations have attempted to resolve the conundrum in various ways, including drafting a constitution as the peace agreement, attaching a constitution to the agreement, creating an interim constitution, or agreeing upon a future process (and timeline) for drafting a new or amended constitution.

In cases where the parties seek to amend the constitution, the existing constitution and corresponding legal framework often plays a significant and complex role in the peace negotiations, its relationship to constitutional reform, and its implementation. The parties are then faced with the conundrum of how to balance the legitimacy of the existing constitutional system with the need for swift changes to accommodate the peace process.

Approaches to Resolving the Constitution/Peace Process Conundrum

During the Dayton Peace Negotiations for Bosnia, the mediators and the parties chose to address this conundrum by agreeing to discuss a full constitution during the negotiations. The aim of so doing was to facilitate a swift end to a particularly violent war. After years of failed talks, and with a high likelihood that the parties would return to fighting in the spring, the mediators designed a dramatic, all-or-nothing negotiation strategy at Dayton. During the talks, the parties initially discussed the possibility of drafting a constitution after the peace agreement. The parties to the peace negotiation, however, perceived a final constitution-drafting process as a way to cement the gains they had made through fighting and chose to draft the constitution during the negotiations.[53] Through shuttle negotiation at Dayton, the parties approved a draft constitution that was attached to the agreement as Annex 4.

By attaching the Bosnian Constitution to the accords, the mediators avoided having to reconvene the parties for contentious negotiations over the future constitution, which may have undermined the tentative peace agreed at Dayton. This choice also averted the potential for one of the parties to withdraw from future negotiations.

The Dayton Accords as a whole achieved an almost impossible feat, ending a war and authorizing the deployment of 50,000 NATO troops to guarantee the peace. Drafting a permanent constitution during these negotiations, however, also ensured that the tensions that existed in the conflict were entrenched in the future governing structure. The short drafting period meant that the parties did not have the time necessary to build trust, move closer together, or envision a common future.[54] Rather than building a cohesive future state, each party focused on ensuring that the other two ethnic groups could not gain what they perceived to be disproportionate power. As a result, the parties failed to design a functional national government.

The strong influence of the parties is reflected throughout the constitution, which effectively served to perpetuate the ethnic tensions present during the negotiations.[55] The power-sharing mechanisms created in the constitution reflect the tense environment and deep ethnic divides present in the drafting process. By creating ethnic proportionality requirements in the new government, the constitution ultimately incentivized the parties to continue to campaign and govern with only the interests of their own ethnic group in mind.[56] This structure ensured that for years to come there was significant support in Bosnia for extreme political parties and little incentive to pursue political reconciliation or moderation.[57]

In South Africa's peace negotiations, which took place after two decades of conflict between state security forces and armed opposition groups, the issue of constitutional reform was a central tenet of discussions. Drafting a new constitution, through a representative process, was a key demand of the African National Congress.[58] In 1993, after two years of multiparty peace talks, the parties produced a peace agreement that also served as an interim constitution until the final constitution was adopted roughly three years later.[59] The interim constitution outlined the timeline and process for drafting a new constitution.[60] The interim constitution also created a Constitutional Court, and empowered the court to review the final draft.[61]

In the interim constitution, the parties agreed on thirty-four constitutional principles that would guide the future constitution, representing an elite consensus on key constitutional issues. These principles were designed to be binding on the future constitution, and covered such issues as antidiscrimination, separation of powers, protecting language diversity, and power-sharing.[62] As part of this peace agreement/interim constitution, the newly formed Constitutional Court was given the power to strike down a draft constitution that did not comply with these principles.[63] This multistep process ensured that the consensus gained in the initial peace negotiations would be retained in the permanent constitution, while also allowing for flexibility and a process that would grow more inclusive over time.[64]

In Colombia, the 2016 peace agreement between the Colombian government and the FARC aimed to achieve constitutional modification and the creation of new institutions geared towards transitional justice. Accomplishing such reforms could not be accomplished through the drafting of a peace agreement alone; unlike many other postconflict states, Colombia has a long history of constitutionalism and judicial review.[65] As such, Colombia's Constitutional Court played a significant role in the implementation of the 2016 peace agreement, producing a "highly judicialized peace process."[66]

During the negotiations, the FARC initially argued for a Constituent Assembly to draft a new constitution, hoping to create deep reforms and to cement the terms of the agreement throughout the constitution. Fearing that reopening the entire constitution could derail the peace process, the Colombian government rejected this proposal. The parties settled on a path through which key provisions of the agreement would be enshrined in the constitution through the traditional amendment process. More specifically, the parties agreed to put the 2016 peace agreement to a popular referendum and then submit it for approval to the Congress and the Constitutional Court.

After failing to win the referendum in October 2016 by less than 1 percent, the parties renegotiated parts of the agreement and signed a new agreement on November 24, 2016. The revised agreement included provisions that required the FARC to declare its assets and hand them over to the government for use in reparation payments and an adjustment of language that religious groups perceived to undermine family values. The revised agreement also imposed a limit of ten years for the transitional justice system, and required the FARC rebels to provide information about drug trafficking.[67] The parties to the peace negotiations chose to avoid the referendum the second time and instead went through the Congress and Constitutional Court, both of which approved the agreement.

By enacting laws associated with the peace agreement as part of the constitution, this process ensured that a high, two-thirds majority in Congress would be needed to undo the agreement. Colombian President Ivan Duque attempted in 2019 to modify the terms of the Special Jurisdiction for Peace included in the peace agreement, in response to public outcry that the mechanism was too lenient on former rebels. This two-thirds majority threshold, however, prevented him from gaining congressional approval, and the Constitutional Court rejected the changes as unconstitutional.[68] By integrating provisions of the peace agreement into the existing constitution through both congressional and Constitutional Court approval, this process also sought to uphold the existing constitution and the legitimacy of the existing rule of law.

When the negotiating parties are unable to agree upon a final constitution during a peace negotiation, an international administration may decide how the state will be governed immediately after the peace agreement is signed and design a process for how the future constitution drafting will take place, as in Kosovo.

In the Kosovo peace process, following months of negotiations to end the armed conflict, the Rambouillet Agreement set forth an interim constitution. The interim constitution established new democratic institutions for Kosovo.[69] The agreement, however, was not signed by the Serbian representatives and this interim constitution did not come into effect. Following a NATO intervention in Kosovo, the UN Security Council adopted Resolution 1244, which set out a path for a transitional international administration of Kosovo.[70]

The international administration governed Kosovo while gradually transitioning responsibility to the interim government. The international administration was also tasked with overseeing the resolution of Kosovo's final status and Kosovo's transition to a permanent, independent government.

In 2005, UN Special Envoy Martti Ahtisaari was assigned to oversee the negotiations for Kosovo's final status. After seventeen rounds of negotiations between Kosovar and Serbian officials, a final report was produced. The report recommended a structure for governance and called for a constitutional commission, to be appointed by the interim legislature.[71] The constitutional commission began drafting shortly thereafter, producing a final draft by the end of 2007. In February of 2008, Kosovo declared independence, announcing that it would approve a constitution within 120 days. After a period of public consultation, the Kosovo Assembly ratified a permanent constitution.

But for the initial stewardship of the international community, it is unlikely that the minority populations in Kosovo would have constructively engaged in the constitution-drafting process. While many, quite reasonably, argue that the delay was unnecessarily long, in the end Kosovo was set on a path of durable peace, and the constitution is well crafted and operates as a framework for an effective and inclusive democracy.

In the case of the Sudanese peace talks, the parties agreed that the constitutional negotiations would begin after the multitrack negotiations were concluded. The constitutional negotiations were naturally designed to include a broader representation of Sudanese society, given that the Juba negotiations were focused on reaching agreement between the state and marginalized regions such as Darfur, Southern Kordofan, the Blue Nile, the north, and the east.

To ensure that the constitutional negotiations did not undo or substantially modify what was settled on in the Juba Agreement, the parties specified that the peace agreed should hold supremacy over the subsequent constitutional decree. The parties decided that the Juba Agreement would be included or annexed to the constitutional decree, and that in the event of a conflict between the peace agreement and the constitutional decree, the decree would be amended to remedy such conflict.[72]

Each method by which parties choose to incorporate constitutional modification into the peace process poses its own challenges. To mitigate the potential risks, the parties face strategic decisions related to the timing of the constitutional process, the kinds of constitutional revisions undertaken, and how the constitutional process is ultimately approved.

Timing

Another early conundrum that parties face during a peace process is the question of how long the constitutional modification process should take, be it a part of the peace negotiation, or a separate process commencing after the signing of a peace agreement. Moreover, if the process for constitutional modification occurs after the signing of the agreement, when should that process begin?

If the constitutional negotiations take place too soon, the legacy of the conflict may overshadow the discussion and the parties may entrench aspects of the conflict in the constitution. Short drafting processes tend to be exclusive or favor former armed groups. One recent empirical study found that a longer period for the constitutional drafting process leads to a more durable peace as the parties have the time to develop trust and to structure functional compromises.[73]

If the parties wait too long to draft a constitution, however, the momentum for key changes may be lost and the conflict may resume. A longer period does not necessarily produce greater inclusion. In some cases, where the conflict features a popular uprising against an exclusive state government, inclusion may be greatest shortly after the conflict ends. In these cases, elite actors may strategically extend the timeframe to make the process more exclusive over time and to reduce momentum for serious forms.

Within the timeline as a whole, the parties must also decide when to negotiate particularly contentious issues. By negotiating divisive issues too soon, intense debate can derail the process or prevent progress on other issues. To avoid these outcomes, the parties frequently defer contentious issues to the future by drafting abstract principles, designing easy amendment processes, or delegating decisions to the future legislature.[74] These approaches can help the parties overcome sticking points to reach an agreement. By deferring issues to a later part of the process, this approach can also create future challenges in interpreting or implementing the constitution.

To balance these competing concerns, the parties and mediators make complex choices and predictions regarding the initiation, length, and sequence of constitutional modification. Often, issues related to timing can be defined by the role of mediators and the legacy of the conflict. In turn, decisions about timing define the extent and nature of reform, as well as the long-term legitimacy of the constitution.

Approaches to Resolving the Timing Conundrum

The Northern Ireland peace negotiations, which included substantial constitutional modification, lasted for twenty-two months. This extended timeline was designed to allow for gradual rolling agreements, and for the inclusion into the process of key nonstate actors. The negotiations initially began with small, interparty talks. Following these talks, elections were held for the public to select negotiators, in a voting system that ensured the inclusion of smaller parties.[75] The gradual inclusion of potential spoilers, smaller parties, and civil society groups also moderated the parties' positions and helped the parties to overcome previous gridlock.[76]

The negotiations also benefited from an incremental, multiyear series of efforts to address drivers of conflict and produce an environment conducive to peace.[77] In the years preceding the negotiations, nonstate armed actors were encouraged to transition to political parties and work within a political process, and the parties made efforts to address root causes of the conflict, including employment discrimination. The process also benefited from changes in British policy, greater coordination between the British and Irish governments, and increased American involvement.[78] The negotiations ended in April 1998, with the announcement of the Good Friday

Agreement. After a one-month campaign period, the agreement was approved in successful referendums in both Northern Ireland and Ireland.[79]

Frequently, however, the parties and mediators may only have a brief window of time to address constitutional issues before the conflict resumes. Following a popular uprising and the outbreak of civil war in Yemen, the Gulf Cooperation Council negotiated an agreement for Yemen's future that outlined a process for a transitional government and a path toward a new constitution.

The timeline for the constitutional process included five months for an inclusive national dialogue and four months for a constitution-drafting process, to be followed by a constitutional referendum and elections.[80] The process was designed to allow a brief window of time for public participation in order to build some sense of national cohesion necessary to create a durable constitution.

Although the National Dialogue extended its mandate to ten months, the large body of 565 participants made it difficult to achieve full agreement on key issues. While the participants agreed on a federal structure, they were unable to agree on the number of substate entities or on the boundaries.[81] Two months after the end of the National Dialogue, President Hadi, the interim president, appointed a seventeen-member Constitution Drafting Committee to draft the new constitution based on the outcomes of the National Dialogue and authorized it to spend a year preparing the new constitution.

In contrast to the positive role that gradual economic improvement played in Northern Ireland, Yemen's economic deterioration gradually eroded trust as the process continued.[82] Shortly after the creation of the Constitution Drafting Committee, the transitional government ended fuel subsidies, leading to mass protests that precipitated a crisis as the Houthis capitalized on unrest to move into Sana'a.[83] Notably, the parties saw the new constitution as essential to restoring peace, and continued the negotiations throughout the renewed conflict, even moving the Constitution Drafting Committee "off-site" to Abu Dhabi in the United Arab Emirates so that the committee could operate in a secure environment. As the Constitution Drafting Committee continued to work on the constitution, Yemen's economy, as well as its security situation, rapidly deteriorated.[84] Two days after the draft constitution was published, the Houthis rejected the proposed federalist structure. Shortly thereafter, armed conflict in Yemen reignited.[85]

Yemen's constitution drafting timeline offered ample time for public participation and expert deliberation. Unfortunately, the parties failed to take advantage of this and were delayed in securing consensus on key governance issues. Moreover, failing to prioritize economic reform in parallel to the reform of the state structure also proved detrimental, as the struggling economy and loss of fuel subsidies undermined the political process.

In East Timor, the transitional administration attempted to resolve this conundrum by deciding on a short, three-month timeline to quickly transition to a new government. In March 2001, the transitional administration issued Regulation 2001/

2, which outlined a constitution-drafting process in which the transitional administration would oversee elections for a Constituent Assembly. The Constituent
Assembly would then have three months to draft the new constitution.[86] Although
the deadline was ultimately extended to six months, East Timor's six-month process
represents one of the shortest constitution-drafting processes to take place outside of
a peace agreement.[87]

With international forces taking over security and administrative responsibilities
during the transition, domestic transitional leadership was able to focus on drafting
the new constitution.[88] This provided for a relatively fast drafting process that was
able to capitalize on momentum for a peaceful transition and quickly establish the
rule of law.

This short time frame also created several challenges for achieving a durable
peace, and disaffected groups criticized the timeline as being designed to fit the
international administration's interests in a quick and low-cost win, rather than the
long-term interests of East Timor.[89] Civil society groups that criticized the process as
rushed also questioned whether the decision to enforce a short timeline was
motivated by a genuine threat of violence or whether the threat of violence was
exaggerated in order to justify a shorter timeline.[90]

The short period allocated for elections for the Constituent Assembly meant that
the former opposition group, Fretilin, won the majority of the seats, while smaller
and newer groups struggled for representation. As a result, the Constituent
Assembly was dominated by one party.[91] With a majority of seats, Fretilin had
little incentive to compromise with other groups or to design constitutional limits
on executive powers.

Additionally, due to East Timor's lack of prior political representation, few
members of the Constituent Assembly had political experience or knowledge of
the key issues to be addressed in the constitution-drafting process. The short timeframe established by the transitional administration gave members little time to
develop these skills and knowledge, leaving some members and their constituencies
disenchanted and marginalized.[92]

In Nepal, the negotiating parties sought to provide sufficient time to enable a
diverse and inclusive constituent assembly to craft a durable constitution. Despite
this, the process was intentionally hindered in order to extend the time even further
as a means to enable elite recapture of the process. The constitution-drafting process
in Nepal began after a ten-year civil war between the monarchy and Maoist rebels
over political and economic exclusion. In 2006, a massive people's movement
tipped the scales of a military stalemate as millions of people participated in protests
and civil disobedience.[93] The momentum achieved through this movement
ensured that the process began with a high degree of inclusivity.

To meet the demands of the Maoists and minority groups, the political parties
agreed to elect a Constituent Assembly to draft the new constitution. The interim
constitution provided for elections for a 601-member body that would have two

years to discuss, debate, and draft the new constitution.[94] The first elected Assembly was remarkably inclusive in terms of regional, ethnic, and gender representation.[95] Civil society groups also advocated for even greater representation by establishing the Women's Commission and five commissions for historically marginalized minority groups.[96]

Political elites unwilling to accept the plans proposed by the majority strategically reduced the momentum over time. Outside of the confines of the peace negotiations, parties such as these elites that did not have much initial leverage, manipulated the agreed process for peace. For instance, by postponing votes in the first Constituent Assembly, elites avoided a vote on the proposed reforms and ran out the clock.[97] After waiting for the election of a second Constituent Assembly, whose participants were less representative of the country than the first Assembly, elites worked with a body whose participants were more amenable to elite interests.[98]

When stalling proved to be an effective tactic for avoiding significant reforms, the process, originally intended to last two years, prolonged into four years. Not until an earthquake literally shook the country and the political establishment did the Constituent Assembly move forward with agreeing to a new constitution.[99]

In South Africa, strategically stalling on a contentious issue proved to be beneficial to moving the constitutional process ahead. The parties to the peace negotiation struggled to reach agreement on issues related to land use and distribution. The African National Congress, representing the majority of black South Africans, believed that land reform was necessary to achieve economic equality. Groups within the African National Congress sought to weaken constitutional protections for existing property and to guarantee future land reform. The National Party, representing white South Africans, remained committed to protecting existing property rights, and they sought international support by predicting that land redistribution would lead to food insecurity.[100]

To resolve this issue, the drafters agreed upon language that highlighted key principles such as "equitable access to land." The drafters gave the future government the ability to take measures to redress historical discrimination in land tenure but did not specify exact programs. This allowed for a system that was amenable to change, defined by the National Assembly, and able to incorporate new information, such as new evidence showing that the National Party's fears of food insecurity had been overstated.[101] By deferring this issue to the future legislature, parties were able to reach an agreement that created a functioning and equitable democracy, while granting the future government the flexibility necessary to meet future challenges.

Another conundrum faced by the parties to a peace negotiation is the question of selecting an interim or permanent constitution as part of postconflict governance reform, a choice closely tied to the many tradeoffs examined in this section on timing.

Permanent versus Interim Constitution

As the parties to a conflict look to design a new constitution to structure their state, they face the conundrum of whether to immediately establish a permanent constitution or design interim structures for the transition period. Either approach can be implemented as part of the peace agreement, or come about as the result of a postagreement process established by the peace agreement.

The parties to a peace negotiation that are set on using a constitutional process to bring about changes to state structure, inclusiveness, and legal reform are often inclined to see a permanent constitution come into being as part of the negotiated agreement, or in the alternative as soon as possible after the conclusion of the negotiations. Yet as the parties increasingly settle conflicts through negotiated agreements rather than outright military victories, it is unlikely that state and nonstate armed actors engaged in armed conflict will readily reach consensus around the core pillars of a new permanent state structure.

Political theorists often conceive of the creation of a constitution as a defining moment in which a populace forms a social contract out of a unified understanding of its "demos, polis and territory." In reality, most states in the immediate aftermath of conflict lack such a unified understanding. Many are still experiencing bouts of violence and are struggling to build sufficient consensus between competing factions to ensure the cessation of hostilities.[102] Trying to establish deep, permanent, structural changes in such a contentious period can be challenging. It may feel "premature" to begin codifying a new constitutional order when many of the immediate security and humanitarian processes set out in the peace agreement have yet to conclude, or perhaps have not even begun.[103]

One way that the parties to peace negotiations have sought to overcome this dilemma is through the adoption of an interim constitution prior to the drafting of a permanent constitution. Interim constitutions are defined as "a constituent instrument that asserts its legal supremacy for a certain period of time pending the enactment of a contemplated final constitution."[104] They can be functionally understood as "temporary political frameworks that allow competing elites to continue negotiating fundamental disagreements in the near future."[105]

According to data from the Uppsala Conflict Data Program, interim constitutions have become significantly more prevalent in the last three decades, especially in states emerging from conflict. Since 1990, two-thirds of all states adopting interim constitutions were emerging from conflict.[106] Interim constitutions can be particularly appealing to states emerging from conflict as they provide an avenue for agreeing upon initial compromises relating to the political framework of a state, while preserving the possibility for renegotiation and allowing the parties time to build trust and consensus.[107]

This is particularly true in situations in which the parties continue to engage in sporadic or low-level violence. The adoption of an interim constitution may create the stability necessary for the parties to buy into the initial structural reforms and participate in a more comprehensive process for long-term reform embedded in a permanent constitution. According to a recent study, the interim period can "give parties a critical window of time during which to rebuild trust; facilitate an iterative process through which consensus can be built around complex or controversial issues; enable constitution-makers to test out new political and institutional arrangements; and allow for more meaningful public participation."[108]

An interim constitution, however, cannot simply serve as a way to pass the time while hoping for peace. In postconflict states, the conflict may have decimated many of the state's institutions. An interim constitution, even if temporary, is still the state's constitution for the transition period. In this way, the interim constitution "may serve the critical purpose of setting out an administrative roadmap to help quickly establish the basic infrastructure of a new governance regime, while still allowing flexibility to test out what works and what does not, before settling on a final form set of institutional arrangements."[109]

The parties to peace negotiations can establish "thick" interim constitutions that provide great detail for how the state should be governed or "thin" interim constitutions that are more limited in the amount of detail and specification they provide.

The parties are likely to arrive at a consensus on a thinner constitution faster than they would on a more extensive document. Depending on the military and political conditions, the parties may consider a thin constitution the only viable option at the time, committing to return to heftier questions when they draft a permanent constitution at a later stage.[110] Even so, relegating the tougher questions to the permanent drafting process can stall the creation of the permanent constitution. The parties may seek to extend the interim period to severely delay or even prevent the passage of key structural reforms.

One benefit that the parties identify in having this period in between the signing of a peace agreement and the drafting of a final constitution facilitated by an interim constitution is the ability to make the process of drafting and ratifying the permanent constitution more inclusive. Historically, constitutions that are quickly drafted immediately following a conflict have been primarily produced by a "small coterie of elites," who are often male, former combatants or unelected technical experts, and not representative of the public writ large.[111] A more participatory process typically requires more time because it necessitates a period of public engagement, education, and/or consultation.[112]

Approaches to Resolving the Permanent versus Interim
Constitution Conundrum

In 2004, Somalia adopted the Transitional Federal Charter of the Somali Republic, which provided a thin interim constitution that guided the transition period.[113] Thorny issues, such as wealth-sharing, were set aside to be determined later via legislation adopted by the transitional government.[114] Somalia then continued negotiating the more challenging issues until it adopted its 2012 Constitution, which was substantially more detailed. The permanent constitution, for instance, had an entire chapter devoted to land, property, and environmental principles that guided the allocation of these resources between the national government and its constituent member states. The constitution also contained significantly greater detail and specificity on topics such as devolution of power, state structure, and parliamentary duties.[115]

In other cases, the parties prefer to negotiate a detailed "thick" interim constitution as part of the peace agreement. For instance, Chapter 1 of the Rambouillet Accords provides a detailed interim constitution for Kosovo. The constitution was robustly designed with enough detail to establish new democratic institutions of self-governance for Kosovo.[116] Such detail was necessitated by the fact that Kosovo had been denied its right of internal self-determination by the Republic of Serbia and did not possess existing democratic institutions, or a functioning impartial and fair judiciary bound by the rule of law at the time of the Rambouillet negotiations.

Opting for a "thin" interim constitution, though often more expedient, can stall more permanent postconflict governance reform, as in Nepal. Nepal's 2007 interim constitution ushered in a new representative governing structure to replace the monarchy, but it did not include agreements on how key governance features of the state would operate. The parties lacked agreement on the federal state structure, electoral system, or judicial entities, amongst other aspects, and the parties negotiated and renegotiated these issues for years without significant progress.[117]

As previously mentioned in the timing conundrum, political elites in Nepal empowered by the interim constitution took the opportunity to stall the process of passing a permanent constitution to retain power as long as possible.[118] Stalling the process of implementing a permanent constitution be particularly problematic when thin interim agreements do not contain sufficient checks, balances, and civil protections.[119]

For instance, the 2011 transitional constitution of the Republic of South Sudan allocated a disproportionate share of power to the executive branch to compensate for the low governance capacity of institutions in the newly independent state. This interim transitional constitution had limited checks on presidential power. The constitution, for instance, specified a four-year term for the president, but set no limit on how many terms the president could serve.[120] Moreover, the constitution only minimally developed more inclusive or participatory bodies that could have potentially offset the executive branch. Combined with imprecision in the process by which a permanent constitution was to be drafted, the weak interim constitution allowed for South Sudanese politicians easily to manipulate it to their advantage.[121]

Many parties try to regulate the time interval between the interim and permanent constitutions by adding provisions to the interim constitution relating to the process by which a final constitution will be produced. The interim constitution for Kosovo included in the Rambouillet Accords, for instance, was written to govern Kosovo for three years, at which point,

> an international meeting shall be convened to determine a mechanism for a final settlement for Kosovo, on the basis of the will of the people, opinions of relevant authorities, each Party's efforts regarding the implementation of this Agreement, and the Helsinki Final Act, and to undertake a comprehensive assessment of the implementation of this Agreement and to consider proposals by any Party for additional measures.[122]

The period between the passage of an interim constitution and that of the permanent constitution varies significantly. Some states, such as Iraq, proceed from interim to final over a one or two-year period, while others, such as Kosovo and Nepal, take closer to a decade, and in certain cases, such as the Democratic Republic of the Congo and Rwanda, the process may exceed ten years.[123] Whether the length of the gap in time between interim and permanent constitutions supports or hinders the establishment of a durable peace depends on the context of the conflict and the conflict drivers the parties seek to confront with postconflict governance reforms.

When considering the adoption of an interim constitution, it is helpful for the parties to bear in mind that the conflict-alleviating potential of an interim constitution cannot be mistaken as a panacea for constitution-making in postconflict states.[124] In fact, between 1990 and 2015, "14 out of the 18–20 countries in which interim constitutions were created in conflict-affected settings either relapsed into conflict or never experienced a lull in conflict."[125] Any state emerging from conflict that seeks new constitutional arrangements will face obstacles. Postconflict constitution modification is an arduous challenge, one in which interim constitutions may be helpful, even while they bring their own difficulties.

Amendments versus Full Constitution

Another major conundrum that parties face when negotiating peace is whether to amend the existing constitution or craft an entirely new constitution. This debate frequently represents deeper disagreements about the nature of postconflict governance reforms. The symbolic importance of an amendment process or new drafting process can also be misused to mislead the parties about the nature of the reforms.

By amending an existing constitution, the drafters begin with the structure established in a previous constitution. This can allow the drafters to focus more narrowly on an amendment tailored to the drivers of conflict. In other cases, grafting an amendment onto the framework of an older constitution can constrain the transformative potential of the process. Constitutional amendment may be particularly palatable if there are only a few constitutional provisions with which one or more of the parties disagree.

A new constitution-drafting process promises a fresh start through which the parties can begin to envision a new future for the country. This more elaborate process also entails significant time, debate, and opportunities for disagreement.

Debating whether to amend the constitution or draft a new constitution may seem at first glance like a technical exercise. This debate frequently reveals deeper conflicts over the nature and scope of the reform necessary to resolve the conflict. The parties with greater power or structural advantages may argue for an amendment process to restrain reform and limit input, while nonstate actors often call for drafting a new constitution through processes that reflect a more inclusive vision of the future state.

Approaches to Resolving the Amendment versus Full Constitution Conundrum

Macedonia's Ohrid Framework Agreement stipulated the modification of Macedonia's existing constitution.[126] In the text of the agreement, the parties agreed on a suite of constitutional amendments that addressed the key drivers of conflict without redrafting the entire constitution.

The agreement modified several articles in the Macedonian constitution to emphasize and codify the "equitable representation of persons belonging to all communities in public bodies at all levels and in other areas of public life."[127] The amendments included formal recognition, protections, and services for speakers of minority languages; an extension of the freedom of religious expression, and clarification of the separation of religion and the state; and the creation of a committee for intercommunity relations.[128]

Rather than redraft the whole constitution, the Macedonian amendments were designed directly to confront the exclusions and omissions of the previous constitution, a driver of societal unrest and fragmentation leading to the outbreak of conflict. By focusing just on the provisions tied to conflict, the amendment process allowed the parties quickly to negotiate the peace and to embed the amendments within the peace agreement.[129]

While constitutional amendments present the potential for a more tailored and efficient process of postconflict governance reform, this is not always the case. In Guatemala's peace process, elites used an amendment process to introduce an overwhelming number of future reforms, confusing voters and obfuscating key reforms.

In Guatemala's 1996 peace agreement, the parties to the peace negotiation drafted fifteen constitutional amendments.[130] These wide-ranging amendments included formally recognizing Guatemala's indigenous peoples, creating reforms related to the role of police and armed forces, fixing the number of deputies in Congress, strengthening the judiciary, creating a career judicial service, specifying the duties of the president over armed forces, and delineating the jurisdiction of military courts.[131]

During congressional deliberations, however, lawmakers added forty-five additional amendments, bringing the total to fifty shortly before the public referendum.[132] By creating dozens of amendments on unrelated issues, the agreement's critics turned the amendments into an overwhelming amount of information that primed voters for the misrepresentation and oversimplification of the amendments in the referendum campaigns.[133] In the referendum, Guatemalans voted on four questions that represented the content of the fifty amendments, as well as the 297-page agreement. Voters ultimately rejected all the proposed amendments.[134]

In other cases, a government may strategically frame constitutional reform as an amendment process to downplay the scope of the reforms to the public, as in the case of South Sudan.

The 2005 Comprehensive Peace Agreement between Sudan and South Sudan included an interim constitution for South Sudan.[135] When South Sudan gained its independence, the new government undertook a process to transform the interim constitution into the transitional constitution.[136] Drafted during the peace negotiations, the interim constitution was drafted primarily by members of one party, the Sudan People's Liberation Movement, along with the government of Sudan. Given the exclusive nature of this process, civil society groups in South Sudan hoped that the transformation of the interim constitution into the transitional constitution would be a more inclusive process.

To avoid opening this process to the public, the new government of South Sudan claimed that the process was not a drafting process for a new constitution, but rather a narrow amendment process. By claiming that the process was only providing a "technical review" to amend the constitution, the government attempted to avoid calls for greater inclusion in the drafting process.[137] Rather than engaging in a more inclusive drafting process, the government instead convened a small Technical Review Committee and appointed members from the Sudan People's Liberation Movement.[138]

In response to pressure, the government allowed several members into the Technical Review Committee from outside of the Sudan People's Liberation Movement, although they remained a minority.[139] The government's claim provided a loose justification for an exclusive process, as the interim constitution had outlined a specific process for amendments that the government was not following.

Frequently, the debate over whether to amend the constitution or draft a new constitution aligns with larger conflicts over the extent of reforms that the parties want to see in the postconflict constitution. This issue became a major dynamic of the Syrian peace process that eventually centered on negotiations over constitutional reform.

In 2012, to appease Arab Spring protestors, the Syrian government appointed a small committee to amend the state's 1973 Constitution. The revised 2012 Constitution allowed for multiple parties and introduced competitive presidential elections. These reforms were considered insufficient by many of the opposition, who also questioned the adoption process. Despite opposition to the amendment process, the government continued to avoid the deeper reforms that would likely come with drafting a new document through a more democratic process.[140]

The question of whether to continue amending the constitution or draft a new constitution remained a major point of contention. In the Intra-Syrian Peace Process in 2019, after five years of peace negotiations, the Syrian regime continued to emphasize that it would only entertain amendments to the preexisting 2012 constitution. The moderate Syrian opposition, on the other hand, remained adamant that an entirely new document was essential to ensure effective and vital reform to the Syrian state.

When the parties engage in a drafting process for a new constitution in a genuine way, with ample time for debate and discussion, however, a new constitution can provide the necessary foundation for a new social bargain. In South Africa, debates over the nature of constitutional reform played a central role in the peace process. From as early as South Africa's independence from Britain, black South Africans resisted racially exclusive constitution-drafting processes. Likewise, opposition groups also resisted government attempts to mollify the opposition by amending some aspects of the constitution while retaining its overall structure. Organizations such as the African National Congress insisted that only a new constitution, drafted in an inclusive process where black South Africans were directly represented, would be sufficient.[141]

After two decades of conflict between state security forces and armed opposition groups, as well as growing external pressure to change, the white South African government relented to secret negotiations with the African National Congress that led to the signing of the National Peace Accord in 1991. To select the members of the new Constituent Assembly, which would also form the constitution-drafting body, the first nonracial elections were held in 1994.[142]

Two years later, the Constituent Assembly produced a new constitution and ratified it on May 1996. The new constitution was hailed as a landmark achievement and a model constitution. The constitution succeeded in transitioning the country into a postapartheid democracy and it introduced an extensive Bill of Rights that featured both political and comprehensive socioeconomic rights.[143]

While the new constitution could not fully remedy the legacies of colonialism that persisted through the unequal distribution of land and wealth, it succeeded in producing a political process through which continued reforms could be peacefully negotiated. The legitimacy of the new constitution and, in particular, the process through which it was drafted, encouraged the continued negotiation of grievances through further amendment processes, providing a new foundation and process for ongoing peaceful reforms.[144]

Structure does not necessarily guarantee a particular outcome or resolve these deeper conflicts. In both amendment and redrafting processes, the legacies of conflict can subvert the expectations and intended goals of the process, limiting or expanding postconflict governance reform in unexpected ways.

Referendums

The parties to peace negotiations that address constitutional issues have increasingly chosen to finalize either the peace agreement or the constitution resulting from a process determined by the agreement, through a public referendum.[145] A public referendum can be a tempting choice, particularly in cases where the public has been excluded from the drafting process. When referendums are successful, they can solidify public agreement at a key moment, providing essential legitimacy that can translate the new constitution into the foundation for the rule of law.

While an attractive option, a public referendum is also a risky choice. Public opinion is ephemeral; in a tense postconflict environment, it can be both difficult to measure and difficult to retain. Notably, it can be difficult to determine the public will, and, in some cases, the parties gravely misinterpret it. When subject to intense "no" campaigns in preparation for a referendum, otherwise solid public approval can slip through the parties' and mediator's grasp. Additionally, in many postconflict societies, there is also no singular "public," but rather multiple distinct identity groups. In these cases, the zero-sum nature of the voting process can reintroduce or reinforce ethnic and political tensions that drove the conflict.

Approaches to Resolving the Referendums Conundrum

Shortly after the signing of the Good Friday Agreement, Northern Ireland held a referendum to vote on the agreement.[146] As the majority of the negotiations had been conducted through secret back-channels, a public referendum was viewed as an important step for gaining public approval and legitimacy.[147]

For the agreement to take effect, a simple majority of the voters had to vote "yes." Given the stark division between Nationalist and Unionist communities, a vote that achieved a majority but revealed a stark divide between the two sides may have deepened divisions. Ultimately, however, the referendum achieved a majority approval overall of 71.1 percent. The agreement also received a majority approval within each community. Additionally, the referendum had a high voter turnout of 81.1 percent, lending legitimacy to the results as a means of translating public will.[148]

The short time frame between the signing of the agreement and the referendum may have contributed to its success, as the popularity of the agreement peaked immediately after it was signed.[149] The robust presence of a civil society-based "yes" campaign, which operated independently from the political parties, may also have helped the referendum avoid a politically divisive environment and result.[150] With majority approval from both communities shortly after the signing of the agreement, the referendum secured legitimacy at a key moment for the constitutional reform negotiated in the Good Friday Agreement.[151]

In divided postconflict societies, however, it can be difficult to determine how best to assess the will of the people in a manner that does not perpetuate divisiveness or disenfranchisement of the minority. Following the US intervention in 2003, Iraq drafted a permanent constitution and put it to a public referendum on October 15, 2005.[152] While the referendum was intended to provide a voice to "the public," Iraq's public remained deeply divided along ethnic lines, and these lines shaped both the referendum's structure and its outcomes.[153]

As the parties debated the referendum's structure during the drafting of the Transitional Administrative Law, Shia Arabs, representing a majority of the population, proposed requiring a simple majority for approval. The Kurdistan National Assembly instead proposed a referendum that would require a majority approval in the region of Kurdistan. As a compromise, the two groups agreed on a "de facto" veto, in which three provinces, such as the three Kurdish provinces of Dohuk, Erbil, and Sulaimania, could reject the constitution if two-thirds of participants in those provinces voted "no." While intended to leverage Kurdish power in the negotiations, this structure also presented the opportunity for a Sunni veto. In response to such a threat, mediators worked feverishly in the days before the referendum to secure enough Sunni votes to pass the referendum.[154]

The referendum was approved by a wide margin in predominately Shia and Kurdish provinces. In the three Sunni-majority provinces, it was voted down.[155] Crucially, the "no" votes exceeded two-thirds in only two of those provinces, one province short of a rejection of the draft.[156] While this outcome allowed the constitutional process to move forward, the divide in the votes also highlighted the continuing ethnic divides just as the permanent constitution was adopted.[157]

The amendments drafted in Guatemala's peace negotiations were also subject to a national referendum, which took place in May 1999. As noted, the referendum featured a series of four questions in which voters were able to approve or reject fifty constitutional amendments.[158] The amendments would have given greater rights, representation, and recognition to the marginalized, indigenous communities through the Agreement on the Identity and Rights of the Indigenous People. The agreement also declared Guatemala to be a "multi-ethnic, multi-cultural, and multi-lingual" state, a significant shift from the country's previous structure, which had marginalized its indigenous majority.[159]

While the referendum was created as a method for achieving public approval of the final agreements, the binary nature of the referendum and the tense political environment surrounding it ultimately subverted this goal. By reducing fifty detailed compromises into zero-sum binaries, the referendum provided critics with the opportunity easily to oversimplify the amendments and what they represented. The "No" campaign capitalized on broad confusion by reducing the content of the accords to familiar ethnic and religious divides and encouraged elites to vote "no" based on racist fears of the indigenous majority.[160]

Additionally, while the referendum was technically open to all registered voters, this access was limited in practice for the indigenous majority, many of whom were located in rural areas. The lack of voter education and outreach, combined with the rapid addition of last-minute amendments, meant that many indigenous Mayans did not understand the referendum or its potential impacts. Of those who did, many could not afford the trips to the municipal centers where the referendum votes were held. Still others stayed home out of legitimate fears of violent reprisals for voting "yes."[161]

As a result, only 18.5 percent of registered voters participated in the referendum, and two-thirds voted "no."[162] Rather than creating greater inclusivity, the referendum process allowed elites effectively to backtrack on prior compromises under the guise of "public opinion" while using the final nature of the referendum effectively to close off future discussion.[163]

In Colombia, the parties chose to hold a referendum on the 2016 peace agreement. Both the FARC and the Colombian government agreed that a form of public approval was necessary to legitimize the agreement and the constitutional reform within it, which had been primarily negotiated behind closed doors. While the FARC preferred a constituent assembly to debate and approve the draft, the Colombian government feared that this might open the door to a redrafting of the whole constitution. The parties agreed instead on a popular referendum.[164] Early polls provided support for this decision, as they predicted a strong "yes" vote based on the public's support for the majority of the agreement's content.[165]

In the months leading up to the referendum, media campaigns from detractors narrowed in on the agreement's most controversial provision, de facto amnesties for former FARC rebels. This emphasis on just the most contentious provision effectively reduced the referendum in voters' minds from a vote on a number of broad issues to a vote on that provision alone, shifting more voters against the agreement. Combined with low voter turnout, this shift helped ensure a narrow rejection of an otherwise popular agreement, significantly reducing its overall legitimacy at a crucial moment.[166] Ultimately, this high-stakes gamble meant "what was gained in peacebuilding was lost in representation."[167] Not every provision was equal in the eyes of the voter. For this reason, voting on a number of provisions accomplishing significant constitutional reforms can be exceedingly difficult.

To solidify public opinion and legitimacy for a new constitution, the parties may be tempted to view referendums as an easy answer. Indeed, the parties have chosen to finalize constitutions through referendums with increasing frequency and are likely to continue to rely on referendums as a tool for public input.[168] Nonetheless, referendums can be risky gambles, in which parties must decide whether they are willing to risk losing the gains that they have won in the drafting process.

Human Rights

This chapter has, until this point, focused on the processes the parties to a peace negotiation agree for postconflict governance reform, including whether and how to incorporate constitutional reform into a peace process, timing, constitution-drafting, amendment-drafting, and referendums. Sometimes, however, the parties consider certain substantive topics within constitutions, such as human rights, to be so important that they are deliberately included in the peace agreement so as to ensure they are embedded in the new postconflict governance structure.

During peace negotiations, the parties are faced with whether and how to incorporate human rights into the agreement. Relatedly, the parties must determine the types of human rights to incorporate into a postconflict constitution, whether solely fundamental human rights or a more expansive view of human rights that also includes socioeconomic rights. In so doing, the parties often seek to balance the relationship between human rights enumerated within international treaties and potential conflicts with existing cultural or religious norms within that state.

Broadly defined, human rights are "the equal protection (within the rule of law) of individuals or groups inside a nation-state by the government, NGOs and private individuals."[169] The violation of human rights, whether political, social, or economic, is often a conflict driver. When discrimination by one group or a government transforms existing societal inequalities or privileges into antagonistic group identities, the potential for collective action and internal conflict within a state emerges.[170] Since the 1990s, as part of attempts to remedy conflict, human rights have become an increasingly integral part of conflict prevention and peacemaking.[171]

The pressures on the peace negotiation itself, related to timing, inclusivity of stakeholders, and the context of the conflict, impact the nature of human rights provisions detailed in the peace agreement. In seeking to resolve the series of conundrums related to incorporating human rights into postconflict constitutions, the parties must contend with a series of tradeoffs. While drafting a peace agreement and postconflict constitution, the parties often face pressure to reach an agreement quickly in order to resolve the conflict, which may inform whether and how human rights are incorporated in the final text. At the same time, the parties drafting a postconflict constitution often aim to create a document that will govern, if not fundamentally transform, the state for years to come.

The ways in which the negotiating parties decide to balance these sometimes-clashing interests can inform whether human rights are specifically enumerated within the constitution or included through references to existing human rights agreements; whether human rights are included through a fundamental or more expansive lens; and whether a domestic cultural context is incorporated.

Drafting Rights or Affirming Existing International Human Rights Law?

Human rights can be individually enumerated within the language of a postconflict constitution or peace agreement to avoid ambiguity and include particular rights specific to the context of the state. This approach enables the parties to the agreement to set their own specific terms with regard to the protection and insurance of human rights and fundamental freedoms.

South Africa's 1993 interim constitution, which marked the end of apartheid and a transition to a democratic South Africa, included a chapter on fundamental rights. This chapter enshrined principles of equality within its twenty-nine sections, detailing such rights and freedoms as to life, dignity, assembly, association, movement, political participation, justice, economic activity, property, and language.[172] This extensive section in the interim constitution sought fundamentally to distinguish the future of South Africa from its apartheid past, which institutionalized racial discrimination and denied the majority of its population human rights. South Africa's 1996 constitution further formalized these human rights in a bill of rights, described in the text of the constitution as "a cornerstone of democracy in South Africa."[173]

Alternatively, some parties choose to cement to human rights and minority protections in postconflict constitutions by drawing from international treaties and covenants.

During the condensed, urgent drafting timeline of the Dayton Accords, human rights took center stage. The Dayton Accords contained annexes on several human rights issues, including the rights of refugees and the displaced.[174] Annex 6 of the Dayton Accords stipulated that the parties would ensure the internationally recognized human rights and fundamental freedoms of all within their jurisdiction, listing sixteen international human rights charters and conventions in an appendix to the annex.[175]

The new constitution for Bosnia laid out in the Dayton Accords asserted that European human rights law "shall apply directly" and "have priority over all other law."[176] The inclusion of this language directly referencing the European Convention for the Protection of Human Rights and Fundamental Freedoms and its Protocols in the new constitution indicated Bosnia's desire fully to integrate into Bosnia's law the highest level of human rights protections. By affirming international human rights agreements in their constitution and peace agreement, the parties at Dayton sought to embed their vision of a postconflict Bosnia within international consensus on the topic of specific human rights, including language on the definition, provision, and protection of those rights.

The issue with implementing this sweeping vision of human rights in Bosnia is the degree to which Bosnian citizens were and are aware of their actual rights. For Bosnia to affirm a suite of treaties in its governing document demonstrates a commitment to human rights, but without enumerating those rights, the populace was less familiar with the precise content of those rights.

Somalia's 2004 thin interim constitution, the Transitional Federal Charter of the Somali Republic, combined these two approaches to incorporating human rights into a postconflict constitution. The charter included a provision that Somalia would recognize and enforce international human rights treaties to which it is a party, and then detailed out an extensive list of specific fundamental and socio-economic human rights.[177] Though this thin constitution did not address all issues motivating the conflict, as noted previously in this chapter, the parties chose to include a detailed enumeration of human rights.

Fundamental or Expansive Rights?

Once negotiating parties decide to include human rights in a postconflict constitution, they must determine the types of human rights that are enumerated: fundamental human rights or more expansive human rights, including socioeconomic rights.

Some parties to peace negotiations decide only to include fundamental rights in their postconflict constitutions. These fundamental rights include such rights as those included in the 1948 Universal Declaration of Human Rights, or political rights, such as those set forth in the International Covenant on Civil and Political Rights.[178]

During the Kosovo peace process in the midst of a devastating ethnic conflict, drafters of the Rambouillet Agreement constitution chose to prioritize fundamental human rights in the accords. The agreement broadly stipulated that all authorities and institutions in Kosovo would ensure and conform to internationally recognized human rights. Notably, the agreement directly provided that the rights and freedoms included in the European Convention for the Protection of Human Rights and Fundamental Freedoms and its protocols, rights which pertain to civil and political rights, would directly apply in Kosovo. In greater specificity, the constitution provided for expanded and concretized political and identity-based rights for Kosovo's national communities, a primary conflict driver. The constitution did not specify economic-based rights, though it provided the opportunity for the Kosovo Assembly to approve internationally recognized human rights agreements.[179]

Other parties to a peace negotiation may choose to incorporate a more expansive view of human rights, including rights to work or to property, in postconflict constitutions. Importantly, should the parties take a more maximalist approach to human rights in a postconflict constitution, but not follow through on implementing all aspects of those rights, the legitimacy of the fundamental rights upon which the expanded rights are based is minimized.

South Africa's 1996 postconflict constitution, cementing the transition away from apartheid, required the inclusion of both fundamental and socioeconomic human rights. The 1996 constitution arose from deliberate, detailed negotiations among the parties committed to creating a solid foundation for a new and democratic South Africa based on principles of equality. The constitution included a bill of rights that ensured fundamental human and political rights, such as equality before the law; freedom of religion, belief and opinion; freedom of assembly; right to political participation; and access to the justice system.[180] From an economic standpoint, the bill of rights included in the 1996 constitution also included freedom of trade, occupation and profession; rights to fair labor practices; rights to organize in unions; and rights to collective bargaining.[181]

Incorporating Cultural or Religious Context

Throughout the postconflict constitution-drafting process, the parties may also need to account for specific cultural or religious contexts when determining which rights to enumerate or reference. This may create tensions as domestic or religious legal frameworks come into conflict with international human rights frameworks.

Yemen's 2015 draft constitution, written as part of the larger peace process, included an expansive view of human rights. The draft constitution included fundamental rights such as equality before the law, as well as a series of detailed socioeconomic rights.[182] This chapter of the draft constitution also included an article that guaranteed all these rights and freedoms as long as they do not conflict with Sharia.[183]

Beyond the relevance of Islamic Sharia to considerations of human rights, Sharia is mentioned several additional times in Yemen's 2015 draft constitution. The draft constitution sought to develop a common understanding of Islamic Sharia, which it defined as the source of legislation. The draft constitution ensured that inheritance, and the defining of Zakat authority, an independent regional institution that collects Zakat (alms) from citizens, were established in accordance with provisions of Sharia. The draft constitution also created the Ifta Council, an institution through which Sharia was to be deliberated.[184]

The establishment of the Ifta Council represented a Yemeni effort within the state's constitution to establish a common understanding regarding the legal relevance of Islamic Sharia. The creation of the Ifta Council addressed disagreement surrounding intent, understanding, and application of Sharia. The council was established to operate as an independent national institution comprised of Sharia scholars from varied jurisprudence doctrines. The aim of the council was to interpret and support the understanding of Islam and Islamic studies, while promoting values of tolerance and moderation.

The two articles of Yemen's 2015 draft constitution that followed the article stipulating that human rights and freedoms were guaranteed (lest they come into conflict with Sharia) provided that assault against these rights would be punished, and all state authorities would enforce and apply the rights and freedoms stated in the constitution.[185] In this case, the parties managed to include both extensive protections of human rights while acknowledging the importance of the domestic cultural and religious context. Because the 2015 Yemeni draft constitution was never implemented and conflict resumed, it has yet to be seen whether a provision like this, when implemented, can allow for both Sharia law and an expansive view of human rights to coexist, or if it would limit the reach of those human rights.

Somalia, likewise, attempted to incorporate both the cultural and religious context of the state and a desire to include greater human rights in its constitution. Somalia's 2004 interim constitution included a chapter entitled "Protection of Fundamental Rights and Freedoms of the People," which detailed equality of citizens before the law regardless of race, birth, language, religion, sex, or political affiliation.[186] Coexisting with these provisions of human rights, Article 8 of the interim constitution marked Islam as the official religion of the state and Sharia as the base source for all national legislation.[187] After the transitional federal charter was adopted, however, violence carried out by insurgents demanding a greater presence of Islam in the government of Somalia continued.

The government formally adopted Sharia as the law governing Somalia in 2009 in an effort to unify the state and quell violence by insurgents using Islam as a justification for antigovernment violence.[188] Attempting to merge a constitutional framework with specific cultural and religious contexts can pose a distinct challenge for states, as codifying this context in law sometimes comes into conflict with a number of provisions of international human rights frameworks.[189] This tension is heightened when there are multiple interpretations of that cultural and religious context, or where a state has a number of primary cultural and religious identities. This challenge is heightened in a state with only a transitional governing authority and ongoing civil unrest, as in Somalia.

Successfully navigating the difficult choices of determining whether to incorporate principles of international human rights law, minimalist or maximalist definitions of human rights, and particular domestic cultural and religious practices into a postconflict constitution can address conflict drivers and pave the path to a durable peace.

CONCLUSION

Addressing constitutional modification, or establishing a process to do so after the coming into force of the peace agreement, can be an effective way of mitigating conflict drivers. Constitutional modification can remedy imbalances in representation, create more inclusive political institutions, enhance the protection of political and socioeconomic rights, and provide for more genuine democratic representation. A postconflict constitution may lay the foundation for a durable peace and equitable governance, but for it to do so, the parties to a peace negotiation must weigh approaches to several distinct conundrums. Despite the risks of committing a misstep while determining the processes for postconflict governance reform, the parties see including constitutional reform as an increasingly important component of peace negotiations.

The parties in postconflict peace negotiations have the opportunity to undertake constitutional modification in a number of ways, depending on the needs and context of the conflict at hand. The parties may agree to strategic amendments, as in the case of Macedonia, which modified the existing legal framework. The parties may also choose to make the peace negotiations and the constitutional negotiations one and the same while momentum exists between the parties to the conflict, as in the case of Bosnia and the Dayton Accords, which resulted in a new constitution for the state attached as an annex to the agreement. Elsewhere, as in Nepal and South Africa, the parties may agree to the creation of an interim constitution to end the violence and put off the negotiation of a permanent constitution to a later, specified or unspecified, date. Notably, though the parties in these contexts selected forms of constitution-making that reflected the political will of their specific situations, each faced its own challenges following peace negotiations, and its own degrees of governmental dysfunction.

As a riskier strategy, the parties may take on postconflict constitution-making processes that are highly ambitious, or that may be easily manipulated to cement the conflict within a state's legal structure. As noted with the case of East Timor, a plan for a six-month constitution-making process set out by the international administration did not leave time for the parties to the constitutional negotiations to develop sufficient expertise. According to some commentators, this resulted in a document that fit the international administration's interests rather than the long-term interests of East Timor. In Guatemala, the parties used peace negotiations as a window of opportunity to catalyze sweeping governance reforms through constitutional amendments, only to have the process coopted and corrupted by the political elite during the amendment referendum process.

The numerous key state practice cases highlighted in this chapter – Bosnia, Colombia, East Timor, Guatemala, Iraq, Kosovo, Macedonia, Nepal, Northern Ireland, Somalia, South Africa, Syria, and Yemen – underscore the mixed outcomes that similar processes for postconflict governance reform can have depending on the particular postconflict setting. As with the cornerstone issues discussed in previous chapters, successfully ensuring that postconflict governance reforms within the larger conversation of a peace negotiation lead to a durable peace and not a return of conflict requires the parties to carefully consider every conundrum they will likely face in the drafting process.

Conclusion

As the introduction notes, no corner of the globe is exempt from the scourge of deadly and durable armed conflict. Yet in the face of seemingly intractable conflicts, state and nonstate parties are time and again able to reach a negotiated compromise that leads to a durable peace. At other times, unfortunately, the process is rushed or misconceived and the peace is short-lived or never reached. In both cases, there are lessons to be learned with regard to how to solve the various puzzles and associated conundrums faced by parties seeking to design resilient peace agreements and establish a durable peace.

When grappling with the puzzle of how best to create a secure environment to contribute to a durable peace, and in particular how and whether to share and/or reestablish a monopoly of force, the parties often recognize that without creating the conditions for an end to armed conflict, deescalating violence, and reestablishing a monopoly of force, resolving the other puzzles discussed in this book would be impossible. Security and the monopoly of force provide the basis for state legitimacy, a key component of establishing power-sharing arrangements, creating resource-sharing structures, enabling postconflict governance, and, if necessary, forming a smooth path to external self-determination.

Prior to the negotiation of a peace agreement, a state often shares its monopoly of force with international actors, such as United Nations peacekeepers, to facilitate bringing about an end to the conflict. A state may then continue to share this monopoly of force with the same or different international actors during the initial stages of peace agreement implementation. This sharing of a monopoly of force by the state may be initiated by the state, or may be, to a degree, forced upon a state.

Negotiations relating to the sharing of force with the international community are multidimensional and occur multiple times throughout the peace process. They often, but not always, involve all the parties to the conflict, and they often also include various representatives of the international community, including the mediators, the UN Security Council, and states providing peacekeeping or peace-enforcing forces.

This sharing of the monopoly of force, which can occur under Chapter VI or VII of the UN Charter, is heavily dependent on the consent of the state and of the nonstate actors, including nonstate armed actors. The sharing of consent with nonstate actors is in and of itself a risky, yet often necessary, dilution of the state's sovereignty. The precise mandate for any international actors sharing a state's monopoly of force, and the configuration of that force and its command structure, must be carefully considered and calibrated by the parties and the relevant international actors. This is necessary to avoid either an insufficiently mandated and configured force, or a force with so much authority that it displaces a state's ability to exercise a monopoly of force, such that the parties in the postconflict setting are unable to rapidly reestablish a state monopoly of force.

As parties discuss whether to reestablish a state's monopoly of force, there is seldom consensus if the monopoly should be regained by the state immediately or shortly after signing a peace agreement as there is frequently deep mistrust between the state and the nonstate armed actors. This animosity makes "losing" parties less willing to relinquish their ability to use force. This is especially true of cases where the state's forces have committed atrocity crimes, which decreases the willingness of the nonstate armed actors to recognize the state's claim to exercise legitimate violence. Given that nonstate armed actors typically come into being specifically to challenge the state's monopoly of force, they are unlikely to readily concede a full return to a state monopoly of force. As such, postconflict states often enter a period of full, yet modified, control over the monopoly of force via the integration of the forces of nonstate armed actors into the national army and police. In these situations, it is imperative to design and implement comprehensive programs for DDR and SSR, and to provide for a nuanced regional or international peacekeeping force.

In other situations, the state is only able to restore limited control over the monopoly of force by permitting nonstate actors to maintain their forces and command structure under the umbrella command of the national forces. These instances are particularly fraught with risk, and often lead to further conflict. To avoid such conflict, it is often helpful to pursue a degree of DDR and SSR in parallel to permitting substate entities to maintain their own armed forces, and to maintain a consensual presence of international forces.

When grappling with the puzzle of how best to craft power-sharing arrangements to secure a durable peace, and in particular how and whether to create vertical power-sharing arrangements, the parties must contend with the fact that nearly all contemporary conflicts are driven in part by political marginalization. This political marginalization amplifies the consequences of economic and cultural marginalization. To craft a durable peace, parties to peace negotiations often spend considerable time and effort crafting power-sharing arrangements that balance the pull of some parties for greater diffusion and devolution of political power with the pull of other parties to maintain a degree of political centralization, both for the sake of efficiency and effectiveness and to preserve their prior political and economic privileges.

If these competing interests are not effectively harmonized, and the agreement not carefully crafted, the structure created by vertical power-sharing arrangements may, in fact, increase the likelihood of a return to armed conflict. Vertical power-sharing is often a tempting panacea to some of the most prominent underlying causes of conflict, including unequal access to resources, representation, and security. Yet a poorly conceived vertical power-sharing arrangement may paralyze the national government, fail to meet the reasonable expectations of the constituents of substate entities, or even embolden some substate entities to seek external self-determination. A well-crafted vertical power-sharing arrangement, however, can significantly contribute to a durable peace. The devolution of power increases the likelihood that the primary parties to the conflict are absorbed into the postconflict governance structure and thereby generates an interest in the immediate and future success of those governance structures.

The parties to conflict frequently determine modifications to a state's structure during the peace process. While the parties to peace negotiations frequently opt for a devolved unitary state structure, negotiating parties increasingly opt for a transformation to a federal state. If parties choose to implement federalism as a method of vertical power-sharing, doing so comes with several risks. Transitioning to federalism can raise serious potential for gridlock and governing inefficiency, slowing essential governance processes and potentially delaying other key reforms. The parties must also grapple with how to pivot to a federalist structure without immediately unraveling an already fragile state that may not have sufficient resources or governing capacity to implement a significant transformation.

In instances where one substate entity is especially focused on decentralization and the remainder of the state's regions are in favor of a unitary system, the parties can opt for an asymmetric state structure. In so doing, the parties must be careful not to undermine the interests of those substate entities not assuming decentralized powers, and also maintain the ability of the state to govern effectively.

States may find asymmetric structures to be particularly beneficial in facilitating decentralization in a manner that is responsive to the differing capacities of substate entities. The negotiating parties have to pay careful attention so that devolving power asymmetrically to one substate entity does not entice previously uninterested substate entities into pushing for their own devolved powers. An asymmetric structure can also breed resentment between substate entities if some entities perceive that others are receiving disproportionate rights and benefits that they are not afforded.

Once the parties have determined the state structure, the next compelling question is the allocation of legislative and executive powers among the various levels of government. The negotiation over the allocation of authorities across various levels of government in a postconflict context reflects the macro-power struggle between the national government, which wishes to retain its grip on power, and substate entities, which agitate for greater autonomy and power. Often, substate entities point to drivers of conflict such as marginalization, lack of autonomy, and underrepresentation in government to support their claims for greater devolution of powers to the substate level in a postconflict system of vertical power-sharing. Meanwhile, the national governments often assert that newly established substate entities lack the capacity to execute the powers devolved to them, supporting their desire to retain power at the national level and transfer powers down to substate entities at a later time.

In many instances, the parties may seek a compromise through an extended list of powers concurrently held by national and substate governments. Concurrent powers may be especially useful in contexts where substate entities are new or have limited governing ability, as is often the case in postconflict states. Concurrent powers may also be needed to handle governance issues in which both the central state and substate entities have a significant interest. Concurrent powers, however, can lead to significant gridlock and destabilization within the state if not effectively managed. As states transition to a decentralized framework, a lack of clarity in defining the authorities allocated to each level of government may create confusion, dysfunction, and a general lack of coordination between jurisdictions, so it is imperative for the parties to establish formal mechanisms for cooperation, coordination, and dispute resolution.

Once the parties decide which levels of government will possess decision-making authority over which powers, they must decide whether that authority includes political, administrative, and fiscal decision-making, or a subset of these three. The debate among the parties often revolves around designing a system that operates effectively and efficiently, or that represents genuine and effective change from an earlier system that perpetuated marginalization.

Initially, the parties representing the substate entities often focus almost exclusively on political decentralization, as they want to reverse political marginalization and exclusion by possessing the power to make decisions on matters of central importance to their region. National government officials are often reluctant to devolve too much political decision-making to the substate entities, as this creates an inconsistent patchwork of laws, rules and regulations across the state, and increases the financial burden on the state to maintain the various parliamentary and executive bodies necessary to carry out this local decision-making. Without a significant degree of political decentralization, however, the substate entities are unlikely to accept an agreement, and thus the parties must carefully design the devolution so that it is narrowly tailored to address the specific drivers of conflict, and not just a general shifting of power from the central to the substate levels of government.

A similar approach must be undertaken with the devolution of the power to implement or administer the political decisions made by the substate entities. Here, again, the parties representing the substate entities will seek to obtain as much control as possible over the implementation of the devolved powers. Often, though, substate entities have a serious lack of capacity to operationalize the powers devolved to them by the national government, creating new governance challenges and gridlock in the provision of basic services. Unfortunately, local governments often lack capacity due to long-term marginalization. Yet to allocate decision-making authority but deny the authority to implement those decisions due to a lack of technical capacity will only serve to perpetuate that lack of technical capacity. The negotiating parties can overcome this by designing a gradual transfer of administrative authority or transfer of national-level personnel coupled with the training of local-level personnel.

Despite the vexing nature of political and administrative devolution, the thorniest issue is how to fund the devolution of power. Successful fiscal decentralization relies on a baseline level of trust between local governments and the national government, something that is often lacking in postconflict states, especially where a substate entity maintains a long-term interest in external self-determination. Without this trust, national control over revenue authority limits the autonomy of substate entities to drive their own policy and may negatively impact their ability to execute political and administrative authorities.

The solution lies in devolving commensurate levels of financial authority with the devolved political and administrative authorities. An unbalanced devolution can undermine the durability of an agreement by granting a sub-state entity political and administrative authority that it is simply unable to implement. Too much fiscal devolution can bankrupt a state and inhibit the ability of the national government to undertake the multitude of reforms often necessary to ensure more inclusive governance and security sector reform. To ameliorate these tensions, states often create formal mechanisms for local integration in national institutions, budgeting committees, or other mechanisms for vertical integration of local representatives at the national level of government.

Having sorted the state structure and identification of devolved powers, the parties must face the question of what timeline will be sufficient to allow the parties to effectively implement their chosen approach to decentralization without delaying implementation so long that one or more of the parties loses confidence in the process, prompting a return to conflict. A consistent undercurrent surrounding the question of timing is the conundrum of whether the state has the capacity or the infrastructure successfully to devolve powers immediately, or whether doing so increases the likelihood that decentralization destabilizes or overwhelms the state. The negotiating parties can overcome this conundrum by benchmarking and sequencing the devolution of power with a plan for devolution in stages, with each stage containing steps necessary to lay the foundation for the next stage of the transition.

When grappling with the puzzle of how best to craft arrangements for natural resource ownership and management and revenue allocation, the parties contend with the fact that access to natural resources and the allocation of revenue generated by resource exploitation is at the core of many conflicts and plays an important role in many others. Efforts to solve the puzzle of whether and how to address natural resource ownership, management, and revenue allocation in a manner that promotes durable peace are complicated by the fact that natural resources can be both a driver of the conflict and a key factor in promoting a durable peace.

When a fragile state possesses an abundance of natural resources (particularly oil and gas), it faces a substantially increased likelihood of intrastate armed conflict, and an increased likelihood that the substate entity involved in the conflict will seek external self-determination as a means to resolve the conflict. Moreover, political elites frequently capture resources, which leads to unaccountable governance structures, which then in turn act as a conflict driver.

The tension relating to the ownership or control of the natural resource often mirrors and is interwoven with other conflict drivers, such as political and economic disenfranchisement. If a general governance issue exists, then there will certainly be a governance issue relating to the ownership and management of natural resources. As such, over time, what starts as a conflict over political rights may evolve into a conflict over the ownership of natural resources.

The effective management of natural resources as the result of a peace agreement, however, can also substantially promote the durability of that agreement. The revenue generated from the management of those resources can serve as a near-immediate and highly visible peace dividend that demonstrates the real and practical value of peace. The funds generated from the management of the natural resources can also provide a ready fund to pay for reconstruction and the implementation of various aspects of the peace agreement.

When the parties seek to negotiate a durable peace in a conflict that entails natural resources, they must first determine if and when to broach the subject in the peace process. Negotiating the ownership, management, and revenue allocation of natural resources during a peace process can help the parties to achieve a durable agreement, especially if tensions over resources drove the conflict. Alternatively, including discussions of natural resources can derail the peace process if it is too contentious an issue among the parties. In some cases, the parties have sorted the issue as the first agenda item in negotiations, creating momentum for resolving the remaining issues, while in others they have left it to the very end of the negotiations so as not to forestall the resolution of other crucial issues. While timing is important for most of the issues in a peace negotiation, natural resources appear to be the issue for which the question of timing is most crucial.

Once the parties determine the timing of discussing natural resources in the broader context of negotiations, they frequently address the technical matters of ownership, management, and revenue allocation. The conundrum of determining natural resource ownership is the most high-profile and emotional puzzle the parties to a peace negotiation can face, yet it is often the least important question they address, making it immensely difficult to negotiate. Often, each party to a conflict desires to have complete ownership of the contested natural resource. No party to the conflict wants to concede ownership of a resource that could prove to be immensely valuable in the future.

While the parties may know or have an idea of the extent of the existing resource reserves, by their nature it is not possible to know the complete extent of future reserves. This can create complications if a substate entity agrees to share ownership with the national government, only to discover years later that oil reserves exist elsewhere, suddenly shifting the incentive to share ownership with the state. Given the complexity of the ownership issues, the negotiating parties sometimes default to opaque language about ownership "by the people." It is, however, exceedingly difficult to implement natural resource ownership by "the people" in a postconflict context.

Other parties opt for national ownership, which, if not coupled with some degree of significant oversight, can perpetuate drivers of conflict such as capture of resource revenue by political elite, and corruption. As such, in postconflict contexts, the parties rarely agree to exclusive ownership of a resource by the national government. In some instances, the parties agree to asymmetrical ownership, which is a form of shared ownership in which one substate entity owns significantly more of a resource than other substate entities, and may have a greater share than the state. Increasingly, the parties to peace negotiations opt for shared national–local ownership, which is designed to enable a higher degree of community and local involvement in exploitation policies and greater control of revenues to spurn local development. With shared ownership, substate entities maintain control over substantial portions of their oil resources, while also allowing the national government to regulate the transportation of oil interregionally and internationally.

When the parties turn to management, they are faced with the conundrum of how to provide for efficient management when an eclectic array of interested parties each seeks to have a role in management processes. Delegating the power of management to a single party may be more efficient, but it is not inclusive of all the interests at play in a peace process. Despite the importance of the question of management, the parties frequently opt not to include any provisions for management in the peace agreement, and rather defer that discussion to the implementation phase of the peace process. This is in large part due to the technical expertise required to reach a consensus on management, and that expertise is seldom at the negotiating table.

If the parties decide to negotiate natural resource management, there are several component parts that are often included in the negotiations, each of which can be negotiated separately and requires a degree of background technical knowledge, including extraction management, existing and future contracts, the authority to contract, and the creation of joint mechanisms. Moreover, each of these components can be placed under the purview of national, regional, or local governments, or a combination of all three.

When the parties turn to the question of revenue allocation, the primary conundrum the parties face is how to allocate revenue in a way that is fair and equitable for all of the parties that perceive an entitlement to a share of those resources. In reaching this determination, the parties must assess the validity of the claims for a share of the resources, deal with the frequent misperception of an abundance of resources, and balance these claims with the need to fund the effective operation of the national government.

Generally, the negotiating parties settle on one of three approaches to revenue collection and allocation: direct collection and retention by national or local governments; collection into a single account and then subsequent sharing based on an agreed formula; or a hybrid approach. The key to a successful allocation of the revenue is transparency and accountability, coupled with a process to reevaluate the allocation formula to align with evolving needs of the state and substate entities, and the depletion of the resource.

When grappling with the puzzle of how best to manage the question of self-determination, and in particular the process for external self-determination, the parties contend with the clash between the principle of sovereignty and the principle of self-determination. When seeking to negotiate a path that contemplates external self-determination, the parties and mediators are often guided by the need to balance the state's desire to design a path that will ultimately preserve the option of retaining the unity of the state, and the substate entity's desire to design a path that will preserve the option for independence. The substate entity also usually seeks to ensure that if the final status is unity, there is extensive internal self-determination for the people of that substate entity.

Moreover, the international community and the substate entity are guided by the desire to ensure that, in the event the substate entity achieves independence, the newly formed state is functional. The parties are also, to a degree, interested in ensuring that statehood for the substate entity does not destabilize neighboring states or lead to further conflict between or within the parent state and new state. To balance these interests, the parties often agree to a process of earned sovereignty, which encompasses a period of shared sovereignty, institution-building, a process for determining final status, the phased assumption of sovereignty, conditions on the assumption of sovereignty, and constraints on the exercise of sovereignty.

When a state and substate entity share sovereignty, the state devolves to the substate entity's specified political, administrative, and financial authority and functions. In some cases, the powers devolved are ones typically associated with a highly autonomous province. In others, nearly all the powers of the state are allocated to the substate entity in partnership with the international community. With each peace agreement, the relevant provisions for shared sovereignty may vary according to the duration of the window of shared sovereignty, the substantive nature of the powers shared, whether the powers are also shared with an international entity, and the purpose of sharing those powers, be it to create an opportunity for capacity-building and institution-building and/or to induce the substate entity to remain a part of the parent state.

In order to carry out shared functions and authorities, it is necessary for the substate entity to establish effective institutions of governance. It is doubly important for the substate entity to create those institutions in the event it opts for independence after the period of shared sovereignty. Effective institutions of democratic governance are also necessary to prevent a return to conflict or to prevent the emergence of a new conflict within a newly independent state. Given the importance of institution-building, peace agreements often seek to provide for the creation of effective institutions from the initial stages of any interim period, and often involve the support or engagement of the international community.

Depending upon the nature and characteristics of the conflict, it may not always be possible to achieve even preliminary power-sharing arrangements, and may thus be necessary to incorporate an element of phased sovereignty. Phased sovereignty involves the measured devolution of sovereign functions and authority from the parent state or international community to the substate entity during the period of shared sovereignty. Phased sovereignty can be useful to promote a smooth transition in those contexts where the adversarial claims of the parties do not allow for immediate devolution of powers. The timing and extent of the devolution of authority and functions may be correlated with the development of institutional capacity and/or conditioned on the fulfillment of certain benchmarks, such as democratic reform and the protection of human rights.

To promote effective implementation of power-sharing through functioning democratic institutions, the transfer of sovereign authority to the substate entity or the determination of final status may be conditioned upon the fulfillment of certain benchmarks. Some peace agreements condition the phasing of sovereignty on the achievement of a satisfactory level of good governance and legal guarantees. This includes protection of human and minority rights, disarmament and demobilization, development of democratic institutions, establishment of the rule of law, and promotion of regional stability.

The most hotly contested conundrum is how to assess the "will of the people" to determine whether a substate entity should remain an autonomous part of the parent state or become an independent state. The answer in its simplest form is that there should be a referendum; from there, it becomes complicated. When should the referendum be held? Who is eligible to vote in the referendum? What is the precise question to be put to the people? What percentage of the people must vote in favor of the question, and is a minimum voter turnout required? Is the outcome of the referendum binding on the parent state? Is it binding on the international community? Can the referendum be repeated at a later point in time? If a new state is established through the referendum, what are the boundaries of the new state?

In order for a substate entity to become a state, it is necessary that it be recognized by other member states of the international community. Given that states that are not parties to the peace agreement play a role through recognition in the transformation of a substate entity to a state, and because the emergence of new states may be destabilizing to the immediate region, the sovereignty of the new state may sometimes be constrained by the international community. The potential for destabilization arises from the fact that the new state, even after a lengthy period of institution-building, remains incapable of exercising effective authority, or from the new state's existence in and of itself, which can create a destabilizing political dynamic. Constrained sovereignty thus involves the imposition of continued limitations on the sovereign authority and functions of the new state. Such constraints include prolonged international administrative and/or military presence and limits on the right of the state to merge with another state.

When grappling with the puzzle of how best to craft a comprehensive legal framework for postconflict governance to secure a durable peace, and in particular whether and how to address a modification of the constitution during peace negotiations, the parties must contend with the fact that the parties often are not able to determine each detail of the system for postconflict governance during the peace negotiations. Rather, the parties often agree to a preliminary set of principles coupled with a general governing framework. They then set forth an agreed process for negotiating, designing and implementing a national dialogue, the drafting or amending of a constitution, and elections. In some limited cases the parties are able to address constitutional amendments or the development of a conflict constitution during the peace negotiations.

When addressing constitutional modification in the negotiations, the parties have attempted to resolve the conundrum in various ways, including drafting a constitution as the peace agreement, attaching a constitution to the agreement, creating an interim constitution, or agreeing upon a future process (and timeline) for drafting a new or amended constitution.

As is to be expected, the parties primarily act out of their self-interest when determining a process for creating and implementing a system for postconflict governance. Notably, however, when negotiating a modification of the constitution, or a process for post-agreement modification of the constitution, it can be exceedingly difficult for the negotiating parties to foresee which options will best serve their interests. With other topics in a peace negotiation, such as external self-determination or a monopoly of force, the consequences of particular choices are more apparent to the parties to the negotiation. The parties thus find it exceptionally difficult to address constitutional modification and to agree upon the ultimate substance of a postconflict constitution.

How the parties approach constitutional modification can either lead to a durable peace or contribute to a relapse of conflict depending on the circumstances. The risks are augmented by the fact that often the parties to a peace negotiation are not entirely inclusive or representative of the wide range of constituent interests in a state, and disproportionately represent security actors. When assessing how to approach constitutional modification during the peace process, the parties are faced with the fact that constitutional modifications focused simply on quickly resolving the immediate conflict may in fact cripple the long-term legitimacy and efficacy of the constitution. Yet a peace process that spends too much time on difficult and contentious constitutional issues may also prolong the conflict or lead an otherwise stable peace process to relapse into conflict.

The contradictory needs of these approaches require the parties to strike a difficult balance. In cases where the parties seek to amend the constitution, the existing constitution and corresponding legal framework often play a significant and complex role in the peace negotiations, its relationship to constitutional reform, and its implementation. The parties are then faced with the conundrum of how to balance the legitimacy of the existing constitutional system with the need for swift changes to accommodate the peace process. As a consequence, the parties must determine how long the constitutional modification process should take, be it a part of the peace negotiation or a separate process commencing after the signing of a peace agreement. If the process for constitutional modification occurs after the signing of the agreement, the parties must also determine when that process should begin.

If the constitutional negotiations take place too soon, the legacy of the conflict may overshadow the discussion and the parties may entrench aspects of the conflict in the constitution. Short drafting processes tend to be exclusive or favor former armed groups. If the parties wait too long to draft a constitution, however, the momentum for key changes may be lost and the conflict may resume. To balance these competing concerns, the parties and mediators make complex choices and predictions regarding the initiation, length, and sequence of constitutional modification. Often, issues related to timing can be defined by the role of mediators and the legacy of the conflict. In turn, decisions about timing define the extent and nature of reform, as well as the long-term legitimacy of the constitution.

The parties often seek to ameliorate these risks by putting the amended, interim, or final constitution to public approval via a referendum. A public referendum can be a tempting choice, particularly in cases where the public has been excluded from the drafting process. When referendums are successful, they can solidify public agreement at a key moment, providing essential legitimacy that can translate the new constitution into the foundation for the rule of law.

While an attractive option, a public referendum is also a risky choice. Public opinion is ephemeral; in a tense postconflict environment, it can be both difficult to measure and difficult to retain. Notably, it can be difficult to determine the public will, and, in some cases, the parties gravely misinterpret it. When subject to intense "no" campaigns in preparation for a referendum, otherwise solid public approval can slip through the parties' and mediator's grasp. Additionally, in many postconflict societies, there is also no singular "public," but rather multiple distinct identity groups. In these cases, the zero-sum nature of the voting process can reintroduce or reinforce ethnic and political tensions that drove the conflict.

In many instances, the parties will also decide during the negotiations to set parameters around how the system of postconflict governance will operate, such as by affirming specific human rights protections. In some postconflict contexts, there are principles that are so important to the resolution of the conflict that the parties articulate them specifically in the peace agreement. The parties may also create supremacy clauses in the peace agreement that provide the peace agreement with priority legal status in relation to the new or amended constitution.

Ironic as it is, armed conflicts are seldom resolved through a military victory; rather, they are settled through negotiations once the parties have concluded that it is not possible to achieve their objectives through the use of force. Unfortunately, many of these negotiated agreements fail to bring about a durable peace. The path to a sustainable peace instead lies in the parties and mediators accurately identifying the puzzles facing the parties, detailing the issues, and then methodically addressing the conundrums that make up these puzzles. Working through each conundrum and agreeing and drafting comprehensive and cogent legal provisions is the most effective path to a lasting peace.

Appendix: Summary of Key Peace Agreements

Aceh–Indonesia
Angola
Bosnia and Herzegovina
Bougainville–Papua New Guinea
Burundi
Colombia
Darfur–Sudan
East Timor–Indonesia
Guatemala
Iraq
Kosovo–Serbia
Macedonia
Mindanao–Philippines
Mozambique
Nepal
Northern Ireland
Rwanda
Sierra Leone
South Africa
Sudan–South Sudan
Western Sahara–Morocco
Yemen

This appendix contains a brief summary of each of the key peace agreements discussed in this book. For each peace agreement, the entry below sets forth the conflict drivers, including the nature of atrocity crimes, if any, the nature of the peace process, the core elements of the peace agreement, and the current status of implementation. This appendix is designed to provide a brief snapshot of the conflicts referenced in this book in order for the reader to have the necessary context to readily move through the substance of the chapters.

The conflict between Aceh and Indonesia was generally rooted in claims that the Acehnese community was not reaping the benefits of the exploitation of the region's widespread oil and gas resources.[1] Historic differences and colonialism operated as additional conflict drivers in the Acehnese armed struggle for independence from Indonesia.[2] Religious differences, concerns over migrants, and widespread human rights abuses further fueled the conflict. Indonesia is not an Islamic state, although nearly 90 percent of Indonesians are Muslim, and the Acehnese sought to uphold and enforce Sharia law, or Islamic criminal law.[3] Mineral resources, such as oil and gas, make Aceh one of the wealthiest provinces in Indonesia, yet it is one of the poorest in terms of per capita income. Social concerns over the increase in Javanese migrants (primarily non-Muslim) to Aceh increased friction with the national government.[4] Finally, the contemporary failure of the national government to address human rights abuses seemed to spark the initiation of armed conflict.[5]

In 1976, the Free Aceh Movement formed as a nonstate armed actor with the mission of securing independence for Aceh.[6] The group received weapons and training from Libya and mounted an aggressive campaign of attacks against Indonesian military and police units. The Indonesian government under President Suharto mounted a counterinsurgency campaign characterized by excessive violence and even more human rights abuses. The resignation of President Suharto brought some measure of hope that the conflict might be peacefully resolved. President Habibie initially agreed to a number of concessions on Acehnese self-government, but failed to agree to hold members of the former administration accountable, which resulted in a return to violence by the Free Aceh Movement. The government stepped up its own attacks and repeated the abuses of the Suharto regime. By 2001, the Free Aceh Movement held control over most of Aceh.[7]

The conflict was particularly brutal, with the government responsible for somewhere between 10,000 and 30,000 deaths, along with extensive torture and sexual violence.[8] The Free Aceh Movement openly admitted to executing people they suspected of betraying the movement or collaborating with government security forces.[9]

Peace negotiations were intermittent throughout the conflict. In 2000, a "Humanitarian Pause" provided a temporary halt to the conflict, but it did not last long.[10] Next, a 2002 "Cessation of Hostilities Agreement" provided some space for negotiations, but ended when the Indonesian government declared a "military emergency" in Aceh in May 2003 and announced that it wanted to destroy the Free Aceh Movement once and for all.[11] In 2004, newly elected President Susilo

Bambang Yudhoyono personally committed to negotiations as a means of ending conflict.[12]

During the initial phases of the talks, Indonesia asserted that the Free Aceh Movement must fully disarm. The Free Aceh Movement refused to hand over its weapons on the basis that there was no means to secure the safety of its forces unless the government also redeployed its forces. The government was unwilling to undertake such a redeployment while the Free Aceh Movement retained its weapons and remained an effective fighting force.[13]

In December 2004, a 9.1-magnitude underwater earthquake caused a tremendous tsunami which devastated Aceh, killing over 128,000 people.[14] A flood of international humanitarian aid to Aceh and surrounding areas elevated calls for action to end the thirty-year conflict.[15] Seeing an opportunity for peace, former Finnish President Ahtisaari succeeded in negotiating a comprehensive peace settlement, the Helsinki Memorandum of Understanding (MoU), signed in August 2005.[16] A total of five rounds took place, with a major breakthrough in February 2005 when the Free Aceh Movement accepted "self-government" as opposed to outright independence, and agreed to disarm in exchange for the redeployment of Indonesian army forces.[17]

The Helsinki Memorandum of Understanding, formally titled the "Memorandum of Understanding Between the Government of the Republic of Indonesia and the Free Aceh Movement," is separated into six different sections: Governing of Aceh (to include political participation, the economy, and rule of law); Human Rights; Amnesty and Reintegration into Society; Security Arrangements; Establishment of the Monitoring Mission; and Dispute Settlement. Given Indonesia's sensitivity regarding sovereignty, the memorandum of understanding was characterized as a product of "private diplomacy." In 2005, the Indonesian parliament enacted legislation implementing the principles of self-government set forth by the memorandum of understanding.

Notably, the memorandum of understanding provided for asymmetrical devolution of all powers related to "public affairs" to the region of Aceh, as well as a number of other power-sharing mechanisms.[18] The central Indonesian government retained specific authority over foreign affairs, external defense, national security, fiscal matters, and freedom of religion.[19] The unitary state of Indonesia was highly reluctant to create any nationwide adjustments to the state structure, as it did not want to encourage or advance self-determination movements in other regions, such as West Papua. The parties thus agreed that the arrangements set forth in the peace agreement would only be applicable to Aceh, and that there would be no horizontal power-sharing with Aceh at the national level. Aceh accepted this limited degree of horizontal power-sharing in exchange for near total control over the oil and other resources on its territory, and the right to implement Sharia law. Aceh was also induced to accept asymmetrical unitary devolution rather than independence as a consequence of the devastating humanitarian and economic effects of the 2004 tsunami.[20]

The agreement also provided for an obligation on the part of Indonesia to facilitate the Free Aceh Movement's entry into politics,[21] the DDR of the movement's forces, and adequate funding for their reintegration into society. The agreement did not provide for the integration of those forces into the national army. Nor did it provide for amnesty for those in the Free Aceh Movement, or for a joint European Union/ASEAN monitoring mission to assist with the implementation of the agreement.

The Aceh peace process is generally considered successful because the government entered the peace negotiations with clear action plans and reasonable offers, including amnesty for the Free Aceh Movement and release of prisoners, and agreed to the substantial devolution of political power and control over natural resources. Moreover, the Indonesian political leadership has remained committed to a lasting peace. International support, negotiation confidentiality, and direct and informal talks between the parties were also key to the success of the negotiations. The agreement has, however, faced substantial criticism for the de jure and de facto amnesty for human rights abuses committed by both of the parties.[22]

ANGOLA

Angola is a former colony of Portugal that gained independence in November 1975 via the Alvor Agreement.[23] The struggle for independence produced three major political opposition groups: the National Front for the Liberation of Angola (FNLA), Popular Movement for the Liberation of Angola (MPLA), and National Union for the Total Independence of Angola (UNITA), whose rivalry significantly contributed to the Angolan civil war.[24] The failure of the power-sharing arrangement included in the Alvor Agreement plunged Angola into a decades-long civil war.[25] Though MPLA and UNITA joined forces to fight the Portuguese for independence, ethnic and ideological differences collapsed the alliance. MPLA was a Marxist organization that was most closely connected to the Portuguese colonial elite and comprised of a mostly urban Umbundu majority. FNLA and UNITA were politically right-leaning and comprised of mostly rural Bakongo and Ovimbundu people, respectively.

The Angolan civil war lasted for twenty-seven years. MPLA controlled the capital and Angola's oil reserves, gaining recognition from several African countries as the legitimate government of Angola.[26] Serving as a proxy conflict for the Cold War, MPLA was also supported by Cuba and the Soviet Union, while UNITA was supported by the United States. The civil war was fraught with atrocities, notably scorched-earth campaigns.[27] Massacres were common, with one of the most infamous being the MPLA massacre of UNITA members in Luanda after the 1992 elections, where some reports place the number killed as high as 30,000. By the end of the conflict, half a million Angolans had been killed, nearly half a million had fled the country, and over three million were internally displaced.[28]

The opposing forces negotiated a series of peace agreements and reached an impasse several times, with UNITA often violating agreements and reigniting conflict.[29] In 1991, the opposing forces signed a ceasefire agreement, the Bicesse Accord, which provided for the immediate integration of the state security forces and the UNITA forces.[30] The agreement collapsed. In 1994, the parties signed the Lusaka Protocol, which established a power-sharing arrangement between MPLA and UNITA within the Angolan government, granted amnesty for all parties for past acts, authorized a UN peacekeeping mission, and again attempted the consolidation of forces into a single national army.[31]

In 1996, the government adopted the Luanda Protocol, which sought to bring into the government those UNITA members that renounced violence and broke from the leadership of Jonas Savimbi.[32] After three iterations of a UN presence, which evolved from observing and monitoring to peacekeeping, Angola requested in January 1999 that the peacekeeping forces withdraw.[33] In 2002, Jonas Savimbi was killed,[34] and the Angolan forces defeated the UNITA forces. The remaining leadership of UNITA signed the Luena Memorandum of Understanding, which was primarily concerned with the demobilization and reintegration of the UNITA forces, bringing an end to the armed conflict.[35] Immediately before the signing of the agreement, parliament unanimously adopted a blanket amnesty for those involved in the conflict.[36]

UNITA successfully transitioned from a nonstate armed actor to a legitimate political party and regularly holds about a quarter of the seats in the Angolan Parliament.[37] One faction present at the time of Angolan independence, FLEC, remains militarized, but their cause is essentially unrelated to the Angolan civil war: They fight to gain independence for the Angolan exclave of Cabinda.[38]

BOSNIA AND HERZEGOVINA

Yugoslavia was once a Socialist Federal Republic comprised of Bosnia and Herzegovina, Croatia, Macedonia, Montenegro, Serbia, and Slovenia, with Kosovo and Vojvodona operating as autonomous provinces within the Republic of Serbia and all under the leadership of President Josip Broz Tito. With the fall of communism throughout Eastern Europe in the early 1990s and the corresponding widespread increase in nationalism, Yugoslavia experienced intense political fragmentation and a subsequent economic crisis.[39]

The rise in nationalism resulted in the Yugoslav wars, including the Bosnian War, which was considered to be the deadliest. Prior to the Yugoslav conflict, Bosnia and Herzegovina was a multiethnic republic within Yugoslavia. In 1991, 44 percent of the population identified themselves as Bosniak Muslims, 32.5 percent identified as Serbs, 17 percent identified as Croats, and 6 percent considered themselves

Yugoslavs.[40] The objective of Serbian nationalists within Bosnia was to obtain and centralize control over the fading Yugoslavian territory. Slobodan Milošević, the leader of Serbia, emerged as the leader of the Serbian nationalist movement that encouraged the forthcoming violence.

In 1989, Serbia adopted various amendments to its constitution that allowed Serbia to have extensive political and economic control of the provinces of Kosovo and Vojvodina. Ultimately, by 1991 the Croatians, Slovenians, and Bosnians all advocated for individual statehood. On June 25, 1991, Slovenia and Croatia declared their independence, which inevitably led to the first of the Yugoslav wars. In 1992, Bosnian citizens voted for independence in a referendum boycotted by Bosnian Serbs who sought their own autonomy.[41] Bosnia and Herzegovina achieved international recognition on April 6, 1992, and the war broke out the next day.

The Bosnian War lasted from April 1992 through November 1995, during which time between 100,000 and 200,000 people were killed and more than 2 million were forced to flee. Over the course of the conflict, Bosnia was essentially divided into two territories. One of these territories was the Republika Srpska, which, through a campaign of genocide and crimes against humanity, ethnically cleansed Bosniaks and Croats from that territory.[42] The second territory was the Federation of Bosnia-Herzegovina, which consisted primarily, but not exclusively, of Bosniaks and Croatians.

As violence peaked in 1995, the international community, acting under Chapter VII of the UN Charter, decided to intervene and essentially assume near-total control over Bosnia's monopoly of force, with NATO authorizing airstrikes designed to bring about an end to the conflict by forcing the Serbian forces into a genuine negotiation process.[43]

The overall crisis in the region is characterized as a genocide, particularly noting the massacre at Srebrenica, the siege of Sarajevo, and other grave human rights abuses that the International Criminal Tribunal has credited to the Serbian forces under the direction of Milošević and others, as evidenced by the indictments, with a small portion being committed by Croatian and Bosniak forces.

In July 1991, the parties to the conflict consented, via the Brioni Declaration,[44] to the creation of an ad hoc European Community Monitoring Mission. The declaration was followed a few days later with a memorandum of understanding, which was essentially a status of forces agreement, signed in Belgrade.[45] The Brioni Declaration launched what was to become a long and tortuous series of negotiations to first forestall, and then to end, the war in Yugoslavia, culminating in the Dayton Accords.

Over the course of its operation from July 1991 to December 2007, the scope of the mission expanded to include Bosnia, Croatia, Macedonia, Montenegro, and Serbia, with the mandate to collect and report to the EU on the military situation, engage in negotiations to resolve local conflicts, assist humanitarian organizations, monitor the human rights situation, and eventually report on violations of the Bosnian no-fly zone.[46] Building from the establishment of this extremely light monitoring mission, the nature and configuration of the international forces haltingly evolved to become increasingly militarized.

During this time, the international community moved from a deployment of 50 military liaison officers to the deployment of 39,000 peacekeepers. The international community then augmented the peacekeepers with an ad hoc, heavily armed Rapid Reaction Force with troops from France, the United Kingdom, and the Netherlands. The international community further augmented the force to include the use of NATO air power: first to enforce a no-fly zone, and then to provide air support for UN peacekeepers. Finally, as authorized by the Dayton peace negotiations, NATO deployed 50,000 troops, anchored by the American First Armored Division, to secure the implementation of the agreement.

After the Srebrenica massacre, sixteen states met in July 1995 at the London Conference to determine how to secure peace in Bosnia. In August 1995, NATO launched "Deliberate Force," which consisted of extensive airstrikes against the Serbian forces. On September 26, 1995, the parties entered into a sixty-day ceasefire, which paved the way for the Dayton peace negotiations. In November 1995, the parties agreed to the Dayton Accords, which were subsequently signed in Paris on December 14, 1995. The accords provided for the deployment of a NATO-led implementation force, and a UN civilian police force to ensure observation of the peace agreement.[47]

The general framework of the Dayton Accords consists of eleven articles, which establish general obligations between its signatories. The bulk of the Dayton Agreement is its eleven annexes that establish more specific details about NATO's involvement, the protection of human rights, vertical and horizontal power-sharing, and the return of refugees and internally displaced persons.[48] The annexes include an Agreement on Military Aspects of the Peace Settlement, Agreement on Regional Stabilization, Agreement on Inter-Entity Boundary Line and Related Issues, Agreement on Elections, Constitution, Agreement on Arbitration, Agreement on Human Rights, Agreement on Refugees and Displaced Persons, Agreement on the Commission to Preserve National Monuments, Agreement on Bosnia and Herzegovina, Agreement on Civilian Implementation, and Agreement on the International Police Force.[49]

Other prominent provisions of the Dayton Accords placed responsibility for key elements of the transition to peace with various international actors. For instance, organizing the first free elections was assigned to the Organization for Security and Co-operation in Europe.[50]

Under the framework established by the Dayton Accords, the Republic of Bosnia and Herzegovina is comprised of the Federation of Bosnia and Herzegovina and the Republika Srpska.[51] These two entities each have their own constitutions and while there are some authorities afforded only to the national government, powers are largely devolved to each of the substate entities. This is complemented by a system of extensive horizontal power-sharing, including a rotating presidency, a vital interest veto, a House of Peoples, and regional quotas in the national government.[52]

Lastly, there was an agreed need for international actors to monitor the implementation of the agreement. NATO's implementation force was deployed after the signing of the agreement in December of 1995. In short, all military aspects of the agreement were transferred to NATO.[53]

The Dayton Accords, and the deployment of 50,000 NATO troops, secured a durable peace in Bosnia. The constitution included with the accords, however, created a highly dysfunctional system of government that has promoted the perpetuation of nationalism, entrenched corruption, and stunted economic growth.

BOUGAINVILLE–PAPUA NEW GUINEA

The opening of the Australian-owned Panguna Mine in 1972 worsened living conditions and created new tensions in Bougainville, a region in Papua New Guinea and part of Australian territory until 1975.[54] Approximately 10,000 workers migrated to Bougainville to work in the mines, which caused economic tensions between Bougainvilleans and non-Bougainvilleans.[55] These tensions were augmented by the environmental destruction caused by the mine, and the failure of the operating company to compensate the local community for the damage, or to implement greater environmental controls at the mine.[56] As a consequence armed secessionists formed the Bougainville Revolutionary Army to seek independence from Papua New Guinea.

The Bougainville Revolutionary Army was initially an environmentalist guerilla group, and later evolved into an ethnonationalist rebellion against the Papua New Guinea police and the Papua New Guinea Defence Force, sparking a nearly ten-year-long civil war from 1988 to 1998.[57] An estimated 20,000 Bougainvilleans, mostly civilians, died in the conflict.[58]

In 1997, the Bougainville Revolutionary Army and Papua New Guinea held peace talks and reached an initial ceasefire called the Burnham Truce; and in January 1998 the Lincoln Peace Conference in New Zealand led to a permanent ceasefire.[59] In August 2001, the government of Papua New Guinea and leaders representing the people of Bougainville signed a joint agreement known as the Bougainville Peace Agreement. The agreement was signed in Arawa, Bougainville and intended to further the objectives of the 1997 Burnham Truce and the 1998 Lincoln and ceasefire agreements.[60]

The agreement focused on ending hostilities by establishing a comprehensive plan to secure Bougainville's autonomy, provide an opportunity for independence, and ensure the demilitarization and demobilization of the nonstate armed actors. The initial phase of autonomy included the creation of a Bougainville constitution, an autonomous Bougainville government, support for human rights, and the reform of the police, prisons, judiciary, and the criminal law code. The agreement also envisioned a program for fiscal independence of Bougainville. The agreement proposed a referendum on Bougainville's future political status, which provided an option for independence and was to be held 10–15 years after the election of the autonomous Bougainville government. The peace agreement granted amnesty for all persons involved in crisis-related activities and did not establish a truth commission or any form of tribunal.[61]

The Bougainville Peace Agreement is largely considered a success. The measures agreed upon within all three pillars (autonomy, referendum, weapons) were implemented and relatively well maintained. The Papua New Guinea Defence Force withdrew in 2001.[62] Bougainville held a nonbinding independence referendum from November 23 to December 7, 2019. Over 180,000 people in Bougainville (98 percent of the vote) voted overwhelmingly in favor of full independence from Papua New Guinea. However, given the referendum is nonbinding, independence for Bougainville must be negotiated between Bougainville and Papua New Guinea leaders, and so Bougainville currently still exists as an autonomous region within Papua New Guinea.[63]

BURUNDI

Burundi has an extensive history of tension among ethnic groups, dating back to precolonial times. German colonial rule from 1893 until 1916 and the subsequent Belgian mandate exacerbated these ethnic tensions. Europeans favored the Tutsi minority at the expense of the Hutus, supporting Tutsi economic and political dominance and affirming the systematic exclusion of the Hutu population. The ethnic hierarchy perpetuated by the Europeans operated as a conflict driver by aggravating the social and economic differences between the Tutsi minority and Hutu majority.[64]

Burundi attained independence in 1962 under Tutsi leadership, prompting thousands of Hutus to flee to avoid ethnic violence. In 1966, ethnic Tutsi Michel Micombero led a successful *coup d'état*, abolished the monarchy, and established a presidential republic.[65]

In 1972 an all-Hutu organization known as the Burundi Workers' Party carried out systematic attacks on ethnic Tutsis, with the intent to eradicate the Tutsi population. The Tutsi military regime responded by targeting Hutus, systematically massacring approximately 150,000 Hutus, forcing thousands into exile, and depriving the Hutu population of political power. The following decades of the postindependence period were increasingly fraught with ethnic violence and political instability.[66]

The Burundi Civil War began in October 1993, after the assassination of the first democratically elected Hutu President Melchior Ndadaye. Approximately 150,000 died in the weeks immediately following the assassination. Violent acts included Hutu-perpetrated massacres against unarmed Tutsis and a Tutsi-led army assault on

Hutu civilians. The conflict in Burundi is remembered for the acts of genocide, crimes against humanity, and war crimes such as premeditated murder, torture, rape, extrajudicial executions, arbitrary arrests and imprisonment, and wanton destruction of public and private property.[67]

The Burundi peace process included a variety of facilitators and successive agreements. In June 1998, the first round of negotiations was held in Arusha, mediated by former Tanzanian President Mwalimu Julius K. Nyerere. Representatives from all the relevant parties to the conflict participated in these negotiations, including the government of Burundi, opposition political parties, nonstate armed actors, and representatives of civil society from commerce, women's, and youth organizations. A temporary cessation of hostilities was considered but not formally agreed.[68]

A second round of negotiations took place in Arusha between 1999 and 2000, mediated by South African President Nelson Mandela. In August 2000, the parties signed the Arusha Peace and Reconciliation Agreement and began the process of implementation and reform.[69]

The 2000 negotiations in Arusha resulted in the Arusha Peace and Reconciliation Agreement, with five protocols spanning ninety-three pages. While the agreement was signed by the Burundi government and sixteen armed movements and political parties in 2000, it was not until 2003 that all major parties to the conflict signed the ceasefire agreement. The comprehensive Arusha Agreement called for a permanent ceasefire, political and constitutional reform, judicial and administrative reform, security and defense reform, power-sharing provisions among relevant political parties, the establishment of transitional institutions, the rehabilitation and resettlement of refugees, and the protection of human rights. The agreement called for a multiparty political system, guaranteed free and fair elections, and created a Ceasefire Commission to ensure the implementation of the ceasefire provisions. The agreement also outlined the role of the international community in the implementation of this agreement, as well as in the social and financial development of Burundi.[70]

The 2000 Arusha Agreement was reinforced by subsequent peace agreements, notably, the 2003 Pretoria Protocols on Political, Defense, and Security Power Sharing in Burundi, which provided positions in the transitional government for the rebel group turned political party, the National Council for the Defense of Democracy-Forces for the Defense of Democracy, that had previously rejected the ceasefire in 2000. The 2003 Global Ceasefire Agreement and the 2006 Dar-es-Salaam Agreement on Principles Towards lasting Peace, Security and Stability in Burundi further supplemented the 2000 agreement.

Since the signing of the Arusha Agreement by all major parties in 2003, the majority of provisions have been fully implemented and Burundi has made significant progress in implementing the social and political systems devised by the peace agreement.[71] While some rebel groups initially resisted the restrictions of the agreement, the primary political parties ultimately agreed to a power-sharing agreement during the transitional period. The parties have continued to respect the agreement, and the negotiations served to mitigate ethnic tensions, build trust between Hutus and Tutsis, and establish more democratic and just state institutions.[72]

Despite such progress, Burundi continues to face challenges of political division and insecurity. Political tensions fall primarily along intra-Hutu divisions, and several political groups lack confidence in the legitimacy of the state's democratic elections. Some commentators accuse the governing party of detaining opposition groups, and several opposition figures have fled the country. This suggests Burundi could conceivably tip back into conflict, though few commentators believe there is an imminent risk.

COLOMBIA

Colombia has been defined by protracted violence and deep political divide across the country's liberal, conservative, and communist forces since the formation of the Conservative and Liberal parties in the mid-1800s.[73] These political tensions culminated in two civil wars in the early twentieth century. In 1899, "The War of the Thousand Days" between Liberals and Conservatives claimed 120,000 lives and lasted until 1902. By 1946, the newly elected Conservative government began reversing previous Liberal reforms and relying upon violent tactics to execute new reforms. The 1948 assassination of Jorge Eliever Gaitain, a Liberal Party presidential candidate seen as a symbol of hope for many Colombian farmers and rural citizens, prompted a series of countrywide uprisings collectively known as *La Violencia*. The violence lasted from 1948 to 1957 and resulted in nearly 300,000 deaths.[74]

By the conclusion of the country's second civil war, the Revolutionary Armed Forces of Colombia (FARC) had risen to national prominence. The FARC, a Marxist–Leninist guerilla group, was founded in 1964 by Manuel Marulanda Vélez and Jacobo Arenas and served as the official armed wing of the Colombian Communist Party established in the 1930s. The FARC deepened the Colombian Communist Party's efforts to organize and politicize Colombian farmers into a local self-defense movement. The aftermath of *La Violencia* in the 1960s and 1970s was also marked by the formation of smaller guerilla groups composed of farmers, students, intellectuals, and communists. These groups attributed their formation to the government's repressive regime, which was felt most acutely by citizens of the country's rural areas due to unequal land distribution. In the late 1970s, Liberal President Julio César Turbay responded to the threat of these guerilla groups, as well as increased drug trafficking, through an intensely repressive regime that inadvertently bolstered the FARC's status and active resistance to the Colombian government.[75] War against drug cartels throughout the 1980s further elevated violence and tension in the region.[76]

In 1996, the FARC began initiating offensive attacks against the Colombian military and other guerilla groups.[77] The resulting conflict was responsible for the forced displacement of more than 6.8 million Colombians and for the deaths of over 215,000 civilians and over 45,000 combatants.[78]

Negotiations for what would become the 2016 Peace Agreement began in October 2012 between President Santos and the FARC leadership in Oslo, Norway, and then moved to Havana, Cuba.[79] Brazil, Chile, Cuba, Norway, and Venezuela participated in negotiations as witnesses and guarantor states.[80]

The final 2016 agreement between the FARC and the Colombian government, signed in November, is a collection of subaccords.[81] The peace deal was endorsed by the United Nations Security Council, which also authorized the deployment of unarmed observers.[82] The agreement has a territorial focus that emphasized the recognition and consideration of the economic, cultural, and social needs, characteristics, and specific features of the territories and communities of Colombia. The final agreement contained six sections, and 578 total commitments. The six points included: rural reform; political participation; cessation of the conflict; solution to the illicit drugs problem; transitional justice reform; and implementation, verification, and public endorsement of the agreement.[83]

The agreement outlined comprehensive development of rural areas by seeking to balance existing forms of production with expectations for commercialization, competition, promotion of investment in rural areas, and an entrepreneurial vision of Colombian rural development. The political participation section sought to provide an expansion of democratic opportunities and allow for new political forces, such as the FARC, to emerge as political parties. The third section addressed the mutual ceasefire and cessation of hostilities and laying down of arms from both sides. That section also contained the accord on the economic, social, and political reintegration of ex-guerilla members into civilian life. The fourth section of the accord addressed efforts to combat narcotics trafficking. The fifth section contained the Victims' Accord and established a comprehensive system for truth, justice, reparation, and nonrepetition with the goal of combating impunity through various judicial mechanisms. The sixth section created the Commission for the Follow-up, Promotion and Verification of Implementation of the Final Agreement. The commission is composed of representatives from the national government and the FARC, and creates mechanisms for the international community to support the implementation of the agreement.[84]

With the signing of the peace agreement, the conflict between the Colombian government and the FARC essentially came to an end in 2016. Since then, the FARC has disarmed and demobilized, and transitioned into an official political party.[85] In 2019, the implementation process for the agreement shifted from short-term commitments towards the implementation of medium- and long-term commitments, requiring significant interinstitutional cooperation and local implementation. More than two-thirds of the commitments in the accord have been initiated, and more than one-third have been completed or have achieved substantial progress, though only 3 percent of the rural reforms had been completed as of April 2019.[86]

Despite notable success in the implementation of the peace agreement, violence and human rights violations persist in Colombia.[87] The murder of FARC ex-combatants and violence by guerillas, former FARC members, and FARC dissidents pose a significant threat to the successful implementation of the 2016 Accords and a durable peace.[88] In August 2019, Ivan Marquez, a former FARC commander, defied the peace agreement and called on supporters to take up arms, leaving the future stability of Colombia uncertain.[89]

DARFUR–SUDAN

The Darfur region, located in Western Sudan, is primarily made up of tribal villages. Traditionally, disputes between members of tribes were settled peacefully by tribal leaders with government mediating as a neutral party when necessary. In the 1970s, President Nimeiry formally abolished the tribal system and implemented a system of government administration. The national government appointed the administrators based on political loyalty, removing the perception of the government as an impartial arbitrator. By 1990, parties settled disputes through a combination of national government and tribal leaders as mediators, but tensions remained and tribal clashes continued. The tensions were heightened after the coup carried out by Omar al-Bashir, who initially was neither able nor willing to address the situation in Darfur.[90]

Between 2001 and 2002, two nonstate armed movement in Darfur, the Sudan Liberation Movement/Army and the Justice and Equality Movement began organizing themselves in opposition to the central government in Khartoum. These groups asserted that the government was the main cause of the socioeconomic and political marginalization of Darfurians and demanded equal participation in government by all groups and regions of Sudan.[91]

In late 2002, in response to attacks by forces aligned with the national government, the armed movements began their first military activities directed at local police offices. The government responded by recruiting nomadic Arab tribes in Darfur to combat the armed movements. These recruits, referred to as the Janjaweed, destroyed villages and committed mass rape and murder against the Darfurians, inciting terror and causing many to flee. In 2004, the conflict was declared a genocide against non-Arab Darfurians, and in 2010 the International Criminal Court issued a warrant for al-Bashir on charges of genocide.[92] An estimated 300,000 civilians were killed in the Darfur region, and 2.7 million have fled to refugee camps, including 250,000 to neighboring Chad.[93]

A hybrid peacekeeping mission comprised of the United Nations and the African Union, UNAMID, was launched in 2007; however, the conflict continued apace.[94] In 2018, protests and demonstrations began in several cities in Sudan calling for the removal of al-Bashir. Protests continued through 2019, and al-Bashir was ousted by a military coup in April 2019. A transitional government was formed.

The Sudanese peace process has involved a series of peace agreements, including the Abuja/Darfur Agreement, the Doha Agreement, and the Juba Agreement, which cover power-sharing, monopoly of force, wealth-sharing, accountability, and protection of human rights. After the Chadian government mediated the Abeche peace talks in September 2003, leading to the first ceasefire agreement between Sudan and the Sudan Liberation Army, the African Union mediated talks in Chad and Ethiopia. Six rounds of peace talks were then held in Abuja, Nigeria, where the Sudan government and a faction of the Sudan Liberation Army led by Minni Minawi signed the Darfur Peace Agreement in May 2006.[95]

The Darfur peace process was deadlocked after the Abuja meetings, as many armed movements in Sudan rejected the Abuja Peace Agreement, claiming it did not sufficiently meet their demands. The Arab League became involved with the peace talks, hosting negotiations in Qatar, and in November 2009 the Darfur civil society representatives participated in the Doha 1 and Doha 2 talks, though these rounds of negotiation also failed to resolve the conflict. In July 2011, the Doha Document for Peace in Darfur was adopted after a series of meetings and negotiations involving the Sudanese government, refugees, internally displaced people, the armed movements, civil society representatives, and international organizations. While most of the major armed movements refused to sign, the government of Sudan and a newly formed coalition of small armed movements, the Liberation and Justice Movement, signed the document.[96]

Both of these agreements contained power-sharing arrangements and wealth-sharing provisions. The Darfur Agreement also allowed for more representation of Darfurians in educational institutions, whereas the Doha Document provided that the Darfur movements would transform themselves into political parties that could participate across government and have representation at all levels of the Sudan armed forces. Both agreements also had provisions on the protection of human rights and for refugees, as well as commitments to remove restrictions on humanitarian assistance.[97] These agreements failed to resolve the conflict.

In October 2020, the parties concluded the multitrack Juba Peace Agreement with the armed movements from Darfur, some of the nonstate parties in Southern Kordofan and Blue Nile, in addition to other intra-Sudan regional parties, unlike the Abuja/Darfur and Doha agreements.[98] These agreements required Sudan to reestablish a federal state, and to provide for substantial vertical power-sharing in the form of devolved powers, residual powers, and the ability to create asymmetric relationships with the national government. The agreement also provided some innovative criteria for dispute resolution relating to the vertical power-sharing. With respect to horizontal power-sharing, the agreement provided for precise regional set-asides for seats in the executive, legislative, and judicial organs.

The failings of the Darfur/Abuja Agreement and the Doha Document for Peace in Darfur created the context for the necessity of the Juba Agreement in 2020.[99] The government of Sudan had blocked the implementation of many provisions from the Doha Document, and the movement factions had limited political and military influence.[100] Further, the document promised compensation, reconstruction, and development for the Darfur region and $2.65 billion from the Sudanese government over a six-year period, but the government allotted only a small portion of that money to Darfur.[101]

Despite the implementation challenges of the Doha Document for Peace in Darfur, Darfur's situation became increasingly stable, which contributed to the signing of the Juba Agreement in 2020. There has been a vast reduction of violent conflict, and the United Nations Security Council reduced the number of peace-keeping troops in the area, a step toward the ultimate goal of full withdrawal. The United Nations African Union Mission in Darfur is slowly shifting its responsibility from peacekeeping to peacebuilding, and shifting responsibility for the security of the region to the Sudanese government.[102] After the signing of the Juba Agreement, Sudan appears to be moving toward implementation of a durable peace.

EAST TIMOR–INDONESIA

After nearly 400 years of colonial rule, East Timor declared its independence from Portugal in the 1970s. Soon thereafter, Indonesia invaded East Timor under the guise of fighting communism, and annexed East Timor as a province.[103] The East Timorese resisted Indonesia's rule and the subsequent repression resulted in violence between pro-independence and pro-Indonesian armed groups. In 1999, East Timor rejected, by referendum, Indonesia's proposal for East Timorese autonomy within Indonesia in favor of independence.[104] Following this vote, pro-integration East Timorese militia, supported by elements of the Indonesia military, propelled East Timor into violent conflict.[105]

The violence prompted the UN to intervene and, with the consent of Indonesia, the UN Security Council authorized Australia in September of 1999 to undertake a Chapter VII authorized mission to lead a multinational force to restore peace and security. The force was to be subsequently replaced by a more traditional UN peacekeeping mission.[106] The Australian command led a combined force of nearly 12,000 troops from twenty-two states and rapidly deployed throughout East Timor to secure the territory. During the mission, the force engaged in combat operations with pro-Indonesian paramilitary forces, and occasionally with Indonesian police forces and suspected Indonesian military forces. Six months after their deployment, the multinational force handed over control to a UN peacekeeping force.

United Nations Security Council Resolution 1272 (1999) decided that a UN Transitional Administration in East Timor (UNTAET) would "be endowed with overall responsibility for the administration of East Timor" and that the UNTAET ought to maintain all authority for governmental functioning, acting within the UN's authority under Chapter VII of the UN Charter to oversee East Timor's transition to independence.[107] The resolution also provided that UNTAET would remain in place until January 2001, following which East Timor was to become independent.[108] East Timor achieved this independence in May 2002.

The resolution highlighted the need to condemn all violence in East Timor and demanded that those responsible for the violence be brought to justice. The resolution stressed that the Indonesian authorities take immediate action to allow displaced East Timorese citizens to return to East Timor by curbing the violence and intimidation. It also provides that UNTAET could take any measures to ensure the mandate is fulfilled and explicitly required that Portugal, Indonesia, and UNTAET cooperate to accomplish the objectives of the mandate.[109]

With international forces taking over security and administrative responsibilities during the transition, the domestic transitional leadership was able to focus on drafting the new constitution.[110] This enabled a relatively rapid drafting process that was able to capitalize on momentum for a peaceful transition and quickly establish the rule of law. The 2002 constitution lays out not only the structure of the government, but also the nation's social goals and the guaranteed rights and freedoms of its citizens.[111] There are seven parts to the constitution: Fundamental Principles; Rights, Duties, Liberties and Fundamental Guarantees; Organization of Political Power; Economic and Financial Organization; National Defense and Security; Guarantee and Revision of the Constitution; and Final and Transitional Provisions.

With the completion of the constitution in February 2002 and international recognition in May 2002, East Timor became a fully sovereign state and continues to maintain its independence, despite minor setbacks the country has encountered as it develops.[112]

GUATEMALA

Approximately 500 years ago, the Spanish colonized Guatemala and embarked on a centuries-long campaign of marginalization of the indigenous Mayan people. Following independence from Spain in 1821, a series of authoritarian military officers led the country. Juan Jose Arevalo became the first elected president of a civilian government in 1944. In 1954, an American-backed coup returned the country to military rule, and nearly six years later civil war broke out. The nonstate armed actor Unidad Revolucionaria Nacional Guatemalteca (URNG) formed with the aim of combating the repression faced by the people at the hands of the military junta. The military responded with strategies that targeted rural civilian populations, particularly indigenous Mayan communities. The civil war lasted from 1960 to 1996, during which an estimated 200,000 people died, and another 500,000 to 1.5 million people fled to escape the violence.[113]

The government entered into direct peace talks with URNG in 1991,[114] with mediation by the United Nations.[115] From 1991 to 1996 the parties reached a number of agreements on matters such as human rights, the return of displaced persons, the rights of indigenous peoples, civilian control over the military, demilitarization of the URNG, and a ceasefire. In 1996, the parties agreed to the Accord for a Firm and Lasting Peace, which ended nearly three decades of conflict.[116] The accord brought all of these prior agreements into force.[117]

The accord called for a new respect for human rights, and invited the United Nations to deploy a verification mission to monitor and assist in the protection of human rights, the integration of URNG into Guatemalan political life, a commission to investigate past human rights violations, the strengthening of laws to protect indigenous people, reforms to the democratic process, and efforts to resettle those displaced by the conflict.[118] The accord also declared Guatemala to be a "multi-ethnic, multi-cultural, and multi-lingual" state, a significant shift from the country's previous structure, which had marginalized its indigenous majority.[119]

The accord also included a series of constitutional amendments which intended to give marginalized and indigenous communities greater rights, representation, and recognition, as well as accomplish key democratic reforms.[120] After the peace agreement was signed, voters participated in a subsequent constitutional amendment referendum process.[121] Shortly before this referendum, lawmakers added forty-five additional amendments, largely on unrelated issues. As a result, voters faced an overwhelming number of amendments, misrepresentation, and oversimplification of particular amendments in the campaigning process, and the referendum failed.[122]

The 1996 Peace Accords remain an aspiration with an uncertain path toward fulfillment by successive Guatemalan governments.[123] This is especially true as patterns of corruption in law enforcement have created a culture of impunity.[124] Indigenous rights and recognition – key components of the agreements – continue to be elusive, with lack of governmental support, placing indigenous communities in similar predicaments as when the war ended.[125]

IRAQ

For over twenty years, Iraq was subject to the authoritarian rule of Saddam Hussein, a dictator who inflicted countless atrocities on both the Iraqi and Kurdish populations, including killings, torture, rape, extrajudicial executions, and forced prostitution.[126] In 1988, Saddam used chemical weapons, primarily mustard gas and nerve agents, against the Kurds in a genocidal campaign, resulting in approximately 50,000–100,000 deaths.[127] Saddam's Arabization campaign also forced Kurds to choose between rejecting their Kurdish identity or losing their property. In addition, Saddam severely restricted the religious practices of Shi'a Muslims in Iraq and displaced nearly 100,000 Kurds, Assyrians, and Turkomans from the oil-rich

Kirkuk region. Hundreds of thousands of citizens in Iraq and neighboring states died as a consequence of Saddam Hussein's regime.[128]

In 2003, following the 2001 terrorist attacks on the World Trade Center and the subsequent war in Afghanistan, a US-led coalition attacked and occupied Iraq, alleging that Saddam was harboring weapons of mass destruction and supported terrorist networks.[129] The initial US military campaign began on March 19, 2003 and lasted only twenty-six days, with Baghdad falling on April 9, 2003.[130]

Following the end of hostilities in 2003, the United States formed the Coalition Provisional Authority (Coalition Authority) pursuant to Security Council Registration 1483 and temporarily operated Iraq's governmental institutions. In July 2003, US officials created the Iraqi Governing Council and appointed its members. The council was intended to serve as Iraq's interim government. The Iraqi Governing Council consisted of twenty-five seats, thirteen reserved for the majority Shiite population and the rest allocated to Iraq's main minorities: the Kurds, Sunni Arabs, Assyrians, and Turkmen. In 2003, the United States also issued two separate orders outlawing Saddam's former political party, the Baath party, and dismissing all Baath members from their government positions while also barring them from participating in Iraq's interim government.[131]

The United States and the Iraqi Governing Council then set forth a two-year timeline by which to establish democracy in Iraq.[132] In accordance with that time-line, the Coalition Authority and Iraqi Governing Council would first produce the Transitional Administration Law as an interim constitution, and establish the Iraqi Interim Assembly.[133] Thereafter, the Coalition Authority and Iraqi Governing Council would develop a new Status of Forces Agreement to govern the US role in Iraq going forward, while the Iraqi Interim Assembly would select an executive and ministers for the interim government. Eventually, the Iraqi people would ratify a permanent constitution dissolving the Coalition Authority and Iraqi Interim Assembly to restore Iraq to full sovereignty.[134]

The Traditional Administrative Law, which operated as an interim constitution, sought to establish a parliamentary-style interim liberal democratic government.[135] The document guaranteed those rights common to most democracies but also included other specific items. The law declared that the transitional government would make amends for Saddam's forced displacement, deprivation of citizenship, loss of finances and property, and dismissal from government for political, racial, or sectarian reasons. Revenues derived from natural resources would be distributed with "due regard" to those areas deprived of funds by Saddam. Women would constitute at least one-quarter of the National Assembly. Baath party members were barred from election except under specified legal procedures. The Transitional Administrative Law also recognized the Kurdistan Regional Government and its control over claimed territories.

In 2005 Iraq, via referendum, adopted a new constitution. The constitution was divided into six sections that define rights, freedoms, governmental structure, and delegation of powers.[136] It largely aligned with the Transitional Administrative Law in laying out a framework for a parliamentary system of government.[137] Of note is that it allowed that any citizen previously deprived of citizenship to demand reinstatement, sought to strengthen the role of civil society, and made provision for integrating minority territories into the federal state. The constitution further declared that oil and gas were owned by all Iraqi citizens in all regions and territories, and revenues from these resources would be fairly distributed in proportion to population size with an adjustment for those areas unjustly deprived by Saddam's former policies. The constitution preserved the Iraqi High Tribunal that was created to prosecute members of Saddam's regime for atrocity crimes, and also preserved the High Commission for De-Baathification. The constitution was amended in 2007 to provide clarity on several issues that had been left relatively unresolved in the 2005 Constitution.

Iraq remains beset with both internal strife and external threats. In 2016, hundreds of thousands of Iraqi citizens took over Iraq's parliament building in a demonstration against the government.[138] At the same time, ISIS occupied a large swath of Iraqi territory until the death of Abu Bakr al-Baghdadi and a combined US, Iraqi, and Kurdish effort to recapture the territory. Iran continued to make inroads into Iraqi politics, with a destabilizing effect on Iraq self-governance.[139] The instability and uncertainty has persisted.

KOSOVO–SERBIA

Some commentators note that the conflict between Kosovo and Serbia harkens back to 1389 defeat of Serbia by the Ottoman Empire in the field of blackbirds located in Kosovo. More recently, however, the conflict stems from the near-apartheid regime imposed by Serbia in Kosovo in 1989 under the direction of Slobodan Milošević.[140]

Within the former Yugoslavia, Kosovo was an autonomous province of Serbia. Under the regime of Yugoslav President Josip Broz Tito, Kosovo was able to preserve an independent government within Serbia and attain a measure of equality with its Serbian counterparts. These developments fueled Albanian nationalism and Serbian resentment toward the "Albanianization" of Kosovo.[141] The death of Tito in May 1980, along with the end of the Cold War, increased political and economic instability in the region.

Slobodan Milošević was elected president of Serbia in 1989 and sought to stoke ethnic nationalism as a means of securing political power. He stripped Kosovo of its autonomy in 1989 and all but extinguished ethnic Albanian political representation within the Serbian government. Kosovar Albanians responded by creating the pacifist Democratic League of Kosovo with the purpose of achieving independence from Serbia. In the face of a highly militarized response, the Kosovo Liberation Army was created as an ethnic-Albanian militia.[142] Serbian military and paramilitary forces responded with a systematic campaign of terror, which included murder, rape, and destruction of cultural heritage.[143] The violence involved well-documented reports of ethnic cleansing, mass rape and sexual violence, and crimes against humanity,[144] resulting in the displacement of over 1.2 million Kosovo Albanians.[145] Eventually NATO undertook a humanitarian intervention in spring 1999 to bring the conflict to an end.

Prior to the NATO intervention, the parties held peace talks at the Rambouillet Chateau outside Paris in February 1999. The Rambouillet Agreement, formally called the Interim Agreement for Peace and Self-Government in Kosovo, provided for a cessation of hostilities, the deployment of an international peacekeeping force, access for humanitarian assistance, the protection of human rights, an interim constitution providing for democratic self-government, the autonomy for Kosovo, the protection of Serbian and other minority rights, reform and reconstitution of the police, internationally monitored elections, and a process for determining Kosovo's final status based on the will of the people.[146]

Albania, the United States, and Britain signed the Rambouillet Agreement, but the Federal Republic of Yugoslavia and Russia refused to do so.[147] In the face of the failed talks and increasing level of atrocity crimes being committed by the Serbian regime, NATO launched the humanitarian intervention, with Milošević accepting NATO's terms to cease combat on June 3, 1999.[148] NATO and Serbia signed a Military Technical Agreement setting out the terms of the cessation of hostilities and obligating Serbia to remove troops and military equipment from Kosovo within eleven days.[149]

The United Nations Security Council adopted Resolution 1244, which provided for the deployment of NATO peacekeeping troops, and the establishment of a UN mission that would carry out most of the sovereign obligations of Kosovo. The UN mission undertook a measured approach of standards before status wherein it worked with the government of Kosovo to create the institutions necessary for self-government prior to Kosovo seeking international recognition. In 2008, Kosovo declared independence from Serbia and was subsequently recognized by over 100 states, but not Serbia or Russia.[150] While not recognized by all member states of the international community, Kosovo remains a relatively stable state[151] and is actively engaged in the international community, participating in various international institutions, such as the International Monetary Fund and World Bank.[152] Notably, the International Criminal Tribunal for the Former Yugoslavia indicted Slobodan Milošević for crimes against humanity in Kosovo, as well as the two co-chairs of the Serbian delegation to the Rambouillet negotiations.[153]

MACEDONIA

Macedonia is considered to be the only nonviolent secession from the former Yugoslavia, yet tensions remained high between Macedonia's ethnic Slavic and ethnic Albanian populations. This tension, coupled with socioeconomic disparity, led to violent conflict in the new state of Macedonia.[154]

After the Allies liberated Macedonia from occupation in mid-1944, the Republic of Macedonia joined the Socialist Federal Republic of Yugoslavia along with Serbia, Croatia, Slovenia, Bosnia and Herzegovina, and Montenegro.[155] Under Yugoslav rule, the Slavic Macedonian majority became increasingly urbanized and dominated the public-sector workforce in the state, while the Albanian minority resided in rural areas, disadvantaged economically by low levels of education and employment.[156] After Macedonia seceded from Yugoslavia by referendum on September 8, 1991, Albanian–Macedonian tensions intensified.[157] Albanians suffered discrimination by the Slavic Macedonian majority and believed themselves to be disadvantaged by the 1991 Constitution.[158] Throughout the 1990s, the Slavic Macedonians ignored the Albanian population's demands for a multiethnic polity, concerned it was the first step toward partition of Macedonia, while continuing to repress Albanian culture by banning the use of the Albanian language and flag.[159] During the war in Kosovo, Macedonia accepted thousands of Albanian refugees fleeing the conflict in Kosovo, putting strain on the economy and increasing anxiety among Slavic Macedonians.

In March 2001, the Albanian rebel group, the National Liberation Army (NLA), initiated armed conflict in the city of Tetovo.[160] The ethnic tensions that had long plagued Macedonia culminated in a six-month internal armed conflict between the ethnic Albanian minority and the ethnic Slavic majority.[161]

After President Boris Trajkovski reached out to the North Atlantic Treaty Organization in June 2001, NATO brokered a ceasefire that went into effect on July 5, 2001.[162] At the United Nations' suggestion, Slavic Macedonian and Albanian leaders worked to adopt a political, rather than military, solution with mediators from the UN, the European Union, and the United States.[163] Partly due to international efforts, the Macedonian conflict ended on August 13, 2001, with the signing of the Ohrid Framework Agreement.[164]

The Ohrid Framework Agreement is a comprehensive peace agreement with eight main provisions and three annexes.[165] The eight provisions addressed basic principles regarding conflict resolution, the cessation of hostilities, the development of a decentralized government, nondiscrimination and equitable representation, special parliamentary procedures, education and the use of languages, the expression of identity, and the implementation of these points.[166] Annex A covered constitutional amendments, Annex B covered legislative modifications, and Annex C covered implementation and confidence-building measures.[167]

The agreement subscribed to the basic principles of peaceful conflict resolution, maintenance of Macedonia's territorial integrity, the preservation of Macedonia's multiethnic society, and commitment to a democratic system of governance. Other principles such as the right to self-government, equal representation in legislative bodies, and nondiscrimination were also present throughout. The parties agreed to declare Macedonian as the official language of Macedonia, as well as any other language spoken by at least 20 percent of the population, including Albanian. The parties also recommitted to the ceasefire of July 5, 2001.[168]

The Ohrid Framework Agreement strengthened Macedonia's democratic institutions with relative success. Aside from instances of voter intimidation, the election process in Macedonia today is free and fair. Political pluralism and participation have been improving, particularly in ensuring representation for the various ethnic communities. Corruption is widespread, with corrupt officials continuing to operate in parliament and in the judiciary, while government transparency is inconsistent. There is relatively equal protection and respect for civil liberties and individual rights.[169]

MINDANAO–PHILIPPINES

Tensions between the Philippines government and Muslim separatist groups in Mindanao, an island group located in the southern Philippines, have plagued the region since the 1970s.[170] Though the Philippines' population is predominately Roman Catholic, the Muslim population has existed in the Philippines as a substantial segment of the country since before the Spanish colonial period began in the early sixteenth century. Colonialization of the Philippines by the United States at the turn of the twentieth century further divided the region's Christian and Muslim inhabitants.

The conclusion of World War II and the Philippines' independence from the United States in 1946 was followed by a series of resettlement programs in the 1950s and 1960s, sponsored by the Christian-dominant government. These programs pushed Christian settlers from the north to relocate to Mindanao, creating significant land scarcity and displacing the Muslim population in the southern Philippines. Population growth in the subsequent decades served to further exacerbate tensions. In 1971, the Moro National Liberation Front (MNLF) was founded to advance the goal of establishing an independent Moro nation.[171]

The enactment of martial law in 1972 by President Ferdinand E. Marcos intensified the Muslim drive for self-determination in the Philippines.[172] In 1981, the Moro Islamic Liberation Front (MILF) was formed as a breakaway faction of the MNLF and ultimately developed into the leading proponent in the fight with the Philippines' government for a separate Islamic state in the Philippines.[173]

Tensions between the national government and Muslim separatist groups, protracted armed conflict, and debilitating underdevelopment in the Mindanao region devastated the Muslim population in the Philippines and deepened social divides within the country.[174] By 2009, over 600,000 civilians had fled their homes and nearly 400,000 were displaced from the region.[175]

In 1987, the Philippines government sought to quell the conflict by amending the constitution to provide for the creation of the Autonomous Region in Muslim

Mindanao. The amendments devolved a number of political powers to the newly established autonomous Mindanao region.[176] Though the MNLF accepted the agreement, it was rejected by the MILF. The subsequent decades of the conflict included additional peace talks which yielded a series of peace agreements.[177]

Peace talks in 2012 between the MILF and the Philippines government were facilitated by Malaysia in Kuala Lumpur. The talks culminated in the signing of the Framework Agreement on the Bangsamoro by the two parties in October 2012.[178] This preliminary peace agreement served as a commitment by both the government of Philippines and the MILF to establish Bangsamoro as a new autonomous political entity to replace the Autonomous Region in Muslim Mindanao that was established in 1989.[179]

Two years later, in 2014, the Comprehensive Agreement on the Bangsamoro was signed by the MILF and the Philippines government. The 2014 agreement incorporated the 2012 agreement and was supplemented with additional annexes on wealth, power-sharing, and arrangements for transition. The agreement enhanced the status of Bangsamoro to that of an autonomous Muslim region. It also provided for the disarmament, demobilization, and reintegration of MILF fighters, the expansion of Sharia courts for Muslim residents, and a reiteration of the protection of democratic and human rights.[180]

The 2012 and 2014 agreements were followed by the Bangsamoro Organic Law in 2018, signed by Philippine President Rodrigo Duterte.[181] The Bangsamoro Organic Law formalized the creation of the Bangsamoro Autonomous Region in Muslim Mindanao and devolved additional fiscal and administrative powers.[182]

Bangsamoro, officially established in 2019 following a plebiscite, exists in the southern Philippines as a fully autonomous region with its own parliament,[183] fiscal autonomy,[184] and over fifty enumerated exclusive powers.[185] The region has formed a fully transitional government which serves as an active governing force in Bangsamoro.[186] It has begun to operate with its own budget and has accomplished the decommissioning of thousands of former combatants.[187]

Despite notable achievements and the conclusion of nearly five decades of bitter conflict between the Philippines government and Moro secessionists, long-term stability in the southern Philippines remains uncertain. As of August 2020, nearly 300,000 individuals remain displaced in Mindanao due to armed conflict, violence, and natural disaster.[188]

MOZAMBIQUE

Mozambique has a long history of foreign control inciting domestic opposition. Portugal assumed control of Mozambique as a colonial power in the late 1890s and consolidated economic and political power in the succeeding decades. By the 1950s and 1960s, an influx of Portuguese settlers entered Mozambique, taking advantage of the economic policies and increased employment opportunities implemented for them, which generated a correspondingly increased national resentment toward Portuguese rule.[189]

In 1962, exiled political groups in opposition to colonial power formed the socialist Mozambique Liberation Front (FRELIMO).[190] Portuguese forces were supported by Rhodesia (modern-day Zimbabwe) and South Africa in resistance to FRELIMO.[191] By 1964, FRELIMO began armed resistance efforts against Portugal's rule and, despite Portuguese military resistance, Mozambique became independent on June 25, 1975.[192] Portuguese troops withdrew from the state and Portugal transferred control of the state to the Marxist insurgency, FRELIMO. There were no elections, and Mozambique became a one-party state.[193]

FRELIMO began its political rule by cracking down on dissidents, forming a single-party system, sending the noncompliant to "reeducation camps," and ousting tribal chiefs who would not cooperate with their vision of a Marxist Mozambique.[194] FRELIMO's rule was met with substantial opposition, heightened national tension, and international interference. States aligned with the anticommunist Cold War bloc quickly became involved. In 1974, Rhodesia supported anti-FRELIMO dissident Mozambican fighters in their effort to form the Mozambican National Resistance (RENAMO).[195] South Africa and the United States provided funding, training, and arms to RENAMO, enabling the group to form remote camps in Mozambique, train and arm fighters, and continuously attack villages, highways, and infrastructure.[196] The ensuing civil war lasted until 1992,[197] and was characterized by systematic and widespread atrocities that left over a million people dead by the end of the fifteen-year civil war.[198]

The Mozambican peace process began with the deceleration of Cold War tensions in the late 1980s, which undermined RENAMO's international support and tempered FRELIMO's Marxist commitments.[199] Peace talks commenced in 1990, facilitated by the Italian government and involved both the FRELIMO-dominated government of Mozambique and RENAMO. The talks ultimately produced the 1992 General Peace Agreement for Mozambique.

The agreement established a power-sharing arrangement between FRELIMO and RENAMO and declared both groups legitimate political parties.[200] It requested the establishment of UN commissions to oversee the transitional government, ensure a successful ceasefire, and observe and enforce demobilization, disarmament, and reintegration. It committed both parties to a pursuit of civil rights, including free travel, press, association, expression, and access to public facilities for all parties, and the return of refugees with restitution for lost property.[201] The agreement also provided complete amnesty to all parties for any crimes committed throughout the conflict, allowing members of RENAMO to run for political office in the future.

The 1992 agreement held for twenty-one years until RENAMO disputed the 2014 election results and demanded control over six provincial elections.[202] The dispute caused a reemergence of conflict and prompted a new round of peace talks between the parties.[203] The talks produced the Accord on Cessation of Hostilities in August 2014 and prompted a new election.[204] This election was also contested and RENAMO threatened to take control of the contested provinces by force. Alleged killings perpetrated by both sides continued until 2017, when a truce was established.[205] Hostility persisted until RENAMO's leader, Afonso Dhlakama, died from a heart attack in 2018.[206] A new peace agreement was signed in 2019 between Mozambique's president and the new RENAMO leader Ossufo Momade.[207]

The success of the 2019 peace agreement remains to be seen.[208] Mozambique faces considerable debt, a number of local insurgencies, and in January 2020 more than half of its population lived below the poverty line.[209] The agreement has, however, been relatively well implemented. The death of RENAMO leader Dhlakama in 2018, the surrender of weapons by RENAMO troops, and the apparent willingness of the opposing parties to seek a peaceful and economically prosperous future offers hope for sustainable peace.[210] FRELIMO is expected to maintain a majority of seats in parliament, while other parties are expected to hold prominent roles. The possibility of economic prosperity is strengthened by Mozambique's access to sea trade routes, proximity to South Africa's strong economy, and rich land and mineral resources.[211]

NEPAL

Nepal was historically closed off from the international community until the 1950s.[212] After centuries of monarchical rule, the caste system embedded within Nepalese culture led to vast socioeconomic inequality. After a brief period of prodemocracy leadership, King Mahendra suspended party politics and replaced the parliamentary system with the party-less democratic Panchayat system that continued until the 1990s. The longstanding socioeconomic inequalities prompted aspiring political parties to launch the People's Movement, a series of street protests that turned violent. As a consequence, the king agreed to reestablish a multiparty democracy, with the first elections taking place in 1991. The people of Nepal had hoped their socioeconomic conditions would improve but saw little change in the years following.[213]

In February 1995, the Communist Party of Nepal (Maoist) submitted a list of demands to the government to address a variety of social and economic issues. The Maoists also warned that if these demands were not met they would resort to violence. A week after the demands were sent, the Maoists began an armed insurgency against the government that tipped Nepal into a decade-long civil war. The primary parties involved were the Maoists and the Nepal police. As the conflict grew, the government deployed the Royal Nepalese Army. From 1996 to 2006, the civil war resulted in at least 13,000 dead and approximately 1,300 missing.[214]

The Maoists and the Nepalese government began peace talks in 2003, but they collapsed as both sides continued to commit violent acts and violate the ceasefire that had been put in place earlier in the year. In November 2005 in Delhi, India, the mainstream political parties, the so-called Seven Party Alliance, met with the Maoists to plan an end to the conflict with a twelve-point letter of understanding. In January 2006, the Maoists broke the four-month ceasefire in protest against the authoritarian rule of the king.

In April 2006, the king implemented the main demand of the Seven Party Alliance and the Maoists by reinstating the House of Representatives and announcing he would be resigning from any active role in politics. The House of Representatives met for the first time and announced a ceasefire in response to the Maoists' own declaration of a unilateral ceasefire. Negotiation teams for both sides met in Kathmandu in May 2006 where they announced a twenty-five-point Ceasefire Code of Conduct. They formed a ceasefire monitoring committee and requested the United Nations to assist in human rights monitoring during the ceasefire. After a series of talks, in November 2006 the Seven Party Alliance and the Maoists signed the Comprehensive Peace Accord.[215]

The Comprehensive Peace Accord is a thirteen-page agreement consisting of eight subcategories of agreements relating to a ceasefire and the implementation of political reforms aimed at reaffirming a multiparty democratic government. The accord provided for placing the Maoist army combatants in cantonments where they would undergo an integrative and rehabilitative process under monitoring by the UN. The UN was also authorized to collect arms and ammunition to be held under its supervision. The accord also addressed the protection of human rights, the operation of an interim parliament, the creation of a constituent assembly to draft a new constitution, the need to transition from a unitary state to a state structure according to the principle of devolution, and a process for abolishing the monarchy by a simple majority of the constituent assembly.[216] The parties also agreed to form a High-Level Commission for State Restructuring, a National Peace and Rehabilitation Commission, and a Truth and Reconciliation Commission.[217] The accord successfully ended the Nepalese Civil War.

In 2007, the reinstated parliament created the interim constitution.[218] The interim constitution outlined the procedure for the negotiation and adoption of the future constitution.[219] Nepal's 2007 interim constitution ushered in a new representative governing structure to replace the monarchy, but it did not include agreements on how key governance features of the state would operate. The parties lacked agreement on the federal state structure, electoral system, and judicial entities, among other aspects, and the parties negotiated and renegotiated these issues for years without significant progress.[220] After several failed attempts to establish the Constituent Assembly designated by the interim constitution to draft the permanent constitution, and facing substantial domestic unrest due to the failed response to the April 2015 earthquake, a permanent constitution was eventually completed in June 2015.[221] The constitution was approved by two-thirds of the second Constitutional Assembly, with the exception of the Madhesh party representing much of southern Nepal.[222]

NORTHERN IRELAND

The island of Ireland had been under partial or complete British control for almost 1,000 years, beginning with the twelfth-century Anglo-Norman Invasion.[223] In the early 1920s, the Anglo-Irish War and the subsequent Irish Civil War resulted in the establishment of an independent Republic of Ireland, with six counties remaining within the United Kingdom as the territory of Northern Ireland.[224] While a majority of the people of Northern Ireland were Protestants loyal to the British crown, a notable minority were Catholics who supported unification with Ireland, referred to as Irish Republicans.[225] In the years leading up to the Northern Ireland conflict, popularly known as the Troubles, pro-Irish Republic citizens of Northern Ireland alleged discrimination by the United Kingdom loyalist majority and the state.[226]

The Troubles were characterized by a resurgence of longstanding tensions between republican supporters of a unified Ireland and the unionist supporters of the British, beginning in the late 1960s.[227] Inspired by the civil rights movement in the United States and student protests in Paris and elsewhere, unionist and nationalist Irish groups began public demonstrations, spawning the violent uprisings.[228] Guerilla-style warfare, including numerous instances of bombings, fires, and shootings by paramilitary forces from both sides, frequently resulted in civilian casualties. The British had also deployed its military to Northern Ireland for use against republican paramilitary forces and civilians.[229]

The most infamous atrocity to occur during the Troubles was a British military attack on Catholic civil rights protesters on January 30, 1972. This attack, known as Bloody Sunday, resulted in the death of fourteen protesters. The British state's final investigation into the attack found that none of the protesters had posed a threat to the British military, prompting UK Prime Minister David Cameron to formally apologize in 2010.[230] Seven months after Bloody Sunday, the Irish Republican Army retaliated with over 20 bombings in Belfast, killing 9 and injuring 130 in what came to be known as Bloody Friday.

In early 1996, the United Kingdom and Ireland announced that all-party peace talks would be held in June of that year in Stormont, contingent on the participants' agreement to abide by the Mitchell Principles laid out by United States Senator George Mitchell.[231] These principles were affirmations from each party designed to reduce violence, and to commit to abiding by the peacefully and democratically determined outcome of negotiations.[232] They agreed to the principles, as well to the decommissioning of paramilitary weapons simultaneously to conducting peace talks.[233] The talks originally commenced without Sinn Féin, a republican Irish political party, but the group later joined in September 1997.

With intermittent interruptions due to continued attacks by the Irish Republican Army, talks continued through 1997 and into 1998, with the parties reaching agreement on Good Friday, April 10, 1998.[234] The agreement was approved by a majority vote in a referendum in Northern Ireland (with both constituencies voting in favor), and in the Republic of Ireland.

The 1998 Good Friday Agreement is a multilateral peace agreement among the United Kingdom, the Republic of Ireland, and the political factions within Northern Ireland. The thirty-five-page agreement set out reforms to the constitutional status of Northern Ireland.[235]

The primary constitutional features of the agreement are that Ireland recognizes Northern Ireland as part of the United Kingdom, the United Kingdom recognizes that a substantial minority in Northern Ireland want reunification with the Republic of Ireland, the United Kingdom commits to cede Northern Ireland should a majority come to support this, and that persons born in Northern Ireland may consider themselves Irish, British, or both as they wish.[236] In addition to these changes to the constitutional status of Northern Ireland, the agreement called for a reduction of British troops in Northern Ireland, the decommissioning of all paramilitary groups, the establishment of a power-sharing devolved government in Northern Ireland in place of direct rule from London, and the establishment of human rights commissions to investigate abuses from both sides of the conflict.

The agreement is a comprehensive peace agreement and recognized the right to self-determination. It contained provisions on constitutional reform, police reform, electoral reform, demobilization, disarmament, reparations, and human rights, among others.[237] The agreement also specifically called for the establishment of a Northern Ireland Victims Commission to memorialize the suffering of victims and seek their participation in efforts to improve relations between the parties moving forward.[238]

While casualties continued into the early 2000s, the Good Friday Agreement largely marked the end of the violence.[239] Neither the Republic of Ireland nor the United Kingdom enforces the Northern Ireland border, allowing citizens of either state to freely travel the entirety of the island.[240] However, the status of the island came into flux as a result of the United Kingdom's decision to exit the European Union. That decision would turn the Northern Irish border into a land border of the European Union, subject to customs checks.[241] The British and Irish states have both expressed their desire to maintain the invisible border between the Republic and Northern Ireland, but it remains deeply contested what arrangement would satisfy both the Good Friday Agreement and the European Union's need for a clear and regulated border. Lingering sectarian tensions about Northern Ireland's relationship with the United Kingdom made this border issue all the more volatile.[242]

RWANDA

Ethnic tension between opposing clans characterize the situation that culminated with the Rwandan genocide. The kingdom of Rwanda, ruled by the Tutsi Nyiginya clan from the 1600s through the late 1800s, imposed repressive conditions on the

Hutu population. German colonists later formed an alliance with the Tutsi king and favored the Tutsis over the Hutus, believing the Tutsis to be racially superior and further stoking the ethnic tension. The ethnic divide was exacerbated by subsequent Belgian colonists when they institutionalized similar practices.[243]

Growing Hutu resentment led to an outbreak of violence in 1959 in which 20,000 Tutsis were killed and hundreds of thousands fled, many of which later formed the Rwandan Patriotic Front.[244] In 1962, Rwanda gained independence from Belgian colonial rule and the Hutus, representing over 80 percent of the population, took control.[245] In the following decades, the economic circumstances of the state worsened and the Tutsi minority was increasingly blamed for Rwanda's troubles, once again increasing the already heightened ethnic divide.[246]

The Rwandan Civil War officially began in October 1990 when the Rwandan Patriotic Front invaded Rwanda. The Hutu government responded with large-scale massacres against the Tutsi population. The violent civil war in Rwanda, lasting three years, involved genocide, crimes against humanity, and war crimes such as recruitment of child soldiers, torture, rape, arbitrary arrests and imprisonment, murder, and destruction of property.[247]

The peace processes between the Rwandan government and the Rwandan Patriotic Front began with a ceasefire in 1992 and a later peace agreement in 1993. The N'sele Ceasefire Agreement, mediated by the Republic of Tanzania, was finalized in July 1992, and was immediately followed by peace negotiations. The ceasefire agreement set forth a framework and timeline to negotiate, sign, and implement a future power-sharing peace agreement between the two opposing parties.[248]

In August 1993, the government of the Republic of Rwanda and the Rwandan Patriotic Front signed the Arusha Peace Agreement, consisting of five protocols: the Protocol of Agreement on the Rule of Law, the Protocol of Agreement on Power-Sharing, the Protocol of Agreement on the Repatriation of Rwandese Refugees and the Resettlement of Displaced Persons, the Protocol of Agreement on the Integration of Armed Forces, and Miscellaneous Issues and Final Provisions.[249]

The Arusha Peace Agreement sought to formally end the conflict and eliminate the root causes of the civil war. The peace agreement, along with the related protocols, detailed political and constitutional reform, security reform, wealth-sharing, and the protection of human rights. The agreement called for the establishment of a transitional government that would include members from the Rwandan Patriotic Front. The power-sharing arrangement included replacing a number of articles of the constitution with provisions of the peace agreement and establishing transitional institutions within thirty-seven days of signing the agreement.[250]

The peace established by the Arusha Peace Accords in 1993 proved unsustainable. Although the accords temporarily ended the civil war, it was unable to resolve the deep-seated ethnic tensions between the Hutus and Tutsis. Hutu extremists, angered by the power-sharing element of the agreement, resisted the agreement's implementation and tipped Rwanda back into conflict in April 1994. Heightened ethnic tensions sparked the Rwandan genocide, with mass systematic killings of Tutsi, Twa, and moderate Hutus. The genocide lasted 100 days, during which an estimated 800,000 ethnic Tutsis and moderate Hutus were slaughtered by the Hutu majority population before the Rwandan Patriotic Front was able to defeat the Rwandan army and associated paramilitaries.[251] The Rwandan Patriotic Front then assumed political control of Rwanda.

Despite indications of greater political pluralism in the 2019 elections, Rwandan efforts to establish democracy, peace, and security, and foster a respect for human rights following the genocide, such as by expanding opportunities for freedom of expression, remain limited. The Rwandan Patriotic Front continues to dominate politically and has been accused of allegations of arbitrary detention, ill-treatment, and torture from those who oppose the government.[252]

SIERRA LEONE

The conflict in Sierra Leone was fueled by an economy twisted by gross inequality due to the favoritism of the postcolonial government to those most loyal, and the struggle over control of the natural diamond reserves, as well as the consequences of an illicit diamond trade.[253] What later became known as "blood diamonds" were key to the onset of the violence between the Sierra Leone government and the armed Revolutionary United Front (RUF) who both wanted to extract profits from the natural resource. Not inconsequentially, the Revolutionary United Front reaped a profit of nearly $200 million a year through the illicit diamond trade and used it to fund its revolutionary movement.[254]

Sierra Leone's economic inequality led to a growing frustration among the population. The government distributed benefits unevenly to those working in the mining industry and granted mining licenses solely to ruling families or loyal government supporters. Further, the government heightened tensions when it made significant funding cuts in health and education, which effectively eliminated payments to teachers or other civil servants and led to fewer students enrolled in school. These circumstances created a pool of marginalized youth who, with little opportunity for education or employment, were susceptible to forced recruitment as child soldiers for the RUF.[255]

The war officially began on March 23, 1991 when the Revolutionary United Front, with the support of Liberian revolutionary forces under the command of Charles Taylor, entered Sierra Leone from Liberia in an effort to take control of the country. Three internal leaders of the Revolutionary United Front – Foday Sankoh, Abu Kanu, and Rashid Mansaray – traveled throughout Sierra Leone and Liberia to recruit combatants. They also made an arrangement with then-Liberian President Charles Taylor to help him siphon diamonds from Sierra Leone in return for his military assistance.[256]

In light of the successes of the RUF, the Sierra Leone army staged a coup in April 1992, and undertook a relatively effective campaign against the RUF. The RUF, however, later regrouped and reoccupied much of Sierra Leone. In March 1995, the president of Sierra Leone hired the South African Executive Outcomes mercenary force to help repel the RUF and was highly successful in pushing back the territorial gains of the RUF and forcing it into peace negotiations in Abidjan. During this time, Sierra Leone also returned to democratic governance with the holding of parliamentary and presidential elections in the spring of 1996. In November 1996, Sierra Leone and the RUF signed the Abidjan Peace Accord; however, it subsequently failed to be implemented and the RUF resumed its attacks on government forces and civilians.[257]

In May 1997, with the failure to implement the peace agreement and the resurgence of the RUF, the Sierra Leone army again staged a coup, but this time joined forces with the RUF to occupy nearly all the territory of Sierra Leone, including the capital of Freetown. The army and the RUF then launched a wave of atrocity crimes against the people of Sierra Leone.[258] In response, the government in exile asked the Economic Community of West African States to send in its military force, the Economic Community Ceasefire Monitoring Group (ECOMOG), to retake the capital. The ECOMOG had previously intervened in a similar situation in Liberia.[259] The ECOMOG force successfully secured Freetown, enabling the government to return. The force was, however, unable to extend its reach much beyond the capital.

The violence inflicted throughout the conflict resulted in the deaths of 50,000–70,000 people and displaced half a million. The Revolutionary United Front and the Armed Forces Revolutionary Council perpetrated the majority of human rights abuses, which ranged from the signature limb amputations to sexual violence. The Sierra Leone government forces also committed serious crimes on a smaller scale, which resulted in the deaths and displacement of civilians. Both government and rebel forces recruited child soldiers and generally failed to distinguish civilians from combatants in attacks.[260]

In the face of intense international pressure, the parties met in Lomé from April through July 1999 to negotiate the Lomé Peace Agreement. The agreement included thirty-seven articles and five annexes, using much of the text from the Abidjan Peace Agreement.[261] The Lomé Agreement created a power-sharing arrangement, setting aside the vice presidency for the leader of the RUF, Foday Sankoh. The agreement also granted him immunity for atrocity crimes.[262] The Lomé Agreement provided for the disarmament of both the RUF and the Sierra Leone army.[263] The disarmament, demobilization, and reintegration process started in October 1998 and was run by the United Nations Mission in Sierra Leone in coordination with a national committee. The mandate for the mission also included protecting civilians under imminent threat of physical violence.[264]

While the Lomé Agreement provided the Sierra Leone government control over the diamond trade, it designated the profits from these resources as public money to be spent on development and postwar rehabilitation and reconstruction.[265] To oversee this arrangement, the agreement created an autonomous body, the Commission for the Management of Strategic Resources, National Reconstruction and Development, in charge of monitoring compliance with the agreement's provisions relating to revenues generated from the sale of diamonds.[266] Notably, the agreement also appointed Foday Sankoh as chairman of the commission. He abused this position to continue to fund the RUF through the illicit trade of diamonds.[267]

The RUF largely ignored the Lomé Agreement and launched an offensive to retake Freetown in May 2000. In May 2000, the United Kingdom, with the consent of Sierra Leone, deployed a military force to initially assist with the evacuation of civilians, but which subsequently shifted its mandate to assist the UN force, and to train and re-equip the Sierra Leone army. The British forces aggressively engaged the RUF, with the assistance of air strikes from the neighboring state of Guinea against RUF strongholds.

The combined action of forces from Sierra Leone, ECOMOG, the UN, Guinea, and the United Kingdom pushed the RUF to essentially surrender via a ceasefire agreement providing for their complete disarmament and demobilization, with the conflict coming to an end in January 2002. The Special Court for Sierra Leone, a hybrid tribunal, subsequently indicted both Foday Sankoh and Charles Taylor for atrocity crimes in Sierra Leone. The tribunal ruled the Lomé amnesty inapplicable to international laws prohibiting atrocity crimes. Foday Sankoh died while awaiting trial, and Charles Taylor was convicted and sentenced to fifty years' imprisonment. It was the first international tribunal to convict defendants on the enlistment and abuse of child soldiers.[268]

SOUTH AFRICA

South Africa's apartheid system stemmed from a history of slavery and exploitation by British and Dutch colonizers starting in the seventeenth century. In 1913, the Afrikaner National Party, led by descendants of European settlers, began systematic- ally expropriating lands from the black majority to give to the white minority. Under the Natives Land Act of 1913, whites expropriated 87 percent of all arable land, leaving 13 percent for the black majority.[269] In the wake of the Great Depression in the 1940s, the National Party ran on a campaign of apartheid in 1948 – Afrikaans for "apartness" – that would allow whites to exploit black labor. From 1949 to 1953, the government passed a series of laws that created a system of racial segregation.

Under apartheid, the white minority controlled the political and economic rights, associations, and movements of the majority black inhabitants and other ethnic groups. The system banned interracial marriage and social integration. The Population Registration Act demanded all South Africans to be registered as white, black, or "colored." The Group Areas Act of 1950 mandated residential and business zones in cities separated for each racial group, in which black residents would be forcibly removed or barred from owning land. In 1974, the Bantu Homeland Citizenship Act forcibly resettled 3 million people in black "homelands." By the end of apartheid, 60,000 white farmers held 86 percent of all farmland, compared to the 13 million black South Africans who held 14 percent of poor-quality land.

For the first two decades, apartheid was resisted through nonviolent activism. Later in the 1960s, some antiapartheid political parties created armed factions, such as the African National Congress' Umkhonto we Sizwe, to force the government to abandon its system of segregation. Subsequently, the African National Congress admitted to using torture, executions, and landmines in fighting against apartheid.[270] In the 1980s, the South African government intensified its violent repression of the antiapartheid movement, leading to an estimated 21,000 almost exclusively black deaths.[271]

On February 2, 1990, facing a rising tide of protests and international pressure, President F. W. de Klerk announced the release of political prisoners and the reversal of the ban on political organizations such as the African National Congress. In 1991, the National Party, African National Congress, and Inkatha Freedom Party, along with church and business representatives, negotiated the National Peace Accord to curb the escalating violence. The agreement, signed by twenty-seven political, trade union, and government leaders, created national, regional, and local peace structures charged with preventing violence in their region or locale.[272]

Formal constitutional negotiations began in 1991 at the Convention for a Democratic South Africa. A negotiated interim constitution would provide for an elected constitutional assembly to pass the final constitution; however, at the second plenary session in May 1992, negotiations broke down citing disagreements over the size of the supermajority required for the assembly to adopt the final constitution.[273]

After the Convention's collapse, in August 1992 the African National Congress and National Party established a "channel bilateral" to maintain communication, which led to considerable progress.[274] The groups later signed a record of understanding on the process to negotiate an interim government and interim constitution, and restarted the negotiation process through a multiparty negotiating process. This process included a plenary body of 208 members from 26 parties to draft an interim constitution. The resulting interim constitution came into force in April 1994.[275]

Later that month, South Africa held its first nonracial, democratic elections to select a transitional government and a new parliament. The African National Congress won the elections, with Nelson Mandela as the first democratically elected president of South Africa.

From 1994 to 1996, the newly elected parliament drafted a final constitution to replace the interim constitution, with a comment period from the public. In December 1996, President Nelson Mandela signed the constitution into law.[276]

The constitution-making process was divided into two phases. The first involved the adoption of the interim constitution, negotiated from March to November 1993 by the multiparty negotiating process. The interim constitution of 1993 was an interim agreement to govern the period of transition. Specifically, the interim constitution provided a blueprint for governing before the adoption of the final constitution, specified the process of adopting the final constitution, and imposed certain requirements for the final constitution including thirty-four constitutional principles.[277] In the second phase, after democratic elections in April 1994, the newly elected parliament would write the final constitution. The phase included a public participation program where ordinary citizens and civil society were invited to comment.[278]

The interim constitution contained thirty-four constitutional principles to be incorporated into the final constitution. The constitutional principles included a multiparty democracy with regular elections and universal adult suffrage, constitutional supremacy, a quasifederal system in place of a centralized government, nonracism and nonsexism, the protection of "all universally accepted fundamental rights, freedoms and civil liberties" in the bill of rights, equality before the law, the separation of powers with an impartial judiciary, provincial and local levels of government with democratic representation, and protection of the diversity of languages and cultures.[279] The new constitutional text was to be tested against these principles by the newly established Constitutional Court. If the text complied with the principles, it would become the final constitution; if it did not, it would be referred back to the Constitutional Assembly.

The final constitution, or the 1996 Constitution of the Republic of South Africa, incorporated the thirty-four principles previously agreed upon. The preamble provided that its aim was to heal the divisions of the past and establish a society based on democratic values, social justice, and fundamental human rights.[280] The 1996 constitution contained fourteen chapters – Founding Provisions; Bill of Rights; Co-Operative Government; Parliament; The President and National Executive; Provinces; Local Government, Courts and Administrative Justice; State Institutions Supporting Constitutional Democracy; Public Administration; Security Services; Traditional Leaders; Finance; and General Provisions – and seven operational schedules and four amendments. South Africa also created a Truth and Reconciliation Commission in 1995, tasked with studying the past brutalities of the apartheid regime committed from 1960 to 1994, and to uncover the truth about the crimes against humanity in exchange for amnesty for the perpetrator.

South Africa's transition to democracy is widely viewed as a success. South Africa's historic 1994 election was largely calm and peaceful. In May 1994, the newly elected South African parliament elected Nelson Mandela as the first president of the new democracy. The international community lifted sanctions and welcomed South Africa back into the United Nations. To date, South Africa receives top scores from Freedom House for upholding high democratic standards.[281] South Africa, however, suffers from gross inequality and ranks among the most unequal nations in the world according to the World Bank.

SUDAN–SOUTH SUDAN

The drivers for the most recent conflict between Sudan and South Sudan were seeded during the first Sudanese civil war. Civil war broke out between Sudan and South Sudan in 1955, a year before Sudan's independence from Great Britain. Some of the tensions creating the conflict were rooted in religious tension between the majority Muslim north and the Christian and animist south. In 1972, the two sides came to a peace agreement, known as the Addis Ababa Accords, ending the conflict. In 1983, the Second Sudanese Civil War began, building off the northern and southern tensions of the previous civil war. Religious tensions escalated when President Nimeiry imposed Sharia law in 1983, angering the predominantly Christian South Sudan.[282] Additionally, South Sudan possessed approximately two-thirds of the oil fields in Sudan, but received only a small share of the revenue generated by oil exports.[283] The government of Sudan used the wealth generated by the oil to expand its military capacity, much of which was used against the south.[284]

In 1983, President Nimeiry abolished South Sudan's autonomy, violating and ending the Addis Ababa Accords.[285] As a result, the Sudan People's Liberation Army led an insurrection for South Sudan.[286] The conflict escalated when Omar al-Bashir, a national government military leader, led a successful coup and became chief of state, prime minister, and chief of the armed forces.[287] Fighting lasted twenty-two years, ending when both parties signed the Comprehensive Peace Agreement in January 2005.[288] The UN estimates that 2 million people died in the conflict, and over 4 million people fled their homes.[289]

The Intergovernmental Authority on Development, a coalition of regional states, mediated peace talks between the government of Sudan and the Sudan People's Liberation Army in the early 2000s. Negotiations took place in Kenya and led to a breakthrough with the signing of the Machakos Protocol in July 2002. The Machakos Protocol became the foundation for the eventual Comprehensive Peace Agreement.[290]

The personal relationship between Vice President Ali Osman al-Taha and Sudan People's Liberation Army chairman Dr. John Garang was a key factor in the negotiations.[291] The two leaders increasingly met together without mediators to discuss and agree key principles.[292] In January 2005, the parties signed the Comprehensive Peace Agreement. The agreement contains six chapters and two annexures, totaling 241 pages. It was the culmination of several smaller agreements settled over the previous few years, starting with the Machakos Protocol, which became chapter one.[293] The agreement on a permanent ceasefire was Annexure I of the Comprehensive Peace Agreement.[294]

Chapter one of the Comprehensive Peace Agreement, the Machakos Protocol, entitled the people of South Sudan to exercise their right of external self-determination through a referendum six years from the signing of the agreement. Chapter two set forth the power-sharing arrangement. Under the arrangement, South Sudan had a high degree of autonomy, as well as substantial representation in the national government, including having the president of South Sudan serve as the first vice president of Sudan. The chapter also enshrined certain rights for the people of Sudan, such as the right to vote, equal rights between men and women, freedom of movement, ownership of land, and freedom of marriage.[295]

Chapter three addressed wealth-sharing and created a framework for the management and development of oil resources in Sudan, including the establishment of the National Petroleum Commission. The chapter also authorized the creation of a National Land Commission to arbitrate competing claims over land and natural resources. A similar Southern Sudan Land Commission was established and had the same responsibilities as the National Land Commission, but with jurisdiction within South Sudan.[296]

Chapter four set out a plan for the final status of Abyei. At the time of the referendum for the south, Abyei would also be entitled to a referendum to determine whether it remained with Sudan or became a part of the south. In the interim, Abyei held special administration status. Chapter five provided similar special administrative status to Southern Kordofan and the Blue Nile states, but with the right to a "popular consultation" in lieu of a referendum on self-determination. Chapter six set out detailed provisions for the maintenance of two separate armies until final status was determined.[297]

In July 2011, South Sudan became an independent state, and in December 2013 it descended into its own civil war, which lasted until February 2020. Somewhat ironically, in 2020 South Sudan hosted the peace negotiations between the national government of Sudan and Darfur, Southern Kordofan, the Blue Nile and other regions in Sudan, which led to the Juba Peace Agreement discussed earlier.

WESTERN SAHARA–MOROCCO

The conflict in Western Sahara originated from nearly a century of colonization by Spain from 1884 to 1975.[298] In 1965, the United Nations called for the decolonization of Western Sahara, which began ten years later in 1975 when Spain withdrew under the Madrid Accords.[299] The United Nations intended for self-determination of the indigenous Saharawi, who had organized themselves into the Polisario Front independence movement in the last years of Spanish rule in Western Sahara when it called for decolonization. But in that same year, Morocco annexed the territory, and relocated 350,000 of its citizens there.[300] The indigenous Saharawi declared the establishment of the Saharan Arab Democratic Republic, and formed the armed Polisario Front, which engaged in armed hostilities with both Morocco and

Mauritania. Consequently, large portions of the population fled to refugee camps in Tindouf, Algeria.

The conflict with Mauritania was settled in 1979, but the conflict with Morocco continued until a ceasefire in 1991. The conflict continues in the political sphere, with occasional eruptions of violence in the many refugee camps.

The peace process in Western Sahara began in 1990 with the United Nations Security Council Resolution 658, also known as the Settlement Plan, which called for the appointment of a special envoy to Western Sahara for peace negotiations.[301] In 1991, the UN brokered a ceasefire between the Polisario Front and Morocco, which included a mandate for Morocco to hold a referendum on Western Sahara's independence, but this referendum has yet to happen.[302] The 1991 agreement also led to the establishment of a UN peacekeeping presence in Western Sahara which continues today,[303] resulting in the Western Sahara conflict becoming one of the oldest "frozen" conflicts.[304] Morocco's failure to implement the referendum has resulted in significant tension with the international community, with Morocco repeatedly condemned by such international organizations as Human Rights Watch and the UN High Commissioner for Human Rights.[305]

In 2000, James Baker III, the UN Secretary-General's envoy to Western Sahara put forward a draft framework agreement, also called the Baker Plan. The plan consisted of a straightforward seven paragraphs over two pages.[306] It proposed a transitional period of five years before holding an eventual referendum on the status of Western Sahara. During this transitional period, a locally elected legislature and executive would carry out all local governance affairs, while the kingdom of Morocco would continue to carry out foreign policy and national security. Any proposed modification to the arrangement would require the consent of the new locally elected legislature and executive.[307] The proposal was not accepted by the parties.

In July 2003 the UN Security Council, acting under Chapter VI in Resolution 1495, endorsed a second plan by James Baker. The Baker Plan II was similar to the original Baker Plan with two noteworthy modifications. The first was that this proposal relaxed the residency requirements to participate in the referendum but tightened the requirements for voting in the election to select the interim government. The second modification was that this proposal detailed the choices for an eventual referendum, including full independence from Morocco, whereas the earlier iteration had not specified what the referendum choices would be.[308] The Polisario approved of the new Baker Plan, but Morocco objected to the independence option in a referendum.[309]

In 2006, Morocco created a Western Sahara Autonomy Proposal, and submitted it to the United Nations in April 2007. The proposal consisted of three pillars: the first reiterated Morocco's wish for a peaceful resolution, the second contained the specific elements of the proposal relating to the autonomy of Western Sahara within the sovereignty of Morocco, and the third called for continuing negotiations and an ultimate referendum on the proposal.[310] The text laid out essentially the same balance of local and national authority as well as responsibility from the Baker Plan's transitional period, although it proposed that this arrangement be permanent.[311] The Polisario rejected the 2003 autonomy plan proposed by Morocco, preferring to continue its pursuit of self-determination and preferably independence from Morocco.[312]

While large-scale violence has not occurred since the 1991 ceasefire, reports of discrimination against pro-independence individuals in Western Sahara continue, such as increased incidence of arrest and brutal treatment by police.[313] In 2018, the United Nations Security Council announced the resumption of peace talks, but in April 2020 the Polisario Front made a public statement condemning the ongoing talks, arguing that the inaction by the United Nations legitimized the encroachment of Morocco into the territory, and reiterating the request that the UN organize a free referendum within Western Sahara on self-governing status.

YEMEN

Tribal leaders historically helped to resolve conflicts amongst Yemenis. However, with the erosion of the tribal system, these conflicts increasingly remained unresolved. With the unification of North Yemen and South Yemen in 1990, Yemen experienced increasing turmoil among both the northern Zaidi and the southern populations. Both groups felt marginalized and discriminated against, with southern Yemenis also believing that the north usurped their natural resources. The Yemeni government has also had to contend with a rising presence of Al-Qaeda in the Arabian Peninsula.[314]

Marginalization and endemic corruption further drove tensions in Yemen from the early 2000s.[315] A crumbling economy and rising unemployment exacerbated these issues.[316] Feeling unheard and unrepresented, marginalized groups rallied against the government when the Arab Spring reached Yemen in 2011.[317] By that time, President Ali Abdullah Saleh had been in power for over thirty years and the Yemeni people wanted change. Consequently, the Yemeni army split between forces loyal to President Saleh and those loyal to his distant cousin Ali Mohsen, the commander of the 1st Armored Division, and Yemen descended into civil war.[318]

To end the conflict, the United Nations and the Gulf Cooperation Council, comprised of Bahrain, Kuwait, Oman, Qatar, Saudi Arabia, and the United Arab Emirates, negotiated the Agreement on the Implementation Mechanism for the Transition Process in Yemen in Accordance with the Initiative of the Gulf Cooperation Council (2011 GCC Initiative).[319] The GCC Initiative outlined a process for a transitional government and new constitution for Yemen. This process included several months for a national dialogue conference, followed by a constitution-drafting process, a constitutional referendum, and elections.[320] The peace process was designed to balance competing desires from southern secessionists, northern Houthi rebels, and a national government wishing to retain a unitary and unified state. The initiative aimed to address these competing interests and form a government of national unity through two phases. First, a transitional mechanism would enter into force and lead to the election of a new interim president to oversee the transitional government. The second phase would involve the beginning of the National Dialogue Conference and drafting of a new constitution. It would end with general elections for a new president under a newly developed constitution, drafted within the interim period.[321]

Following the 2011 GCC Initiative, President Saleh stepped down and his vice president, Abd Rabbo Mansour Hadi, was elected to the position of interim president, intending to lead the transitional government for a two-year term. Mr. Hadi was elected to the position of interim president via a ballot which listed him as the only candidate standing for election. Almost immediately, former President Saleh sought to undermine the ability of President Hadi to implement the GCC Initiative.[322]

Nevertheless, President Hadi convened the National Dialogue Conference and mandated it to propose a set of recommendations to mitigate the conflict drivers and design a process for the democratic transformation of Yemen.[323] According to the GCC Initiative, the National Dialogue Conference was to draft guidelines for constitutional reform, address issues of tension in Yemen (such as the southern question, human rights issues, and strengthening the rights of vulnerable individuals), design a path for moving toward a democratic system while focusing on national reconciliation and transitional justice, and recommend initiatives for reconstruction and sustainable economic development.[324] The National Dialogue Conference operated for nine months and produced a comprehensive document with over 1,800 recommendations relating to the democratic transformation of Yemen.[325]

Broadly speaking, the outcomes recommended the substantial sharing of political, administrative, and fiscal decision-making among four levels of government: the creation of transitional justice mechanisms, the reformation of the parliament and the Shura Council so that the northern and southern provinces would each have 50 percent representation, enhanced protections for freedom of religion, special status for Sana'a and Aden, and substantial local control over natural resources.

Two months after the end of the National Dialogue, President Hadi, the interim president, appointed a seventeen-member Constitution Drafting Committee to draft the new constitution based on the outcomes of the National Dialogue.[326] During the first series of meetings, the drafting committee identified over 1,200 recommendations made by the National Dialogue that were deemed constitutional in nature.

As the Constitution Drafting Committee continued to work on the constitution, Yemen's economy, as well as its security situation, rapidly deteriorated.[327] The committee completed a draft constitution in 2015. The constitution was intended to transform Yemen from a unitary to a federal state, and provided for the devolution of substantial political and fiscal authority. In particular, the constitution provided that each of the regions, *wilaya*, and districts would enjoy financial independence.[328] The draft constitution also provided for the creation of a National Revenue Fund, to be managed by a board that included representatives from each level of government.[329] The constitution also included an expansive view of human rights. It included fundamental rights such as equality before the law, as well as a series of detailed socioeconomic rights,[330] so long as these rights did not conflict with Sharia.[331]

The process of democratic transformation reached a tipping point when the special committee created by the president to determine the boundaries of the regions released its conclusions. The committee created two regions in the south, which rendered the potential for future secession more difficult, and ensured that the region associated primarily with Houthi territory had limited access to important economic assets in the form of oil and coastal resources.[332] The party of former President Saleh also rejected the six-region solution, arguing instead for the creation of more numerous and smaller governorates, which would be less likely to seek self-determination.

Two days after the details of the constitution leaked, the Houthis rejected the proposed federalist structure[333] and abducted the secretary of the Constitution Drafting Committee, who was on his way to deliver the draft to the interim parliament for approval.[334] Yemen then slipped into a multidimensional armed conflict characterized by deep political dysfunction and humanitarian catastrophe.[335] The conflict is characterized by widespread food insecurity, with nearly half of the population facing famine-like circumstances;[336] frequent indiscriminate artillery and missile attacks by the Houthi forces; and inexplicably imprecise airstrikes by the Saudi-led coalition which hit homes, markets, hospitals, schools, and mosques;[337] the widespread use of child soldiers;[338] and the obstruction of humanitarian assistance.[339]

Notes

CHAPTER 1

1 *See* Stockholm International Peace Research Institute, SIPRI YEARBOOK 2008: ARMAMENT, DISARMAMENT AND INTERNATIONAL SECURITY (Oxford University Press, 2008) 72.
2 LOTTA HARBOM, STINA HÖGBLADH, and PETER WALLENSTEEN, "Armed Conflict and Peace Agreements" (2006) 43(5) JOURNAL OF PEACE RESEARCH 617, 623–624. One hundred and forty-four total agreements (1989–2005) are recorded in the Uppsala Conflict dataset. Forty-four had disarmament provisions. Twenty-three included the deployment of peacekeepers. Thirty-eight called for the integration of armed forces.
3 For more information on security arrangements in postconflict contexts and peace processes, *see generally* Craig Valters et al., "Security in Post-Conflict Contexts: What Counts as Progress and What Drives It?" (Overseas Development Institute, Apr. 2014); Alan Bryden et al., "Shaping a Security Governance Agenda in Post-Conflict Peacebuilding" (Geneva Centre for the Democratic Control of Armed Forces, Nov. 2005); "Security Arrangements before, during, and after Negotiations" (Berghof Foundation, Oct. 2012); ROLF SCHWARZ, "Post-Conflict Peacebuilding: The Challenges of Security, Welfare, and Representation" (2005) 36(4) SECURITY DIALOGUE 429–446.
4 DAVID A. BACKER, RAI BHAVNANI, and PAUL K. HUTH, PEACE AND CONFLICT 2016 (Routledge, 2016) 94. There were sixteen total agreements in this period, with civil war recurrence avoided in seven out of the eight in which the provisions were fully implemented.
5 MAX WEBER, THE VOCATION LECTURES (Rodney Livingstone, David Owen, and Tracy B. Strong eds., Hackett, 2004) 33.
6 THOMAS HOBBES, LEVIATHAN (Edward White and David Widger eds., Project Gutenberg EBook, Jan. 25, 2013) Part II, Ch. X7.
7 Benjamin Brast, "Liberal Statebuilding Interventions and the Monopoly on Violence" (PhD thesis, Bremen International Graduate School of Social Sciences, 2015) 25.
8 *See generally*, Laura Kasinof, "Why the World Missed Yemen's Downward Spiral" (Foreign Policy, Apr. 20, 2015).

237

9 Brast, *supra* note 7 at 25.
10 Sovereignty is defined in public international law as "the basic international legal status of a state that is not subject, within its territorial jurisdiction, to the governmental, executive, legislative, or judicial jurisdiction of a foreign state or to foreign law other than public international law." *See* HELMUT STEINBERGER, "Sovereignty," MAX PLANCK INSTITUTE FOR COMPARATIVE PUBLIC LAW AND INTERNATIONAL LAW, ENCYCLOPEDIA FOR PUBLIC INTERNATIONAL LAW (1987) vol. 10, 414.
11 "Providing Security in Times of Uncertainty: Opting for a Mosaic Security System" (Monopoly on the Use of Force 2.0?, Report of the Global Reflection Group, Friedrich Ebert Stiftung, 2017) 2.
12 Charter of the United Nations [UN Charter] (San Francisco, June 26, 1945), 3 Bevans 1153, 59 Stat. 1031, TS No. 993, entered into force Oct. 24, 1945, Ch. I, art. 2 (1, 4, 7).
13 Sofía Sebastián and Aditi Gorur, "U.N. Peacekeeping & Host-State Consent: How Missions Navigate Relationships with Governments" (Stimson Center, 2018) 13, 15.
14 UN Charter, *supra* note 12.
15 PAUL WILLIAMS and MICHAEL SCHARF, "The Letter of the Law" *in* WITH NO PEACE TO KEEP ... UNITED NATIONS PEACEKEEPING AND THE WAR IN THE FORMER YUGOSLAVIA (Ben Cohen and George Stamkoski eds., Grainpress, 1995) 34, 35.
16 United Nations Peacekeeping, "Mandates and the Legal Basis for Peacekeeping" (undated).
17 UN Department of Peacekeeping Operations, "United Nations Peacekeeping Operations: Principles and Guidelines" [Capstone Doctrine] (Jan. 18, 2008) Part I, Ch. 2, p. 17.
18 *Id.*, Part I, Ch. 2, p. 18.
19 *Id.*
20 *Id.* at 34–35.
21 *Id.* at 18.
22 UN Charter, *supra* note 12, Ch. VI, arts. 33–38.
23 "United Nations Peacekeeping Operations: Principles and Guidelines" (UN Department of Peacekeeping Operations, 2008) 1.4, 2.3, 2.4.
24 UN Charter, *supra* note 12, art. 25.
25 MARKO DIVAC ÖBERG, "The Legal Effects of Resolutions of the UN Security Council and General Assembly in the Jurisprudence of the ICJ" (2005) 16 EUROPEAN JOURNAL OF INTERNATIONAL LAW 879, 885; KWADWO APPIAGYEI-ATUA, "United Nations Security Council Resolution 1325 on Women, Peace, and Security – Is It Binding?" (2011) 18(3) HUMAN RIGHTS BRIEF 1, 2–6.
26 This reading was codified in the International Court of Justice's 1971 opinion on South Africa's presence in Namibia. The International Court of Justice found that: "Article 25 is not confined to decisions in regard to enforcement action but applies to 'the decisions of the Security Council' adopted in accordance with the Charter. Moreover, that Article is placed, not in Chapter VII, but immediately after Article 24 in that part of the Charter which deals with the functions and powers of the Security Council. If Article 25 had reference solely to decisions of the Security Council concerning enforcement action under Articles 41 and 42 of the Charter, that is to say, if it were only such decisions which had binding effect, then Article 25 would be superfluous, since this effect is secured by Articles 48 and 49 of the Charter." *Advisory Opinion on the Legal Consequences for States*

of the Continued Presence of South Africa in Namibia, Advisory Opinion, ICJ Rep. 1971 (June 21) art. 113.

27 Capstone Doctrine, *supra* note 17, Part I, Ch. 1, pp. 13–14. "United Nations peacekeeping operations have traditionally been associated with Chapter VI of the Charter. However, the Security Council need not refer to a specific Chapter of the Charter when passing a resolution authorizing the deployment of a United Nations peacekeeping operation and has never invoked Chapter VI."

28 *See generally*, Giandomenico Picco, "The U.N. and the Use of Force" (Foreign Affairs, Sep./Oct. 1994).

29 UN Charter, *supra* note 12, art. 42.

30 *Id.* at art. 2(7).

31 "Security Council Action under Chapter VII: Myths and Realities" (Security Council Report, June 23, 2008).

32 SC Res. 83, UN SCOR, 5th Year, Resolutions and Decisions of the Security Council, 1950, UN Doc. S/1511 (1950).

33 *Id.*

34 SC Res. 161, UN SCOR, 16th Year, Resolutions and Decisions of the Security Council, 1961, UN Doc. S/RES/161 (1961).

35 TREVOR FINDLAY, THE USE OF FORCE IN UN PEACE OPERATIONS (Stockholm International Peace Research Institute, Oxford University Press, 2002) 87, 125. To track the evolution of the scope of the mandate of peacekeeping forces from one of the nonuse of force except in self-defense to a scope that allowed for the use force in the defense of the mandate, including civilian populations, in an effort to create the conditions necessary for a peace process, *see* "Report of the Panel on United Nations Peace Operations," GAOR, 55th Session, at viii–ix, UN Doc. A/55/305 (2000).

36 SC Res 1244, UN SCOR, UN Doc. S/RES/1244 (1999) para. 3.

37 UN Charter, *supra* note 12, art. 52.

38 *Id.* at art. 53.

39 The Alvor Agreement between Portugal and the Angolan Liberation Movements [Alvor Agreement] (Alvor, Jan. 15, 1975) *in* "Decolonization" (United Nation Department of Political Affairs, Trusteeship and Decolonization, Mar. 1975) Vol. II, No. 4, 17–28.

40 "Angola: Civil War" (World Peace Foundation at the Fletcher School, Aug. 7, 2015).

41 Peace Accords for Angola (Lisbon, May 1, 1991), People's Republic of Angola and UNITA, UN SCOR S/22609, Attachment IV, § III, arts. 3.1–3.2, § VI.A, art. 1.

42 "Angola: Civil War," *supra* note 40; Peace Accords for Angola, *supra* note 41.

43 Lusaka Protocol, Government of the Republic of Angola and UNITA (Lusaka, July 23, 1999).

44 SC Res. 1229, UN SCOR, UN Doc. S/RES/1229 (1999).

45 Luena Agreement, Government of the Republic of Angola and UNITA (Apr. 26, 2002).

46 "Former Yugoslavia: UNPROFOR" (United Nations Department of Public Information, Sep. 1996).

47 Ivo H. Daalder, "Decision to Intervene: How the War in Bosnia Ended" (Brookings Institution, Dec. 1, 1998).

48 The General Framework Agreement for Peace in Bosnia and Herzegovina (Dayton, Nov. 21, 1995).

49 *Id.* at Annex 4, art. V.10.a.

50 "Ministry of Defense and the Armed Forces of Bosnia and Herzegovina: Brochure 2015" (Public Relation Office of the BiH Ministry of Defense, July 2015) 4–5.

51 "Burundi Profile – Timeline" (BBC News, Dec. 3, 2018); Henri Boshof and Waldemar Vrey, "A Technical Analysis of Disarmament, Demobilisation, and Reintegration: A Case Study from Burundi" (ISS Monograph Series, Aug. 2006) 3.

52 "Country Overview: Burundi" (United Nations Disarmament, Demobilization and Reintegration Resource Center, undated).

53 "Mozambique: Civil War" (World Peace Foundation, Mass Atrocity Endings, Aug. 7, 2015).

54 General Peace Agreement for Mozambique (Rome, Oct. 4, 1992) Republic of Mozambique and RENAMO, UN SCOR S/24635, Protocol IV, art. VI.i.1.

55 "Mozambique Political Leaders Sign Peace Pact" (*Deutsche Welle*, Aug. 1, 2019).

56 Alex Vines, "Prospects for a Sustainable Elite Bargain in Mozambique: Third Time Lucky?" (Chatham House, 2019).

57 Bougainville Peace Agreement (Arawa, Aug. 30, 2001) arts. 4, 60, 329.

58 *Id.* at art. 312; 'Referendum Results' (Bougainville Referendum Commission, Dec. 11, 2019).

59 "Rwanda Assessment" (Country Information and Policy Unit, Immigration and Nationality Directorate of the Home Office of the United Kingdom, Oct. 2000); Kathryn Reid, "1994 Rwandan Genocide, Aftermath: Facts, FAQs, and How to Help" (World Vision, Apr. 1, 2019).

60 NINA WILÉN, "From Foe to Friend? Army Integration after War in Burundi, Rwanda and the Congo" (2016) 23(1) INTERNATIONAL PEACEKEEPING 79, 81–82.

61 *See generally*, "Getting Away with Murder, Mutilation, Rape: New Testimony from Sierra Leone" (Human Rights Watch, July 1999).

62 Economic Community of West African States Monitoring Group.

63 Peace Agreement between the Government of Sierra Leone and the Revolutionary United Front of Sierra Leone [Lomé Agreement] (Lomé, July 7, 1999) art. IX, annexed in SC Res. S/1999/77; Ibrahim Abdullah, "Between Democracy and Terror: The Sierra Leone Civil War" (Council for the Development of Social Science Research in Africa, 2004) 213.

64 The Comprehensive Peace Agreement between the Government of the Republic of the Sudan and the Sudan People's Liberation Movement/Sudan People's Liberation Army (2005) Ch. VI, art. 1.

65 Virginia Page Fortna, "Where Have All the Victories Gone? Peacekeeping and War Outcomes" (Working Paper Prepared for Presentation at the Annual Meeting of the American Political Science Association, Aug. 2009) 1, 24.

66 *Id.*

67 *See* FRIEDRICH SOLTAU, "The Right to Participate in the Debates of the Security Council" (2000) 5(13) ASIL INSIGHTS ("Under Article 31 of the Charter any member of the UN may participate, without the right to vote, in the discussion before the Council, if the Council 'considers that the interests of that member are specially affected'").

68 *See generally*, "Status of Forces Agreement" (US Department of State, undated).

69 Sebastián and Gorur, *supra* note 13 at 16.

70 "Summary of AG-050 Department of Peacekeeping Operation (DPKO) Office of the Under-Secretary-General (OUSG) (1992–present)" (United Nations Archives and Records Management Section, 2007) 420.

71 Mozambican National Resistance (in Portuguese, Resistência Nacional Moçambicana, undated).

72 General Peace Agreement for Mozambique (Rome, Aug. 7, 1992), UN Doc. S/2463 (1992).

73 "General Peace Agreement" (Mozambique – ONUMOZ Background, UN, undated).

74 Letter dated Oct. 4, 1992 from the President of the Republic of Mozambique addressed to the Secretary-General (Enclosure), at 2, UN Doc. S/24635 (Oct. 8, 1992).

75 "Mozambique – UNUMOZ: Facts and Figures" (UN Peacekeeping, undated).

76 "General Peace Agreement" (Mozambique – ONUMOZ Background, UN, undated).

77 SC Res. 1590, UN SCOR, UN Doc. S/RES/1590 (2005).

78 Humanitarian Ceasefire Agreement on the Conflict in Darfur (N'djamena, 2004).

79 "UNMIS Facts and Figures" (UN Peacekeeping, undated).

80 Darfur Peace Agreement (Abuja, 2006) arts. 184, 241, 270.

81 UN Doc. S/2006/591 (2005).

82 SC Res. 1706, UN SCOR, UN Doc. S/RES/1706 (2006).

83 Sebastián and Gorur, *supra* note 13 at 15.

84 "About UNAMID" (United Nations–African Union Hybrid Operation in Darfur); SC Res. 1769, UN SCOR, UN Doc. S/RES/1769 (2007).

85 Letter dated Mar. 15, 2004 from the Permanent Representative of Burundi to the United Nations addressed to the President of the Security Council, UN Doc. S/2004/208 (Mar. 15, 2004).

86 SC Res. 1545, UN SCOR, UN Doc. S/RES/1545 (May 21, 2004).

87 Letter dated Nov. 26, 1991 from the Permanent Representative of Yugoslavia to the United Nations addressed to the President of the Security Council, UN Doc. S/23240 (Nov. 26, 1991).

88 SC Res. 713, UN SCOR, UN Doc. S/RES/713 (Sep. 25, 1991).

89 Paul R. Williams, "UN Members Share Guilt for Genocide in Bosnia" (Christian Science Monitor, Aug. 8, 1995).

90 Paul R. Williams, "Why the Bosnian Arms Embargo Is Illegal" (Wall Street Journal Europe, June 15, 1995).

91 Carol J. Williams, "News Analysis: Conflicting Approaches to Ending Balkans War Forge Odd Alliances" (Los Angeles Times, Aug. 13, 1994).

92 "Angola – MONUA Background" (UN Peacekeeping, undated).

93 National Union for the Total Independence of Angola (Portuguese: União Nacional para a Independência Total de Angola, undated).

94 SC Res. 1229, UN SCOR, UN Doc. S/RES/1229 (1999).

95 "Waging War to Keep the Peace: The ECOMOG Intervention and Human Rights" (June 1993) 5(6) HUMAN RIGHTS WATCH, https://www.hrw.org/reports/1993/liberia/#3.

96 SC Res. 1973, UN SCOR, UN Doc. S/RES/1973 (Mar. 17, 2011) arts. 4, 6, 8.

97 Agreement on a Ceasefire between the Government of the Democratic Socialist Republic of Sri Lanka and the Liberation Tigers of Tamil Eelam (Sri Lanka, Feb. 22, 2002) art. 3.2.

98 "NORWAY: Sri Lankan Rebel Tamil Tigers Demand that European Union Members Be Withdrawn from a Five-Nation Truce Monitoring Mission at Talks in Oslo" (Screen Ocean Reuters, June 24, 2006).

99 "SLMM Tipped-Off LTTE" (Daily Mirror, Oct. 1, 2014).

100 "Iceland 'Apologises' to Sri Lanka" (BBC Sinhala, Oct. 4, 2007).

101 "TIMELINE: Collapse of Sri Lanka's Troubled Ceasefire" (Reuters, Jan. 8, 2008).

102 "War Crimes in Sri Lanka" (International Crisis Group Report, May 17, 2010).

103 San José Agreement on Human Rights Signed between the Government of El Salvador and the Frente Farabundo Martí para la Liberación Nacional (San José, 1990).

104 SC Res. 693, UN SCOR, UN Doc. S/RES/693, paras. 2–4 (May 20, 1991).

105 Peace Agreement [Chapultepec Agreement] (Mexico City, Jan. 16, 1992) Government of El Salvador and Frente Farabundo Martí para la Liberación Nacional, UN GAOR A/46/864, Ch. VII, 26–29.

106 SC Res. 729, UN SCOR, UN Doc. S/RES/729 (1992).

107 SC Res. 832, UN SCOR, UN Doc. S/RES/832 (1993).

108 "El Salvador – ONUSAL: Facts and Figures" (UN Peacekeeping, 2003).

109 SC Res. 991, UN SCOR, UN Doc. S/RES/991 (1995).

110 University of Notre Dame Peace Accords Matrix, "Chapultepec Peace Agreement" (2015).

111 Brioni Declaration (Ljubljana, 1991).

112 Memorandum of Understanding on the Monitor Mission to Yugoslavia (Ljubljana, 1991).

113 "European Community Monitoring Mission in the Former Yugoslavia" (Government of Canada, 2018).

114 SC Res. 770, UN SCOR, UN Doc. S/RES/770 (1992).

115 SC Res. 776, UN SCOR, UN Doc. S/RES/776 (1992).

116 Agreement on the OSCE Kosovo Verification Mission (Belgrade, Oct. 16, 1998), as published in 73(4) DIE FRIEDENS-WARTE 503–533. *See also* https://www.youtube.com/watch?v=e6-nmgPZ_7Y.

117 SC Res. 1203, UN SCOR, UN Doc. S/RES/1203 (1998).

118 "OSCE Kosovo Verification Mission/OSCE Task Force for Kosovo (Closed)" (OSCE, undated).

119 "Kosovo Verification Mission" (Government of Canada, 2018).

120 Carlotta Gall, "Serbs' Killing of 40 Albanians Ruled a Crime against Humanity" (New York Times, Mar. 18, 1999).

121 Second Amended Indictment, *Prosecutor v. Milosevic, Milutinovic, Sainovic, Ojdanic, and Stojiljkovic* (IT-99-37-PT), Oct. 16, 2001.

122 SC Res. 1244, UN SCOR, UN Doc. S/RES/1244 (1999).

123 Letter dated Dec. 11, 1996 from the Permanent Representative of Sierra Leone to the United Nations Addressed to the Secretary-General, UN Doc. S/1996/1034 Annex – Peace Agreement between the Government of the Republic of Sierra Leone and the Revolutionary United Front of Sierra Leone, signed at Abidjan on Nov. 30, 1996, art. 11 (Dec. 11, 1996).

124 *See generally*, Lansana Gberie, "First Stages on the Road to Peace: The Abidjan Process (1995–96)" (Conciliation Resources, Sep. 2000).

125 Letter dated Dec. 11, 1996 from the Permanent Representative of Sierra Leone to the United Nations Addressed to the Secretary-General, *supra* note 123.

126 *See* SEAN CREEHAN, "Soldiers of Fortune 500" (2002) 23(4) HARVARD INTERNATIONAL REVIEW 6–7; Elizabeth Rubin, "Saving Sierra Leone, at a Price" (New York Times, Feb. 4, 1999).

127 To authorize this expansion, the Economic Community adopted a protocol that provided the legal basis for the body to serve in peacekeeping, peacebuilding, disarmament, and demobilization capacities through their Ceasefire Monitoring Group. ECOWAS, Protocol Relating to the Mechanism for Conflict Prevention, Management, Resolution, Peacekeeping and Security (Lomé, Dec. 10, 1999) A/P.1/12/99, arts. 17, 22.

128 Lomé Agreement, *supra* note 63.

129 *Id.* at art. IX.

130 *Id.* at Annex, art. 5.

131 *Id.* at arts. XIII and XIV.

132 SC Res. 1270, UN SCOR, UN Doc. S/RES/1270 (1999).

133 SC Res. 1313, UN SCOR, UN Doc. S/RES/1313 (2000).

134 SC Res. 1343, UN SCOR, UN Doc. S/RES/1343 (2001).

135 SC Res. 1346, UN SCOR, UN Doc. S/RES/1346 (2001).

136 SC Res. 1264, UN SCOR, UN Doc. S/RES/1264 (1999).

137 *See* David Rieff, Slaughterhouse: Bosnia and the Failure of the West (Touchstone, 1996).

138 Williams and Scharf, *supra* note 15 at 35.

139 *Id.*

140 *See generally,* Ivo H. Daalder, "Decision to Intervene: How the War in Bosnia Ended" (Brookings Institute, Dec. 1, 1998).

141 SC Res. 721, UN SCOR, UN Doc. S/RES/721 (1991); SC Res. 727, UN SCOR, UN Doc. S/RES/727 (1992).

142 SC Res. 743, UN SCOR, UN Doc. S/RES/743 (1992); SC Res. 749, UN SCOR, UN Doc S/RES/749 (1992).

143 SC Res. 762, UN SCOR, UN Doc. S/RES/762 (1992).

144 SC Res. 769, UN SCOR, UN Doc. S/RES/769 (1992).

145 SC Res. 743, UN SCOR, UN Doc. S/RES/743 (1992); SC Res. 749, UN SCOR, UN Doc S/RES/749 (1992).

146 SC Res. 908, UN SCOR, UN Doc. S/RES/908 (1994).

147 SC Res. 958, UN SCOR, UN Doc. S/RES/958 (1994).

148 Williams and Scharf, *supra* note 15 at 38.

149 Findlay, *supra* note 35 at 263.

150 Williams and Scharf, *supra* note 15 at 38.

151 SC Res. 770, SCOR, 47th Year, Resolutions and Decisions of the Security Council, 1992, at 24, UN Doc. S/RES/770 (Aug. 13, 1992) art. 2.

152 Williams and Scharf, *supra* note 15 at 34, 38.

153 SC Res. 816, UN SCOR, UN Doc. S/RES/816 (1993) paras. 3–4.

154 SC Res. 836, UN SCOR, UN Doc. S/RES/836 (1993) paras. 5–6, 9.

155 "The Fall of Srebrenica and the Failure of UN Peacekeeping" (Human Rights Watch, Oct. 15, 1995).

156 SC Res. 795, UN SCOR, UN Doc. S/RES/795 (1992).

157 SC Res. 842, UN SCOR, UN Doc. S/RES/842 (1993).

158 The General Framework Agreement for Peace in Bosnia and Herzegovina (Dayton, Nov. 21, 1995), Annex 1.

159 John Pomfret and Lee Hockstader, "In Bosnia, a War Crimes Impasse" (Washington Post, Dec. 9, 1997).

160 "War Criminal Arrested" (NATO, Apr. 21, 2000).

161 *See generally* Mimmi Soderberg Kovacs, "From Rebellion to Politics: The Transformation of Rebel Groups to Political Parties in Civil War Peace Processes" (PhD thesis, Uppsala University, 2007); JEROEN DE ZEEUW ed., FROM SOLDIERS TO POLITICIANS: TRANSFORMING REBEL MOVEMENTS AFTER CIVIL WAR (Lynne Rienner, 2008).

162 W. ANDY KNIGHT, "Disarmament, Demobilization, and Reintegration and Post-Conflict Peacebuilding in Africa: An Overview" (2008) 1(1) AFRICAN SECURITY 24, 34.

163 *Id.* at 47–48.

164 "DDR in Peace Operations: A Retrospective" (UN Department of Peacekeeping Operations, 2010) 4.

165 Chapultepec Agreement, *supra* note 105, Chs. 7, 11.

166 Peace Accords for Angola (Lisbon, May 1, 1991), People's Republic of Angola and UNITA, UN SCOR S/22609, Annex I, § C.

167 Cotonou Agreement (Cotonou, July 25, 1993) Liberia, UN Peacemaker S/26272, Annex, Part I sec. F, art. 7, para. 1.

168 "DDR in Peace Operations: A Retrospective" (UN Department of Peacekeeping Operations, 2010) 4.

169 Rotokas Record (Togaru, May 3, 2001) Bougainville Revolutionary Army and the Bougainville Resistance Force; *see also* "Arms Surrender" (Post-Courier, May 9, 2001).

170 Bougainville Peace Agreement (Arawa, Aug. 30, 2001).

171 Rotokas Record (Togaru, May 3, 2001) Bougainville Revolutionary Army and the Bougainville Resistance Force, Weapons Disposal Plan.

172 Bougainville Peace Agreement (Arawa, Aug. 30, 2001) Annex: Statement of Commitment to Unified Structures.

173 Rotokas Record (Togaru, May 3, 2001) Bougainville Revolutionary Army and the Bougainville Resistance Force, Weapons Disposal Plan; Bougainville Peace Agreement (Arawa, Aug. 30, 2001) Annex: Peace Process Consultative Committee Resolution on Weapons Disposal.

174 Bougainville Peace Agreement (Arawa, Aug. 30, 2001) arts. 60, 312.

175 *See* Jo Woodbury, "The Bougainville Independence Referendum: Assessing the Risks and Challenges before, during and after the Referendum" (Australian Defence College Centre for Defence and Strategic Studies, Jan. 2015).

176 *See e.g.* Final Agreement to End the Armed Conflict and Build a Stable and Lasting Peace (Bogota, 2016) Chs. 3, 2.1.2.1.c.

177 VÉRONIQUE DUDOUET, "Nonstate Armed Groups and the Politics of Postwar Security Governance" in MONOPOLY OF FORCE: THE NEXUS OF DDR AND SSR (Melanne A. Civic and Michael Miklaucic eds., Institute for National Strategic Studies, National Defense University, 2011) 9. For other, earlier, efforts at DDR in Colombia, *see generally* STEVEN JONES-CHALJUB, "Peace Negotiations in Colombia and the DDR Challenge" (2013) 5(11) COUNTER TERRORIST TRENDS AND ANALYSES 14–16 and Sergio Jaramillo et al., "Transitional Justice and DDR: The Case of Colombia" (International Center for Transitional Justice, June 2009).

178 Final Agreement to End the Armed Conflict and Build a Stable and Lasting Peace (Bogota, 2016) Ch. 3.

179 "Colombia FARC Rebel Dissidents Number 1,200, Military Says" (Reuters, Mar. 20, 2018).

180 NINA WILEN, "From Foe to Friend? Army Integration after War in Burundi, Rwanda and the Congo" (2016) 23(1) INTERNATIONAL PEACEKEEPING 79, 81–82.

181 Yemen National Dialogue Outcomes (2014) Ch. II, Working Group on Good Governance, Annex 7, art. 1, p. 92.

182 *Id.* at Ch. II, Working Group on Building the Foundations for the Security and Military Institutions, Decisions on Constitutional Principles, art. 1, p. 95.

183 *See generally,* "Rethinking Peace in Yemen" (International Crisis Group, July 2, 2020).

184 SC S/20346, UN SCOR, UN Doc. S/20346 (Dec. 22, 1988) Annex, Agreement among the People's Republic of Angola, the Republic of Cuba, and the Republic of South Africa.

185 "Angola: United Nations Angola Verification Mission I" (United Nations Department of Public Information, 2000).

186 Lomé Agreement, *supra* note 63, art. XVIII. For a detailed examination of DDR efforts in Sierra Leone as related to a broader program of transitional justice, *see generally* Mohamed Gibril Sesay and Mohamed Suma, "Transitional Justice and DDR: The Case of Sierra Leone" (International Center for Transitional Justice, June 2009).

187 Agreement on a Comprehensive Political Settlement of the Cambodia Conflict (Paris, Oct. 23, 1991) sec. IV, art. 8.

188 General Peace Agreement for Mozambique (Rome, Oct. 4, 1992) Republic of Mozambique and RENAMO, UN SCOR S/24635, Protocol IV, arts. VI.i.1–3.

189 Dudouet, *supra* note 177 at 10.

190 Peace Accords for Angola (Lisbon, May 1, 1991), People's Republic of Angola and UNITA, UN SCOR S/22609, Annex I, Appendix 4, 5(a).

191 Chapultepec Agreement, *supra* note 105, Ch. VII, 29.

192 Cotonou Agreement (Cotonou, July 25, 1993) IGNU, NPFL and ULIMO, UN Peacemaker S/26272, Annex, Part I, sec. E, art. 6.

193 Dudouet, *supra* note 177 at 9.

194 Memorandum of Understanding between the Government of the Republic of Indonesia and the Free Aceh Movement (Helsinki, 2005) 4.2.

195 *See* AGUS WANDI, "Guns, Soldiers and Votes: Lessons from DDR in Aceh" in POST-WAR SECURITY TRANSITION PROCESSES: PARTICIPATORY PEACEBUILDING AFTER ASYMMETRIC CONFLICTS (Véronique Dudouet et al. eds., Routledge, 2011). For more on DDR in Aceh, *see generally* Tommi Niemi, "Reintegration in Aceh Indonesia" (Crisis Management Centre Finland Yearbook, 2009) 92–109.

196 Bairbre de Brún, "The Road to Peace in Ireland" (Berghof Transition Series No. 6, 2008) 16.

197 Dudouet, *supra* note 177 at 10.

198 "El Salvador – ONUSAL Background" (United Nations Peacekeeping, undated).

199 PAUL R. WILLIAMS and MATTHEW T. SIMPSON, "Drafting in Doha: An Assessment of the Darfur Peace Process and Ceasefire Agreements" in MONOPOLY OF FORCE: THE NEXUS OF DDR AND SSR (Melanne A. Civic and Michael Miklaucic eds., Institute for National Strategic Studies, National Defense University, 2011) 50–52.

200 Sean McFate, "The Link between DDR and SSR in Conflict-Affected Countries" (USIP Special Report 238, May 2010).

201 Bernard Koucher, SRSG, "On the Establishment of the Kosovo Protection Corps" Regulation No. 1999/8, UN Doc. UNMIK/REG/1999/8 (Sep. 20, 1999) para. 1.1.

202 Ramadan Qehaja, Kosum Kosumi, and Florian Qehaja, "The Process of Demobilization and Integration of Former Kosovo Liberation Army Members – Kosovo's Perspective" (Kosovo Centre for Security Studies, Apr. 2010).

203 Mark Knight, "SSR: Post-conflict Integration" (Global Facilitation Network for Security Sector Reform, Aug. 2009) 19.

204 MARK SEDRA, "Introduction: The Future of Security Sector Reform" in THE FUTURE OF SECURITY SECTOR REFORM (Mark Sedra ed., Centre for International Governance Innovation, 2010) 16.

205 SC Res. 2151, UN SCOR, UN Doc. S/RES/2151 (Apr. 28, 2014) para. 5.

206 Dylan Hendrickson, *Understanding and Supporting Security Sector Reform* (Department for International Development, 2002) 7.

207 "What Is Security Sector Reform" (African Security Sector Network, 2018).

208 For more on the complexities of SSR, *see generally* Sean McFate, "Securing the Future: A Primer on Security Sector Reform in Conflict Countries" (United States Institute of Peace, 2008).

209 Williams and Simpson, *supra* note 199 at 50–52.

210 Peace Accords for Angola (Lisbon, May 1, 1991), People's Republic of Angola and UNITA, UN SCOR S/22609, Attachment IV – Protocol of Estoril § VI.A., arts. 1, 5, 9.

211 Vegard Andersen, "Disarmament Demobilization and Reintegration (DDR) of Ex-combatants in Angola" (University of Bergen, Nov. 2011) 42, 44.

212 G. EUGENE MARTIN, "Managing DDR and SSR Programs in the Philippines" in MONOPOLY OF FORCE: THE NEXUS OF DDR AND SSR (Melanne A. Civic and Michael Miklaucic eds., Institute for National Strategic Studies, National Defense University, 2011) 185.

213 Arusha Peace and Reconciliation Agreement, Ch. II, arts. 14 (1, 2) (Aug. 28, 2000).

214 *Id.* at art. 14.1.b. (The quotation refers to the national defense force, and the language is mirrored in art. 14.2.b. with regard to the national police force: "The national police shall include members of the current national police, combatants of the political parties and movements and other citizens who meet the requirements".)

215 *Id.* at art. 14 (1.g., 2.e.).

216 Cyrus Samii, "Military Integration in Burundi, 2000–2006" (Columbia University, June 8, 2010) 11–12.

217 Pretoria Protocol on Political, Defence, and Security Power Sharing in Burundi (Pretoria, Oct. 8, 2003) art. 1.3.1.

218 Pretoria Protocol on Outstanding Political, Defence and Security Power Sharing Issues in Burundi (Pretoria, Nov. 2, 2003).

219 Final Agreement to End the Armed Conflict and Build a Stable and Lasting Peace (Bogota, 2016) 3.2.1.

220 General Peace Agreement for Mozambique (Rome, Aug. 7, 1992), UN Doc. S/2463 (1992) Protocol IV.I.

221 *See id.* art. 6; Protocol VI.

222 Dudouet, *supra* note 177 at 14.

223 SC Res. 1556, UN SCOR, 59th year, Resolutions and Decisions of the Security Council, Aug. 1, 2003–July 31, 2004, UN Doc. S/RES/1556 (2004); Human Rights Situation in Sudan, UN Doc. A/HRC/7/HGO/21 (Feb. 21, 2008) 3.

224 "'They Were Shouting "Kill Them"': Sudan's Violent Crackdown on Protesters in Khartoum" (Human Rights Watch, Nov. 17, 2019).

225 Juba Declaration for Trust Building Procedures and Runup for Negotiations (Juba, 2020) sec. B.

226 Two Areas Track Agreement between the Transitional Government of Sudan and Sudan People's Liberation Movement-North/Sudan Revolutionary Front (Juba, 2020) sec. C, Chs. 2–3.

227 Agreement between Sudan and the Sudan People's Liberation Movement-North/Sudan Revolutionary Front (SPLM-N/SRF) (Juba, 2020) para. 18.

228 Darfur Agreement between the Transitional Government of Sudan and Darfur Parties to Peace (Juba, 2020) sec. I. Ch. 4, arts. 26.4–6.

229 *Id.* at sec. I. Ch. 4, art. 22.6; For more information related to DDR and SSR in peace processes on the African continent, *see generally* W. ANDY KNIGHT, "Linking DDR and SSR in Post Conflict Peace-Building in Africa: An Overview" (2010) 4(1) AFRICAN JOURNAL OF POLITICAL SCIENCE AND INTERNATIONAL RELATIONS 29–54.

230 The Comprehensive Peace Agreement between the Government of the Republic of the Sudan and the Sudan People's Liberation Movement/Sudan People's Liberation Army (2005), Ch. II, part II, art. 2.3.5.

231 *Id.* at Ch. I, art. 2.3.5–8.

232 *Id.* at Ch. VI, art. 1b.

233 *Id.* at Ch. VI, art. 3.

234 "Sudan's Spreading Conflict (I): War in South Kordofan" (International Crisis Group Africa Report No. 198, Feb. 14, 2013) 23n/140.

235 The Comprehensive Peace Agreement between the Government of the Republic of the Sudan and the Sudan People's Liberation Movement/Sudan People's Liberation Army (2005), Ch. VI, art. 1a and art. 4.

236 *Id.* at Ch. VI, art. 5.

237 Aly Verjee, "Sudan's Aspirational Army: A History of the Joint Integrated Units" (Centre for International Governance Innovation, SSR Issue Papers No. 2, May 2011) 6.

238 *Id.* at 4.

239 *Id.* at 7.

240 The General Framework Agreement for Peace in Bosnia and Herzegovina (Dayton, Nov. 21, 1995) Annex 1-A, art. I.2.a; Annex 4, art. V.10.a.

241 Mark Knight, "SSR: Post-Conflict Integration" (Global Facilitation Network for Security Sector Reform, Aug. 2009) 27; *see also* Sgt. Peter Fitzgerald, "The Armed Forces in Bosnia and Herzegovina" (NATO, Nov. 28, 2001) 127 SFOR Informer.

242 "Ministry of Defense and the Armed Forces of Bosnia and Herzegovina: Brochure 2015" (Public Relation Office of the BiH Ministry of Defense, July 2015) 4–5.

243 "Relations with Bosnia and Herzegovina" (NATO, Feb. 3, 2020).

244 *See* "Armed Forces of Bosnia and Herzegovina" (Ministry of Defense and Armed Forces of BiH, 2015).

245 Joint Agreement (Addis Ababa, Sep. 3, 2020) para. 4.
246 Permanent Ceasefire and Final Security Agreement Protocol (Juba, 2020) Ch. 4, arts. 29, 29.4.1, 29.5.2, 29.6.

CHAPTER 2

1 ANNA JARSTAD and DESIRÉE NILSSON, "From Words to Deeds: The Implementation of Power-Sharing Pacts in Peace Accords" (2008) 25 CONFLICT MANAGEMENT AND PEACE SCIENCE 206, 215.
2 *See* Benjamin A. T. Graham, Michael K. Miller, and Kaare W. Strøm, "Powersharing and Democratic Survival" (HIS Political Science Series Working Paper 141, 2016) 6.
3 EGHOSA E. OSAGHAE, "A Reassessment of Federalism as a Degree of Decentralization" (1990) 20(1) PUBLIUS 83.
4 For more information on the role of horizontal power-sharing arrangements in peace-building processes, *see generally* ULRICH SCHNECKENER, "Models of Ethnic Regulation: The Politics of Recognition" in MANAGING AND SETTLING ETHNIC CONFLICTS (Ulrich Schneckener and Stefan Wolff eds., Hurst, 2004); KRISTIN HENRARD, "Minority Protection Mechanisms as Means to Prevent and Settle Sovereignty Disputes: The Growing Recognition, Protection and Promotion of Participatory Rights of Minorities" in SOVEREIGNTY AND DIVERSITY (Miodrag Jovanovic and Kristin Henrard eds., Eleven International Publishing, 2008).
5 For more information on the role of power-sharing arrangements in peacebuilding processes, *see generally* David Lanz et al., "Negotiations, Continued: Ensuring the Positive Performance of Power-Sharing Arrangements" (USIP, 2019); MELANI CAMMETT and EDMUND MALESKY, "Power Sharing in Postconflict Societies: Implications for Peace and Governance" (2012) 56 JOURNAL OF CONFLICT RESOLUTION 982–1016; CAROLINE HARTZELL and MATTHEW HODDIE, "Institutionalizing Peace: Power Sharing and Post-Civil War Conflict Management" (2003) 47 AMERICAN JOURNAL OF POLITICAL SCIENCE 318–332.
6 CAMMETT and MALESKY, *supra* note 5 at 983.
7 Joseph Siegle and Patrick O'Mahony, "Assessing the Merits of Decentralization as a Conflict Mitigation Strategy" (USAID Office of Democracy and Governance 2006) i.
8 *Id.* at 1.
9 *Id.*
10 Nancy Bermeo, "Position Paper for the Working Group on Federalism, Conflict Prevention and Settlement" (Paper prepared for the International Conference on Federalism, Brussels, 2005) as cited in Siegle and O'Mahony, *supra* note 7 at 6.
11 Siegle and O'Mahony, *supra* note 7 at 6.
12 STEPHEN M. SAIDEMAN, THE TIES THAT DIVIDE: ETHNIC POLITICS, FOREIGN POLICY, AND INTERNATIONAL CONFLICT (Columbia University Press, 2001) as cited in Siegle and O'Mahony, *supra* note 7 at 6.
13 NICOLE HERTHER-SPIRO, "Can Ethnic Federalism Prevent Recourse to Rebellion – A Comparative Analysis of the Ethiopian and Iraqi Constitutional Structures" (2007) 21 EMORY INTERNATIONAL LAW REVIEW 321, 329.

14 James Manor, "The Political Economy of Democratic Decentralization" (World Bank, 1999) 10.

15 *See* Seigle and O'Mahony, *supra* note 7.

16 *See generally* PAUL WILLIAMS, TIFFANY SOMMADOSSI, and AYAT MUJAIS, "A Legal Perspective on Yemen's Attempted Transition from a Unitary to a Federal System of Government" (2017) 33(84) UTRECHT JOURNAL OF INTERNATIONAL AND EUROPEAN LAW 4–22.

17 Osaghae, *supra* note 3 at 85.

18 PIPPA NORRIS, DRIVING DEMOCRACY: DO POWER-SHARING INSTITUTIONS WORK? (Cambridge University Press, 2008) 168.

19 Spain Constitution (1978 rev. 2011) Ch. 3 & Transitional Provision 5. *See also* "Spain Profile" (OECD, 2016) 1.

20 Italy Constitution (1948) § II, arts. 114, 117.

21 *See* Paola E. Signoretta, John Foot et al., "Italy: Regional and Local Government" (Encyclopædia Britannica, July 15, 2020).

22 Italy Constitution (1948) § I, arts. 55–57 and § II, art. 116.

23 "Federalism" (Forum of Federations), http://www.forumfed.org/federalism/introduction-to-federalism/

24 Osaghae, *supra* note 3 at 85.

25 Ronald L. Watts, "Comparing Federal Systems in the 1990s" (Institute of Intergovernmental Relations, 1999) 1.

26 *See* Sujit Choudhry et al., "Decentralization in Unitary States: Constitutional Frameworks for the Middle East and North Africa" (Center for Constitutional Transitions, 2016) 11–12.

27 *Id.*

28 Constitutional Act, 1867, 30 & 31 Vict., c. 3, II and VI Part 2.

29 *See* Yukon Act, RSC 1985, c. Y-2; Northwest Territories Act, RSC 1985, c. N-27; Nunavut Act, SC 1993, c. 28.

30 Constitutional Act, 1867, 30 & 31 Vict., c. 3, subsec. 51(2) and VI Part 2.

31 Malaysia Constitution, Part I, art. 1(4); Part VI, Ch. 1, art. 73; Schedule Nine, List I, art. 6.

32 United Arab Emirates Constitution (2004) Preamble; art. 23; art. 46.

33 "Swiss Political System – Facts and Figures" (Swiss Confederation, undated).

34 "The Swiss Confederation: A Brief Guide" (Swiss Confederation Federal Chancellery, 2020) 13.

35 "Swiss Federalism" (Democracy: The Swiss Political System, Swiss Confederation, undated).

36 Act No. 577 – "The Greenland Home Rule Act" (Denmark, Nov. 29, 1978).

37 "What Are the Powers of the Scottish Parliament?" (Scottish Parliament, undated).

38 "Reserved Powers Model" (Senedd Cymru Welsh Parliament, undated).

39 "Guidance: Devolution Settlement: Northern Ireland" (Gov.UK, Sep. 23, 2019).

40 Claude Bélanger, "Quebec, the Constitution and Special Status" (Marianopolis College, 1998).

41 Constitutional Act, 1867, 30 & 31 Vict., c. 3, § 91.

42 Canadian Constitutional Act of 1982, art. 5 (Canada, 1982).

43 *Id. See also* Bélanger, *supra* note 40.

44 *See* M. Govinda Rao and Nirvikar Singh, "Asymmetric Federalism in India" (Santa Cruz Center for International Economics, 2004).

45 *See* K. Venkataramanan, "Explained: India's Asymmetric Federalism" (The Hindu, Aug. 11, 2019).

46 "The Netherlands" (Division of Powers, European Committee of the Regions, undated).

47 "France" (Division of Powers, European Committee of the Regions, undated).

48 Germany Constitution (1949) art. 74.

49 *Id.* at art. 73.

50 *Id.* at art. 30.

51 Canada Constitution (1867) § 91.

52 "Political Decentralization" (World Bank Group, 2001).

53 AREND LIJPHART, PATTERNS OF DEMOCRACY (Yale University Press, 2012) 33.

54 "Swiss Federalism" (swissfederalism.ch.ch, undated).

55 South Africa Constitution (1996) Ch. 6.

56 "Administrative Decentralization (World Bank Group, 2001).

57 J. Tyler Dickovick and Tegegne Gebre-Egziabher, "Comparative Assessment of Decentralization in Africa: Ethiopia Desk Study" (USAID, July 2010) 10.

58 "Democratic Decentralization Programming Handbook" (USAID, June 2009) 13.

59 "Administrative Decentralization (World Bank Group, 2001).

60 "Democratic Decentralization Programming Handbook" (USAID, June 2009) 13.

61 William F. Fox, "Fiscal Decentralization in Post Conflict Countries" (USAID Best Practice Paper, 2007) 9. *See e.g.* Robin Broadway and Ronald Watts, "Fiscal Federalism in Canada" (2000) 7.

62 "Fiscal Decentralisation in EU Applicant States and Selected EU Member States" (OECD, 2002) Ch. 1, Table 1.4.1.

63 Roy Bahl and Jorge Martinez-Vazquez, "Sequencing Fiscal Decentralization" (Policy Research Working Paper, World Bank, May 2006) 35.

64 Sean Muller, "Fiscal Decentralization in Switzerland" (Institute of Federalism, University of Fribourg, Aug. 2008) 14.

65 Switzerland Constitution (1999) art. 142.

66 Barnard Dafflon, "Fiscal Federalism in Switzerland: A Survey of Constitutional Issues, Budget Responsibility and Equalisation" (University of Fribourg Working Paper, 2006) 6, 24; Muller, *supra* note 64 at 14.

67 Muller, *supra* note 64 at 17.

68 "Democratic Decentralization Programming Handbook" (USAID, June 2009) 13.

69 Julio López-Laborda, Jorge Martinez-Vazquez, and Carlos Monasterio, "The Practice of Fiscal Federalism in Spain" (Georgia State University International Studies Program Working Paper 06-23, Oct. 2006) 36.

70 THOMAS D. GRANT, "Internationally Guaranteed Constitutive Order: Cyprus and Bosnia and Predicates for a New Nontraditional Actor in the Society of States" (1998) 8 JOURNAL OF TRANSATLANTIC LAW & POLICY 3, 4–5.

71 Bosnia and Herzegovina Constitution (1995) art. I, § 3 (Annex 4 to General Framework Agreement for Peace and in Bosnia and Herzegovina with Annexes [Dayton, Dec. 14, 1995]).

72 *See id.*, arts. III–V.

73 Siegle and O'Mahony, *supra* note 7 at 28.

74 Final Agreement to End the Armed Conflict and Build a Stable and Lasting Peace (Bogota, 2016) Ch. 6.

75 Memorandum of Understanding between the Government of the Republic of Indonesia and the Free Aceh Movement (Helsinki, Aug. 15, 2005) Part 1, § 1.1.2.

76 Jonathan Morrow, "Weak Viability: The Iraqi Federal State and the Constitutional Amendment Process" (United States Institute of Peace, 2006) 2.

77 Iraq Constitution (2005) arts. 1 and 116.

78 *Id.* at art. 121.

79 Ohrid Framework Agreement (Macedonia, 2001) § 3.

80 *See* Comprehensive Peace Agreement between the Government of Nepal and the Communist Party of Nepal (Maoist) (2006).

81 Philippines Constitution (1987) art. 10, § 20.

82 William Depasupil, "'Yes' Vote Prevails in 4 of 5 Provinces" (Manila Times, Jan. 23, 2019).

83 South Africa Constitution (1996) Ch. 6.

84 *Id.* at Scheds. 4–5.

85 *See* Williams, Sommadossi, and Mujais, *supra* note 16.

86 *See id.*

87 *See* Siegle and O'Mahony, *supra* note 7.

88 "Asymmetric Decentralization: Policy Implications in Colombia" (OECD, 2019) 5, 23.

89 Herther-Spiro, *supra* note 13 at 331.

90 "Census of Population, Households and Dwellings in the Republic of Macedonia, 2002 Final Data" (Republic of Macedonia State Statistical Office, 2005) 34, 35.

91 Marija Aleksovksa, "Trust in Changing Institutions: The Ohrid Framework Agreement and Institutional Trust in Macedonia" (2015) 43(1) East European Quarterly 55, 57, 84.

92 Ohrid Framework Agreement (Ohrid, 2001).

93 Cvete Koneska, "Vetoes, Ethnic Bidding, Decentralisation: Post-Conflict Education in Macedonia" (2012) 11(4) Journal on Ethnopolitics and Minority Issues in Europe 28, 33.

94 Ohrid Framework Agreement (Ohrid, 2001) Annex B(7), Annex C(6.1).

95 *Id.* at Annex A.

96 George Anderson, "Yemen's Failed Constitutional Transition: 2011–2015" (Forum of Federations Occasional Paper Series 41, 2019) 5–6.

97 Officially known as the People's Democratic Republic of Yemen.

98 Agreement on a Just Solution to the Southern Question, Subcommittee of the Southern Working Group (2013) part III.

99 Yemen Draft Constitution (2015) Ch. III, § IV, arts. 264, 273.

100 Anderson, *supra* note 96 at 18.

101 *See* Williams, Sommadossi, and Mujais, *supra* note 16.

102 Mareike Transfeld, "The Failure of the Transitional Process in Yemen" (German Institute for International and Security Affairs, 2015) 1.

103 Mohammed Ghobari and Agnus McDowall, "Houthis Abduct Yemeni Official amid Wrangling over Constitution" (Thomson Reuters Africa, Jan. 17, 2015).

104 Transfeld, *supra* note 102 at 1.
105 Darfur Agreement between the Transitional Government of Sudan and Darfur Parties to Peace (Juba, 2020) § B, para. 25.1.
106 *Id.*
107 *Id.* at § B, para. 25.3.
108 *Id.* at § B, para. 25.4.
109 The General Framework for Peace in Bosnia and Herzegovina (Dayton, 1995) Annex 2.
110 *See* "Bosnia: Serb Ethnic Cleansing" (DCI Interagency Balkan Task Force, Central Intelligence Agency, Dec. 1994).
111 In February 2020, Milorad Dodik, the Serb member of Bosnia's joint presidency, repeatedly called for a referendum on Republika Srpska independence. Dodik had previously called for an independence referendum and submitted a formal referendum proposal to the Republika Srpska Assembly in April 2011. Dodik withdrew the referendum in exchange for a "Structured Dialogue on Justice" among the institutions of Bosnia and the EU, which would discuss the grievances of Republika Srpska authorities toward the Bosnian judiciary. *See* "Dodik's Repeated Calls for Republika Srpska Session Raise Alarm" (Al Jazeera, Feb. 18, 2020) and Eldin Hadzovic and Drazen Remikovic, "Bosnia: Dodik Agrees to Drop Disputed Referendum" (BalkanInsight, May 13, 2011).
112 Washington Agreement (Washington, DC, 1994).
113 The Vance–Owen Plan (New York, Mar. 25, 1993) art. I.
114 Washington Agreement (Washington, DC, 1994) Framework Agreement for the Federation.
115 ROLAND SLYE, "The Dayton Peace Agreement: Constitutionalism and Ethnicity" (1996) 21(2) YALE JOURNAL OF INTERNATIONAL LAW 459, 463–464.
116 The General Framework Agreement for Peace in Bosnia and Herzegovina (Dayton, 1995) Annex 4, art. IV(11e, f); art. V(7d).
117 SLYE, *supra* note 115, 463–464.
118 JAMES O'BRIEN, "The Dayton Constitution of Bosnia and Herzegovina" in FRAMING THE STATE IN TIMES OF TRANSITION (Laurel E. Miller with Louis Aucoin eds., USIP, 2010) 347.
119 C. Bryson Hull and Bill Tarrant, "Tale of War and Peace in the 2004 Tsunami" (Reuters, Dec. 17, 2009).
120 Memorandum of Understanding between the Government of the Republic of Indonesia and the Free Aceh Movement (Helsinki, Aug. 15, 2005) Part 1, § 1.1.2.
121 Markku Suksi, "Aceh: Unclear Implementation of the Settlement," in *Sub-State Governance through Territorial Autonomy: A Comparative Study in Constitutional Law of Powers, Procedures and Institutions* (Springer, 2011) 355, 357.
122 *See* Iraq Constitution (2005) art. 116, § 5.
123 *See* ASHLEY S. DEEKS and MATTHEW D. BURTON, "Iraq's Constitution: A Drafting History" (2007) 40(1) CORNELL INTERNATIONAL LAW JOURNAL 1, 77.
124 *Id.* at 75, 77.
125 *Id.* at 80–81.
126 Iraq Constitution (July 22, 2005 draft) § 4, art. 20.
127 *See* Iraq Constitution (July 28, 2005 draft) Ch. 1, art. 3; §§ 6, 11; arts. 60–61.

128 *See* Law of Administration for the State of Iraq for the Transitional Period (Mar. 8, 2004) Ch. 8.

129 *See id. See also* Deeks and Burton, *supra* note 123 at 75.

130 Iraq Constitution (2005) art. 114.

131 Law of Administration for the State of Iraq for the Transitional Period (Mar. 8, 2004) Ch. 8, art. 53(C).

132 Deeks and Burton, *supra* note 123 at 81.

133 Iraq Constitution (2005) § Five, Ch. 1, art. 118.

134 *Id.* at § Five, Ch. 1, art. 119.

135 *See* "Basra Votes in Favour of Being Autonomous Region in Iraq" (Middle East Monitor, Apr. 3, 2019).

136 "Fact Sheet: About the Kurdistan Regional Government" (Kurdistan Regional Government, undated).

137 Iraq Constitution (2005) § 6, Ch. 2, art. 141.

138 Law of Administration for the State of Iraq for the Transitional Period (Mar. 8, 2004) Ch. 8, art. 53(C).

139 Iraq Constitution (2005) § 6, Ch. 2, art. 140.2.

140 *See* Deeks and Burton, *supra* note 123 at 82.

141 *See* Mina Aldroubi, "President of Iraqi Kurdistan Says Independence Vote Is Due to Failure of Unity" (The National, Sep. 8, 2017).

142 David Zucchino, "Iraqi Forces Sweep into Kirkuk, Checking Kurdish Independence Drive" (New York Times, Oct. 16, 2017).

143 Ahmed Rasheed and Raya Jalabi, "Iraqi Court Rules Kurdish Independence Vote Unconstitutional" (Reuters, Nov. 20, 2017).

144 *See* Chloe Cornish, "Protestors Seek End of Sectarian Power-Sharing in Iraq and Lebanon" (Financial Times, Nov. 4, 2019).

145 "Kurd Parties Contest Iraq Presidency for First Time" (AFP, Oct. 1, 2018).

146 GODWIN RAMOUS and KWAME EGBENYA, "The Effectiveness of Decentralization Policy in Ghana: A Case Study of Komenda-Edina-Eguafo-Abrim (KEEA) and Abura-Asebu-Kwamankese (AAK) Districts in Ghana" (2010) 4 AFRICAN JOURNAL OF POLITICAL SCIENCE AND INTERNATIONAL RELATIONS, 13, 14; *see* Adalbert Engel, "Decentralization, Local Capacity and Regional Rural Development: Experiences from GTZ-Supported Initiatives in Africa" (Southern Region GTZ, 1997).

147 The General Framework for Peace in Bosnia and Herzegovina (Dayton, 1995) Annex 4, art. 3.9.

148 *Id.* at Annex 4, art. 3.13.

149 *Id.* at Annex 4, art. 3.13.a.

150 *Id.* at Annex 4, art. 3.13.a.

151 *See id.* at arts. 5–8.

152 *Id.* at Annex 4, art. 3.13.b.

153 *Id.* at Annex 4, art. 3.10–11.

154 "Bosnia and Herzegovina" (Division of Powers, European Committee of the Regions, undated).

155 *Id.*

156 "Bosnia and Herzegovina: Background and U.S. Policy" (Congressional Research Service, Apr. 15, 2019) 7.

157 *Id.*

158 Nepal Constitution (2015) Sched. 5.

159 *Id.* at Scheds. 5–9.

160 Bishal Chalise, "Nepal's Uncertain Transition to Federalism" (Livemint, June 18, 2018).

161 "Constitutional History of South Africa" (ConstitutionNet, International IDEA, undated).

162 South Africa Constitution (1993) Sched. 6.

163 *See id.* at Sched. 4 XXI–XXIV.

164 South Africa Constitution (1996) Sched. 4, Part A; Sched. 5, Part A; Ch. 4, art. 44(2).

165 South Africa Constitution (1993) arts. 60, 67.

166 *See* JAAP DE VISSER, "Concurrent Powers in South Africa" in CONCURRENT POWERS IN FEDERAL SYSTEMS (Nico Steytler ed., Brill | Nijhoff, 2017).

167 Doha Document for Peace in Darfur (Doha, 2011) Ch. II, art. 10(60).

168 "Sudan Sets Date for Darfur Administrative Status Referendum" (Reuters, Jan. 12, 2016).

169 "Darfur Referendum: 'States Option' Wins by a Landslide" (Dabanga, Apr. 23, 2016).

170 Darfur Agreement between the Transitional Government of Sudan and Darfur Parties to Peace (Juba, 2020) § B, para. 25.6.

171 *Id.* at § B, para. 25.6.4.

172 *Id.* at § B, para. 25.6.

173 *Id.* at § B, para. 25.7.

174 *Id.* at § B, para. 32.

175 *Id.* at § B, paras. 30–31, 33.

176 Agreement on National Issues between the Transitional Government of Sudan and Signatory Parties to this Agreement (Juba, 2020) para. 1.29.

177 *Id.* at paras. 4–6.

178 Darfur Agreement between the Transitional Government of Sudan and Darfur Parties to Peace (Juba, 2020) § B, para. 27.1.

179 *Id.* at § B, para. 24.

180 *See* Two Areas Track Agreement between the Transitional Government of Sudan and Sudan People's Liberation Movement – North/Sudan Revolutionary Front (Juba, 2020).

181 Joint Declaration (Khartoum, 2020) para. 3.

182 *See* ERKMEN GIRAY ASLIM and BILIN NEYAPTI, "Optimal Fiscal Decentralization: Redistribution and Welfare Implications" (2017) 61 ECONOMIC MODELLING 224.

183 "Democratic Decentralization Programming Handbook" (USAID, June 2009) 13–14.

184 "The Process of Decentralization in Macedonia: Prospects for Ethnic Conflict Mitigation, Enhanced Representation, Institutional Efficiency and Accountability" (Institute for Regional and International Studies, 2006) 9.

185 The Ohrid Framework Agreement (Ohrid, 2001) § 3, art. 3.1.

186 *Id.*

187 *Id.* at Annex B, § 4.

188 *Id.* at § 3, art. 3.3.

189 *Id.* at § 1.5.

190 *Id.* at Annex B, § 2.

191 "Ohrid Framework Agreement: Review on Social Cohesion" (European Institute of Peace, 2015) 15.

192 *Id.* at 16.

193 *Id.* at 15.

194 TZIFAKIS NIKOLAOS, "The Bosnian Peace Process: The Power-Sharing Approach Revisited" (2007) 28 PERSPECTIVES 85, 86–87.

195 Alberto Nardelli, Denis Dzidic, and Elvira Jukic, "Bosnia and Herzegovina: The World's Most Complicated System of Government?" (The Guardian, Oct. 8, 2014).

196 "Bosnia and Herzegovina: Background and U.S. Policy" (Congressional Research Service, Apr. 15, 2019) 7.

197 "Constitutional History of Bosnia and Herzegovina" (ConstitutionNet, International IDEA, undated).

198 "Bosnia and Herzegovina: Background and U.S. Policy" (Congressional Research Service, Apr. 15, 2019) 7.

199 Fox, *supra* note 61 at 15. *See also* RADENKA GRGIC and SAUDIN TERZIC, "Tax Evasion in Bosnia and Hercegovina and Business Environment" (2014) 119 PROCEDIA – SOCIAL AND BEHAVIORAL SCIENCES, 957–966.

200 Fox, *supra* note 61 at 15.

201 "Local Governance and Service Delivery in Bosnia and Herzegovina" (World Bank, Jan. 2009) 21.

202 Fox, *supra* note 61 at 15.

203 Presidential Decree No. 1083 (Philippines, 1977).

204 Philippines Constitution (1987) art. 10, § 20.

205 Republic Act No. 6734 (Philippines, 1989) art. V, § 2.

206 Mindanao Final Agreement (Philippines, 1996) arts. 132, 144.

207 *Id.* at art. 27(c).

208 *See* Comprehensive Agreement on the Bangsamoro (Manila, 2014).

209 *See* Republic Act No. 11054 (Philippines, 2017).

210 J. C. Gotinga, "Philippines' Muslim Region Votes on New Autonomy Law" (Al Jazeera, Jan. 20, 2019).

211 Republic Act No. 11054 (Philippines, 2017) art. VII, § 5; arts. XII and V.

212 *Id.* at art. X.

213 Yemen Draft Constitution (2015) Ch. III, § III, arts. 250, 258; Ch. VII, arts. 358, 365–367.

214 *Id.* at Ch. I, § II, art. 17; Ch. VII, art. 355.

215 *Id.* at Ch. VII, art. 355.

216 *Id.* at Ch. VII, art. 357.

217 "Constitutional History of Colombia" (ConstitutionNet, International IDEA, undated).

218 CAROLINE MOSER, "Violence in Colombia: Building Sustainable Peace and Social Capital" in COLOMBIA: ESSAYS ON CONFLICT AND DEVELOPMENT (Andrews Slimano ed., World Bank, Dec. 2000) 21.

219 Colombia Constitution (1991) Title VII, art. 227.

220 Siegle and O'Mahony, *supra* note 7 at 27–28.

221 *Id.* at 28.

222 ISMAIL MOMONIAT, "Fiscal Decentralisation in South Africa: A Practitioner's Perspective" in MANAGING FISCAL DECENTRALIZATION (Ehtisham Ahmad and Vito Tanzi eds., Routledge, 2002) 4, n7.

223 "Inter-governmental Relations and Planning in Government" (Education and Training Unit, undated).

224 John-Mary Kuazya, "Political Decentralization in Africa: Experiences of Uganda, Rwanda, and South Africa" (United Nations Department of Economic and Social Affairs, Dec. 2007) 5.

225 DAWID VAN WYK, RIGHTS AND CONSTITUTIONALISM: THE NEW SOUTH AFRICAN LEGAL ORDER (Oxford University Press, 1996) 139.

226 South Africa Constitutional Act 200 (1993) arts. 68–74, 245.

227 Interim Constitution of South Africa (1993) arts. 243–244.

228 South Africa Intergovernmental Fiscal Relations Act (2005) arts. 39–45.

229 Mindanao Final Agreement (Philippines, 1996) art. 2.

230 *Id.* at arts. 2–3.

231 The Implementation of Federalism: Comparative Findings from Four Countries (Harvard Law & International Development Society, 2011) 6, 14, 21, 28.

232 Andreo Calonzo, "Govt, MILF Agree to Create 'Bangsamoro' to Replace ARMM" (GMA News Online, Oct. 7, 2012).

233 Memorandum of Understanding between the Government of Indonesia and the Free Aceh Movement (Helsinki, 2005) art. 1.2.

234 "Indonesia: How GAM Won in Aceh" (International Crisis Group, Mar. 22, 2007) 1.

235 The Ohrid Framework Agreement (Ohrid, 2001) § 3.

236 The Comprehensive Peace Agreement of the Government of Nepal and the Communist Party of Nepal (Maoist) (2006) 3.4–3.5.

237 Interim Constitution of Nepal (2007) Part 17, art. 138,

238 *See* The Comprehensive Peace Agreement of the Government of Nepal and the Communist Party of Nepal (Maoist) (2006).

239 Nepal Constitution (2015) Part 33, art. 295.

240 *See* Jarstad and Nilsson, *supra* note 1.

CHAPTER 3

1 UNEP, "From Conflict to Peacebuilding: The Role of Natural Resources and the Environment" (United Nations Environment Programme, 2009) i.

2 UN DPA and UNEP, "Natural Resources and Conflict: A Guide for Mediation Practitioners" (United Nations Department of Political Affairs and United Nations Environment Program, 2015) 46.

3 *Id.*

4 Phillipe Le Billon, "Resources for Peace? Managing Revenues from Extractive Industries in Post-Conflict Environments" (Political Economy Research Institute Working Paper Series Number 167, Apr. 2008) i.

5 UNEP, *supra* note 1.

6 MICHAEL L. ROSS, "How Do Natural Resources Influence Civil War? Evidence from Thirteen Cases" (2004) 58(1) INTERNATIONAL ORGANIZATION 35; *see also* MICHAEL L. ROSS, "What Do We Know about Natural Resources and Civil War?" (2004) 41(3) JOURNAL OF PEACE RESEARCH 337, as cited in Simon J. A. Mason, Damiano A. Sguaitamatti, and María del Pilar Ramirez Gröbli, "Stepping Stones to Peace? Natural

Resource Provisions in Peace Agreements" in GOVERNANCE, NATURAL RESOURCES, AND POST-CONFLICT PEACE BUILDING (Carl Bruch, Carrol Muffett, and Sandra S. Nicholas eds., Routledge, 2016) 71, 75.

7 *Id.*

8 Mauricio O. Ríos, Florian Bruyas, and Jodi Liss, "Preventing Conflict in Resource-Rich States" (World Bank, June 2015) 7.

9 UN DPA and UNEP, *supra* note 2 at 28.

10 UNEP, *supra* note 1 at 8.

11 For more analyses about the relationship between natural resources, peace, and security, *see generally* BENJAMIN SMITH, "Resource Wealth as Rent Leverage: Rethinking the Oil-Stability Nexus" (2017) 34(6) CONFLICT MANAGEMENT AND PEACE SCIENCE 597–617; PAUL COLLIER and ANKE HOEFFLER, "Resource Rents, Governance, and Conflict" (2005) 49(4) JOURNAL OF CONFLICT RESOLUTION 625–633; NILS PETTER GLEDITSCH, "Environmental Change, Security, and Conflict" in LEASHING THE DOGS OF WAR (Chester A. Crocker et al. eds., United States Institute of Peace, 2007); SANJEEV KHAGRAM and SALEEM ALI, "Environment and Security" (2006) 31(1) ANNUAL REVIEW OF ENVIRONMENT AND RESOURCES, 395–411; Christine Bell, "Economic Power-Sharing, Conflict Resolution and Development in Peace Agreements" (Political Settlements Research Programme, 2018); SANDRA S. NICHOLS et al., "When Peacebuilding Meets the Plan: Natural Resource Governance and Post-Conflict Recovery" (2011) 12(1) WHITEHEAD JOURNAL OF DIPLOMACY AND INTERNATIONAL RELATIONS 9–24.

12 UN DPA and UNEP, *supra* note 2 at 10–12.

13 JIMMY D. KANDEH, "Ransoming the State: Elite Origins of Subaltern Terror in Sierra Leone" (1999) 26 REVIEW OF AFRICAN POLITICAL ECONOMY 349.

14 JESSE SALAH OVADIA, "The Reinvention of Elite Accumulation in the Angolan Oil Sector: Emergent Capitalism in a Rentier Economy" (2013) 25 CADERNOS DE ESTUDOS AFRICANOS 33.

15 UN DPA and UNEP, *supra* note 2 at 19.

16 Ian Smillie, Lansana Gberie, and Ralph Hazleton, "The Heart of the Matter: Sierra Leone, Diamonds & Human Security" (Partnership Africa Canada, 2000).

17 Thailand's official policy on the Khmer Rouge was that of noncooperation. Due to this, the Thai government required that any timber it imported from Cambodia be obtained by the Phnom Penh authorities rather than the Khmer Rouge. The Cambodian government "charged loggers operating in Khmer Rouge zones a flat rate of USD 35 per cubic meter for the provision of these certifications, enabling their enemy, the Khmer Rouge, to raise the funds to pursue their war effort," eventually leading to millions of US dollars per month paid out to the Khmer Rouge. THE KHMER ROUGE AND THE FUNDING OF THE CIVIL WAR (Global Witness Publishing, 1996); UNEP, *supra* note 1 at 13.

18 Nicholas Haysom and Sean Kane, "Negotiating Natural Resources for Peace: Ownership, Control, and Wealth-Sharing" (Centre for Humanitarian Dialogue Briefing Paper, Oct. 2009) 5.

19 UN DPA and UNEP, *supra* note 2 at 28.

20 Ethiopia Constitution (1994) arts. 51, 52.

21 "State of the World's Minorities 2006 – Ethiopia" (Minority Rights Group International, Dec. 22, 2005).

22 Kaleyesus Bekele, "Ministry of Mines, South West to Sign PSA for Gambella Block" (The Reporter, Jan. 7, 2012).

23 GEORGETTE GAGNON, "Targeting the Anuak: Human Rights Violations and Crimes against Humanity in Ethiopia's Gambella Region" (2005) 17(3) HUMAN RIGHTS WATCH 6–7.

24 Felix Horne, "Forced Displacement and 'Villagization' in Ethiopia's Gambella Region" (Human Rights Watch, Jan. 16, 2012).

25 "State of the World's Minorities 2006 – Ethiopia" (Minority Rights Group International, Dec. 22, 2005).

26 UN DPA and UNEP, *supra* note 2 at 12.

27 *Id.* at 96.

28 UNEP, *supra* note 1 at 20–21.

29 UN DPA and UNEP, *supra* note 2 at 96.

30 *Id.* at 95.

31 Le Billion, *supra* note 4 at 14; UN DPA and UNEP, *supra* note 2 at 29.

32 THE KHMER ROUGE AND THE FUNDING OF THE CIVIL WAR (Global Witness Publishing, 1996); UNEP, *supra* note 1 at 13.

33 Sadaf Lakhani, "Extractive Industries and Peacebuilding in Afghanistan: The Role of Social Accountability" (United States Institute of Peace, Oct. 30, 2013) 4–7; *see also* Javed Noorani, "Afghanistan's Emerging Mining Oligarchy" (United States Institute of Peace, Jan. 22, 2015) 7–8; UN DPA and UNEP, *supra* note 2 at 29.

34 . Noorani, *supra* note 33 at 7.

35 UNEP, *supra* note 1; UN DPA and UNEP, *supra* note 2.

36 SIMON J. A. MASON, DAMIANO A. SGUAITAMATTI, and MARÍA DEL PILAR RAMIREZ GRÖBLI, "Stepping Stones to Peace? Natural Resource Provisions in Peace Agreements" in GOVERNANCE, NATURAL RESOURCES, AND POST-CONFLICT PEACE BUILDING (Carl Bruch, Carrol Muffett, and Sandra S. Nicholas eds., Routledge, 2016) 71, 92; UN DPA and UNEP, *supra* note 2 at 29.

37 Haysom and Kane, *supra* note 18 at 28.

38 Mason, Sguaitamatti, and Gröbli, *supra* note 36 at 100; *see also* Haysom and Kane, *supra* note 18 at 28.

39 Lakhani, *supra* note 33 at 4–5.

40 Le Billion, *supra* note 4 at 122.

41 Haysom and Kane, *supra* note 18 at 91–101.

42 UN DPA and UNEP, *supra* note 2 at 91.

43 *Id.* at 10–12.

44 *Id.* at 95.

45 Mohammed Ghobari and Agnus McDowall, "Houthis Abduct Yemeni Official Amid Wrangling over Constitution" (Thomson Reuters Africa, Jan. 17, 2015).

46 Haysom and Kane, *supra* note 18 at 10.

47 Kazakhstan Constitution (1995) art. 6(3).

48 Venezuela Constitution (1999) Ch. VII, art. 113.

49 Kuwait Constitution (1962) art. 21.

50 Nigeria Constitution (1999) art. 44(3).

51 Qatar Constitution (2003) art. 29.

52 Syria Constitution (1973) art. 14(1).

53 Middle Eastern and African oil-producing states include Algeria, Angola, Chad, Egypt, Iran, Kuwait, Libya, Nigeria, Oman, Qatar, Saudi Arabia, Syria, the United Arab Emirates, and Yemen.

54 "United Arab Emirates Country Analysis Brief" (US Energy Information Administration, undated).

55 United Arab Emirates Constitution (1996) art. 23.

56 Argentina Constitution (1994) § 124; ANN L. GRIFFITHS ed., HANDBOOK OF FEDERAL COUNTRIES (McGill-Queen's University Press, 2005).

57 Argentina Constitution (1994) § 124.

58 *See* Canada Constitution (1867) Ch. 6, art. 92(A).

59 *Id.* at Ch. 6, art. 91, cl. 2 (this provision establishes the authority of the Parliament of Canada to regulate trade and commerce).

60 "Reconciling the Irreconcilable: Addressing Canada's Fiscal Imbalance" (Council of the Federation, 2006) 6.

61 PAUL BOOTHE, "Taxing Spending, and Sharing in Federations: Evidence from Australia and Canada" in FISCAL RELATIONS IN FOUR COUNTRIES: FOUR ESSAYS (Paul Boothe ed., Forum of Federations, 2003) 9.

62 *See* Canada-Nova Scotia Offshore Petroleum Resources Accord (1986) arts. 12–13.

63 UNEP, *supra* note 1 at 5.

64 Petroleum (Submerged Lands) Act 1967 (Australia), § 8(a) (although the Offshore Petroleum Act repeals the Petroleum (Submerged Lands) Act 1967, it maintains the structure and most of the powers of the Joint Authorities. *See* Offshore Petroleum Act 2006 (Australia)).

65 "Mineral and Petroleum Exploration & Development in Australia: A Guide for Investors" (Department of Industry, Tourism and Resources, 2005) 1.

66 Nova Scotia Offshore Petroleum Resources Accord (1986) art. 3.

67 Canada-Nova Scotia Offshore Petroleum Resources Accord (1986) arts. 12–18.

68 "Legal Foundations" (Website of Bureau of Minerals and Petroleum, Greenland, no date).

69 Ehtisham Ahmad and Eric Mottu, "Oil Revenue Assignments: Country Experiences and Issues" (International Monetary Fund Working Paper, 2002) 203.

70 United Arab Emirates Constitution, 1971 (rev. 2009) art. 127 (in reality, only the oil-rich Abu Dhabi Emirate and the economically strong Dubai Emirate fund the federal budget).

71 *See* Canada Constitution (1867) Ch. 6, art. 92A.

72 Boothe, *supra* note 61.

73 Law No. 22/2001 Petroleum and Natural Gas (Nov. 23, 2001); *see also* MARK TURNER, "Implementing Laws 22 and 25: The Challenge of Decentralization in Indonesia" (2001) 8 ASIAN REVIEW OF PUBLIC ADMINISTRATION 69, 73.

74 Turner, *supra* note 73 at 72.

75 *See* The World Bank, "Chad–Cameroon Petroleum Development and Pipeline Project"(Apr. 13, 2000), https://documents.worldbank.org/en/publication/documents-reports/documentdetail/234181468743694143/chad-and-cameroon-petroleum-development-and-pipeline-project

76 In 2006, the Norwegian government changed the fund's name to the "Government Pension Fund"; Norges Bank Investment Management (Norway GPFG)" (SWF Institute, undated), https://www.swfinstitute.org/profile/598cdaa60124c9fd2d05b9af

77 Benn Eifert, Alan Gelb, and Nils Borje Tallroth, "The Political Economy of Fiscal Policy and Economic Management in Oil-Exporting Countries" (World Bank Policy Research Working Paper 2899, 2002) 10.

78 "Republic of Kazakhstan: Selected Issues" (International Monetary Fund, 2005) 14.

79 Alaska residents receive an annual tax dividend that is allocated from the state's oil revenue through the Alaska Permanent Fund. This dividend is called the "Permanent Fund Dividend" and is distributed to qualifying Alaska residents; "The Permanent Fund Dividend" (Alaska Permanent Fund Corporation, undated), https://apfc.org/

80 Inflation-proofing is the annual transfer (by legislative appropriation) of a portion of fund income to the principal to protect the value of the principal from inflation.

81 GA Res. 1803, UN GAOR, 17th Session, UN Doc. A/RES/1803 (XVII 1962).

82 *See* Lillian Aponte Miranda, "The Role of International Law in Intrastate Natural Resource Allocation: Sovereignty, Human Rights, and Peoples-Based Development" (2012) 45(3) Vanderbilt Journal of Transnational Law 785, 787.

83 *Id.* at 840.

84 "Free, Prior and Informed Consent" (Food and Agriculture Organization of the United Nations, no date), http://www.fao.org/family-farming/detail/en/c/899936/

85 *Id.*

86 UN DPA and UNEP, *supra* note 2 at 29.

87 Franziska Bieri, From Blood Diamonds to the Kimberley Process: How NGOs Cleaned Up the Global Diamond Industry (Routledge, 2016) 1.

88 J. Andrew Grant and Ian Taylor, "Global Governance and Conflict Diamonds: The Kimberley Process and the Quest for Clean Gems" (2004) 93(375) The Round Table: The Commonwealth Journal of International Affairs 385, 387.

89 Bieri, *supra* note 87.

90 "About" (KimberleyProcess.org).

91 Grant and Taylor, *supra* note 88 at 392.

92 "Briefing: Aceh" (Minority Rights Group International, 2001).

93 Memorandum of Understanding between the Government of the Republic of Indonesia and the Free Aceh Movement (Helsinki, 2005).

94 Haysom and Kane, *supra* note 18 at 32.

95 Iraq Constitution (2006) art. 111 ("Oil and gas are owned by all the people of Iraq in all the regions and governorates").

96 The Constitution of the Autonomous Region of Bougainville (2004) Part 3, 23.

97 Id.

98 Ian Smillie, Lansana Gberie, and Ralph Hazleton, "The Heart of the Matter: Sierra Leone, Diamonds & Human Security" (Partnership Africa Canada, 2000).

99 Lomé Peace Agreement (Lomé, 1999) art. VII (1–6).

100 "Implementing the Lomé Peace Agreement" (Conciliation Resources, 2000) 39.

101 Haysom and Kane, *supra* note 18 at 30.

102 *Id.*

103 Sujit Choudhry and Richard Stacey, "Oil and Natural Gas: Constitutional Frameworks for the Middle East and North Africa" (Center for Constitutional Transitions, International IDEA and the United Nations Development Programme, 2014) 75.

104 Charles Schmitz, "Building a Better Yemen" (Carnegie Endowment, 2012) 1.

105 Yemen Draft Constitution (2015) arts. 357, 387–390.

106 *Id.* at arts. 387–390.

107 DARIN JOHNSON, "Conflict Constitution-Making in Libya and Yemen" (2017) 39(2) UNIVERSITY OF PENNSYLVANIA JOURNAL OF INTERNATIONAL LAW 293, 325.

108 Haysom and Kane, *supra* note 18 at 26.

109 "Briefing: Aceh" (Minority Rights Group International, 2001).

110 C. Bryson Hull and Bill Tarrant, "Tale of War and Peace in the 2004 Tsunami" (Reuters, Dec. 17, 2009).

111 Haysom and Kane, *supra* note 18 at 30.

112 *See* Machakos Protocol (Machakos, 2002).

113 Comprehensive Peace Agreement, Agreement on Wealth Sharing (Sudan, 2005) Ch. III.

114 Bougainville Peace Agreement (Arawa, 2001) Introduction, arts. 1–3.

115 Paul R. Williams and Carly Fabian, "Bougainville's Faustian Bargain" (The Diplomat, Nov. 7, 2019).

116 The Constitution of the Autonomous Region of Bougainville (2004) Part I, art. 23.

117 Williams and Fabian, *supra* note 115.

118 RNZ, "Bougainville Mining Plan Meets with Outrage" (RNZ, Feb. 6, 2019).

119 Iraq Constitution (2006) art. 111.

120 ASHLEY S. DEEKS and MATTHEW D. BURTON, "Iraq's Constitution: A Drafting History" (2007) 40 CORNELL INTERNATIONAL LAW JOURNAL 1, 66.

121 Sharon Otterman and Lionel Beehner, "Iraq: Drafting the Constitution" (Council on Foreign Relations, Apr. 27, 2005).

122 Iraq Constitution (2006) art. 111.

123 Ruba Husari, "Iraqi Oil Law Puts Elections before State-Building" (Middle East Institute, Apr. 26, 2018).

124 National Dialogue Conference Outcomes Document (Yemen, 2013–14) § I, art. II(8).

125 Yemen Draft Constitution (2015) Ch. VIII, art. 381.

126 BRYONY LAU, "The Philippines: Peace Talks and Autonomy in Mindanao" in TERRITORY AND POWER IN CONSTITUTIONAL TRANSITIONS (George Anderson and Sujit Choudhry eds., Oxford University Press, 2019), 20.

127 Philippines Constitution (1987) arts. 10(15–21), art. 12(2).

128 *Id.* at art. 10(20).

129 Lau, *supra* note 126 at 210.

130 Republic Act No. 11054 (Manila, 2017) art. V, § 2(d).

131 "Profile: Aceh's Separatists" (BBC News, Dec. 9, 2002).

132 STATE OF THE WORLD 2006: SPECIAL FOCUS: CHINA AND INDIA (WorldWatch Institute, 2006) 123.

133 "Indonesia: A Reconstruction Chapter Ends Eight Years after the Tsunami" (World Bank, Dec. 26, 2012).

134 Achim Wennmann and Jana Krause, "Resource Wealth, Autonomy, and Peace in Aceh" (Center on Conflict, Development, and Peacebuilding Working Paper 3, 2009) 5.

135 Memorandum of Understanding between the Government of the Republic of Indonesia and the Free Aceh Movement (Helsinki, 2005) art. 1.3.3.

136 Wennmann and Krause, *supra* note 134, as cited in UN DPA and UNEP, *supra* note 2 at B, 81.

137 *Id.*

138 Comprehensive Peace Agreement, Agreement on Wealth Sharing (Sudan, 2005) Ch. III, art. 2.1.

139 UN DPA and UNEP, *supra* note 2 at Part B, 81.

140 Darfur Agreement between the Transitional Government Sudan and Darfur Parties to Peace (Juba, 2020) § C, para. 2.

141 *Id.* at §, C para. 22.1.

142 UN DPA and UNEP, *supra* note 2 at 91.

143 UNEP, *supra* note 1.

144 Lomé Peace Agreement (Lomé, 1999) art. VII(1).

145 Lomé Peace Agreement (Lomé, 1999) Part I, art. VII(5), art. VII(1).

146 "Implementing the Lomé Peace Agreement" (Conciliation Resources, 2000) 28, 30–33, 39.

147 Iraq Constitution (2005) art. 112.

148 The Federal Oil & Gas Draft Law – The Iraqi Government Version English Translation, as Compiled by the Federal Ministry of Oil (2011) arts. 1–2, 5.

149 *Id.* at art. 5.

150 Christopher M. Blanchard, "Iraq: Oil and Gas Legislation, Revenue Sharing, and U.S. Policy" (Congressional Research Service, Nov. 3, 2009) 25.

151 *Id.* at 10; The Federal Oil & Gas Draft Law, *supra* note 148, art. 14.

152 Blanchard, *supra* note 150 at 13.

153 Tara Patel, "Total Chief Says Kurdistan Oil Contracts 'Better' than Iraq" (Kurd Net, Feb. 11, 2012).

154 "Iraq Approves $560 Mln for Kurdistan Oil Payments" (Kurd Net, Apr. 1, 2012).

155 Yemen Draft Constitution (2015) Ch. VIII, art. 381; National Dialogue Conference Outcomes Document (Yemen, 2013–14) § I, art. II(8).

156 National Dialogue Conference Outcomes Document (Yemen, 2013–14) § I, art. II(8).

157 Yemen Draft Constitution (2015) arts. 387–388.

158 *Id.* at art. 389.

159 National Dialogue Conference Outcomes Document (Yemen, 2013–14) Introduction Decisions art. 42.

160 Comprehensive Peace Agreement, Agreement on Wealth Sharing (Sudan, 2005), Ch. III, B, art. 3.4.

161 *Id.* at art. 3.3 a–d.

162 Agreement on Wealth Sharing (Sudan, 2004) art. 3.3 b–d.

163 Darfur Agreement between the Transitional Government Sudan and Darfur Parties to Peace (Juba, 2020) § C, para. 23.1.

164 *Id.*

165 *Id.* at § C, para. 24.1.

166 *Id.* at § C, para. 24.

167 Law on the Governing of Aceh (2006) Law No. 11/2006, Ch. XXXIX, art. 252(A).

168 *Id.* at Part 4, art. 160.

169 *Id.* at Ch. XXXIX, art. 252(A).

170 Haysom and Kane, *supra* note 18 at 23.

171 *Id.* at 23.

172 *Id.* at 24.

173 Lomé Peace Agreement (Lomé, 1999) Part I, art. VII(6).

174 "Implementing the Lomé Peace Agreement" (Conciliation Resources, 2000) 39.

175 "Natural Resource Management: Lomé Peace Agreement" (University of Notre Dame Peace Accords Matrix, undated).

176 The Mines and Minerals Act (Sierra Leone, 2009), Part XVI.

177 Jared Schott et al., "Development from the Ground Up? Mining Community Development Agreements in Sierra Leone" (World Bank, 2015).

178 Comprehensive Peace Agreement (Sudan, 2005) Ch. III, art. 5.

179 "Natural Resource Management: Sudan Comprehensive Peace Agreement" (University of Notre Dame Peace Accords Matrix, undated).

180 *Id.*

181 "Sudan 'Stealing Oil' from South – Pagan Amum" (BBC News, Dec. 1, 2011).

182 Ulf Laessing and Khalid Abdelaziz, "Sudan Says Taking Some South Sudan Oil but Won't Close Pipe" (Reuters, Jan. 15, 2012).

183 "Sudan 'Stealing Oil' from South – Pagan Amum" (BBC News, Dec. 1, 2011).

184 Anne W. Kamau and Witney Schneidman, "South Sudan: Resolving the Oil Dispute" (Brookings Institute, 2012).

185 Laessing and Abdelaziz, *supra* note 182.

186 The Cooperation Agreement between the Republic of the Sudan and the Republic of South Sudan (Addis Ababa, 2012).

187 *Id.*

188 Agreement between the Government of the Republic of South Sudan and the Government of the Republic of the Sudan on Oil and Related Economic Matters (Addis Ababa, 2012) arts. 4, 7, 9, 10, 12.

189 Darfur Agreement between the Transitional Government Sudan and Darfur Parties to Peace (Juba, 2020) § C, paras. 23.2, 25.1–2.

190 Memorandum of Understanding between the Government of the Republic of Indonesia and the Free Aceh Movement (Helsinki, 2005).

191 "Aceh: Can Autonomy Stem the Conflict?" (International Crisis Group, 2001) 8, as cited in Wennmann and Krause, *supra* note 134; MICHELLE A. MILLER, "What's Special about Special Autonomy in Aceh?" in VARANDAH OF VIOLENCE: THE BACKGROUND TO THE ACEH PROBLEM (Anthony Reid ed., Singapore University Press, 2006) 297 as cited in Wennmann and Krause, *supra* note 134.

192 CRAIG THORBUN, "Building Blocks and Stumbling Blocks: Peacebuilding in Aceh" (2012) 93 INDONESIA 83, 89.

193 Fergus Jensen, "Indonesia's Arun LNG Project to Ship Final Cargo, Imports Due Soon" (Reuters, Oct. 14, 2014).

194 "Aceh: Can Autonomy Stem the Conflict?" (International Crisis Group, 2001) 8, as cited in ACHIM WENNMANN, "Breaking the Conflict Trap? Addressing the Resource Curse in Peace Processes" 17(2) GLOBAL GOVERNANCE 265, 271.

195 Yemen Draft Constitution (2015) art. 357.

196 *Id.* at art. 390.

197 "Yemen's Houthis Reject Draft Constitution" (Project on Middle East Democracy, Jan. 9, 2015).

198 Chris Johnston, "Yemeni President's Chief of Staff Seized by Gunmen" (The Guardian, Jan. 17, 2015).

199 Iraq Constitution (2006) arts. 111, 112.

200 *Id.* at art. 112(1).

201 *Id.* at art. 121(3).

202 Serena Chaudhry and Mariam Karouny, "Iraq Approves $560 Mln for Kurdish Oil Payments" (Reuters, Mar. 27, 2012).

CHAPTER 4

1 Monty G. Marshall and Ted Robert Gurr, "Peace and Conflict 2005: A Global Survey of Armed Conflicts, Self-Determination Movements, and Democracy" (Center for International Development & Conflict Management, 2005) 21, 84–90.

2 *Id.* at 26.

3 *See* Memorandum of Understanding between the Government of the Republic of Indonesia and the Free Aceh Movement (Helsinki, 2005).

4 *See* Yemen Draft Constitution (2011).

5 For more perspectives on self-determination and conflict resolution, *see generally* HURST HANNUM et al. eds., NEGOTIATING SELF-DETERMINATION (Lexington Books, 2005); Patricia Carley, "Self-Determination: Sovereignty, Territorial Integrity, and the Right to Secession" (United States Institute of Peace, 2018).

6 JANE M. O. SHARP, "Appeasement, Intervention and the Future of Europe, in Military Intervention in European Conflicts" in MILITARY INTERVENTION IN EUROPEAN CONFLICTS (Lawrence Freedman ed., Blackwell, 1994) 49; ED VULLIAMY, "Bosnia: The Crime of Appeasement" (1998) 74(1) INTERNATIONAL AFFAIRS 88.

7 *See* The Treaty of Westphalia (1648).

8 CHARLES R. BEITZ, POLITICAL THEORY AND INTERNATIONAL RELATIONS (Princeton University Press, 1979).

9 UN CHARTER, c. I, art. 2(4).

10 *See* "Territorial Integrity" (Commission on Security and Cooperation in Europe – US Helsinki Commission, undated).

11 "The Legal Issues Involved in the Western Sahara Dispute: The Principle of Self-Determination and the Legal Claims of Morocco" (New York City Bar Association Committee on the United Nations, 2012) 41.

12 *See* Betty Miller Unterberger, "Self-Determination" (Encyclopedia of American Foreign Policy, 2002).

13 *See* GA Res. 1514, UN SCOR, UN Doc. A/RES/1514 (XV 1960) (Declaration on the Granting of Independence to Colonial Countries and Peoples).

14 *Id.*

15 *Id.*

16 A. Cristescu (Special Rapporteur of the of the Sub-Commission on Prevention of Discrimination and Protection of Minorities), "The Right to Self-Determination: Historical and Current Development on the Basis of United Nations Instruments," UN SCOR, UN Doc. E/CN.4/Sub.2/404/Rev. 1 (1981) paras. 31, 46.

17 SIDI M. OMAR, "The Right to Self-Determination and the Indigenous People of Western Sahara" (2008) 21(1) CAMBRIDGE REVIEW OF INTERNATIONAL AFFAIRS 41–57, 44; *see* Advisory Opinion on Western Sahara, Advisory Opinion, ICJ Rep. 1975, p. 12, paras. 75–83.

18 *Case Concerning the Frontier Dispute (Burkina Faso/Republic of Mali)*, Judgment, ICJ Rep. 1986 (Dec. 22) para. 20.

19 JAN C. JANSEN and JÜRGEN OSTERHAMMEL, DECOLONIALIZATION: A SHORT HISTORY (Princeton University Press, 2017) 29.

20 Ng Tze Lin Tania, "Rendel Commission" (Singapore Infopedia); Constitution Commission, "Report of the Constitutional Commission, Singapore" (Singapore: Government Printing Office, 1954) 5.

21 *See* "Compacts of Free Association" (Department of the Interior Office of Insular Affairs, undated).

22 *See* "Federated States of Micronesia, Republic of the Marshall Islands, and Palau" (US Citizenship and Immigration Services, 2019).

23 UN CHARTER, Ch. XII.

24 *See* UN Doc. T/RES/2200 (LXI 1994).

25 *See* Agreements Relating to Algerian Independence [Evian Accords] (Evian, Mar. 18, 1962).

26 "1961: French Vote for Algerian Freedom" (BBC News on This Day, undated).

27 *See* Evian Accords, *supra* note 25.

28 *Id.*; Andrew H. Bellisari, "The Evian Accords: An Uncertain Peace" (Origins, Mar. 2017).

29 WILLIAM E. WATSON, TRICOLOR AND CRESCENT, FRANCE AND THE ISLAMIC WORLD (Greenwood Publishing, 2003) 242; DIETER NOHLEN, PHILIP STÖVER, ELECTIONS IN EUROPE: A DATA HANDBOOK (Oxford University Press, 2010) 674.

30 *See* Evian Accords, *supra* note 25.

31 *Id.* at Ch. I(D–E).

32 *Id.* at Ch. I(G).

33 *Id.* at 23.

34 "Algeria – Oil and Gas – Hydrocarbons: Algeria Country Commercial Guide" (Export. gov, undated).

35 "Self Determination" (Minority Rights Group International, Aug. 26, 2015).

36 International Covenant on Civil and Political Rights (New York, Dec. 16, 1966) 999 UNTS 171 and 1057 UNTS 407, *entered into force* Mar. 23, 1976, art. 25.

37 International Covenant on Economic, Social and Cultural Rights (New York, Dec. 16, 1966) 993 UNTS 3, *entered into force* Jan. 3, 1976, art. I.

38 International Covenant on Civil and Political Rights (New York, Dec. 16, 1966) 999 UNTS 171 and 1057 UNTS 407, *entered into force* Mar. 23, 1976, art. I.

39 PAUL R. WILLIAMS, "Earned Sovereignty: The Road to Resolving the Conflict over Kosovo's Final Status" (2003) 31(3) DENVER JOURNAL OF INTERNATIONAL LAW AND POLICY 387, 399.

40 *Id.*

41 Art. 2 CE.

42 Constitution Act of Finland (July 17, 1919) § 3.

43 577/1978 Greenland Home Rule Act, 1 luku, 1(1)§.

44 *Accordance with International Law of the Unilateral Declaration of Independence in Respect of Kosovo*, Advisory Opinion, ICJ Rep. 2010, § 79.

45 Helsinki Final Act (Organization for Security and Co-operation in Europe, Aug. 1, 1975).

46 Decision of the Supreme Court of Canada in the Matter of Section 53 of the Supreme Court Act, RSC 1985, c. s. 26; and in the matter of a Reference by the Governor in Council Concerning Certain Questions Relating to the Secession of Quebec from Canada, as set out in Order in Council PC 1996–1497, Sep. 30, 1996, para. 154.

47 The General Framework for Peace in Bosnia and Herzegovina (Dayton, 1995) Annex 10.

48 "PIC Bonn Conclusions" (OHR, 1998) art. 11.

49 Bougainville Peace Agreement (Arawa, 2001) art. 2.

50 "Bougainville Referendum Commission" (Bougainville Referendum Commission); Kate Lyons, "Bougainville Referendum: Region Votes Overwhelmingly for Independence from Papua New Guinea" (The Guardian, Dec. 10, 2019).

51 Seth Mydans, "In East Timor, Decisive Vote for a Break from Indonesia" (New York Times, Sep. 4, 1999).

52 *See* IAN MARTIN, SELF-DETERMINATION IN EAST TIMOR: THE UNITED NATIONS, THE BALLOT AND INTERNATIONAL INTERVENTION (Lynne Rienner, 2001) 15; TANIA VOON, "Closing the Gap between Legitimacy and Legality of Humanitarian Intervention: Lessons from East Timor and Kosovo" (2002) 7 UCLA JOURNAL OF INTERNATIONAL LAW FOREIGN AFFAIRS 31.

53 SC Res. 1272, UN SCOR, 53rd Sess., UN Doc. S/RES/1272 (1999); SC Res. 513, UN SCOR, at Annex II at 24 and Annex III, UN Doc. S/1999/513 (1999).

54 SC Res. 1272, at art. 1, UN SCOR, 53rd Sess., UN Doc. S/RES/1272 (1999).

55 James Bennett, "U.S. and Partners Present Proposal for Mideast Peace" (New York Times, May 1, 2003); Proposal for "Final and Comprehensive Settlement to Middle East Conflict" (New York Times, May 1, 2003).

56 US Department of State, "Roadmap for Peace in the Middle East: Israeli/Palestinian Reciprocal Action, Quartet Support" (2003).

57 "The 'Road Map'" (Foundation for Middle Eastern Peace, 2003).

58 Rambouillet Agreement (Rambouillet, 1999) Ch. 2, art. I, para. 2; SC RES 1244, UN SCOR, UN Doc. S/RES/1244 (1999).

59 "UNMIK Fact Sheet" (United Nations Peacekeeping, undated).

60 SC Res. 1244, UN SCOR, UN Doc. S/RES/1244 (1999).

61 Belfast Agreement [Good Friday Agreement] (Belfast, 1998) arts. 2–5.

62 *Id.* at art. 3.

63 Serbia and Montenegro Constitution (Feb. 4, 2003) art. 60.

64 Nicholas Wood, "Montenegro Votes to Secede from Serbia" (New York Times, May 21, 2006).

65 Comprehensive Peace Agreement between the Government of Sudan and the SPLM/SPLA (Kenya, 2005) Part B, 2.5.

66 SC Res. 565 [Baker Plan II], UN SCOR, at Annex II, S/2003/565 (2003); *see generally* YAHIA H. ZOUBIR, "The West Saharan Conflict: A Case Study in Failure of

Prenegotiation and Prolongation of Conflict" (1996) 26(2) CALIFORNIA WESTERN INTERNATIONAL LAW JOURNAL 173.

67 Anna Theofilopoulou, "The United Nations and Western Sahara: A Never-Ending Affair" (United States Institute of Peace Special Report 166, 2006) 9.

68 *Id.* at 12; *see* SC Res. 1495, UN SCOR, UN Doc. S/RES/1495 (2003).

69 This section draws from the author, Dr. Paul R. Williams', previous work including: PAUL R. WILLIAMS and FRANCESCA JANNOTTI PECCI, "Earned Sovereignty: Bridging the Gap between Sovereignty and Self-Determination" (2004) 40 STANFORD JOURNAL OF INTERNATIONAL LAW 347; PAUL R. WILLIAMS, "Earned Sovereignty: The Future of Sovereignty-Based Conflict Resolution" (2011) 40 DENVER JOURNAL OF INTERNATIONAL LAW & POLICY 128.

70 Baker Plan II, *supra* note 66, at Annex II para. 8(b); UN Doc. UNTAET/REG/1992/2 (1999) § 1, 5.

71 *See* Serbia and Montenegro Constitution (Feb. 4, 2003) art. 19.

72 *Id.* at arts. 35, 42.

73 Bougainville Peace Agreement (Arawa, 2001) B, arts. 1–15.

74 *See* Good Friday Agreement, *supra* note 61.

75 *See* Serbia and Montenegro Constitution (Feb. 4, 2003) arts. 3, 42.

76 Good Friday Agreement, *supra* note 61 at § 5(d).

77 *Id.* at Strand 3, para. 2.

78 UN Doc. UNTAET/REG/1992/2 (1999) § 5.

79 Baker Plan II, *supra* note 66 at paras. 4, 15, 21.

80 *Id.* at paras. 15, 21.

81 "A Performance-Based Roadmap to a Permanent Two-State Solution to the Israeli–Palestinian Conflict" (The Quartet, Apr. 30, 2003).

82 "South Sudan: The Comprehensive Peace Agreement on Life Support" (Hearing and Briefing before the Subcommittee on Africa and Global Health of the Committee on Foreign Affairs House of Representatives, 110th Congress, 1st Session Serial No. 110-2, Jan. 24, 2007) 62.

83 UN Doc. UNMIK/REG/2001/9 (2001) Ch. 1, art. 1.

84 *See* Good Friday Agreement, *supra* note 61.

85 A Performance-Based Roadmap, *supra* note 81 at 34.

86 *See* Bougainville Peace Agreement (Arawa, 2001) B, arts. 1–15.

87 *See* Agreement on Principles of Relations between Serbia and Montenegro within the State Union (Belgrade, Mar. 14, 2002).

88 DANILO TÜRK, "Declaration on the Guidelines on the Recognition of New States in Eastern Europe and in the Soviet Union: A Comment" (1993) 4(1) EUROPEAN JOURNAL OF INTERNATIONAL LAW 72, 72.

89 "A Performance-Based Roadmap," *supra* note 81; *see also* US President George W. Bush, "Address at the Rose Garden" (June 24, 2002).

90 *See* Good Friday Agreement, *supra* note 61.

91 Standards before Status; UN Doc. UNMIK/PR719 ("Address to the Security Council by Michael Steiner Special Representative of the Secretary-General in Kosovo") (Apr. 24, 2002).

92 *See* Bougainville Peace Agreement (Arawa, 2001) C, para. 312b.

93 Baker Plan II, *supra* note 66 at paras. 15, 21; Machakos Protocol (Machakos, 2002) Part B, para. 2.2.

94 Serbia and Montenegro Constitution (Feb. 4, 2003) art. 60.

95 Bougainville Peace Agreement (Arawa, 2001) art. 312(a).

96 Baker Plan II, *supra* note 66 at para. 2.

97 Machakos Protocol (Machakos, 2002) Part. B, para. 2.2.

98 Good Friday Agreement, *supra* note 61, Strand 2, Annex Nos. 1, 2.

99 *Id.* at art. I(iii).

100 *See* Rambouillet Agreement: Interim Agreement for Peace and Self-Government in Kosovo (Rambouillet, 1999).

101 "Republic of Montenegro, Referendum on State-Status, May 2006, OSCE/ODIHR Referendum Observation Mission Final Report" (Office for Democratic Institutions and Human Rights, Aug. 4, 2006) 8.

102 Bougainville Peace Agreement (Arawa, 2001) C, art. 315.

103 SC Res. 513 at Annex II(C), UN SCOR, UN Doc. S/1999/513 (1999).

104 "Southern Sudan Referendum Act 2009" (2010) 5(1) INTERNATIONAL JOURNAL OF AFRICAN RENAISSANCE STUDIES – MULTI-INTERN- AND TRANSDISCIPLINARY 192, 205, Part II(25).

105 AMY H. HANDLIN, "Response and Order Effects in Referendum Voting: Exploring the Influence of Contextual Bias on Public Policy" (1994) 30(1) JOURNAL OF BUSINESS RESEARCH 95, 96.

106 Law on the Referendum of Legal Status (Montenegro, 2006) I, art. 5.

107 SC Res. 513, UN SCOR, at Annex II(B), UN Doc. S/1999/513 (1999).

108 "Question Agreed for Bougainville's independence referendum" (RNZ, Oct. 13, 2018).

109 Andrew Heavens, "Observers Approve South Sudan Independence Vote" (Reuters, Jan. 17, 2011).

110 *See* MATT QVORTRUP, "Voting on Independence and National Issues: A Historical and Comparative Study of Referendums on Self-Determination and Secession" (2015) XX(2) FRENCH JOURNAL OF BRITISH STUDIES.

111 *See* European Convention for the Protection of Human Rights and Fundamental Freedoms (Rome, Nov. 4, 1950).

112 International Covenant on Civil and Political Rights (New York, Dec. 16, 1966) 999 UNTS 171 and 1057 UNTS 407, *entered into force* Mar. 23, 1976, art. 25.

113 Serbia and Montenegro is a party to Protocol No. 1 to the European Convention for the Protection of Human Rights and Fundamental Freedoms, Article 3 of which provides that "[t]he High Contracting Parties undertake to hold free elections at reasonable intervals by secret ballot, under conditions which will ensure the free expression of the opinion of the people in the choice of the legislature." Protocol to the European Convention for the Protection of Human Rights and Fundamental Freedoms (Mar. 20, 1952) art. 3. The European Commission on Human Rights has interpreted this provision as applying only to institutions established by the constitutions of the contracting parties which possess inherent rule-making power. *See Polacco & Garofalo v. Italy* (inadmissible), No. 23450/94, ECHR 1997; *Mathieu-Mohin & Clerfayt v. Belgium*, No. 9267/81 A/113 ECHR 1987, 23.

114 *See* Agreement Regarding the Modalities for the Popular Consultation of the East Timorese through a Direct Ballot, between the Government of Indonesia and Portugal and the Secretary General of the United Nations (New York, 1999).

115 Comprehensive Peace Agreement between the Government of Sudan and the SPLM/SPLA (2005) Part B, 2.5.

116 Bougainville Peace Agreement (Arawa, 2001).

117 *See* Baker Plan II, *supra* note 66 at § II, para. 3.

118 Law on the Referendum of Legal Status (Montenegro, 2006) art. 37.

119 *See* Law of the USSR of Apr. 3, 1990 (1990) 13 Register of the Congress of the People's Deputies of USSR and Supreme Soviet of USSR 252.

120 *Id.* at art. 6.

121 *See* Jaak Treiman, "The Soviet Secession Law Is a Sham" (Wall Street Journal Europe, July 3, 1990).

122 *See* "Report on Ukraine's Referendum on Independence and Presidential Election" (Commission on Security and Cooperation in Europe, Presidential Elections and Independence Referendums in the Baltic States, the Soviet Union and Successor States, Dec. 1, 1991) 103.

123 Rambouillet Agreement (Rambouillet, 1999) Ch. 8, art. I, para. 3.

124 Julian Duplain, "Q&A: East Timor Referendum" (BBC, Aug. 24, 1999).

125 *See* MILENA STERIO, "On the Right to External Self-Determination: 'Selfistans,' Secession and the Great Powers' Rule" (2010) 19 MINNESOTA JOURNAL OF INTERNATIONAL LAW 137–176.

126 Republic of Montenegro, Referendum on State-Status, May 2006, OSCE/ODIHR Referendum Observation Mission Final Report" (Office for Democratic Institutions and Human Rights, Aug. 4, 2006) 4–5.

127 *Order on Provisional Measures in the Case Concerning the Frontier Dispute (Burkina Faso/Mali)*, Provisional Measures Order, ICJ Rep. 1986 25 ILM 146, 565–569.

128 ENVER HASANI, "Uti Possidetis Juris: From Rome to Kosovo" (2003) 27 FLETCHER FORUM OF WORLD AFFAIRS 85, 88.

129 *Order on Provisional Measures in the Case Concerning the Frontier Dispute (Burkina Faso/Mali)*, Provisional Measures Order, ICJ Rep. 1986 25 ILM 146, 565–569; Conference on Yugoslavia Arbitration Commission, Opinion No. 3 (Jan. 11, 1992).

130 *See* STEFAN TALMON, "The Constitutive versus the Declaratory Theory of Recognition: Tertium Non Datur?" (2004) 75(1) BRITISH YEARBOOK OF INTERNATIONAL LAW 101–181; JURE VIDMAR, "Explaining the Legal Effects of Recognition" (2012) 61(2) INTERNATIONAL AND COMPARATIVE LAW QUARTERLY 361–387; "Recognition in International Law: A Functional Reappraisal" (1967) 34(4) UNIVERSITY OF CHICAGO LAW REVIEW 857–883.

131 *See generally* RICHARD CAPLAN, A NEW TRUSTEESHIP? THE INTERNATIONAL ADMINISTRATION OF WAR-TORN TERRITORIES (Routledge, 2002) (analyzing the emergence of neotrusteeships in postconflict settings); General Framework for Peace in Bosnia and Herzegovina (Dayton, 1995) Annex 1(A), art. I.

132 UN Doc. SC/7400 (2002).

CHAPTER 5

1 *See* Peter Harris and Ben Reilly, "Democracy and Deep-Rooted Conflict: Options for Negotiators" (International IDEA, 1998) 253; *see also* Katia Papagianni, "Civil Society Dialogue Network Discussion Paper No. 3: National Dialogue Processes in Political Transitions" (Centre for Humanitarian Dialogue, Jan. 23, 2014) 1.

2 *See* "United Nations Peacebuilding Commission Working Group on Lessons Learned, Chair's Summary: Lessons Learned from National Dialogue in Post-Conflict Situations" (United Nations Peacebuilding Support Office, Nov. 2009).

3 *See e.g.* Ecuador Constitution (2008) art. 424; Ethiopia Constitution (1994) art. 9.1; Swaziland Constitution (2005) Preamble; *see also* "What Is a Constitution?" (University College London: Constitution Unit, undated).

4 Jamal Benomar, "Constitution-Making after Conflict: Lessons for Iraq" (2004) 15 Journal of Democracy 81, 82.

5 *See* Charlotte Fielder, "Why Writing a New Constitution after Conflict Can Contribute to Peace" (German Development Institute Briefing Paper, Nov. 2019).

6 For a broader examination of topics related to postconflict governance, *see generally* Louis Anten, "Strengthening Governance in Post-Conflict Fragile States" (Netherlands Institute of International Relations Conflict Research Unit, June 2009); Garth Glentworth, "Post-Conflict Reconstruction: Key Issues in Governance" (DFID – Governance Department, 2002); Daniel G. Ogbaharaya, "(Re-)Building Governance in Post-Conflict Africa: The Role of the State and Informal Institutions" (2008) 18(3) Development in Practice 395–402; Jonathan P. Worboys, "Electoral Laws and Electoral Reform" in Research Handbook on Post-Conflict State Building (Paul R. Williams and Milena Sterio eds., Edward Elgar, 2020); Betsy Popken, "Vetting the Public Sector" in Research Handbook on Post-Conflict State Building (Paul R. Williams and Milena Sterio eds., Edward Elgar, 2020); Jennifer Trahan, "Judicial Reform and Rebuilding" in Research Handbook on Post-Conflict State Building (Paul R. Williams and Milena Sterio eds., Edward Elgar, 2020).

7 Hallie Ludsin, "Peacemaking and Constitution-Drafting: A Dysfunctional Marriage" (2011) 33(1) University of Pennsylvania Journal of International Law 239, 242.

8 *See* Darin Johnson, "Post-Conflict Constitution-Making" in The Research Handbook on Post-Conflict State Building (Paul R. Williams and Milena Sterio eds., Edward Elgar, 2020).

9 *Id.*

10 *Id.*

11 *Id.*

12 Vicki C. Jackson, "What's in a Name? Reflections on Timing, Naming, and Constitution-Making" (2008) 49(4) William and Mary Law Review 1249, 1250.

13 Louise Olivier, Constitutional Review and Reform (Open Society Initiative for Southern Africa, 2007) 6.

14 International Covenant on Civil and Political Rights (New York, Dec. 16, 1966) 999 UNTS 171 and 1057 UNTS 407, *entered into force* Mar. 23, 1976 (the provisions of art. 41 (Human Rights Committee) *entered into force* Mar. 28, 1979).

15 *Id.*

16 Office of the High Commissioner for Human Rights, General Comment 25, art. 6 (57th session, 1996), UN Doc CCPR/C/21/Rev. 1/Add. 7 (1996).

17 NOHA IBRAHIM ABDELGABAR, "International Law and Constitution Making Process: The Right to Public Participation in the Constitution Making Process in Post Referendum Sudan" (2013) 46(2) VERFASSUNG UND RECHT IN ÜBERSEE/LAW AND POLITICS IN AFRICA, ASIA AND LATIN AMERICA 131, 135.

18 *Mi'kmaq Tribal Society v. Canada*, UN Doc. CCPR/C/43/D/205/1986 (1990) 3.1.

19 *Id.* at 2.2.

20 *Id.* at 5.3

21 UN Doc. CCPR/C/BiH/CO/1 (2006) para. 8.

22 *Id.*

23 *See* Jason Gluck and Michele Brandt, "Participatory and Inclusive Constitution Making: Giving Voice to the Demands of Citizens in the Wake of the Arab Spring" (United States Institute for Peace, 2015) 105 PEACEWORKS 5, 5–6.

24 *See* Johnson, *supra* note 8; *see also* VIVIAN HART, "Constitution-Making and the Transformation of Conflict" (2001) 26 PEACE AND CHANGE 153, 154.

25 Abdelgabar, *supra* note 17 at 134–135.

26 These include: the UN Declaration of Human Rights, the Convention on the Elimination of All Forms of Racial Discrimination, the Convention on the Elimination on All Forms of Discrimination Against Women; *see* Abdelgabar, *supra* note 17 at 133–134.

27 These include: the African Charter on Human and Peoples' Rights, the Asian Charter of Rights, the European Convention on Human Rights, the American Convention on Human Rights, and the Inter-American Democratic Charter; *see* Abdelgabar, *supra* note 17 at 133–134.

28 JAMES O'BRIEN, "The Dayton Constitution of Bosnia and Herzegovina" in FRAMING THE STATE IN TIMES OF TRANSITION (Laurel E. Miller and Louis Aucoin eds., United States Institute of Peace, 2010) 333–335.

29 The General Framework for Peace in Bosnia and Herzegovina (Dayton, 1995) Annex 4.

30 Final Agreement to End the Armed Conflict and Build a Stable and Lasting Peace (Bogota, 2016) 3.2.1.2.

31 *Id.* at Other Agreements and the Draft Law on Amnesty, Pardon and Special Criminal Treatment: Agreement of Nov. 7, 2016, I.

32 SC Res 1272, UN SCOR., UN Doc. S/RES/1272 (1999).

33 MARKUS BENZING, "Midwifing a New State: The United Nations in East Timor" (2005) 9 MAX PLANCK YEARBOOK OF UNITED NATIONS LAW 295, 304.

34 UN Doc. S/1997/114 (1997) Annex II: Agreement on a Firm and Lasting Peace (1996).

35 Agreement on the Identity and Rights of Indigenous People (1995).

36 LAUREN MARIE BALASCO and JULIO F. CARRIÓN, "Required Consultation or Provoking Confrontation? The Use of the Referendum in Peace Agreements" (2019) 55 (2) REPRESENTATION 141, 146.

37 "Q&A: Drafting Iraq's Constitution" (New York Times, Aug. 17, 2005).

38 "Constitutional History of Iraq" (ConstitutionNet, International IDEA, 2016).

39 "Constitutional History of Kosovo" (ConstitutionNet, International IDEA, 2016).

40 Kosovo Constitution (2008).

41 The Ohrid Framework Agreement (Ohrid, 2001) Annex A.

42 Nanako Tamaru and Marie O'Reilly, "A Women's Guide to Constitution Making" (Inclusive Security, Mar. 2018) 8.

43 "Nepal's Constitutional Process" (International Crisis Group, 2007).

44 Interim Constitution of Nepal (2007) 70(1).

45 "Constitution-Making Process in Nepal: A Look Back at the Achievements in 2014–2015" (UNICEF: Children's Fund, 2014) 1.

46 "Nepal's Constitution Building Process: 2006–2015: Progress, Challenges, and Contributions of International Community" (International IDEA, 2015) 10.

47 JOANA AMARAL, MAKING PEACE WITH REFERENDUMS: CYPRUS AND NORTHERN IRELAND (Syracuse University Press, 2019) 90–94.

48 CATHERINE BARNES and ELDRED DE KLERK, "South Africa's Multi-Party Constitutional Negotiation Process" (2002) 13 ACCORD 26, 31.

49 ALBIE SACHS, "Constitutional Developments in South Africa" (1996) 24 NEW YORK UNIVERSITY JOURNAL OF INTERNATIONAL LAW & POLICY 695, 698.

50 *See* Sudan Interim Constitution (2005).

51 The Comprehensive Peace Agreement between the Government of the Republic of the Sudan and the Sudan People's Liberation Movement/Sudan People's Liberation Army (2005).

52 DARIN JOHNSON, "Conflict Constitution-Making in Libya and Yemen" (2017) 39 UNIVERSITY OF PENNSYLVANIA JOURNAL OF INTERNATIONAL LAW 293, 321.

53 O'Brien, *supra* note 28 at 335.

54 FIONNUALA NI AOLAIN, "The Fractured Soul of the Dayton Agreement: A Legal Analysis" (1998) 19(4) MICHIGAN JOURNAL OF INTERNATIONAL LAW 957, 970–973.

55 Robert M. Hayden and R. Bruce Hitchner, "Constitution Drafting in Bosnia and Herzegovina" (Wilson Center, July 2011).

56 NIKOLAOS TZIFAKIS, "The Bosnian Peace Process: The Power-Sharing Approach Revisited" (2007) 28 PERSPECTIVES 85, 88.

57 KIRSTI SAMUELS, "Post-Conflict Peace-Building and Constitution-Making" (2006) 6(2) CHICAGO JOURNAL OF INTERNATIONAL LAW 663, 675.

58 "A History of South Africa: 1910–1996" (South African History Online, Mar. 21, 2011).

59 Christine Bell and Kimana Zulueta-Fülscher, "Sequencing Peace Agreements and Constitutions in the Political Settlement Process" (International IDEA Policy Papers No. 13, Nov. 2016) 14.

60 South Africa Interim Constitution (1993) arts. 40(1), 48(1), 73(1).

61 Bell and Zulueta-Fülscher, *supra* note 59 at 25.

62 South Africa Interim Constitution (1993) Schedule 4.

63 Barnes and De Klerk, *supra* note 48 at 31.

64 Bell and Zulueta-Fülscher, *supra* note 59 at 26.

65 Manuel José Cepeda Espinosa, "The Peace Process and the Constitution: Constitution Making as Peace Making?" (IACL-AIDC Blog, July 5, 2016).

66 David Landau, "Constitutional Implications of Colombia's Judicialized Peace Process" (ConstitutionNet, July 29, 2016).

67 "Colombia Signs New Peace Deal with Farc" (BBC News, Nov. 24, 2016).

68 Helen Murphy and Julia Symmes Cobb, "Colombian High Court Rules FARC Peace Law Must Be Sanctioned" (Reuters, May 29, 2019).

69 *See* Rambouillet Accords (1999), Ch. 1, including legislative, executive, and judicial organs.
70 UNSC Res. 1244, UN SCOR, UN Doc. S/RES/1244 (June 10, 1999).
71 Kimana Zulueta-Fülscher and Sumit Bisarya, "(S)electing Constitution-Making Bodies in Fragile and Conflict-Affected Settings" (International IDEA Policy Paper No. 16, 2018) 24.
72 Darfur Agreement between the Transitional Government of Sudan and Darfur Parties to Peace (Juba, 2020) § B, art. 24.1.
73 *See* Fielder, *supra* note 5.
74 ROSALIND DIXON and TOM GINSBURG, "Deciding Not to Decide: Deferral in Constitutional Design" (2011) 9 INTERNATIONAL JOURNAL OF CONSTITUTIONAL LAW 636, 652–654.
75 ACCORD: STRIKING A BALANCE, NORTHERN IRELAND PEACE PROCESS (Conciliation Resources, 1999) 33.
76 Amaral, *supra* note 47 at 90–94.
77 ACCORD: STRIKING A BALANCE, NORTHERN IRELAND PEACE PROCESS (Conciliation Resources, 1999) 36; JENNIFER TODD, "Northern Ireland: Timing and Sequencing of Post-Conflict Reconstruction and Peacebuilding" in BUILDING SUSTAINABLE PEACE: TIMING AND SEQUENCING OF POST-CONFLICT RECONSTRUCTION AND PEACEBUILDING (Arnim Langer and Graham K. Brown eds., Oxford University Press, 2016) 1.
78 Todd, *supra* note 77 at 3.
79 Amaral, *supra* note 47 at 90–94.
80 George Anderson, "Yemen's Failed Constitutional Transition: 2011–2015" (Forum of Federations Occasional Paper Series 41, 2019) 5–6.
81 JASON GLUCK, "Constitution-Building in a Political Vacuum: Libya and Yemen" (2014) ANNUAL REVIEW OF CONSTITUTION-BUILDING PROCESSES 43, 50; Anderson, *supra* note 80 at 3.
82 Anderson, *supra* note 80 at 18.
83 *Id.* at 3.
84 *Id.* at 18
85 Mareike Transfeld, "The Failure of the Transitional Process in Yemen" (German Institute for International and Security Affairs, 2015) 1.
86 United Nations Transitional Authority for East Timor, Directive No. 2001/3, On the Establishment of Constitutional Commissions for East Timor, UN Doc UNTAET/DIR/2001/3 (Mar. 31, 2001).
87 Jennifer Widner, "Constitution Writing & Conflict Resolution: East Timor" (Princeton University and United States Institute of Peace, 2004).
88 Benzing, *supra* note 33 at 365; JIM DELLA-GIACOMA, SELF-DETERMINATION AND PEACE OPERATIONS IN TIMOR-LESTE (Crisis Group, May 28, 2012).
89 Michele Brandt, "Constitutional Assistance in Post-Conflict Countries: The UN Experience: Cambodia, East Timor & Afghanistan" (United Nations Development Programme, June 2005) 9, 16.
90 LOUIS AUCOIN and MICHELE BRANDT, "East Timor's Constitutional Passage to Independence" in FRAMING THE STATE IN TIMES OF TRANSITION: CASE STUDIES IN CONSTITUTION-MAKING (Laurel Miller and Louis Aucoin eds., USIP, 2010) 245, 256–257.

91 *Id.*

92 *Id.* at 255–258.

93 KANAK MANI DIXIT, "The Spring of Dissent: People's Movement in Nepal" (2006) 33(1) INDIA INTERNATIONAL CENTRE QUARTERLY 113, 114.

94 "Nepal's Constitution Building Process: 2006–2015: Progress, Challenges, and Contributions of International Community" (International IDEA, Nov. 1, 2015) 8, 16.

95 *Id.* at 10; Tamaru and O'Reilly, *supra* note 42 at 8.

96 Hari Phuyal, "Nepal's Constitution: 65 Years in the Making" (The Diplomat, Sep. 18, 2015).

97 Mahendra Lawoti, "Prolonged Transition and Setback in Reforms: Timing, Sequencing, and Contestations over Reforms in Post-Conflict Nepal" (Centre for Research on Peace and Development Working Paper No. 43, 2015) 19–20.

98 "Nepal's Constitution Building Process: 2006–2015: Progress, Challenges, and Contributions of International Community" (International IDEA, Nov. 1, 2015) 19.

99 "Constitution-Making Process in Nepal: A Look Back at the Achievements in 2014–2015" (UNICEF: Children's Fund, 2014) 1.

100 Dixon and Ginsburg, *supra* note 74 at 647.

101 *Id.* at 657–648,

102 CHARMAINE RODRIGUES, "Letting Off Steam: Interim Constitutions as a Safety Valve to the Pressure-Cooker of Transitions in Conflict-Affected States" (2017) 6(1) GLOBAL CONSTITUTIONALISM 33, 61–62.

103 Michele Brandt, Jill Cottrell, Yash Ghai, and Anthony Regan, "Constitution-Making and Reform: Options for the Process" (Interpeace, 2011) 67.

104 Kimana Zulueta-Fülscher, "Interim Constitutions: Peacekeeping and Democracy-Building Tools" (International Institute for Democracy and Electoral Assistance, Policy Paper, Oct. 2015) 9.

105 *Id.* at 6.

106 *Id.* at 3.

107 Rodrigues, *supra* note 102 at 41, 61.

108 *Id.* at 40–41, 43.

109 *Id.* at 46.

110 Zulueta-Fülscher, *supra* note 104 at 4.

111 Rodrigues, *supra* note 102 at 50.

112 *Id.*

113 Though Somalia is a failed state, its peace process contains important approaches to resolving the conundrums related to postconflict governance and constitution-making.

114 The Transitional Federal Charter of the Somali Republic (Feb. 2004, Nairobi) art. 13 (1).

115 The Federal Republic of Somalia Provisional Constitution (Aug. 1, 2012, Mogadishu) Ch. 3, arts. 43–45; Chs. 5–10.

116 Rambouillet Accords, *supra* note 69 at Ch. 1, Perambulatory Cl. 4.

117 Rodrigues, *supra* note 102 at 53.

118 *Id.* at 52.

119 Zulueta-Fülscher, *supra* note 104 at 4.

120 The Transitional Constitution of the Republic of South Sudan (2011) Part Six, Ch. II, art. 100.

121 Rodrigues, *supra* note 102 at 57.

122 Rambouillet Accords, *supra* note 69 at Ch. 8, art. I(3).

123 Zulueta-Fülscher, *supra* note 104 at 14.

124 Rodrigues, *supra* note 102 at 62.

125 Zulueta-Fülscher, *supra* note 104 at 15.

126 Ohrid Agreement (Ohrid, 2001) Annex A.

127 *Id.* at art. 8.

128 *Id.* at arts. 7, 19, 78.

129 STEFAN ANDONOVSKI, "The Effects of Post-Conflict Constitutional Designs: 'The Ohrid Framework Agreement' and the Macedonian Constitution" (2018) 81 CROATIAN INTERNATIONAL RELATIONS REVIEW 23, 25.

130 GA Res. 526, UN GAOR, UN Doc. A/54/526 (Nov. 11, 1999).

131 GA Res. 776, UN GAOR, UN Doc. A/51/776 (Jan. 20, 1997).

132 LAUREN MARIE BALASCO and JULIO F. CARRIÓN, "Required Consultation or Provoking Confrontation? The Use of the Referendum in Peace Agreements" (2019) 55 (2) REPRESENTATION 141, 146.

133 *Id.*

134 GA Res. 526, UN GAOR, UN Doc. A/54/526 (Nov. 11, 1999); Balasco and Carrión, *supra* note 132 at 142.

135 The Comprehensive Peace Agreement between the Government of the Republic of the Sudan and the Sudan People's Liberation Movement/Sudan People's Liberation Army (2005).

136 "South Sudan: Constitutional Structure" (International Commission of Jurists, June 16, 2014).

137 Remember Miamingi, "South Sudan's Endless Transition: The Illusive Search for a 'Permanent' Constitution" (International IDEA ConstitutionNet, 2015).

138 "South Sudan: Constitutional Structure" (International Commission of Jurists, 2014).

139 Miamingi, *supra* note 137.

140 Nicholas Norberg, "A Primer on Syria's Constitutional Committee" (Lawfare, Dec. 22, 2018).

141 "A History of South Africa: 1910–1996" (South African History Online, Mar. 21, 2011).

142 Kroc Institute for International Peace Studies, University of Notre Dame, "South Africa Interim Constitution Accord" (Peace Accords Matrix, undated).

143 "Constitutional History of South Africa" (International IDEA ConstitutionNet, undated).

144 *See* Marianne Merten, "Land Expropriation Amendment Moves Forward in South Africa, Will Likely Pass" (ConstitutionNet, Nov. 15, 2018).

145 MICHEL STEPHAN, "Majority Rules in Constitutional Referendums" (2017) 70(3) INTERNATIONAL REVIEW FOR SOCIAL SCIENCES 402, 403.

146 Amaral, *supra* note 47 at 84.

147 IAN SOMERVILLE and SHANE KIRBY, "Public Relations and the Northern Ireland Peace Process: Dissemination, Reconciliation and the 'Good Friday Agreement' Referendum Campaign" (2012) 1(3) PUBLIC RELATIONS INQUIRY 231, 233.

148 Amaral, *supra* note 47 at 85.

149 *Id.* at 87.

150 Somerville and Kirby, *supra* note 147; Amaral, *supra* note 47 at 97.

151 Stephen Tierney, "Reflections on Referendums" (International IDEA Discussion Paper, 2018) 13.
152 MAKAU MUTUA, "The Iraq Paradox: Minority and Group Rights in a Viable Constitution" (2006) 54 BUFFALO LAW REVIEW 927.
153 Joost R. Hiltermann, "Elections and Constitution Writing in Iraq, 2005" (International Crisis Group, Middle East at a Crossroads, 2006) 39–40.
154 *Id.*
155 Edward Wong, "Iraqi Constitution Vote Split on Ethnic and Sect Lines; Election Panel Reports No Major Fraud" (New York Times, Oct. 23, 2005).
156 Mutua, *supra* note 152.
157 Hiltermann, *supra* note 153 at 39–40.
158 Balasco and Carrión, *supra* note 132 at 147.
159 Agreement on the Identity and Rights of Indigenous People (1995) IV(A).
160 SUNG YONG LEE and ROGER MAC GINTY, "Context and Postconflict Referendums," 18(1) NATIONALISM AND ETHNIC POLITICS 43, 54–55; Balasco and Carrión, *supra* note 132 at 147.
161 Lee and Mac Ginty, *supra note* 160.
162 Balasco and Carrión, *supra* note 132 at 147.
163 Lee and Mac Ginty, *supra* note 160 at 58.
164 Balasco and Carrión, *supra* note 132 at 148.
165 SUSANNE JONAS, OF CENTAURS AND DOVES: GUATEMALA'S PEACE PROCESS (Westview Press, 2000) 198.
166 Balasco and Carrión, *supra* note 132 at 147–148.
167 *Id.* at 152.
168 Stephan, *supra* note 145 at 403.
169 E. IKE UGODU, HUMAN RIGHTS, THE RULE OF LAW, AND DEVELOPMENT IN AFRICA (University of Pennsylvania Press, 2004) 83.
170 OSKAR N. T. THOMS and JAMES RON, "Do Human Rights Violations Cause Internal Conflict?" (2007) 29(3) HUMAN RIGHTS QUARTERLY 674, 692.
171 "Human Rights in Peace Negotiations" (1996) 18(2) HUMAN RIGHTS QUARTERLY 249.
172 South Africa Constitution (1993) Ch. 3.
173 *Id.* at Ch. 2, § 7(1).
174 O'Brien, *supra* note 28 at 338.
175 The General Framework for Peace in Bosnia and Herzegovina (Dayton, 1995) Annex 6, Appendix.
176 *Id.* at Annex 4, art. II.
177 The Transitional Federal Charter of the Somali Republic (Nairobi, 2004) Ch. 5.
178 International Covenant on Civil and Political Rights (adopted Dec. 16, 1966, entered into force Mar. 23, 1976) 999 UNTS 171 (ICCPR).
179 Rambouillet Accords, *supra* note 69 at Ch. 1, arts. VI (1–3), art. VII.
180 South Africa Constitution (1996) Ch. 2.
181 *Id.* at Ch. 2(23).
182 Yemen Constitution (2015) Ch. II.
183 *Id.* at Ch. II, art. 135.
184 *Id.* at Ch. I, arts. 4, 25; Ch. III, arts. 295–297, 306–307.

185 *Id.* at Ch. II, arts. 136–137.
186 The Transitional Federal Charter of the Somali Republic (Nairobi, 2004) Ch. 5.
187 *Id.* at Ch. 1, art. 8.
188 Mohamed Ibrahim, "Somalia Adopts Islamic Law to Deter Insurgency" (New York Times, Apr. 18, 2009).
189 RAN HISCHL, "The Theocratic Challenge to Constitution Drafting in Post-Conflict States" (2008) 49(4) WILLIAM & MARY LAW REVIEW 1179, 1185.

APPENDIX

1 "Briefing: Aceh" (Minority Rights Group International, 2001).
2 *See* MOHAMMAD HASAN ANSORI, "From Insurgency to Bureaucracy: Free Aceh Movement, Aceh Party and the New Face of Conflict" (2012) 1 STABILITY INTERNATIONAL JOURNAL OF SECURITY AND DEVELOPMENT 31–44.
3 *See* MICHELLE ANN MILLER, "The Conflict in Aceh: Context, Precursors, and Catalysts" (2008) 20 ACCORD: AN INTERNATIONAL REVIEW OF PEACE INITIATIVES 12, 15.
4 *See* Ansori, *supra* note 2.
5 "Indonesia: The War in Aceh" (Human Rights Watch Report, 2001) 7.
6 *See* Ansori, *supra* note 2.
7 "Indonesia: The War in Aceh," *supra* note 5 at 7–9.
8 "A 'Lost Decade' for Victims of Indonesia's Aceh Conflict" (Amnesty International, Aug. 13, 2015).
9 *Id.*
10 Joint Understanding on Humanitarian Pause for Aceh (Bavois, 2000).
11 Cessation of Hostilities Framework Agreement between Government of the Republic of Indonesia and the Free Aceh Movement (2002).
12 Edward Aspinall, "The Helsinki Agreement: A More Promising Basis for Peace in Aceh" (East–West Center Policy Studies No. 20, 2005).
13 VÉRONIQUE DUDOUET, "Nonstate Armed Groups and the Politics of Postwar Security Governance" in MONOPOLY OF FORCE: THE NEXUS OF DDR AND SSR (Melanne A. Civic and Michael Miklaucic eds., Institute for National Strategic Studies, National Defense University, 2011) 9.
14 JUDITH LARGE et al., "Introduction: The Forging of Identity, the Imperative of Political Voice, and Meeting Human Needs" (2008) 20 ACCORD 6, 7.
15 *Id.* at 9.
16 Memorandum of Understanding between the Government of the Republic of Indonesia and the Free Aceh Movement (Helsinki, 2005).
17 KONRAD HUBER, "Aceh's Arduous Journey to Peace" (2008) 20 ACCORD 16, 20.
18 Memorandum of Understanding, *supra* note 16, Part 1, § 1.1.2.
19 *Id.*
20 C. Bryson Hull and Bill Tarrant, "Tale of War and Peace in the 2004 Tsunami" (Reuters, Dec. 17, 2009).
21 Memorandum of Understanding, *supra* note 16, § 1.3.
22 FAISAL HADI, "Human Rights and Justice in Aceh: The Long and Winding Road" (2008) 20 ACCORD 66.

23 The Alvor Agreement between Portugal and the Angolan Liberation Movements [Alvor Agreement] (Alvor, Jan. 15, 1975) *in* "Decolonization" (United Nation Department of Political Affairs, Trusteeship and Decolonization, Mar. 1975) Vol. II, No. 4, 17–28.

24 World Peace Foundation, "Mass Atrocity Endings: Documenting Declines in Civilian Casualties – Angola: Civil War" (Mass Atrocity Endings, Aug. 7, 2015); "Angola" (Uppsala Conflict Data Program Conflict Encyclopedia, undated).

25 World Peace Foundation, *supra* note 24.

26 THOMAS J. NOER, "International Credibility and Political Survival: The Ford Administration's Intervention in Angola" (1993) 23 PRESIDENTIAL STUDIES QUARTERLY, 771, 776–777.

27 "Forgotten Fighters: Child Soldiers in Angola" (Apr. 2003) 15(10) Human Rights Watch; "Atrocities by Angolan Forces Described by Refugees" (New York Times, Nov. 13, 1976); "Angolans Describe Human Rights Abuse during Civil War" (Christian Science Monitor, June 3, 1983).

28 "Armed Conflicts Report, Angola" (US Department of Justice, Sept. 2003).

29 World Peace Foundation, *supra* note 24.

30 Peace Accords for Angola (Lisbon, May 1, 1991), People's Republic of Angola and UNITA, UN SCOR S/22609, Attachment IV, § III, art. 3.1–3.2, § VI.A., art. 1.

31 Lusaka Protocol, Government of the Republic of Angola and UNITA (Lusaka, July 23, 1999).

32 Luanda Protocol (Luanda, 1999).

33 SC Res. 1229, UN SCOR, UN Doc. S/RES/1229 (1999).

34 LINDA HEYWOOD, "Angola in the Violent Years 1975–2008: Civilian Casualties" (2011) 19 PORTUGUESE STUDIES REVIEW, 311, 328.

35 Luena Agreement, Government of the Republic of Angola and UNITA (Apr. 26, 2002); CYNTHIA ARNSON, RETHINKING THE ECONOMICS OF WAR: THE INTERSECTION OF NEED, CREED, AND GREED (Woodrow Wilson Center Press, 2005) 17, 120; AARON GRIFFITHS, "The End of the War: The Luena Memorandum of Understanding" (2004) 15 ACCORD 24–27.

36 *See* Griffiths, *supra* note 35 at 24–27.

37 *See* Inge Amundsen and Markus Weimer, "Opposition Parties and the 2008 Parliamentary Elections in Angola" (Chr. Michaelson Institute Working Paper, 2008).

38 ALI AL'AMIN MAZRUI, THE WARRIOR TRADITION IN MODERN AFRICA (Brill, 1977) 227; "UNPO Resolution Concerning the Cabinda Enclave" (Unrepresented Nations and Peoples Organization, July 7, 2005).

39 "The Conflicts" (United Nations International Criminal Tribunal for the Former Yugoslavia site, undated).

40 "1991 Census" (Federalni savod Za Statistiku, 1991).

41 "The Conflicts," *supra* note 39.

42 *See* "Bosnia: Serb Ethnic Cleansing" (DCI Interagency Balkan Task Force, Central Intelligence Agency, Dec. 1994).

43 Ivo H. Daalder, "Decision to Intervene: How the War in Bosnia Ended" (Brookings Institution, Dec. 1, 1998).

44 Brioni Declaration (Ljubljana, 1991).

45 Memorandum of Understanding on the Monitor Mission to Yugoslavia (Lubljana, 1991).

46 "European Community Monitoring Mission in the Former Yugoslavia" (Government of Canada, 2018).

47 The General Framework Agreement for Peace in Bosnia and Herzegovina (Dayton, 1995) Annex 4, art. V.10.a.

48 *See id.*

49 *Id.* at Annex 1a–11.

50 *Id.* at Annex 3, art. 3.

51 Bosnia and Herzegovina Constitution, art. I, § 3 (Annex 4 to General Framework Agreement for Peace and in Bosnia and Herzegovina with Annexes (Dayton, 1995)).

52 *See id.* at arts. III–V.

53 The General Framework Agreement, *supra* note 47 at art. 1.

54 "History: Bougainville's Journey to the Present" (Autonomous Bougainville Government, undated).

55 ANTONIO ADAMO, "A Cursed and Fragmented Island: History and Conflict Analysis in Bougainville, Papua New Guinea" (2018) 29 SMALL WARS & INSURGENCIES 164, 169; ANTHONY REGAN, "Towards Peace for Bougainville" (1998) 9 ASIA-PACIFIC MAGAZINE 13.

56 "Bougainville: The Peace Process and Beyond" (Parliament of Australia, Sep. 27, 1999).

57 *Id.*; Adamo, *supra* note 55 at 170.

58 "History: Bougainville's Journey to the Present," *supra* note 54.

59 JOHN BRAITHWAITE et al., "The Architecture of the Peace" in RECONCILIATION AND ARCHITECTURES OF COMMITMENT: SEQUENCING PEACE IN BOUGAINVILLE (John Braithwaite et al., ANU Press, 2010) 51, 52.

60 "History: Bougainville's Journey to the Present," *supra* note 54.

61 Bougainville Peace Agreement (Arawa, Aug. 30, 2001) arts. B, C, F.1.

62 Braithwaite et al., *supra* note 59 at 51, 56.

63 Referendum Result (Bougainville Referendum Commission, 2020).

64 "International Commission of Inquiry for Burundi: Final Report" (July 23, 1996) UN Doc. S/1996/682.

65 *Id.*

66 *Id.*

67 *Id.*

68 Declaration by the Participants to Peace Negotiations on Burundi (Arusha, 1998).

69 Arusha Peace and Reconciliation Agreement (Arusha, 2000).

70 *Id.*

71 *Id.*

72 Howard Wolpe, "Making Peace after Genocide: Anatomy of the Burundi Process" (United States Institute of Peace, Mar. 2011) 58.
"International Commission of Inquiry for Burundi: Final Report" (July 23, 1996) UN Doc. S/1996/682.

73 GARRY LEECH, THE FARC: THE LONGEST INSURGENCY (Zed Books, 2011) 8–12.

74 "Colombia Profile – Timeline" (BBC News, Aug. 8, 2019).

75 Leech, *supra* note 73 at 2, 9, 11, 23.

76 "Colombia Profile – Timeline," *supra* note 74.

77 Leech, *supra* note 73 at 2.

78 César Romero, "262.197 Muertos Dejó el Conflicto Armado" (Centro Nacional de Memoria Histórica, Aug. 2, 2018).

79 Juan Forero, "Colombia Explores Peace Talks with FARC" (Washington Post, Aug. 28, 2012).

80 Julia Symmes Cobb, "Colombia, ELN Rebels Say Peace Talks Will Be Moved to Cuba" (Reuters, May 5, 2018).

81 Final Agreement to End the Armed Conflict and Build a Stable and Lasting Peace (Bogota, 2016).

82 SC Res. 2307, UN SCOR, UN Doc. S/RES/2307 (2016).

83 Final Agreement to End the Armed Conflict, *supra* note 81.

84 *Id.* at Accords 1–6.

85 Michel Forst, "End of Mission Statement on the Situation of Human Rights Defenders in Colombia" (Dec. 3, 2018).

86 "State of Implementation of the Colombian Final Accord December 2016" (Kroc Institute for International Peace Studies, Apr. 2019).

87 Forst, *supra* note 85.

88 "World Report 2020: Colombia" (Human Rights Watch, 2019) 143.

89 "Colombia Profile – Timeline," *supra* note 74.

90 *See generally* "Report of the International Commission of Inquiry on Darfur to the United Nations Secretary-General" (United Nations, Jan. 25, 2005) para. 59.

91 *Id.*

92 *Id.* at para. 69.

93 "Thousands of Darfur Refugees Trapped by Fighting" (CNN, May 6, 2008).

94 *Id.*

95 Abdullahi Shuaibu, "Darfur Peace Agreements: Challenges and Opportunities" (UNAMID – Voices of Darfur, July 2012) 8.

96 *Id.* at 9–10.

97 Darfur Peace Agreement (Abuja, 2006) paras. 23–43; Doha Document for Peace in Darfur (Doha, 2011) at 59.

98 Darfur Agreement between the Transitional Government of Sudan and Darfur Parties to Peace (Juba, 2020).

99 Doha Document for Peace in Darfur (Doha, 2011) para. 318.

100 "Sudan's Spreading Conflict (III): The Limits of Darfur's Peace Process" (International Crisis Group, Africa Report No. 211, Jan. 27, 2014) i.

101 *Id.* at 8.

102 Mohamad Almahady, "UN Officials Urge Support as Darfur Attempts to 'Turn the Page' from Conflict to Peace" (UN News, Sep. 28, 2018).

103 "Modern Conflicts: Conflict Profile, East Timor – Indonesia (1975–1999)" (Political Economy Research Institute, University of Massachusetts Amherst, undated).

104 Seth Mydans, "In East Timor, Decisive Vote for a Break from Indonesia" (New York Times, Sep. 4, 1999).

105 *See* IAN MARTIN, SELF-DETERMINATION IN EAST TIMOR: THE UNITED NATIONS, THE BALLOT AND INTERNATIONAL INTERVENTION (Lynne Rienner, 2001) 15; TANIA VOON, "Closing the Gap between Legitimacy and Legality of Humanitarian Intervention: Lessons from East Timor and Kosovo" (2002) 7 UCLA JOURNAL OF INTERNATIONAL LAW FOREIGN AFFAIRS 31.

106 SC Res. 1264, UN SCOR, UN Doc. S/RES/1264 (1999).

107 SC Res. 1272, UN SCOR, UN Doc. S/RES/1272 (1999) paras. 1–2.

108 *Id.* at para. 17.

109 *Id.* at para. 1.

110 Markus Benzing, "Midwifing a New State: The United Nations in East Timor" (2005) 9 Max Planck Yearbook of United Nations Law 295, 365; Jim Della-Giacoma, Self-Determination and Peace Operations in Timor-Leste (Crisis Group, May 28, 2012)

111 East Timor Constitution (2002).

112 Ali MC, "East Timor between Hope and Unease 20 Years after Referendum" (Al Jazeera, Aug. 29, 2019).

113 *See generally* "Guatemala" (Center for Justice & Accountability, undated); "Guatemala's Crippled Peace Process: A Look Back on the 1996 Peace Accords" (Council on Hemispheric Affairs, May 10, 2011); Donald J. Planty, "Guatemala: An Unfulfilled Promise" in Research Handbook on Post-Conflict State Building (Paul R. Williams and Milena Sterio eds., Edward Elgar, 2020).

114 *See* David Holiday, "Guatemala's Precarious Peace" (2000) 99(634) Current History 78–84.

115 "MINUGUA – Background" (UN Peacekeeping, undated).

116 *See* Susanne Jonas, "Democratization through Peace: The Difficult Case of Guatemala" (2000) 42(4) Journal of Interamerican Studies and World Affairs 9–38.

117 UN Doc. S/1997/114 (1997) Annex II: Agreement on a Firm and Lasting Peace (1996).

118 Secretary-General, "The Situation in Central America: Procedures for the Establishment of a Firm and Lasting Peace and Progress in Fashioning a Region of Peace, Freedom, Democracy and Development" (1997) UN Doc. S/1997/114 paras. 2–14; *see also* Margriet Poppema, "Guatemala, the Peace Accords and Education: A Post-Conflict Struggle for Equal Opportunities, Cultural Recognition, and Participation in Education" (2009) 7(4) Globalisation, Societies, and Education 383–408.

119 Agreement on the Identity and Rights of Indigenous People (1995).

120 *Id.*

121 Lauren Marie Balasco and Julio F. Carrion, "Required Consultation or Provoking Confrontation? The Use of the Referendum in Peace Agreements" (2019) 55 (2) Representation 141, 146.

122 *Id.*

123 Alessandro Preti, "Guatemala: Violence in Peacetime – A Critical Analysis of the Armed Conflict and the Peace Process" (2002) 26(2) Disasters 99–119.

124 Marie-Louise Glebbeek, "Police Reform and the Peace Process in Guatemala: the Fifth Promotion of the National Civilian Police" (2001) 20(4) Bulletin of Latin American Research 431–453.

125 Poppema, *supra* note 118.

126 "Life under Saddam Hussein: Past Repression and Atrocities by Saddam Hussein's Regime" (US Dept. of State Fact Sheet Archive, Apr. 4, 2003).

127 "Introduction" in *Genocide in Iraq: The Anfal Campaign against the Kurds*, A Middle East Watch Report (Human Rights Watch, 1993).

128 "Life under Saddam Hussein," *supra* note 126.

129 This US military force was launched on Mar. 19, 2003, under the name Operation Iraqi Freedom. *See* "Iraq and Weapons of Mass Destruction" (National Security Archive, Feb. 11, 2004).

130 Max Boot, "The New American Way of War" (Foreign Affairs, Jul./Aug. 2003).

131 "Iraq: Debaathification" (Council on Foreign Relations, Feb. 22, 2005).

132 Kenneth M. Pollack, "After Saddam: Assessing the Reconstruction of Iraq" (Foreign Affairs, Jan. 12, 2004).

133 Law of Administration for the State of Iraq for the Transitional Period (Mar. 8, 2004).

134 Pollack, *supra* note 132.

135 Law of Administration, *supra* note 133 at art. 4.

136 Iraq Constitution (2005) art. 1.

137 *Id.*

138 Ranj Alaaldin, "Saving Iraq" (Foreign Affairs, May 9, 2016).

139 Hamdi Malik, "Iraq Can Now Wrest Its Sovereignty from Iran" (Foreign Affairs, May 25, 2020); Maysam Behravesh, "Soleimani Was More Valuable in Politics than in War" (Foreign Affairs, Jan. 8, 2020).

140 For a comprehensive review of the history of Kosovo, see NOEL MALCOM, KOSOVO: A SHORT HISTORY (Pan Macmillan, 1999).

141 Steven Woehrel, "Kosovo: Historical Background to the Current Conflict" (Congressional Research Service, June 3, 1999).

142 "The Kosovo Case, 1998–1999" (SENSE Transitional Justice Center, June 5, 2020).

143 "Under Orders, War Crimes in Kosovo" (Human Rights Watch, Oct. 26, 2001).

144 *Id.*

145 "The Kosovo Case, 1998–1999," *supra* note 142.

146 Interim Agreement for Peace and Self-Government in Kosovo (Rambouillet, 1999).

147 "NATO's Role in Relation to the Conflict in Kosovo" (NATO, July 15, 1999).

148 *Id.*

149 Military Technical Agreement between the International Security Force and the Governments of the Federal Republic of Yugoslavia and the Republic of Serbia (1999) art. 1.

150 "Recognition List" (Republika Kosoves Ministria E Puneve Te Jashtme Dhe Diaspores, June 15, 2020).

151 Promoting Security, Stability, and Respect for Human Rights in Kosovo (United Nations Peacekeeping, June 5, 2020).

152 European Neighbourhood Policy and Enlargement Policy (European Commission, June 5, 2020).

153 "The Kosovo Case, 1998–1999," *supra* note 142.

154 Violeta Petroska-Beska and Mirjana Najcevska, "Macedonia: Understanding History, Preventing Future Conflict" (United States Institute of Peace, Feb. 2004) 1, 2–3; JAMES DOBBINS et al., "Macedonia" in EUROPE'S ROLE IN NATION-BUILDING: FROM THE BALKANS TO THE CONGO (James Dobbins et al., Rand Corporation, 2008) 49, 52.

155 Petroska-Beska and Najcevska, *supra* note 154 at 1, 3.

156 *Id.* at 1, 3–4.

157 John Tagliabue, "Macedonians Vote for Independence from Yugoslavia" (New York Times, Sep. 10, 1991).

158 Dobbins et al., *supra* note 154 at 49, 52.

159 *Id.*

160 "Macedonia: The Last Chance for Peace" (International Crisis Group, June 20, 2001) 1, 5.

161 Dobbins et al., *supra* note 154,at 49.

162 "NATO Brokers Ceasefire in Macedonia" (The Guardian, July 5, 2001); "Peace Support Operations in North Macedonia" (NATO, Mar. 24, 2020).

163 George A. Tsukatos, "The Republic of Macedonia: Implementing the Ohrid Framework Agreement and Reforming the State" (MA thesis, Naval Postgraduate School, Sep. 2008) 1, 33.

164 The Ohrid Framework Agreement (Ohrid, 2001); For a comprehensive review of the peace process by the chief negotiator, *see* JAMES PARDEW, PEACEMAKERS: AMERICAN LEADERSHIP AND THE END OF GENOCIDE IN THE BALKANS (University of Kentucky Press, 2018).

165 The Ohrid Framework Agreement (Ohrid, 2001) art. 2.

166 *Id.*

167 *Id.*

168 *Id.* at arts. 1, 2, 3, 6.

169 "Freedom in the World 2020: North Macedonia" (Freedom House, 2020).

170 "Guide to the Philippines Conflict" (BBC, Oct. 8, 2012).

171 *Id.*

172 Zachary Abuza and Luke Lischin, "The Challenges Facing the Philippines' Bangsamoro Autonomous Region at One Year" (United States Institute of Peace Special Report, June 10, 2020).

173 "Guide to the Philippines Conflict," *supra* note 170.

174 Fermin Adriano and Thomas Parks, "The Contested Corners of Asia: Subnational Conflict and International Development Assistance – The Case of Mindanao, Philippines" (Asia Foundation, 2013).

175 "Armed Conflicts Report – Philippines-Mindanao" (US Department of Justice, Jan. 2009).

176 Philippines Constitution (1987) art. 10, § 20.

177 "Guide to the Philippines Conflict," *supra* note 170.

178 Framework Agreement on the Bangsamoro (Kuala Lumpur, 2012).

179 *Id.*

180 "Guide to the Philippines Conflict," *supra* note 170.

181 Richard Javad Heydarian, "Bangsamoro Organic Law Can Be Duterte's Greatest Legacy" (Al Jazeera, Aug. 1, 2018).

182 "Fast Facts on the Bangsamoro Organic Law" (Republic of the Philippines: Philippine Information Agency, undated).

183 Republic Act No. 11054 (2017) art. VII, § 5.

184 *Id.* at art. XII.

185 *Id.* at art. V.

186 "Mindanao Displacement Dashboards" (UNHCR, Aug. 2020).

187 Abuza and Lischin, *supra* note 172.

188 "Mindanao Displacement Dashboards," *supra* note 186.

189 "Mozambique: History" (TheCommonwealth.org, undated).

190 "Mozambique Country Profile" (BBC, Jan. 17, 2020).

191 GEORGI DERLUGUIAN, SURE ROAD? NATIONALISMS IN ANGOLA, GUINEA-BISSAU, AND MOZAMBIQUE (Brill, 1997) 81–95.

192 "Mozambique" (Encyclopedia Britannica, undated).

193 WILLIAM FINNEGAN, A COMPLICATED WAR: THE HARROWING OF MOZAMBIQUE (University of California Press, 1992) 112–118.

194 JOAO CABRITA, MOZAMBIQUE – THE TORTUOUS ROAD TO DEMOCRACY (Palgrave, 2001) 80–99.

195 WILLIAM MINTER, APARTHEID'S CONTRAS: AN INQUIRY INTO THE ROOTS OF WAR IN ANGOLA AND MOZAMBIQUE (Zed Books, 1994) 11–16.

196 JAMIE MILLER, AN AFRICAN VOLK: THE APARTHEID REGIME AND ITS SEARCH FOR SURVIVAL (Oxford University Press, 2016) 122–126.

197 Tom Hartley, "RENAMO and the LRA: The History and Futures of African Child Soldiers" (New Histories, Oct. 30, 2011).

198 Tom Bowker, Simon Kamm, and Aurelio Sambo, "Mozambique's Invisible Civil War" (Foreign Policy, May 6, 2016); "World Report 1990" (Human Rights Watch, Jan. 1, 1991).

199 BARRY MUNSLOW, "Mozambique: Marxism-Leninism in Reverse, the Fifth Congress of Frelimo" (2007) 6 JOURNAL OF COMMUNIST STUDIES 109, 109–112.

200 General Peace Agreement for Mozambique (Rome, Oct. 4, 1992).

201 *Id.* at arts. 1–5.

202 Elsa Buchanan, "Negotiations between Frelimo and Renamo Suspended as Mozambique War Escalates" (London International Business Times, Aug. 1, 2016).

203 Paul Fauvet, "Mozambique's Renamo Kills Three on Highway" (IOL, June 4, 2014).

204 Paul Fauvet, "Mozambique: Renamo Claims Victory in Elections" (All Africa, Oct. 29, 2014).

205 Joseph Hanton, "Mozambique: Indefinite Truce – Debt Guarantee Confirmed" (All Africa, May 5, 2017).

206 "Mozambique's Opposition Leader Alfonso Dhlakama Dies Aged 65" (Al Jazeera, May 3, 2018).

207 "Mozambique Rivals Sign Peace Deal" (Mail & Guardian, Aug. 8, 2019).

208 "Mozambique Signs Peace Accord with Rebel Leader" (Associated Press, Aug. 6, 2019).

209 "Mozambique Country Profile," *supra* note 190.

210 "Mozambique's Former Civil War Foes Sign Landmark Peace Deal" (France24, Aug. 1, 2019).

211 "Mozambique Overview" (World Bank, Sept. 30, 2019).

212 "Nepal Country Profile" (BBC News, Feb. 19, 2018).

213 "Nepal Conflict Report" (UN OHCHR, Oct. 2012) 15.

214 *Id.* at 14.

215 *Id.*, at 14.

216 Comprehensive Peace Agreement between the Government of Nepal and the Communist Party of Nepal (Maoist) (2006).

217 *Id.*, at § 8.

218 Interim Constitution of Nepal (2007).

219 *Id.* at 70(1).

220 CHARMAINE RODRIGUES, "Letting Off Steam: Interim Constitutions as a Safety Valve to the Pressure-Cooker of Transitions in Conflict-Affected States" (2017) 6(1) GLOBAL CONSTITUTIONALISM 33, 53.

221 "Constitution-Making Process in Nepal: A Look Back at the Achievements in 2014–2015" (UNICEF: Children's Fund, 2014) 1.

222 "Nepal's Constitution Building Process: 2006–2015: Progress, Challenges, and Contributions of International Community" (International IDEA, 2015) 10.

223 *See generally* J. F. O'DOHERTY, "The Anglo-Norman Invasion, 1167–71" (1938) 1(4) IRISH HISTORICAL STUDIES 154–157.

224 Sean Kay et al., "Ireland" (Encyclopedia Britannica, undated).

225 "Northern Ireland" (Minority Rights Group International, undated).

226 "Key Events – Civil Rights Campaign (1964–1972)" (CAIN, Ulster University, undated).

227 "Northern Ireland Profile" (BBC News, Jan. 17, 2013).

228 "Accord: Striking a Balance, The Northern Ireland Peace Process" (Conciliation Resources, 1999) 16.

229 Jeff Wallenfeldt, "The Troubles" (Encyclopedia Britannica, undated).

230 *Id.*

231 "The Mitchell Principles" (Irish Times, May 21, 1996).

232 *Id.*

233 "Accord: Striking a Balance," *supra* note 228 at 33.

234 "George Mitchell Transcript" (United States Institute of Peace, undated).

235 Belfast Agreement [Good Friday Agreement] (Belfast, 1998).

236 *Id.*

237 *See* MADHAV JOSHI, JASON MICHAEL QUINN, and PATRICK M. REGAN, "Annualized Implementation Data on Comprehensive Intrastate Peace Accords, 1989–2012" (2015) 52 JOURNAL OF PEACE RESEARCH 551–562.

238 Good Friday Agreement, *supra* note 235.

239 Malcolm Sutton, "Sutton Index of Deaths" (CAIN, Ulster University, no date).

240 "Irish Border Checks Will Be Impossible after Brexit, Says Ambassador" (The Guardian, Feb. 8, 2017).

241 Amanda Sloat, "Protecting the Good Friday Agreement from Brexit" (Brookings Institute, Oct. 22, 2019).

242 Lisa O'Carroll, Rowena Mason, and Jennifer Rankin, "Boris Johnson and Leo Varadkar Say They 'See Pathway' to Brexit Deal" (The Guardian, Oct. 10, 2019).

243 GÉRARD PRUNIER, "Rwandese Society and the Colonial Impact: The Making of a Cultural Mythology (1894–1959)" in THE RWANDA CRISIS: A HISTORY OF GENOCIDE (Columbia University Press, 1999) 1–35.

244 "Rwanda: How the Genocide Happened" (BBC, May 17, 2011).

245 "Rwanda Profile – Timeline" (BBC, Sep. 17, 2018).

246 *Id.*

247 "Final Report of the International Commission of Investigation on Human Rights Violations in Rwanda Since 1990" (International Commission of Investigation on Human Rights Violations in Rwanda, Mar. 1993) 3–6.

248 N'sele Ceasefire Agreement between the Government of the Republic of Rwanda and the Rwandese Patriotic Front (Arusha, 1992).

249 Peace Agreement between the Government of the Republic of Rwanda and the Rwandese Patriotic Front (Arusha, 1993).

250 *Id.*

251 "Rwanda Genocide: 100 Days of Slaughter" (BBC, Apr. 4, 2010).

252 "World Report 2019: Rwanda" (Human Rights Watch, 2019) 491.

253 *See* Young Jang, "The Causes of the Sierra Leone Civil War" (E-International Relations, Oct. 25, 2012).

254 *Id.* at 2.

255 *Id.* at 1, 3, 4.

256 *Id.* at 9.

257 Letter dated December 11, 1996 from the Permanent Representative of Sierra Leone to the United Nations Addressed to the Secretary-General, UN Doc. S/1996/1034 Annex – Peace Agreement between the Government of the Republic of Sierra Leone and the Revolutionary United Front of Sierra Leone, signed at Abidjan on November 30, 1996 [Lomé Agreement] (Dec. 11, 1996).

258 Priscilla Hayner, "Negotiating Peace in Sierra Leone: Confronting the Justice Challenge" (Centre for Humanitarian Dialogue/International Center for Transitional Justice Report, Dec. 2007) 8; Mary Kaldor et al., "Evaluation of UNDP Assistance to Conflict-Affected Countries: Sierra Leone Case Study" (UN Development Programme Evaluation Office, undated).

259 To authorize this expansion, the Economic Community adopted a protocol that provided the legal basis for the body to serve in peacekeeping, peacebuilding, disarmament, and demobilization capacities through their Ceasefire Monitoring Group. ECOWAS, Protocol Relating to the Mechanism for Conflict Prevention, Management, Resolution, Peacekeeping and Security (Lomé, Dec. 10, 1999) A/P.1/12/99, arts. 17, 22.

260 "The Armed Conflict in Sierra Leone" (Human Rights Watch, Apr. 11, 2012); Mary Kaldor et al., *supra* note 258.

261 *See* Lomé Agreement, *supra* note 257.

262 *Id.* at art. IX.

263 *Id.* at Annex, art. 5.

264 SC Res. 1270, UN SCOR, UN Doc. S/RES/1270 (1999).

265 Lomé Agreement, *supra* note 257 at art. VII (1–6).

266 *Id.* at art. VII (1).

267 "Implementing the Lomé Peace Agreement" (Conciliation Resources, 2000) 39.

268 Carolyn A. Dubay, "The Special Court for Sierra Leone (Revisited)" (International Judicial Monitor, 2012).

269 HARVEY M. FEINBERG, "The 1913 Natives Land Act in South Africa: Politics, Race, and Segregation in the Early 20th Century" (1993) 26 INTERNATIONAL JOURNAL OF AFRICAN HISTORICAL STUDIES 65–109.

270 Suzanne Daley, "Party Led by Mandela Now Owns Up to Atrocities" (New York Times, May 13, 1997).

271 MAX COLEMAN ed., A CRIME AGAINST HUMANITY: ANALYZING THE REPRESSION OF THE APARTHEID STATE 235 (Human Rights Committee of South Africa, 1998).

272 CATHERINE BARNES, "Owning the Process: Public Participation in Peacemaking" (Conciliation Resources, Dec. 2002) 13 ACCORD.

273 HASSEN EBRAHIM and LAUREL E. MILLER, "Creating the Birth Certificate of a New South Africa: Constitution Making after Apartheid" in FRAMING THE STATE IN TIMES OF TRANSITION: CASE STUDIES IN CONSTITUTION MAKING (Laurel E. Miller with Louis Aucoin eds., United States Institute of Peace, 2010) 111, 112.

274 *Id.* at 119.

275 *Id.*

276 *Id.*

277 *Id.* at 120.

278 *Id.* at 134.

279 South Africa Constitution (1993).

280 South Africa Constitution (1996); Promotion of National Unity and Reconciliation Act 34 of 1995 (South Africa).

281 "Countries and Territories: Global Freedom Scores" (Freedom House, July 26, 2020).

282 Samuel Momodu, "First Sudanese Civil War (1955–1972)" (BlackPast.org, Jan. 22, 2020).

283 ANA ELISA CASCÃO, "Resource-Based Conflict in South Sudan and Gambella (Ethiopia): When Water, Land and Oil Mix with Politics" in STATE AND SOCIETAL CHALLENGES IN THE HORN OF AFRICA CONFLICT AND PROCESSES OF STATE FORMATION, RECONFIGURATION AND DISINTEGRATION (Alexandra Magnólia Dias ed., Centro de Estudos Internacionais, 2013) para. 14.

284 *Id.* at para. 13.

285 Dr. Daniel Thabo Nyibong, "History of Southern Sudan" (Pachodo, Oct. 6, 2010).

286 *Id.*

287 "Sudan: The Quick and the Terrible" (Frontline/World, PBS, Jan. 2005).

288 "Sudan Peace Agreement Signed 9 January" (United Nations News, Feb. 8, 2005).

289 "Mass Atrocity Endings: Sudan 1985–2005" (World Peace Foundation, Aug. 7, 2015).

290 MOHAMMED EL-MUKHTAR HUSSEIN, "Negotiating Peace: The Road to Naivasha" (2006) 18 ACCORD 18–19.

291 *Id.* at 19.

292 *Id.* at 19.

293 Comprehensive Peace Agreement (Sudan 2005) Ch. 1.

294 *Id.* at Annexure I.

295 *Id.* at Chs. 1–2.

296 *Id.* at Ch. 3.

297 *Id.* at Chs. 4–6.

298 "Western Sahara Profile" (BBC News, May 14, 2018).

299 *Id.*

300 *Id.*

301 SC Res. 658, UN SCOR, UN Doc. S/RES/658 (1990).

302 "Western Sahara" (Oct. 1995) 7(7) Human Rights Watch.

303 "MINURSO Fact Sheet" (United Nations Peacekeeping, Jan. 21, 2020).

304 Daniel Samet, "The Western Sahara Dispute Drags On after 27 Years in Limbo" (Freedom House, Jan. 9, 2019).

305 "Western Sahara," *supra* note 302; "Report of the OHCHR to Western Sahara & the Refugee Camps in Tindouf 2006" (UN Office of the High Commissioner for Human Rights, 2006).

306 Secretary-General, "Report of the Secretary-General on the Situation Concerning Western Sahara," UN Doc. S/2001/613 (June 20, 2001) Annex I, paras. 1–7; "Western Sahara" (Congressional Research Service, Feb. 15, 2011).

307 Secretary-General, *supra* note 306 at Annex I, paras. 1–7.

308 *See* Anna Theofilopoulou, "The United Nations and Western Sahara: A Never-Ending Affair" (United States Institute of Peace Special Report 166, 2006).

309 *Id.*

310 "Full Text of the Moroccan Initiative for an Autonomy Plan" (Kingdom of Morocco, undated).

311 *Id.*

312 "Morocco's Proposal for Western Sahara" (Center for American Progress, May 17, 2007).

313 "2019 Country Reports on Human Rights Practices: Western Sahara" (US Department of State, 2019).

314 "Yemen: Drivers of Conflict and Peace" (Chatham House, Nov. 2016) 4.

315 Shoqi Maktary and Katie Smith, "Pathways for Peace & Stability in Yemen" (Search for Common Ground, 2017) 12.

316 Angus McDowall and Ghaida Ghantous, "Why Yemen Is at War" (Reuters, Apr. 27, 2020).

317 Maktary and Smith, *supra* note 315 at 14.

318 Haydee Dijkstal, "Yemen and the Stockholm Agreement: Background, Context, and the Significance of the Agreement" (American Society of International Law, May 31, 2019).

319 Agreement on the Implementation Mechanism for the Transition Process in Yemen in Accordance with the Initiative of the Gulf Cooperation Council (GCC) (Yemen, 2011) art. 1(a).

320 George Anderson, "Yemen's Failed Constitutional Transition: 2011–2015" (Forum of Federations Occasional Paper Series 41, 2019) 5–6.

321 Agreement on the Implementation Mechanism, *supra* note 319 at arts. 5, 7, 20.

322 McDowall and Ghantous, *supra* note 316.

323 Yemen National Dialogue Outcomes (2014) 2.

324 Agreement on the Implementation Mechanism, *supra* note 319 at art. 21.

325 Yemen National Dialogue Outcomes (2014).

326 Darin Johnson, "Conflict Constitution-Making in Libya and Yemen" (2017) 39 University of Pennsylvania Journal of International Law 293, 321.

327 Anderson, *supra* note 320 at 18.

328 Yemen Draft Constitution (2015) Ch. III, § III, arts. 250, 258.

329 *Id.* at Ch. VII, art. 358.

330 *Id.* at Ch. II.

331 *Id.* at Ch. II, art. 135.

332 *See* Paul Williams, Tiffany Sommadossi, and Ayat Mujais, "A Legal Perspective on Yemen's Attempted Transition from a Unitary to a Federal System of Government" (2017) 33(84) Utrecht Journal of International and European Law 4.

333 Mareike Transfeld, "The Failure of the Transitional Process in Yemen" (German Institute for International and Security Affairs, 2015) 1.

334 Mohammed Ghobari and Agnus McDowall, "Houthis Abduct Yemeni Official amid Wrangling over Constitution" (Thomson Reuters Africa, Jan. 17, 2015).

335 Transfeld, *supra* note 333 at 1.

336 Dijkstal, *supra* note 318.

337 "Yemen: Events of 2018" (Human Rights Watch, 2019).

338 "Yemen: Events of 2019" (Human Rights Watch, 2020).

339 Ammar Al-Ashwal, "Where Is the Yemen War Heading?" (Carnegie Endowment for International Peace, Apr. 15, 2020).

Index

Indonesia (cont.)
Cessation of Hostilities Agreement (2002), 198
disarmament, 199
disarmament, demobilization, and reintegration
(DDR), 109, 200
East Timor independence, 134
external self-determination, 114
Free Aceh Movement, 40, 198
Helsinki Memorandum of Understanding
(2005). *See* Memorandum of Understanding
(2005)
Humanitarian Pause (2000), 198
Islam, 198
joint European Union/ASEAN monitoring
mission, 200
joint natural resources management, 118
Law on the Governing of Aceh (2006), 91, 118
Memorandum of Understanding (2005), 74, 91,
106, 114, 120, 198–200
migration, 198
monopoly of force, 40
natural resources, 106, 198
natural resources ownership, 114
natural resources revenue sharing, 121
oil revenue, 104
power-sharing, 199
shared sovereignty, 137
tsunami (2004), 114, 199
unitary state, 64
West Papua, 74
interim constitution, 169
thick interim constitution, 170–171
thin interim constitution, 170–171
international administration, 163
International Court of Justice, 128
Advisory Opinion of Western Sahara (2008). *See*
Western Sahara
International Covenant on Civil and Political
Rights, 131, 146, 181
Article 25(a), 155
International Covenant on Economic, Social and
Cultural Rights, 131
International Criminal Tribunal for the Former
Yugoslavia, 28, 216
International Monetary Fund, 29
Iraq, 64, 75–76, 213–215
Coalition Provisional Authority, 214
Constitution (2005), 64, 75–76, 112, 116, 122, 215
constitutional referendum, 158, 177
constitution-drafting process, 158
de-Ba'athification, 214
horizontal power-sharing, 64, 76
interim constitution, 75. *See also* Transitional
Administrative Law (2004)

Iraqi Governing Council, 214
joint management council, 116
Kurdistan, 75–76, 107, 113, 117,
121
natural resources, 96, 107
natural resources management, 116–117
natural resources ownership, 113
natural resources revenue sharing, 122
oil, 76
Saddam Hussein, 213
Saddam Hussein, atrocities, 213
Transitional Administrative Law (2004), 64, 76,
158, 214
United States occupation of, 214
Israel, 134
phased sovereignty, 141
Roadmap for Middle East Peace in 2003, 134,
139
Italy
devolution, 55

Kazakhstan
intergenerational fund, 105
Korean War, 13
Kosovo, 13, 18, 215–216
Albanian nationalism, 215
Ambassador William Walker, role in Kosovo
Verification Mission, 28
conditional sovereignty, 142
Constitution (2008), 158, 164
Constitutional Framework for Provisional
self-government, 158
constitution-drafting process, 158,
164
crimes against humanity, 28
Democratic League of Kosovo, 215
final status negotiations, 164
independence, 127, 135, 158
independence referendum, 143
interim constitution, 158, 163, 171–172
international observation mission, 28
Kosovo Liberation Army, 41, 215
Kosovo Verification Mission, 28
monopoly of force, 23, 27, 41
NATO intervention, 163, 216
NATO, role in peace process, 23, 28
phased sovereignty, 140
Provisional Constitutional Framework for
Kosovo, 140
Rambouillet Agreement (1999), 134, 163,
171–172, 216. *See* interim constitution
Rambouillet Agreement (1999) and human
rights, 181
shared sovereignty, 137